The Origins of Canadian and American Political Differences

Jason Kaufman

HARVARD UNIVERSITY PRESS

Cambridge, Massachusetts

London, England

2009

Library of Congress Cataloging-in-Publication Data

Kaufman, Jason Andrew, 1970–
    The origins of Canadian and American political differences / Jason Kaufman.
        p. cm.
    Includes bibliographical references and index.
    ISBN 978-0-674-03136-4
    1. United States—Relations—Canada.   2. Canada—Relations—United
States.   3. United States—Politics and government.   4. Canada—Politics
and government.   5. National characteristics, American.   6. National
characteristics, Canadian.   7. Political culture—United States.   8. Political
culture—Canada.   9. Jurisdiction—United States—History.
10. Jurisdiction—Canada—History.   I. Title.
    E183.8.C2K28 2009
    327.73071—dc22   2008031411

Dedicated in loving memory
to
Linda Hertan Kaufman (1940–2004)

Contents

Preface

This book stems from the desire to understand why politics might vary between a country and its neighbor, particularly when people, ideas, money, and material readily pass between them. It rests on the somewhat irrational belief that macrohistorians like me can identify and explain social processes that span a century or more. It takes seriously the premise that ideas do not just "travel" but are transmitted and transformed by real people and organizations, customs and procedures.

I sometimes refer herein to early residents of colonial North America as "Americans" or "Canadians," even though those nationalities were not yet born. I do the same for the countries "Canada" and the "United States," as well as for colonies, provinces, and states-to-be. This is for the sake of simplicity and is not meant to imply determinism or "destiny" of any kind.

Original spellings and quotations, for the most part, have been recrafted into modern English. Dates for the colonial period can be complicated by changes made to the calendar in early modern Europe. I have worked diligently to iron out the details, but a number of errors, or at least disputed claims, may nevertheless have found their way into this account. In recompense, I have taken the unusual step of quoting *directly* from many of the works referenced here—allowing authors to speak for themselves rather than paraphrasing their work and potentially misleading you to think it is my own.

It has been a great pleasure to share the company of so many scholars, both living and deceased. I apologize in advance to all those whose work I have trampled, ignored, or otherwise misrepresented. At the same time, I ask you to remember that this is a piece of scholarship concerned less with recounting history in all its exacting detail than with gleaning from it basic lessons about human social process. In other words, we seek the forest, not the trees. Hopefully, I have contributed meaningfully to the study of Canada and the United States by distilling thousands of pages of professional history down into a unique and meaningful reading of the parallel political development between two nations. Much of this information is controversial, contentious, and/or uncertain, but I hope at least to stir new debates and proffer new questions. I welcome the skepticism of those inclined to see things differently.

In exploring the parallel history of these two nations, I have dodged some sticky moral issues underlying their creation. For instance, many thousands of Native Americans lost their lives because of the European presence, and tribal life was irrevocably changed as a result. Though I have endeavored to incorporate native affairs into my research, mine is ultimately a story about Europeans and their ventures in northern North America. Native Americans do not receive the full attention they deserve in this account, nor do slaves, women, or minorities of any sort. Québécois, specifically, may take issue with certain aspects of my account of their "national" struggles. My goal is to understand the historical, as opposed to the moral or existential, nature of political claims such as theirs.

This book would not have come to fruition without the help of numerous people, including the staff members of many learned institutions, including the National Library of Canada, the Provincial Archives of British Columbia, the New Brunswick Public Library, the Loyalist House and Museum (St. John, New Brunswick), the Massachusetts State Archives, Widener and Langdell Libraries (Harvard University), and the Massachusetts Historical Society. Harvard University's William F. Milton Fund, Weatherhead Center for International Affairs, Center for American Political Studies, Department of Sociology, and Faculty of Arts and Sciences all provided much-needed financial and clerical support. Audiences and discussants at the American Sociological Association; Social Science History Association; Harvard/MIT Economic Sociology Seminar; Harvard Center for American Political Studies (CAPS); Harvard/Weatherhead Workshop on Religion, Political Economy, and Society (PRPES); Harvard/Weatherhead Canada Seminar; and the Sociology Departments at the Universities of Wisconsin, Michigan, Massachusetts, Pennsylvania, and Western Ontario deserve thanks for their thoughtful comments on various parts of this manuscript. Several paragraphs have been adapted from my article "Corporate Law and the Sovereignty of States," published in the *American Sociological Review,* June 2008.

About halfway through this project, the Canadian government kindly took me under its wing through Project CONNECT, a mentoring program for young Americans interested in the study of Canada. André Senecal of the University of Vermont and Chris Kirkey of SUNY Plattsburgh designed the program, and I thank them for hosting our first meeting in Ottawa, as well as for introducing me to so many great members of the wider Canadian Studies community. Harvard's Weatherhead Center for International Affairs also helped by providing funds to hold a special workshop dedicated to early drafts of the manuscript. Dan Carpenter, Evan Haefeli, Michele Lamont, Theda Skocpol, and Robert Vipond generously agreed to serve as discussants, and Monet Uva helped organize the meeting. Ian Steele also read chapters at this stage.

The other scholars I consulted on this project are too many to name, but a few deserve special mention for taking time out of their already overbooked schedules to lend a helping hand: historians Liz Cohen, Chris DeSan, Colleen Dunlavy, Robert Gordon, Dirk Hartog, Andrew Johnston, Stan Katz, Rob MacDougall, Ken Mack, Pauline Maier, Bill Novak, Bob Steinfeld, and Alan Taylor; sociologists Julia Adams, Andy Andrews, Bayliss Camp, Lis Clemens, Claude Fischer, Marshall Ganz, Ed Grabb, Neil Gross, Ann Orloff, Orlando Patterson, Lyn Spillman, Ann Swidler, and Chuck Tilly; economists David Cutler, Ben Friedman, and David Laibson; and political scientists Frank Bryan, Andrea Campbell, Iain Johnston, Richard Simeon, and Richard Winters. Frank Dobbin, my former dissertation advisor, has remained a staunch but constructive critic, as well as an amazingly supportive friend and mentor. Marco Gonzalez was an invaluable research assistant on this project, as were Lydia Bean, Jacob Model, and Mike Nguyen. Mary Quigley, Katsch Belash, Cheri Minton, and Suzanne Washington were also a great help. Kathleen McDermott of Harvard University Press was a tough but steadfast editor.

I am an American, born and raised, and I knew next to nothing about Canadian history or politics when I began this project. It has been my great fortune to meet so many wonderful people and to visit so many amazing places in the process of coming to know what I have found to be one of the most admirable societies on earth. My hosts in Victoria and Vancouver, the Stull family, were unusually kind—it was a special privilege to share the stage with Caleb Stull and his amazing band, The Parlour Steps.

Dan Torop, a good friend and fine photographer, was a wonderful companion on a road/research trip to Canada. Greig Cranna was a gold mine of Canadiana, as well as travel advice.

My new son, Louis Joseph, has been a joy and a savior, and I thank him and his mother, Heather Caldwell, for their help and forbearance in so many ways. Mark Stewart has been a trusted friend and mensch. Gamelan Galak Tika, my local world music clique, provided useful distraction over the long haul.

My beloved mother, Linda Hertan Kaufman, passed away during the course of this project. I miss her dearly. This book is dedicated to her loving memory, and to the many friends and family who have helped her and us during these difficult years.

*The Origins of Canadian and American
Political Differences*

Introduction

The whole continent of North America appears to be destined by Divine Providence to be peopled by one nation, speaking one language, professing one general system of religions and political principles, and accustomed to one general tenor of social usages and customs.

—John Quincy Adams (1811)

Among the many compelling but untrue statements made by Alexis de Tocqueville in his nineteenth-century classic *Democracy in America* is: "Neighboring democratic peoples do not only become alike . . . but in the end come to be alike in almost all matters."[1] By "democratic peoples," Tocqueville meant those whose law does not recognize class or caste-based distinctions, and by this standard, the United States and Canada were relatively democratic polities by the time he visited them in 1831.

Tocqueville offered this observation in support of an idea first posited by Immanuel Kant, that democratic nations are generally loath to wage war on one another: "If two neighboring nations have the same democratic social condition, they cannot fail at once to adopt similar opinions and manners, for the spirit of democracy tends to assimilate people." John Adams agreed; along with many of the Founding Fathers, he believed the United States would one day include the provinces that comprise contemporary Canada.[2]

Tocqueville, Kant, and Adams were right in one respect: Though Canadians and Americans did wage several vicious wars against one another in the eighteenth and early nineteenth centuries, and while plans are still said to exist for an American invasion of Canada, the two countries have been at peace since at least the mid-nineteenth century.[3] We might thus expect them to be "alike in almost all matters"—neighboring peoples with "similar opinions and manners."

This book attempts to explain why this is *not* so—why two peoples with so much in common have come to disagree so consistently over issues like the separation of church and state, the relationship between federal and subnational government, the responsibility of government for the welfare of all, or the right to smoke marijuana, marry a same-sex partner, or own a high-powered assault rifle.

Comparing the United States and Canada allows us to track the parallel development of two modern nation-states from their earliest origins, thus affording an unusually complete picture of the puzzles of political development and differentiation. In other words, what are the really big, long-term factors that underlie the contemporary political differences between the two countries, and what do these say about the general properties of political development in the face of intercultural exchange?

Canada and the United States are not only geographically proximate but also economically and demographically interdependent societies. Relatively open borders plus a common language have encouraged an astonishing amount of transmigration between the two countries. Despite ebbs and flows, the United States and Canada also share one of the closest economic and diplomatic relationships in the world.

Culturally, too, these nations have long been remarkably well integrated. Prior to the creation of transatlantic telegraph service, for example, European news often reached American media outlets via Halifax, Nova Scotia, a major port for the British merchant marine. Athletic, scholarly, and artistic exchanges were also common between the two countries in the nineteenth century. Today, practically every television in Canada receives at least one American network, and news regarding the domestic public policy of the United States features prominently in Canadian media, as do American sports stories and celebrity gossip. Though Americans are not nearly as familiar with Canadian affairs—or with the affairs of other nations—Canadians have long been an unusually common presence in American television and film, news media, music, literature, academe, and the fine arts.

"Passing" being, perhaps, the most existentially real marker of cultural similarity, it is worth noting the ease with which Americans can "pass" as Canadians almost anywhere in the world—save border crossings and curling matches. Conversely, "American" rock stars Neil Young and Joni Mitchell are Canadian, as well as television newsmen Morley Safer and the late Peter Jennings. Countless "American" television and film actors are Canadian, too, including Matthew Perry, Pamela Anderson, Jim Carrey, William Shatner, and Donald Sutherland, as was "America's Sweetheart" Mary Pickford. *Jeopardy* quizmaster Alex Trebek is Canadian. Even basketball was invented by a Canadian, although he was living in Massachusetts at the time.

Overall, Canadians and Americans are so culturally similar that their separate nationality is virtually undetectable, though Canadians do often complain of mistaken identity, largely for political reasons. Nuances and regional particularities exist—francophone Canada is the most obvious example—but the social customs, cultural knowledge, interactional style, and (English) dialect of these two populations are, in comparative terms, remarkably similar.

By Tocqueville's logic, these similarities are not surprising—interaction breeds emulation. However, Tocqueville predicted that political convergence would precede cultural convergence. The United States and Canada appear to have defied this prediction, converging in almost every area *but* politics. In fact, they appear to be *diverging* in terms of both public opinion and public policy. Regional disparities notwithstanding, Canadians and Americans think about politics quite differently, and their respective governments support starkly different kinds of regulation, responsibility, and social support.

It is puzzling that two countries so culturally, economically, and demographically interdependent would be so dissimilar in the realm of politics.

In contrast to much of the extant literature, which tends to work backward from present to past, I approach the question of US/Canadian political differences inductively. First, I document initial conditions in the earliest North American colonies—most historical accounts begin only with the American Revolution. Then, I follow these colonies through time, watching for the proverbial forks in the road (rather than assuming them based on present knowledge). Ultimately, my depiction of US/Canadian political differences is not significantly different from information offered elsewhere. My *explanation* of those differences, however, diverges sharply in its focus on the causal import of *legal institutions,* as opposed to cultural, demographic, organizational, economic, geographic, or geopolitical factors.

One thing a legal perspective does is focus our attention on *relationships* instead of specific organizations and interest groups. This demands that we account for the ways in which various political domains are interdependent, thus highlighting their tensions and complementarities. The resulting analyses are quite complicated, but also unusually revealing.[4]

One might counter that "relationalism" is nothing but a fancy way of talking about power, or the ability to get one's way in a conflict of wills. This is a fair complaint, except for the nuance that political power is more than the exertion of will; it is exertion *with constraints*. Law codifies rules regarding contests of will, as well as many other types of relationships. Family law, for example, imposes standards of behavior on husbands, wives, parents, and children. Labor laws outline the things employers and employees can and cannot do in competing for control over the workplace.

Jurisdiction is a simple but useful term for the legal delineation of such relationships, referring to the legal ambit of political actors—the things they are formally charged with doing. Jurisdictional rules define constraints and opportunities for persons and organizations of many different stripes, from husbands and wives to the executive, judicial, and legislative branches of government. More important, jurisdictional rules circumscribe what can be done in one domain *relative to another.* If, for example, a certain task—say the routine maintenance of bridges—is allocated to one government agency, then the actions of all other agencies are thereby constrained. This is exactly where politics get so complicated, because our aforementioned bridge agency may have some duties that are clearly assigned to it and others that are not, thereby begging the question of who should be responsible for identifying, defining, and completing undefined, unallocated tasks. Such questions are not always easily answered; rival agencies might covet the same task. Jurisdictional ambiguity tends to create opportunities for political innovation, as well as chaos, conflict, and conquest.

The political histories of the United States and Canada are filled with examples in which the character, clarity, and contentiousness of their respective jurisdictional regimes has had landmark, though often unintended, consequences for their political development. Consider the fact that the US Constitution is fairly clear about the powers and limitations of state and federal government but virtually silent on the governance of *cities*—places where many of the nation's most pressing social problems converge. American cities are formally subject to their encompassing American states, but these relationships are vague and often quite contentious. Furthermore, federal programs that target cities and city dwellers often circumvent state governments.

The overall relationship between American city, state, and federal government is loosely and ambiguously defined. Washington, DC, is an archetypal case. The District of Columbia is not part of an American state; its municipal government is under the direct jurisdiction of Congress, although its elected congressperson has no formal vote in Congress, much to the chagrin of Washingtonians. The Canadian Constitution, in contrast, places city affairs under the *direct* stewardship of the provinces. There is relatively little ambiguity regarding government responsibility for urban affairs. This simple difference goes a long way toward explaining disparities in Canadian and American urban history.[5]

In both cases, moreover, matters are complicated by the fact that each municipality is not a single jurisdiction but many overlapping and sometimes conflicting jurisdictions—counties, boroughs, school districts, regional development and transportation zones. Each of these subjurisdictions contains its own mix of well- and poorly defined features. Politics are complicated, indeed.

One conceptual key here is the role of ambiguity in institutional scripts, or the all-too-common situation where political means and ends do not match. Many scholars treat institutions as rigid organizational forms that are constrained and constraining from the outset. In point of fact, most political institutions are much more malleable than this. In this book, I illustrate the feedback effects of institutional action on ordinary civilians, who often respond to state action in unpredictable ways (something we might jargonize as *extra-institutional compensation*). I also observe the cascade effect of institutional "memory" on political action, such as when large-scale successes or failures are considered evidence of the viability of entire domains of institutional action (*institutional imprinting*). Finally, I frequently have cause to note the reconfiguration of state institutions in light of changed or otherwise unanticipated circumstances (*institutional recoupling*). These are some institutional mechanisms by which state action cumulates over time, thereby creating national political "styles."

Technical parlance usually limits use of the term "jurisdiction" to intergovernmental relations, but I see it as an appropriate term of reference for state-supervised deliberation about autonomy and control of any kind. A dispute between neighbors over *property rights* would be an example where government must serve as a de facto mediator between individual property owners. In fact, property deeds and titles only exist because of government support and enforcement. So-called *intermediary associations*—corporations, partnerships, trusts, clubs, and congregations—also play an important role in this respect; they owe their existence to state action recognizing them as such. Nation-states themselves can be viewed as "legal fictions" of a sort—they are legal constructs that hold power over subsidiary legal constructs. Seen this way, national societies resemble vast amalgamations of overlapping legal entities that act and react to one another through time and space.[6]

Explaining how these vastly complicated, always-changing legal regimes come to be is no easy task. We might err in interpreting national legal regimes as products of national character or ideology. This would be unwarranted, for laws are *not* direct emanations of collective values or cultural "repertoires," though they certainly do help shape them. The legal infrastructure of any given society is comprised of multiple, often uncoordinated judicial and legislative actions that are subsequently interpreted, implemented, resisted, and/or transformed by the members of society.

Comparative Political Development and Jurisdictional Law

Four observations have led me to believe that law is a useful place to start thinking about international variation in the political development of nation-states: (1) law is geographically bounded, as are nation-states; (2) legal regimes constitute sets of ideas about social life that serve as "scripts" for legitimate (that is, acceptable) action; (3) law is fundamentally historical and, with institutional support, can easily span centuries, as the Roman legal tradition has done in much of Europe; and (4) laws shape human action—collective and individual—in ways that are verifiable, common, explainable, and concrete. The intractable puzzle of national political differences is thus reduced to the highly tractable trajectories of comparative sociolegal development.

In the case of the United States and Canada, our obvious starting points are the English and French legal systems established in the original North American settlements (Spanish law demands some attention here as well). Unlike their Anglo-Canadian counterparts, Anglo-Americans treated English common law with an unusually free hand. Though most American states formally adopted common law after the Revolution, early American legislators, lawyers, and jurists felt free to pick and choose from British precedent as they saw fit, thus radically redesigning the system.

One crucially important feature of the early American jurisdictional landscape, for example, is the fact that the separate colonies were chartered independently, on different legal grounds, and with virtually no plan for handling matters pertaining to intercolonial cooperation and conflict. For instance, the colonies of Massachusetts, Connecticut, and Rhode Island were founded as private, for-profit corporations, whereas others, such as Pennsylvania and Maryland, were established as private estates granted to one or a few proprietors to do with as they wished. Efforts to wrest the corporate charters from the New England colonies created a legacy of anti-imperial hostility and covetous regard for legislative autonomy there. In the proprietary colonies, settlers resented and often protested the political power of their landed masters, thus ignoring demands that they stay within prescribed areas of settlement. In the remaining "royal colonies," disputes between domestic legislators and colonial executives fomented power struggles of their own. Combined, these experiences helped push the American colonies toward revolution, while their Canadian counterparts *voluntarily* remained part of the British Empire.

Because the founding American states were as suspicious of one another as they were of their new central government, they drafted a constitution filled with details about what national government should *not* be allowed to do and left the actual responsibilities of government for the states to decide. The Dominion of Canada, by contrast, was created through active negotiation between the would-be federal government and the existing provinces. The resulting arrangement tried to strike a balance between local and federal power and carefully laid out the responsibilities of each.

These differences in the federalist structure of political power have had great ramifications for the political development of each nation.

Over time, the responsibility of Congress for vast expanses of western territory both nurtured the growth of American federal government and fomented powerful suspicion of it. In Canada, by contrast, provincial autonomy was protected by concessions made to Quebecers as early as 1774. What evolved in Canada was a careful, sometimes tense system of federal-provincial power sharing that fostered both landmark policy experimentation at the local level (for example, single-payer health insurance was the idea of a small coterie of Saskatchewan bureaucrats) and "equalization" schemes that redistribute tax dollars from richer to poorer provinces. Though interprovincial tensions still run high in Canada, its unique federalist system helps preserve peace and equity in the midst of deep, sometimes fractious cultural differences.

A second landmark distinction between Canadian and American jurisdictional law regards the role and regulation of private corporations. In the aftermath of the American Revolution, the so-called corporate colonies—Massachusetts, Connecticut, and Rhode Island—reconceptualized a key aspect of the "legal fiction" of corporations: *the ability to incorporate.* Whereas English common law conceived of corporations as monopoly rights granted by the sovereign, these new American states made incorporation something that nearly anyone could acquire. Canada maintained the British system of restricted incorporation until the late nineteenth century, when American standards of "freedom of incorporation" were already spreading around the world. In the meantime, a single corporation, the Hudson's Bay Company, held a legal monopoly over nearly all trade and governance in central and western Canada. The United States and Canada deployed very different legal conceptions of intermediary associations for much of their early history. Remnants of those differences still remain, particularly in the realms of corporate taxation and regulation, as well as church-state relations, higher education, and campaign finance law.[7]

The nature and enforcement of *property law*, particularly as it relates to private land claims, is another key component of the contrasting jurisdictional landscape of the United States and Canada. Because land grants and colonial charters were issued in the thirteen colonies without much regard for consistency or legal enforceability, settlers and colonies clashed over land boundaries with unusual frequency. Much litigation followed, which prompted the emergence of new legal norms, as well as the formal American profession of law. This prompted more civil litigation and more legal development, which ultimately had profound consequences for American political development, particularly with respect to the connection between legal institutions and ordinary people. An American legal culture evolved rife with litigation and mutual suspicion. Combined with the fact that the colonial governments themselves were often in dispute over their shared borders, this helped plant the seeds for an American revolution in law, both in terms of the number of lawyers employed and the scope and volume of civil cases brought before American jurists.

Early settlement in Canada, by contrast, was centrally organized by the French colonial government, thus precluding the contentiousness of the early American system. New France had its own problems—a sagging economy and poor military defenses—but it did not suffer from the kind of overexpansion and contention extant in the American colonies. Similarly, the land grant system in early Ontario was corrupt and inefficient, but titles at least were clear and property rights sacrosanct. The conservatism inherent in English land law, as well as the bureaucratic fastidiousness of early nineteenth-century English colonialism, helped forestall the chaos of the American scene.

Consider the example of two towns settled by New Englanders in the 1760s—Liverpool, Nova Scotia, and Machias, Maine. These two towns were both easily accessible by sail from Boston, Halifax, and London, making them equally susceptible to imperial influence. Both towns were also populated by the same stock of hardy, Protestant New Englanders. Nonetheless, the Mainers willingly joined the American Revolution whereas the Nova Scotians stayed out of the fray. Understanding why is a key part of our mission.[8]

Much of the difference seems to revolve around the contrasting jurisdictional frameworks of the two settlements. The province of Nova Scotia was governed by the British in a way that reinforced the legitimacy of colonial rule. Both the symbols and the structures of governance were integrated in order to provide maximum continuity between local, provincial, and imperial authority. Thus, Nova Scotians never had cause to question their link to the empire. New Englanders, however, doubted their imperial status from the very beginning. "The provincial governments of the colonies that rebelled had weaker and more contested vertical linkages with the metropolitan government," notes historian Elizabeth Mancke, "and colonists in them insisted they were not so much provinces within an empire, but discrete overseas provinces of the Crown." At the provincial and local levels in New England, political integration was equally unstable. Regional and even intraprovincial conflict was common. Maine, a subjurisdiction of Massachusetts until 1820, was doubly disadvantaged in this respect—Mainers were subjects of both the Crown *and* Massachusetts, neither of which they were eager to recognize as sovereign. Thus, long before the Revolution, the seeds of rebellion were sown.[9]

These differences were exacerbated by contrasting systems of property and associational law. In Nova Scotia, land was partitioned evenly and distinctly, and township autonomy was constrained by provincial oversight. This differed sharply from the New England township system, in which land companies and township corporations were given free rein to acquire and partition colonial territory. As a result of New England's agonistic system of property and commercial law, lawsuits and civil disputes were unusually common. In Nova Scotia, they were relatively rare.

It is a stretch to generalize from jurisdictional structure to civic character, but the subsequent reputation of New Englanders as a contentious people, aloof and hostile to outsiders, seems noteworthy in this regard. In the timeless words of an acquaintance of New England poet laureate Robert Frost, "Good fences make good neighbors." Good fences were historically more reliable than legal title, which could always be challenged in court, as colonial New Englanders were wont to do. Nova Scotians, and English Canadians more generally, had a far more peaceable reputation; historically and comparatively speaking, they seemed determined to leave politics to the politicians and get on with the long, hard business of hauling nets, tilling fields, trapping, and trading.[10]

This focus on jurisdictional differences thus helps us answer several key questions about comparative American and Canadian politics: Why, given common ties to England and comparable reasons for independence therefrom, did the various colonies of British North America break apart rather than forge a single confederation? Why did the successful American revolutionaries choose to found the "first new nation" in the particular way they did? And how did this differ from comparable efforts in Canada?

After explaining and digesting the ramifications of the American Revolution, I then explore differences in the way both countries expanded west, accessioning indigenous land and erecting new extensions of the polity. Finally, I endeavor to understand the remarkably complex twentieth century, during which each country underwent remarkable and sometimes unpredictable change.

It is not my intention to argue that nation-states deploy consistent, unitary visions of jurisdictional law, but instead to create a comprehensive rubric with which to understand the role of the state as creator and arbiter of legal relationships in government and civil society. These relationships, I argue, shape the prevailing scope and style of political *and* civic behavior in democratic societies. In the case of Canada and the United States, these relationships developed in stages: an incipient stage in which well-developed European legal standards were adapted to totally new circumstances; an intermediary stage in which domestic affairs began to accommodate and transform those European standards; and a "modern" stage in which these new legal cultures emerged in full. Though the legal systems of these two countries have converged in some important ways, basic differences in their jurisdictional makeup and legal culture will likely continue to drive them farther apart, politically speaking.

How Are Canada and the United States Different?

In searching for apt generalizations about Canada and the United States, most scholars put much stock in the respective creeds of their federal governments: "Peace, Order, and Good Government" in Canada; "Life, Liberty, and the Pursuit of Happiness" in the United States. My own analysis finds this a fitting comparison. The interesting and controversial question is what exactly these creeds mean. Here, again, a deeply historical account of contemporary differences proves most useful, for it shows not only the roots and ramifications of such differences but also the intent and meaning endowed them by their creators.[11]

Despite so much evidence to the contrary, not everyone agrees that the United States and Canada are all that different, politically or otherwise.[12] Some scholars have focused on regional instead of national differences; the northern United States is more ideologically similar to the Canadian provinces than to comparable states in the American South. Some have argued for four distinct northern North American political-cultural "zones"; others for nine.[13] I maintain that *national* differences exist and merit study in their own right. Without denying the relevance of regional differences—I consider them frequently herein—my focus is on the transformation of colonies into nation-states.

After studying more than four centuries of North American comparative political development, I agree with others in concluding that the United States is a particularly individualistic, competitive, and litigious society. It is also home to a comparatively entrepreneurial, voluntarist, and high-minded (that is, morally righteous) people. The political culture of contemporary Canada, however, more closely resembles the Western European nations in its tradition of statist paternalism, social liberalism, and fiscal collectivism. For example, Canadians support proactive state social programs and endorse relatively high tax rates, whereas welfare and taxes are anathema in the United States. Unionization rates are far higher in Canada than the United States, as are strikes and collective bargaining agreements. America stands alone in the paramount role its courts play in dispute resolution and compensation for damages. In stark contrast, the US penal system is comparatively larger and far more extreme than Canada's. Compared to the United States, Canadian law has also evolved in ways more tolerant of "deviant" behaviors such as homosexuality, prostitution, and drug use. Legalized abortion, though controversial in both societies, has largely passed muster in Canada but remains a flash point in the United States. These differences are exactly why political scientists and sociologists have been fascinated for so long with the American/Canadian comparison: There are no two more culturally similar nations in the world; yet in terms of their political cultures, they are miles apart.

To avoid under- or overestimating the scale and scope of these differences, I focus on five specific areas in which there are clearly documented, long-standing distinctions between Canada and the United States:

Economic development. Historically, the American economy has been uncommonly robust, creative, and entrepreneurial. Structurally, it is also unique among developed nations in the leeway granted businesses and nonprofit organizations, both in terms of government regulation and requisite taxation. American employers have unusually strong legal rights vis-à-vis workers, and labor unions in general have an embattled history in the United States. Canada has followed its European counterparts, particularly England, in forging a "middle path" between a state-planned and a free market economy.[14]

Collectivism, social services, and voter alignment. Canadians generally support government income assistance and social service programs more than their American counterparts. For example, each Canadian province runs its own mandatory health system, something no American state has achieved (despite repeated efforts and considerable electoral support). Electorally speaking, the political-ideological mix in Canada skews farther left than that in the United States. Canada's center-left Liberal Party dominated national politics for much of the twentieth century, and even Canada's conservative parties are fairly liberal by American standards. At the provincial level in Canada, furthermore, bona fide socialist parties have actually held majorities for sustained periods of time. This has never occurred in the United States.[15]

Comparative federalism. The relationship between national and subnational governments varies greatly between the United States and Canada. In Canada, writes Smith, "the provinces have evolved a degree of autonomy unimagined by the Fathers of [Canadian] Confederation and unexcelled elsewhere by units of a federal system." In the United States, state governments are fairly weak relative to the federal government. Ironically, each nation was conceived around exactly the *opposite* type of federalism it currently practices. The United States was born out of a desire to protect the rights of the states; Canada was founded around the desire to build the strongest possible central government and relatively weak provincial governments. A central task of this volume is to explain this strange reversal.[16]

Individual and civil rights. America has an unusually litigious legal culture in which legal action is often seen as the first means of settling disputes. Individual rights are protected to an extent not seen in most other legal systems. Canada, by contrast, has adhered much more closely to the English common law standard of balancing individual rights and freedoms with matters of collective and governmental concern. Group rights, rather than those of the individual, are the legal standard in Canada.[17]

Identity politics. While there are about as many Spanish-speaking inhabitants in the United States as there are French-speaking inhabitants in Canada (on a per capita basis), Canada is unique in both protecting the linguistic rights of French speakers and offering them territorial enfranchisement in the Province of Quebec. Neither policy would be tolerable in the United States. There are also salient differences in the ways these two nations approach issues of religion, race and ethnicity, citizenship, and aboriginal rights. Contemporary Canada is generally considered a more multicultural, less assimilationist society than the United States. There is no legal separation of church and state in Canada, as there is in the United States. Canada also lacks America's history of intense and sometimes militant patriotism.[18]

Many claim that the chief difference between the United States and Canada is that one is a "socialist" country and the other is not. I believe this view overstates the scope of state social programs and income redistribution in Canada relative to those of other developed nations.[19] It also understates the extent of social welfare programs in the United States—particularly if America's enormous prison population is included—and overlooks the long and varied history of Socialist Party activity in the United States. Socialism itself is a relatively new concept, historically speaking, as is the conception of the modern "welfare state." Many of the most salient political differences between Canada and the United States predate these ideas and institutions. There must be larger, more durable factors at play.

Alternative Explanations of the "Continental Divide"

In general, efforts to explain differences between the United States and Canada fall into three or four different camps, each of which has something to offer but fails to bear the weight alone. I attempt here to adjudicate between better and worse formulations while drawing on each perspective.

It is true, for example, that Canada's long-lasting ties to Great Britain say a lot about its political trajectory in comparison to the United States. However, the meaning of these ties is more difficult to discern; simply being "connected" to a country through the reins of empire leaves a lot to account for. Canadians are not overly enthusiastic about cricket, for example, nor are they particularly British in their diet, dialect, or demeanor (though they do insist on a select few Britishisms). We know that the Canadian political system is modeled after the British "Westminster" parliamentary system, but so are those of many countries, including some with notably atypical political cultures, such as Singapore and India. In sum, we cannot genuinely expect countries to "look alike" simply because they were designed by, or modeled after, the same political system. In fact, we should probably expect more similarities among the Commonwealth countries than actually exist—at the level of political culture, how much do Jamaica, South Africa, India, and England have in common? One of my primary goals in this book is to think hard about the ways a nation's political roots shape its subsequent political development.

Before proceeding, we need to dispel another common explanation of US/Canadian differences: that Canada's cold weather distinguishes it from the United States. This overlooks the fact that, historically, a large percentage of the American population has lived in quite cold climes, from icy New England to the frigid Great Lakes and northern prairies. Canada *is* a cold country, and inclement weather may have some effect on political development, but myriad factors trump the importance of weather. Climate is not destiny. Significant parts of coastal British Columbia have temperate weather similar to Washington State and Oregon, for example, and there are political differences aplenty there.

Dissimilarities between the United States and Canada are frequently explained by the unusual role of the United States as a global superpower. Certainly, America's geopolitical status has shaped its domestic politics. By contrast, Canadian geopolitics have been subsumed by British imperial policy until recently, and this too has had important ramifications on Canada's domestic affairs. Canadians, moreover, complain mightily about American influence on their political, cultural, and economic development. It is important to remember, however, that these are largely twentieth-century outcomes, things that are happening well into the maturity of both countries. The historicist perspective taken here asks that we attempt to account for such differences in a manner consistent with our larger explanatory apparatus. It just so happens, for example, that an important feature of contemporary American geopolitics—the desire to control other countries through a combination of military aggression and support for local insurgents—is a direct avatar of the way the early United States was settled. Geopolitical position and power are as much outcomes of political development as they are drivers, at least in long-term, macro-historical perspective.

Another set of explanations looks to uncover the *sociodemographic roots* of each nation and their political ramifications: For example, one feature of American history more "exceptional" than any other is the country's ugly experience with race. Overlooking the impact of slavery on the American national experience would be both irresponsible and unwise. Nonetheless, we might still wonder exactly which features of "American exceptionalism" are related to the African-American experience. Race has shaped the political development of the United States with regard to issues such as property rights, civil rights, federalism, and domestic and foreign policy. Racial tensions in the United States have also undermined efforts to build classwide social movements in support of workers' rights and social welfare programs.[20]

Nevertheless, we must not forget that a number of America's counterparts—England, France, and Brazil, for example—have similar track records with regard to racial exclusion, discrimination, and subjugation. Even gentle, multicultural Canada has experienced serious and sometimes violent tumult as a result of race-based sociopolitical divisions—for example, francophones were once considered a distinct "race" of people and slavery existed in Canada throughout the eighteenth century. The United States retained and defended slavery far longer than its counterparts, however. A key question for our inquiry is to explain slavery's persistence in the United States. Moreover, why did white Americans subsequently develop such fraught relationships with their freed slaves? The answers, I argue, revolve around the unusual approach of American law to the issues of private property and states' rights.

A related sociodemographic view of North American political differentiation hovers around the issues of immigration and religious and ethnic diversity. For instance, one often hears the assertion that Canadian national culture is a simple by-product of its immigrant roots; that hardy, hardworking, politically unadventurous Scottish, Irish, and English settlers gave Canada its distinctive character. While appealing in the abstract, this argument is easily refuted: First, it entirely overlooks the impact of French Canadians, as well as aboriginals, *Métis*, Ukrainians, Russians, Italians, Jews, Americans, Chinese, and countless other groups on Canadian national development. Second, it makes the rather untenable argument that the supposed political characteristics of these ethnic groups prevailed over the centuries despite the countervailing trends of assimilation, integration, and intermarriage. And third, it mistakes ethnic stereotypes for sound characterizations, thus allowing observers to see whatever it is they are looking for in a particular group. To give but one example, Scotch-Irish immigrants have been associated with *both* the bellicose individualism of the United States *and* the pacifist, workmanlike spirit of English Canada. Likening contemporary Canada to "old world" Britain is hardly a sound basis for sociopolitical analysis.[21]

Similarly, a literature on the United States equates regional political culture with ethnic stereotypes of its original settlers—"socialist" Wisconsin and its central and northern European settler population, for example. This so-called American mosaic argument twists and turns in trying to account for the country's long and storied history of immigration: Scandinavian farmers pacified the Great Plains; Scotch-Irish rebels created the wild, craggy culture of rural Appalachia; stolid central European laborers instilled the blue-collar ethos of the urban Midwest; urban ethnics fought and competed in ways that rendered socialism all but impossible in the United States; and so on.[22] These types of argument are questionable on several accounts: First, they assume, as do "ethnic" accounts of Canada, that ethnic behavioral patterns not only manifest themselves in political ways but also that such preferences last and spread despite the countervailing pressures of assimilation and integration. Second, while it is true that the United States has institutionalized ethnicity in unique ways, America is not the world's only—or even foremost—immigrant society. France, Australia, Canada, and Argentina all have roughly equivalent histories of in-migration, though often with contrasting results, particularly regarding issues of cultural assimilation and political representation.[23]

All these issues point to the fact that immigration is a major feature of national political development that deserves explanation, not just commentary and description. How did distinct political niches develop around immigrant communities in different parts of Canada and the United States? How and why were these niches more or less durable and influential?

I apply the same principle to the related issue of population size, or the fact that demographically (and economically) speaking, the United States is simply a much larger country than Canada. Size accounts for some differences in the political development of the United States and Canada, but it is also part and parcel of those differences, an outcome of historically different immigration and settlement policies, as well as emerging variations in the economic, social, and political life of each nation. There is no a priori reason why Canada, the world's second-largest country—Canada is slightly larger than the United States by landmass—is today one-tenth as populous as the United States. Given its large percentage of "frozen" territory, Canada is probably destined to be somewhat less populous than the United States, but the current gap is more a product of human history than climate. Many thousands of immigrants landed in Canada only to move on to the United States, which generally welcomed a greater percentage of newcomers into its population than Canada—a trend that is rapidly reversing today. I endeavor here to portray these differences in immigration and population size as both products and drivers of national political development.

A stronger counterpart to this demographic strain of thinking lies in the often-fraught presence of francophone peoples in Canada's midst. If not for the Anglo-American victory in the Seven Years' War, all of Canada may have evolved as part of *la francophonie* (the term French speakers use when referring to the former colonies of France). As it stands, one major Canadian province—Québec—considers itself a "nation within a nation" and occasionally threatens to secede. French Canadians, however, are not altogether unique: Belgians face a similar national rift over language; Spanish Catalans couple linguistic nationalism with their larger pursuit of independence; and numerous other countries contain large linguistic subcultures—the 2000 US Census found, for example, that nearly one in five Americans speaks a language other than English in their home. Seen from the perspective of the US/Canadian question, then, the key point about Canadian biculturalism is not the presence of a sizable linguistic minority, but the fact that it is territorially enfranchised as a subnational jurisdiction—the *Province* of Québec. Oddly enough, there is little political solidarity between Québecers and francophone Canadians living outside of Québec, further evidence that the Canadian biculturalism debate is less about language than it is about provincial (that is, jurisdictional) autonomy.

Finally, there is the question of religious differences: The British colonial government of Canada sought to institute England's state religion, Anglicanism, in most of Canada. Though the presence of the Anglican Church might thus appear to be a key factor in explaining Canada's differences with the United States, Anglicans were actually rather rare in early English Canada. Methodists, Presbyterians, Baptists, and members of other Protestant denominations were far more prevalent, especially in frontier regions, where itinerant preachers were willing to travel muddy back roads and rural constituents were uncomfortable with stuffy, university-educated Anglican clergymen. Many "barnstorming" non-Anglican ministers actually hailed from the United States (as did many of their constituents). Their influence on Canadian Protestants later waned, but the Canadian/American story is nonetheless far more complicated than Anglicans versus "others" in English Canada.[24]

We also should consider the *political-structural approach* taken by many scholars of comparative political development. As already mentioned, Canada is governed under a federalist parliamentary system in which executive power is exercised by the controlling party in the legislature. The structure of the Canadian political system thus contrasts sharply with that of the United States, wherein a strict separation of powers is meant to protect the "ship" of state and two political parties "share the helm." Despite having a multiparty system in Canada, the centrist Liberal Party has dominated Canadian politics for much of its history, thus driving conservatives to continually reconstitute themselves in search of a nationally viable coalition. In contrast, the American two-party system has had a formative role in the evolution of American political ideology— those with extremist political views must infiltrate the centrist parties in order to have influence.[25]

Similarly, the Canadian justice system has been subject to dramatic change under the 1982 Charter of Rights and Freedoms, but Canada still lacks an American-style "independent judiciary" inclined to veto decisions made by the legislative and executive branches. Until 1949, the Judicial Committee of the British Privy Council had veto power over Canadian court decisions, and the British government had similar veto powers over the Canadian parliament (although in both cases, these powers were only rarely invoked).[26]

Another, more significant difference between the political systems of these two countries is their comparative histories of voting rights. The United States offered suffrage to all (white) men before any other country in the world, albeit with legal loopholes that kept many eligible voters away from the polls. Canada, by contrast, only gradually adopted manhood suffrage, more or less in line with its western European counterparts. Political scientists argue that this is significant because voting privileges offered would-be American radicals deliberative venues denied their working-class brethren elsewhere. Suffrage, in other words, dampened working-class radicalism in the United States.[27]

Existing studies have much to tell us about the structural organization of the US and Canadian political systems; the pressing question is what role these differences played in the actual course of national political development. Are they causes of difference or its effects? Remember that the formal construction of the Canadian and American national polities occurred sometime in the *middle* of the historical trajectory we are considering here—both were colonies long before they became independent nation-states. Political-organizational structure is only the shell of nations; the meat and bones lie within, activated by the lifeblood of custom and procedure.

This latter view reflects what is now a prominent approach to studying comparative political development: *historical institutionalism,* or a focus on the role of scripts, rituals, routines, and cognitive schema in political action. Tocqueville's predictions about the convergence of Canadian and American societies can be seen as an early form of this kind of thinking: like many institutionalist scholars today, Tocqueville was interested in processes whereby ideas, preferences, and procedures spread across proximate social spaces—"institutional isomorphism" in the parlance of contemporary social science. My "jurisdictional" approach to the relational apparatus of statecraft fits directly in this tradition. We share a concern with the ways ideas and behaviors are transmitted through time and space. In each case, moreover, there is strong interest in the impact that historical events have on the way present-day people think, the manner in which modern organizations function, and the rationales used by both to justify what they're doing and why. Institutionalists consider cultural scripts and organizational structures to be socially constructed remnants of past experiences—instead of regarding political interests and actions as pure, rational, context-neutral things in themselves.

Historical institutionalism contributes significantly to my analysis of Canadian and American political differences: for example, rather than attributing the revolutionary impulse in the American colonies to some fixed set of preferences or goals, I explore the specific experiences and beliefs that cumulated to give revolutionary Americans their particular view of the situation.[28]

One final type of explanation focuses on *political ideology* rather than on demographics or politics. In the mid-twentieth century, legendary scholars like Samuel Huntington, Gabriel Almond, and Sidney Verba launched a long and venerable tradition of scholarship into the personal, affective components of political order. Their work was built around the belief that the ultimate source of political culture is the psychological disposition of individuals within the polity. They believed that all significant institutions of national life reflect in microcosm the central values of the society in which they circulate.

Seymour Martin Lipset and Louis Hartz are two influential scholars who have tried to apply this perspective directly to the study of the United States and Canada. In his landmark book *The Liberal Tradition in America,* Hartz argues that the United States owes its political distinctiveness to "skipping the feudal stage of history," thus allowing the English "liberal" tradition of political philosophy to evolve in America undisturbed by the influences of Bolshevism and socialism, both common products of class conflict in Europe. The chief difference between England and Canada stems from the sustained role of Tory political ideas in Canada, which, when combined with American liberalism, produced a hybrid political culture. While compelling in the abstract, this account falls short on several accounts. To begin with, class-based political subjugation, if not outright feudalism, *was* present in the colonies of the future United States and Canada, thus providing every opportunity for the sorts of class conflict that led to collectivist ideology in Europe. For Hartz, furthermore, ideas are the engines of history, though we learn relatively little from his account about actual efforts to promote and disseminate such ideas, let alone translate them into actual practice.[29]

Lipset's account of "American exceptionalism" is a bit more causally oriented. He argues that Canadians have historically had a more "deferential" outlook toward authority and government than their American counterparts, and that these differences stem from the ideological self-selection that took place after the American Revolution, when deferential "loyalists" went to Canada and defiant "republicans" stayed in the nascent United States.[30] Unfortunately, Lipset's thesis also falters in several respects. Historically speaking, his account of the "Tory exodus" is quite misleading—many loyalists returned to the United States once hostilities ceased, and many Americans subsequently migrated to Canada under false pretenses, signing loyalist oaths in return for free land. Furthermore, several empirical studies have cast doubt on the very notion that Canadians are more "deferential to authority" than Americans—in fact, an analysis of data from two 1984 electoral surveys found just the opposite.[31]

For our purposes, it is not significant whether a random sample of Americans were more or less trustful of government than a comparable sample of Canadians in 1984, but it does matter that analyses like

Lipset's suffer from a form of tautological reasoning common to the social science of his generation: national ideology is both cause and effect in his (and Hartz's) model. Though this type of reasoning is acceptable in intellectual history, where scholars want to know how specific ideas and philosophical positions developed over time, it is less useful when our subject matter is not political philosophy or personal ideology but the political development of huge agglomerations of people with vastly different experiences, preferences, and interests. We gain little by declaring cultural differences to be self-evident and then using them as explanations for the eccentricities of national political development.[32]

We should also be careful to distinguish political culture from "culture" more generally, the latter being too amorphous and variegated for our purposes. American political culture does have a distinct, perhaps "exceptional" profile in comparative historical perspective, but there is scant reason to believe that this is the result of anything as discrete as the fact that, in Seymour Martin Lipset's words, "the United States is the country of the revolution, Canada of the counter-revolution." Nor does "American individualism" get us far in understanding the roots of this particular disposition.[33]

Fortunately, social scientists since Lipset have made significant strides in advancing our understanding of political culture. Process and procedure are focal points of many contemporary studies of comparative political development, a literature I draw upon frequently in this account.[34]

Jurisdictional Law and Legal Culture

In considering the effects of jurisdiction on political culture, what we are really asking is how certain aspects of a given society's legal institutions shape its larger social and political climate. Unlike explanatory accounts of national political culture based on "national values," "political structure," or "cultural repertoires," a jurisdictional perspective lends itself particularly well to analyses of continuity and change. Courts, legislators, and litigants are all agents in the jurisdictional process.

The concept of "legal culture"—a subset of the larger concept of political culture—has a long and murky history. Though commonly referred to and debated by legal scholars, few standards have evolved concerning its proper usage and form. Law professor Lawrence Friedman's definition of legal culture is quite useful for our purposes; he defines it as "the network of values and attitudes relating to law, which determines when and why and where people turn to law or government, or turn away," and he adds a series of empirical questions we might ask in trying to characterize a given society's legal culture:

> Who goes to court and why? Who occupies legal roles—lawyers, judges, policemen—and what do the role-players do? What is the conversion process of the legal system; that is, how are demands handled, by whom, and how are decisions made? Which officials have discretion; which do not? What questions are matters of rule, and what are matters of discretion? Are various parts of the system bureaucratic or flexible? What are the effects of the outputs on the population and how can we measure them? What is the source of the legitimacy of various parts of the system? Who is supposed to make law; who is supposed to carry it out? Is there much corruption and maladministration and why?[35]

Friedman differentiates this approach to studying comparative law from: (a) lineal accounts based solely on the historical origins of a given legal system (for example, "common law" versus "civil law" countries); and (b) those based primarily on analysis of court procedure (for example, "trial by jury" versus other systems). Friedman's legal culture approach thus has the benefit of considering not just technical differences in legal systems but also their connection to wider patterns of social behavior. It acknowledges, for example, the complex relationships between norms and rules, customs and laws. It also endorses sensitivity to issues such as variance in the degree to which law "penetrates" society, as well as the extent to which constituents participate in the creation and enforcement of law. Though empirical work in this vein is only beginning to bear fruit, it seems an appropriate way to think about the question of the effects of law on political culture, broadly understood.[36]

Nevertheless, our contemporary concept of law should be only the beginning of a search for the origins of national political development. Future scholarship will, we hope, circle back to the question of how modern nation-states came to be defined by law in the first place, as well as the manner in which that development shaped and socialized individuals under respective jurisdictions. Furthermore, we must take seriously the objection that even within the most highly codified legal systems, there are variations in the actual consistency of enforcement. Jurisdiction is a useful concept in that it embraces the idea that task management is often contentious and that political organizations some-times fail at the tasks assigned them. This is exactly where the present inquiry into the comparative political development of the United States and Canada gains traction, for here we find inconsistencies in the evolution and enforcement of jurisdictional law that do, in fact, tell us much about the way social relations and state power developed in northern North America.

1

Origins of the Colonial System

The presiding myths of early American history are largely false. National myths and rituals do not reflect history as much as they help make it interesting; they represent embellished wishes for vision, purpose, and national character. National holidays epitomize this process—false celebrations of falsely reported events.[1]

For example, most Americans think the first North American Thanksgiving Day was celebrated in 1621 at Plymouth Plantation in modern-day Massachusetts. In fact, it was more likely observed in 1578, by British explorers in modern-day Canada. Moreover, that first celebration at Plymouth was not really a thanksgiving at all, at least not in terms the Pilgrims would have understood. It was something more like a giving thanks, and it was probably not held until 1623. "Thanksgivings" were strictly religious holidays in England; formal in aspect and demeanor, they usually involved fasting, not feasting.

The Pilgrims were not the first English settlers in North America, but they are, perhaps, the most well known. Unhappy in the Netherlands, where they had taken refuge from Anglican religious persecution, the Pilgrims sought a new home. Noting the ambling success of the Jamestown settlement in Virginia, where private enterprise had taken route under draconian, quasi-military rule during the 1610s, the Pilgrims sought their own contract to settle in the New World. At the same time, the Virginia Company, host to the Jamestown settlement, was in dire financial straits and looking to issue "special privileges and patents to groups of undertakers, who," in historian Charles Andrews' words, "either would go to Virginia themselves or would send over tenants and servants for the purpose of setting up private plantations." After a long spell of contract arbitration and legal entanglement (according to one authoritative account, a last-minute contract dispute on the eve of departure nearly killed the journey) a deal was made to issue the Pilgrims a grant of land in Virginia where, as we now well know, they never arrived.[2]

In the late fall of 1620, after a long journey and several false starts, the captain of the *Mayflower* decided to drop anchor at Cape Cod and reconnoiter. A Pilgrim landing party found Plymouth Harbor about a month later, and it was decided that this would be an appropriate place to settle. Fortunately, the local natives were friendly and their numbers were unusually small, having suffered an outbreak of epidemic disease several years earlier, most likely caused by exposure to itinerant European fishermen who made occasional stops along the coast to dry fish and take on fresh water.

Because this was not their original destination, the Pilgrims had no legal title to the land on which they were attempting to settle, a major legal complication that required their backers in London to negotiate impromptu terms with the Virginia Company's northern branch, the Council for New England. Construction on the colony's first building began, appropriately enough, on December 25, 1620 (though the Pilgrims did not celebrate "pagan" holidays like Christmas).[3]

The Pilgrims almost did not survive their first winter at Plymouth. They had arrived poorly supplied, and they had yet to receive fresh provisions from their London backers, who wished to see solid profits from the colony before spending any more on the venture. (The colony was funded as a for-profit endeavor, though many of the original investors also shared the religious sympathies of the Pilgrims). Thus, when the harvest of 1621 proved bountiful, a celebration was in order. According to contemporary records:

> Our Governour sent foure men on fowling, that so we might after a more speciall manner reioyce together, after was had gathered the fruit of our labours. They foure in one day killed as much fowle, as with a little helpe beside, served the Company almost a weeke, at which time amongst other Recreations, we exercised our Armes, many of the Indians coming amongst vs, and amongst the rest their greatest King Massasoyt, with some ninetie men, whom for three days we entertained and feasted, and they went out and killed fiue Deere, which they

brought to the Plantation and bestowed upon our Governour, and upon the Captaine, and others.[4]

This was the occasion of American lore now remembered as the first Thanksgiving Day.

Keeping in mind the gross solemnity with which the Pilgrims practiced their faith, one can hardly mistake this 1621 harvest celebration for a formal thanksgiving. The practice of such rituals was so carefully regulated that they were not held on Fridays or Mondays, which were traditional Catholic and Anglican days of fasting and thanksgiving.[5] Another now-exploded myth concerns the warm, friendly relations between the Pilgrims and the local natives that are memorialized during the American Thanksgiving Day holiday. Mistrust, war, and betrayal ran rife in the region for most of the next century and a half—until the local natives were all but eliminated.

The first actual Thanksgiving Day was apparently held in late July 1623, following a long period of drought that threatened to leave the Pilgrims hungry for yet another winter. A day of fasting had been called to beckon rain and the arrival of two ships bearing settlers and provisions from Leyden. Whether by coincidence or divine intervention, the rain began to fall the very next day and continued for two weeks, until about July 30, when a genuine day of thanksgiving was held. A day or two later, the missing ships arrived from Leyden.[6]

Good fortune and happy tidings aside, the story of the Pilgrims is actually quite emblematic of several important trends in American political development: From the outset, the Pilgrims were without clear title to the land they inhabited, and they did not have a royal charter incorporating them as a trading company. "The colonists were squatters, destitute of legal rights of settlement," notes one account. This kind of jurisdictional ambiguity and territorial hubris remained a hallmark of American settlement policy for the next three hundred years.[7]

Their community was also far from the egalitarian, democratic society exalted in American national mythology. From the start, the Pilgrims knew that it would not be easy to preserve the religious tenor of their settlement. According to Andrews' account:

The Pilgrims were a small group—but the dominating group—within the larger body of passengers on board, and they realized the necessity, if their religious integrity were to be preserved, of keeping in their own hands the entire control of affairs. . . . Before going ashore, where the rebellious members of the company might become less manageable than on shipboard, they drafted a solemn agreement, which was signed in the cabin of the *Mayflower* by forty-one [out of a total of one hundred and one] adults.

The now-famous Mayflower Compact is hardly an emblem of inclusive self-government; it was explicitly drafted to keep control of the colony in the hands of the devout.[8]

The Pilgrims were also very concerned with their rights and responsibilities as a business enterprise. As long as they remained under contract to the Council for New England, they had no independent control over their destiny. In 1626, the enterprise's principal investors sold their interest in the colony to the Puritans for £1,800. Plymouth had failed in its principal mission as a for-profit trading center. The colonists toiled on, concerned with their religious mission as well as their financial stake.[9]

The colony's legal status remained as much of a problem as its ailing finances. It never obtained a royal charter of incorporation, though, notes Andrews, "they ardently desired to do so and made many attempts and spent much money to that end." It is not entirely clear why such efforts failed, but Andrews' reading of the colonial correspondence indicates that it was probably due to poor legal representation and the lack of money needed to procure a charter. This was risky. "The want of a legal right to exist proved its ultimate undoing," says Andrews. Plymouth was ultimately annexed to Massachusetts in 1691, thus losing any legal autonomy it had established during its prior seventy-one years of existence. Possession of legal title via royal fiat was a key concern of the Pilgrims, one with far greater resonance than their faith, hope, and vision.[10]

Thus, we reconcile the past and present histories of Plymouth Plantation. The first thanksgivings had little to do with prosperity or intercultural understanding. They were wholly devout affairs that expressed appreciation to God for removing and rescuing Nonconformists from the perils of harsh weather, stormy seas, and the dual tempests of Catholic and Anglican hostility. The practice of holding annual harvest festivals like the modern Thanksgiving Day feast did not become a regular affair in New England until the 1660s, nearly forty years after its supposed origins. President Abraham Lincoln made Thanksgiving Day an official

American national holiday in 1863, in an effort to institutionalize, and thereby propagate, his desired ideal of intercultural acceptance and exchange among mutually suspicious, potentially warring peoples.

Tellingly, the first official *Canadian* Thanksgiving Day occurred soon thereafter, on April 15, 1872. (In fact, many important events in Canadian political history occurred in response to US precedent.) Prior to that, the colonial governors of the separate Canadian provinces had declared their own days of thanksgiving. Canada had only been declared a nation in 1867, but, notably, this first Canadian Thanksgiving Day in 1872 was *not* observed to honor the new nation but to celebrate the recovery of the Prince of Wales from serious illness. This is indicative of Canadian national history, or the lack of it; Canadians have a strong national identity and a unique cultural patrimony, but not a strong sense of collective history.

For example, there is no compelling narrative of the origins of the Canadian Thanksgiving Day holiday other than the rather uninteresting fact that it is now celebrated more than a month earlier than America's—presumably owing to the early onset of winter in the North. In fact, the first documented thanksgiving in North America was held in Canada several decades before the Pilgrims' famous harvest fête. Sir Martin Frobisher ordered the first thanksgiving prayer during a 1578 voyage off Baffin Island, during which he unknowingly discovered the entrance to Hudson's Bay (Frobisher named the mouth of Hudson's Bay "Mistaken Strayts").[11]

Frobisher's three voyages to the New World were dismal failures that resulted in financial ruin and embarrassment for nearly everyone involved—he was knighted only for his subsequent efforts as a British naval captain. In addition to the several Inuit hostages that Frobisher brought back with him from his first two voyages were some black rocks that he thought might contain silver or gold. When assayers declared that these rocks were chock-full of precious metal, "gold fever" overtook England. An expensive smelting plant was built in anticipation of the torrents of gold waiting to be harvested in Canada. The Spanish government even sent a spy to keep an eye on the venture, suspecting that the English might finally have discovered their own source of American gold.

Alas, Frobisher and his fleet of fifteen ships returned with nothing more than hardship stories and several tons of useless rock, some of which was used to build a stone wall around the Queen's manor house in Dartford, England—the rocks are still there today. Regardless, Frobisher's "discovery" of Baffin Island prompted what would later become England's colonial toehold in northern North America.[12]

Surprisingly, none of this seems to surface when Canadians discuss the origins of their national Thanksgiving Day holiday. Thus, we see the forgetfulness of nations, as well as the private, for-profit origins of England's claim to northern North America. In both the forgotten story of Martin Frobisher and the more contemporary one of thanksgiving in October, Canada gives thanks to bureaucrats and businessmen, not dreamers and ideologues. America's thanksgiving story, in contrast, is one of love and death, danger and redemption; a story that masks the business of colonial profiteering in a veil of accommodation and piety.

Foundational myths notwithstanding, these rival stories also hold important clues about the legal-organizational structure of the earliest European settlements in the New World, as well as the economic and agricultural systems erected to support them. Some of these features became the basis of the jurisdictional makeup of these colonies in subsequent years: In colonial New England, the "legal fiction" of the private, for-profit corporation served as the basis for colonial endeavor at the regional level. Though intended as a means of providing royal sanction to capital-intensive overseas speculation, the corporate organizational form was used by the New England Puritans in new and untested ways, thus fomenting 150 years of legal conflict with the Crown. Elsewhere, the Jamestown Colony in Virginia failed and came under royal supervision, thus creating another model of colonialism in the proto-United States. In proto-Canada, meanwhile, the French were making their first forays into missionary activity and trade among the natives. Much changed in subsequent periods, but the basic concept underlying each colonial endeavor largely remained: conjoint diplomacy in New France; aggressive entrepreneurialism in New England; and agrarian paternalism in Virginia.

Strategy and Structure in British North America

While the Pilgrims held their "thanksgivings" and the Jamestown settlement muddled along, there was still no substantive British presence in modern-day Canada. British settlement in New Scotland—or Nova Scotia, as it was named in its 1621 charter—lasted only three short years. Britain did not regain jurisdiction of this region until 1713, when much of the Maritime Provinces were granted them by France as part of the Treaty of Utrecht. Newfoundland remained only sparsely populated by English and French fishermen until the late eighteenth century. The only other exception was the southern area of Hudson's Bay, then known as Rupert's Land, where the Hudson's Bay Company, chartered in 1670, began slowly but surely to steal the fur trade from the French.[13]

Prior to 1670, the bulk of England's colonial efforts in North America centered on the Atlantic coast of what would later become the United States. Having been in contact for a long while with the Spanish colonies in Central and South America, the English targeted nearby shores along the Atlantic. English merchant companies were already active in India, the Baltic, and the Mediterranean, so a ready means existed to mobilize capital and manpower for foreign settlement. For the English Crown, moreover, there now emerged the imperative to block other European powers on the new, still largely unexplored continent. Mercantilist economics dictated the need to secure natural resources, and potentially tariffs from trade, in the New World.[14]

The English, in contrast to the French and Spanish, were not overly intent on evangelizing native North Americans; they saw no need to establish frontier outposts where clergy could live among them. English settlement thus proceeded only gradually into the American interior. Despite the relative density of settlement, however, governance of the English colonies was far less centralized than in the French and Spanish colonies at both the local and imperial levels. Until the late seventeenth century, little thought was given to coordinated strategy among the separate British colonies in North America.[15]

Because the British colonists never had a clear sense of legitimate imperial order, they were perpetually mired in speculation about their rights and responsibilities as British subjects. Subsequent attempts to rationalize administration of the American colonies fomented high levels of resistance to royal oversight. The original lack of British colonial policy lent the American colonists an unusually strong sense of autonomy and anomie, both of which helped fuel the spiral of dissent that typified prerevolutionary America. Even in the heat of the Revolution, however, American colonists still felt quite "British."

Unlike the French and Spanish efforts of the time, the English sought to build small but permanent agricultural settlements in North America.

England was already far ahead of its European rivals in domestic economic development and sought places to export surplus population and import surplus grain. Because of its geography, England did not require a land army the size of its continental rivals; instead, naval power was the focus of English might, a strategy that dovetailed well with the erection of overseas colonies. This mix of surplus population, ready sea power, and a vastly growing need for natural resources, oriented English colonial strategy in directions not taken by the continental powers. Unlike the earlier Spanish model of colonialism, which crafted a one-way transfer of resources and manpower from west to east, the British anticipated a bidirectional system in which new axes of "domestic" development would be nurtured in the New World, relations that would be maintained by regular sea traffic. Increasingly sophisticated capital exchange markets facilitated these aims by providing a steady stream of private investors ready and willing to take risks on overseas development.

Nonetheless, the decision to take up this new form of colonialism was not made by royal fiat but by the unwitting agglomeration of market forces, religious dissent, and entrepreneurialism. British North America evolved piecemeal. In the (thirteen) colonies that later made up the United States, three different models of English colonialism were employed: The Pilgrims and Puritans brought to New England a "corporate" form of colony based on the English model of the common-law corporation. *Corporate colonies* were those in which a group of private investors received monopoly rights from the king to a fixed parcel of land. The assorted colonies of New England—Massachusetts Bay (including Maine), Connecticut, and Rhode Island—were founded as corporate colonies. English reliance on private trade corporations for these purposes became a hallmark of British North America, and it was through this organizational form that many of the original ideas inhabiting the contemporary American political-legal system were hatched.[16]

In *proprietary colonies,* by contrast, similar rights were bestowed by the king upon a single individual or small group of individuals (as opposed to a "corporation"). Unlike the corporate colonial form, which placed said corporations under strict legal obligation to the king, a proprietary grant gave its bearers virtually absolute power over their holdings. The colony was held and governed by the "proprietors" as their private fief. New York, New Jersey, Pennsylvania, Maryland, Georgia, and the Carolinas were originally founded as proprietary colonies.

In the *royal colonies,* the king retained direct ownership of the land, as well as the right to govern without reservation. New Hampshire was chartered as a royal colony. Virginia was originally chartered as a private corporation, but after persistent failure, the king soon changed it to a royal colony. Interestingly, Delaware was never actually chartered; it was technically part of Pennsylvania until the Revolution, when it unilaterally seceded from Pennsylvania, as did Vermont from New York.

The surprising array of legal administrative means that were used to create and organize the British North American colonies in the seventeenth century merit a closer look; they provide key insights into the jurisdictional origins of the United States.

The Virginia Company—Jamestown and Plymouth Settlements

The Virginia Company was granted a corporate charter in 1606, which gave it monopoly rights to all the land between modern-day Maine and Georgia—the extent and vagueness of this grant subsequently caused much conflict. Originally organized as a private joint stock company, the Virginia Company was actually comprised of two separate groups of investors: one from London, the other from the southwestern port town of Plymouth. Two different American colonies were planned—one by the London branch at Jamestown in southern Virginia and the other by the Plymouth group at Sagadahoc in Maine. The Sagadahoc settlement lasted only a year, though the Plymouth group retained the right to plant future settlements there.[17]

Jamestown did survive, but barely. The general plan for settlements of this type was for investors to send a group of colonists overseas to create and inhabit a small agricultural plantation. The colonists were generally offered no remuneration except the rights to a plot of land in the new settlement should they survive the ocean passage and the initial rough years.

The organizational form of the joint stock company had been widely used in England to finance speculative ventures to foreign ports, but the merchant adventurers of the time had little experience actually colonizing new land. None among them seemed to know much about indigenous crop and soil conditions, let alone the extreme weather patterns of the New World. Several hundred settlers—many of whom were there out of desperation, most without firsthand knowledge of how to build cabins, clear fields, or greet natives—were expected somehow to build a successful village in the wilds.

The Virginia Company was issued a new charter in 1609 that reorganized governance of the company and authorized the formal purchase and sale of its stock. (Legal wrangling over charters and charter rights is a persistent theme in American political development.) Though there was less dissent among the colonists as a result, material conditions were scarcely improved. Disease, hunger, and skirmishes with the natives continued to decimate the population of Jamestown. The charter was redrafted again in 1612, this time expanding the colony's jurisdiction to include Bermuda, which solidified the rule of law through a regular court system, and bolstered the investors' power to raise funds for the colony through annual lotteries that were held in England. In addition, the Virginians had some success growing tobacco on their plantations. Though it was no match for the tobacco being produced in the Spanish colonies to the south, Virginia tobacco was granted tax support by the king.

Virginia quickly became dependent on tobacco as a cash crop, despite the fact that the king himself found it a "noxious weed." Because it brought in so much tax revenue, instead of lobbying for its prohibition, the king had all tobacco farms banned from England and Ireland, thus increasing the Virginians' dependence on monoculture. Nonetheless, quips Herbert L. Osgood, "English statesmen of the time always deprecated the fact that the Virginians devoted so much of their labor to the raising of tobacco, and spoke with regret or protest against a plantation being founded so largely on smoke."[18]

Indeed, acrimony over the organization of the tobacco trade soon brought the Virginia Company's Bermuda and Virginia factions into a disagreement so fierce that their corporate charter was revoked in 1642, and Virginia reorganized as a royal colony.

As with many of England's North American ventures, neither the king nor his council had very clear ideas about how best to govern Virginia. In fact, a clear set of instructions for the operation of the Virginia colony was not drafted until 1638. One of its most important provisions was permission for the colonists to continue to convene a general assembly, or legislature. Ironically, Charles I was concurrently trying to govern England without the input of its legislature. His decision to grant Virginia legislative representation is thus a testament to the unusual autonomy granted the earliest British colonies; presumably, this was done so that England would not have to expend excessive time and energy governing them. The promise of profits from the tobacco farms of Virginia was also a likely motivation for appeasing the settlers, as the Crown stood to gain much revenue from taxes on this increasingly popular commodity. Regardless of his motivation, Charles had created an important precedent in Virginia "according to which the people of any royal colony were assured of their right to share in the making of laws, the levying of taxes," and so forth.[19]

This hardly settled matters. Both by lack of design and the internal turmoil then consuming England, consistent administration of the colonies was still a long way off. Though most of the thirteen colonies came to resemble the Virginia model in part by the early eighteenth century, the remainder of the seventeenth century brought various experiments in self-government and colonial rule. The corporate colonies of Puritan New England deserve special mention in this respect. These intervening events, so often ignored by students of American political development, actually say more about the pending Revolution and its aftermath than the tax and tariff controversies of the 1760s and 1770s.

"Corporate" Colonialism in Puritan New England

Unlike Virginia, which lost its corporate charter early on, several settlements in colonial New England had more success as private corporations. For instance, settlers from the Massachusetts Bay Company colony, centered in Boston, subsequently went on to form the corporate colonies of Connecticut and Rhode Island, as well as usurp other independent colonies such as New Haven and Plymouth.

Like the Pilgrims who settled Plymouth Plantation, the Massachusetts Puritans left England because they feared for their future under King Charles I, a monarch devoted to restoring many of the Catholic appendages of Christian worship. Recognizing that it was nonetheless in Charles's interest to continue promoting the English settlement of North America, a group of Puritans under the leadership of a modest provincial lawyer, John Winthrop, applied for and gained a charter to settle near the existing settlements of the Plymouth Plantation. This new Puritan colony was not Winthrop's idea, but he was chosen to lead the first party of settlers because of his extensive connections in the English Puritan community, as well as his legal training, which soon came in handy.[20]

As was so often the case in British North America, there were legal complications aplenty for the colonists. The legitimacy of the Massachusetts Bay Company's charter was suspect from the start. The actual plot of land granted by the king to the Massachusetts Bay Company in 1629 had previously been offered to the Council for New England, which had established a corporation called the Dorchester Company to settle the area. The Dorchester Company had tried and failed to create a series of fishing villages along the coast to the north of Boston Harbor. Arrangements were supposedly made to transfer title of this land from the Council of New England to a new concern, the New England Company (a predecessor of the Massachusetts Bay Company), but the legality of the deed was contested at the time and no documentation of it remains—in fact, some believe that the proprietors of the Massachusetts Bay Company destroyed these documents, realizing that they might otherwise be used against them in legal proceedings.[21]

Members of the rival Council for New England repeatedly tried to have the Massachusetts Bay Company charter revoked, a battle that continued well past the American Revolution, when inhabitants of Maine disputed Massachusetts's claim to their territory via these early eighteenth-century land grants. Furthermore, there was great hostility in England toward the religious goals of the colony. In 1633, a special Commission for Regulating Plantations (colloquially referred to as the Laud Commission, after its head, William Laud, bishop of London) was convened to investigate claims that the colonists were religious extremists who violated church policy. For a short time, the Laud Commission tried to restrict emigration to the colony. In July 1634, they demanded that the Massachusetts Bay Company's charter be submitted to them for inspection.[22]

The company's response is significant because it entails a landmark departure from both English colonial policy and corporate law. In response to the request to deliver the charter to England for scrutiny, the company's governing council resolved "not to return any answer or excuse." They forestalled a second request by claiming that they could not respond until the next meeting of the colony's legislative assembly, which would take several months. When the Laud Commission threatened to send a military envoy to seize their charter by force, the Massachusetts Bay colonists raised a tax to build military fortifications in strategic locations, one of which was a sentry post at "Beacon Hill," the current site of the Massachusetts State House.

Though no such convoy ever arrived, the very fact that the company refused assent to a royal order was a violation of the common-law understanding of corporate privilege. Corporations served "at the king's pleasure," meaning that their special privileges were granted with the proviso that they remain directly accountable to the king. The leaders of the Massachusetts Bay Company were able to resist such intrusions in part because they had taken the unusual step of bringing the corporate seal—literally, a medallion used to stamp all official corporation documents—with them across the Atlantic. As long as they possessed the seal, they held de facto power to act as a corporation. This, coupled with the migration of a majority of the corporation's officers, unified the colony and the corporation in a single place. "This removal was a fact of the greatest importance not only in the history of New England," writes historian Herbert Osgood, "but in the development of modern governmental forms."[23]

One reason for moving the corporate council from England to the colony in Massachusetts Bay was the company's desire to evade government oversight. Anything London might seek to do with regard to the colony would first have to travel over several thousand miles of ocean. While this distanced the Puritans from a government that technically and actually held the power to revoke their charter and remove them from Massachusetts, it added greatly to their legal expenses. A legal representative was almost perpetually employed in London to represent the colony in legal and business affairs, arrange shipments of durable goods back to Massachusetts, fend off creditors and intrusions, and take the general temperature of England in a time of great religious and political ferment.

The Massachusetts Bay Company's charter technically allowed for the "removal" of the corporate council because it failed to stipulate a "place of residence" for the corporate seal, an oversight that historian Charles Andrews feels must have been inadvertent, since the charter would never have been granted if any such intention had been evident. The charter itself was probably only granted because of the money and influence of its chief backers—for example, Mathew Cradock, first governor of the new colony, remarked that they had obtained the charter "from his Majesty's especiall grace, with great cost, favor of personages of note and much labor."[24]

Regardless, under Winthrop's guidance, these Puritans had special zeal for the corporate organizational form. Corporations did not have many of the legal powers vested in them today, but it was nonetheless a legal shell within which community property could be aggregated and protected. This suited the Puritans' specific religious preference: unlike many Protestants, who sought to organize allied churches within a collective presbytery, the Massachusetts Puritans sought a congregationalist model within which each individual church would be autonomous and self-governing—much like a private corporation. This was a controversial idea at the time, even among staunch Puritans, so Winthrop and his associates kept it rather quiet. During that time, the Massachusetts Bay government used the corporate organizational form more as a conceptual model than as an actual legal structure. They relied on this model for organizing churches and townships, as well as a small theological seminary called Harvard College, which today remains the oldest continually operating corporation in North America.[25]

The leaders of the Massachusetts Bay colony wasted no time in exercising their rights as members of a chartered corporation. Using company funds, they offered bounties to entrepreneurs who were willing to establish mines, textile mills, and iron mongeries in the colony. In addition, townships were conceived and settled—also well within the rights of the colonists. However, when the company decided to legally incorporate Harvard College in 1650, they markedly changed the path of American history.

Though originally founded in 1636, the subsequent incorporation of Harvard College granted it a number of rights, privileges, and immunities not otherwise available: The corporation would have "perpetual succession," or the right to pass itself from one set of administrators to another, thus guaranteeing that the institution would outlive its founders. The charter also established the college's right to buy and sell property, "sue and plead or be sued and impleaded," as well as choose "officers and servants." The colonial legislature also granted the college and its staff some exemption from "taxes and rates" and some civil offices, such as "military exercises," "watchings and wardings." A few years later, following a brawl between Harvard students and Cambridge residents, it was also determined that local law enforcement officials would have only limited power on campus, thus establishing the precedent of "campus police" and internal discipline in all but the most extreme cases.[26]

The college charter itself is a rather lavish affair, including not only elaborate calligraphy but also drawings of the college arms and a young man shooting a squirrel while his dog looks on expectantly. The legal language incorporated in the charter resembles that of earlier English universities, such as those of Emmanuel College in Cambridge, England. "The phrases in question were common to all corporate grants and would have been known by heart by a man like [Richard] Bellingham," who, as "the only trained lawyer then in a position of authority in Massachusetts," is believed to have drafted the actual legal language in the charter.[27]

It also should be noted that the incorporation of a college was, in itself, nothing unusual under English law. Universities had long been considered private concerns worthy of legal institutionalization, thereby providing their members some means of conducting collegiate affairs while assuring the "perpetual" life of the college. What is noteworthy about the incorporation of Harvard College is the circumstance under which it was incorporated. Technically, English corporations such as the Massachusetts Bay Company were expressly forbidden from chartering corporations; this was a privilege reserved for the king, and later Parliament. Though overseas trade companies may have been granted more leeway to organize subsidiary companies in their midst, such powers were not expressly granted to the government of Massachusetts Bay, nor thereafter to the governments of Connecticut and Rhode Island. However, the fact that the Bostonians were overstepping the terms of their charter was temporarily overlooked—they chartered Harvard during a period of jurisdictional uncertainty in England following the execution of Charles I.

Ultimately, the law caught up with the colonists. In 1684, a judgment was passed before the Lord Chancellor that revoked both the colony's and the college's corporate charters.[28] Where did this leave them, legally speaking?

Increase Mather, president of Harvard at the time, sought the answer to this question during a trip to England in the spring of 1688. Mather traveled to London as ambassador for *both* the college and the company, their fates being legally and symbolically intertwined. His trip lasted three years, during which time King James II was deposed and William of Orange was crowned in his place. Despite repeated requests that the college finally be recognized by royal charter, "Answer was made," Mather writes, "that it should be so if I desired it, but that a better way would be for the General Court of the Massachusetts Colony to incorporate their

College, and to make it an University, with as ample privileges as they should think necessary."[29]

Unfortunately, no one in Massachusetts was convinced that colonial charters had the same force of law as those issued directly from England— as late as 1772, for example, the royal governor of Massachusetts, Thomas Hutchinson, wrote to the Lords of Trade pleading for some resolution on this matter. As Hutchinson rightly observed, there was nothing in the by-laws of the colony that stated whether royal or colonial charters held pre-eminence. Hutchinson asked that the colonial charter be revised "to abridge or restrain the Prerogative which is in the Crown of creating Corporations" and stressed that every time the colonial assembly passed such acts itself, it only strengthened "the exception that is taken to this part of the Prerogative [that is, royal monopoly over the power to grant corporate charters]." Hutchinson was, in fact, correct. The Board of Trade clearly stated that "Incorporation should arise from the bounty of the Crown by letter patent, rather than by act of [colonial] Assembly." However, enforcement of this policy was inconsistent; most colonial corporations were either overlooked or simply tolerated by royal authorities.[30]

Equally pressing is the question of the colonists' desire to defend their legally defined charter rights. Provincial charters were important to New England colonists not only for legal protection from the king but also from their neighboring colonies—that is, one another. Ambiguity in charters regarding territorial boundaries was a huge source of anxiety and contentiousness during the early colonial and postrevolutionary periods. Charter rights were thus perceived as a vital component of inter-state, as well as international, political autonomy. Rhode Island, for example, was a corporate colony founded by religious dissenters looking to escape persecution in Puritan Massachusetts. Possession of a corporate charter was key to their pursuit. Though granted such a charter in 1643 by King Charles I, Rhode Islanders sought recertification of their corporate status following Charles's execution. Religious freedom was permanently instituted in Rhode Island's new 1663 charter, granted by Charles II, which also allowed unprecedented autonomy from the Crown and gave the legislative assembly almost complete control over colonial affairs. In addition, the new charter was seen as an important safeguard in fending off territorial incursions initiated by Rhode Island's neighbors, Massachusetts and Connecticut. By putting its legal status and territorial jurisdiction in a legally binding contract with the king, Rhode Island thus secured protection from its always-predacious neighbors. Much later, following the American Revolution, the commitment of Rhode Islanders to jurisdictional autonomy almost kept them from ratifying the new US Constitution—they saw its model of confederation as a potential threat to local autonomy. Despite widespread dissent, Rhode Island actually retained its 1663 charter until 1842, thus signifying the extent to which the original charter rights were regarded as sacrosanct and immutable, a constituent part of Rhode Island's existence as a polity.[31]

The case of Connecticut is equally telling: For example, the movement for Connecticut's corporate charter was spearheaded by settlers from Massachusetts who were seeking new land. In so doing, they literally coerced the independent colony of New Haven to join them—New Haven lacked a corporate charter and thus had sparse legal means to defend its jurisdictional autonomy. Thereafter, Connecticut's corporate charter was wielded as an important weapon in boundary disputes with New York, Rhode Island, and Massachusetts.[32]

Another important controversy that revolved around the corporate status of the early New England colonies involved the system of land grants and their instituted townships. Though many scholars, from Alexis de Tocqueville to Robert Putnam, have extolled the virtues of New England township democracy, new historical research on the seventeenth-century township system reveals quite a different story. The Massachusetts Bay Company knew that settling the wilderness would require not only hearty souls but also prudent financing, and therefore issued dozens of land grants to a handful of investors willing to front the capital necessary for successful appropriation. The towns thus resembled corporations in all but name. Governance of towns remained firmly in the hands of the shareholders, despite the fact that many were actually only absentee landlords.

Though shares could be bought and sold—and women actually held shares in a number of cases—participation in seventeenth-century town government required ownership of shares. Shareholders were referred to as "inhabitants," and they "controlled both the town meeting and the land corporation and excluded [nonshareholding] residents from participation in either." In some cases, town meetings were not even held in town, owing to the disparate location of the township proprietors. Historian John Frederick Martin describes this system as "a complex public sponsorship of private enterprise, in which a land corporation undertook the organizational and financial responsibilities for starting new towns in return for substantial land ownership, apportioned among its share-holders according to their shares." He adds:

> From the beginning of colonization, New Englanders used shares to apportion rights and responsibilities in towns. They divided land by shares, taxed themselves by shares, and based political participation upon the holding of shares. In some places, they even voted by shares [thus granting major shareholders disproportionate "say" in town affairs]. Shares shaped the essential relationships between individuals and their towns. They gave to the towns a strong business character by reflecting the principle that rights were anchored by investment.[33]

The nature of this system itself was not controversial, but the fact that the Massachusetts Bay Company granted such privileges was disputatious. Here again, we see pending conflict over the nature of political jurisdiction in seventeenth-century New England. In this case, English authorities objected to the fact that New England townships were acting like corporations "even though they lacked the authority to do so." By the 1680s and 1690s, royal envoys began noting that "the institutions of New England towns were anomalous, without precedent, and unlawful." Though the Massachusetts Bay Company was legally entitled to issue land grants in the king's name, many towns were illegally established through land deals between speculators and tribal leaders—technically, only representatives of the king could "treat" with natives for accession of their lands. Later, in the mid-eighteenth century, many existing New England land grants were declared null and void by the royal authorities on related grounds. Moreover, many towns were stripped of the corporate veneer they had adopted for themselves. "As such," comments Martin, "there was no established way that a 'town' could hold land, grant land, or restrict the number of landowners. For that matter, there were no legal grounds for the holding of town meetings, which were actually banned for a short time.[34]

Puritan townships often acted quite independently of the colonies that had created them: For example, townships around the modern-day Massachusetts/Rhode Island/Connecticut border played fast and loose with colonial jurisdiction. As a matter of convenience, they sometimes decided to "affiliate" first with one colony and then another. Since land titles were sometimes spurious and often contested, favorable attention from colonial legislatures could make the difference between profit and peril. In some cases, moreover, land companies offered shares to prominent statesmen like John Winthrop Jr. in exchange for efforts to secure favorable jurisdiction. The powerful Atherton Company did exactly this in Rhode Island. Fearing that Rhode Island authorities would not recognize their claim to land in Narragansett Bay, they "hoped that by giving Winthrop a share in the venture he would work to bring the land under Connecticut jurisdiction and confirm the company title to it."[35]

In sum, the early New England settlers perceived the law as a malleable, contestable entity. No legal title was beyond question. Colonists were as willing to challenge the legitimacy of their local governments as they were their neighbors' land claims. Roger Williams, one of the so-called founders of Rhode Island, attacked the legality of the Massachusetts Bay charter on repeated occasions. He and other religious dissenters rightly objected to the colony's conflation of political and religious authority, as well as its irregular system of government, which privileged moneyed elites in Boston and Cambridge over elected deputies who represented the towns. Andrews notes:

> In 1634, Israel Stoughton wrote a long letter to his brother in England, declaring that the people at large had never seen the [Massachusetts Bay Company] charter and did not know the extent of their own prerogatives, and he charged Winthrop with such arbitrary conduct of his office that he had "lost much of the applause" he had heretofore received, raising "very many hands" against himself, who were admonishing him to look a little more circumspectly into his way of doing things.

Winthrop was repeatedly charged with abuse of power. He defended himself with recourse to the business model of the colony's founding charter.[36]

Winthrop also did not feel constrained by the letter of the law as given in the company's charter. Under his guidance, the Massachusetts General Court (that is, the colony's legislative assembly) violated English law in issuing taxes, rescheduling elections, minting currency, and formulating its own penal code. Despite the knowledge that they had no legal right to do so, the colony formally declared itself an independent commonwealth in 1652. Governor Winthrop boldly declared, "Our allegiance binds us not to the laws of England any longer than while we live in England, for the laws of the parliament of England reach no further, nor do the king's writs under the great seal go any further." Winthrop was equally mistrustful of the general will of the colony: there was no democracy in Israel, he noted, nor should there be in Massachusetts. "The best part [of a community] is always the least and of that best part the wiser part is always the lesser."[37]

This issue of the colony's actual legal status became increasingly controversial in the eighteenth century. Though the English were ostensibly aware of the wayward climate prevalent New England, they had more pressing domestic problems until the 1680s. Perhaps bolstered by the success of the Calvinist revolutionaries in England, the Puritans drafted ever more draconian schemes of religious rule and repression in Massachusetts Bay. Though Presbyterians were largely sympathetic to the religious predispositions of Puritanism, they were briskly driven out of the colony in the mid-1640s, their complaints to Parliament ignored amid the domestic controversies of Great Britain. Baptists received even worse treatment; despite their ideological solidarity with the Puritans, they denied the sanctity of infant baptism, insisting that baptism was a right that should be reserved for sentient adults. A 1644 Massachusetts Bay statute ordered that anyone who would condemn or oppose the baptism of infants (that is, all Baptists) should be banished from the colony.

Most despised by the Puritans were the Quakers, who, despite persistent threats of jailing, beating, and execution, insisted on entering Massachusetts to preach their own particular brand of religious individualism. At least a handful of defiant Quakers entered the colony knowing that they would be punished with death, but even summary execution failed to quell the flame. Herbert Osgood remarks:

> Instead, in May, 1661, a new law was passed providing that Quakers who came into the colony should first be whipped at the cart's tail from town to town till they reached the border, and then should be expelled. If they returned three times, they should be dealt with in the same way each time, or at the discretion of the court be branded. Should they return a fourth time, they might be put to death. Under this act Christison [a Quaker who defiantly welcomed martyrdom for his beliefs] and twenty-seven others were released and expelled from the colony.

Fines were even instituted against ship captains who knowingly transported Quakers to the colony. "Penalties were also affixed to the importation and sale of Quaker books, and to the defense of their opinions."[38]

Though some dissenters returned to England after being banished from Massachusetts, most of them simply moved elsewhere, often to unsettled land outside the colony's jurisdiction. For example, Exeter, New Hampshire, was settled by an antinomian supporter of Roger Williams, and Williams himself helped found Rhode Island. Had the Puritans been more tolerant of their fellow Protestants, the course of British North American settlement may have been entirely different. Boston, like Quebec City to the north, might have remained the central seat of authority over a small, tightly organized rural hinterland. Instead, the American colonies, unlike their Canadian counterparts, spread and morphed into a sprawling network of villages, towns, and provinces covering the Atlantic seaboard from Portsmouth to Baltimore.[39]

However, English settlement might have spread on its own accord. New Haven, for example, was founded by devout Puritans who simply desired a colony of their own. The central obstacle to greater political coordination among these settlements was the arbitrariness of their land claims. In other words, who owned which colony? Though the Plymouth and Massachusetts Bay colonies received explicit (but ambiguous) grants of land from England, many others were established by possession alone.

Regardless of the outcome, the Crown was being circumvented in ways that had substantial repercussions for American political development for centuries to come. The corporate organizational form continued to spread and solidify in its new surroundings, the culmination of a legal revolution with respect to citizens' access to the means of incorporation. Litigation and land speculation ran rife. The New England provinces, repeatedly provoked in their efforts to negotiate self-government with the Crown, eventually led the American colonies into open rebellion.

French and Spanish Settlements in the New World

French, English, Spanish, and Portuguese fisherman all sailed the North Atlantic coast in the sixteenth century. Word of the copious quantities of fish to be found in the ocean off Newfoundland prompted European interest in northern North America—Norse fisherman had been sailing there for centuries. Settlement, however, remained limited to temporary summer "fishing stations" where codfish could be cured before the trip back to Europe.

Around Newfoundland and Gaspé, European fishermen occasionally met and traded with coastal natives; they particularly coveted the natives' beautiful fur robes. Such furs were quite valuable in Europe, where defor-estation had long since limited the supply of wild animals, especially beaver, whose pelts were prized as material for warm, waterproof hats. Such pelts became more valuable in Europe as the climate cooled during the Little Ice Age. Most valuable, ironically, were older, well-worn furs that had shed their outer layer of hair and taken on a sort of greasy veneer— they were worth far more than fresh pelts on the European market. Natives thus found that their used blankets and clothing could be traded for modern weapons, textiles, trinkets, and metalware.[40]

The introduction of European-made goods and the need to find re-newable supplies of fur to trade for them had an irrevocable effect on the native people of the region: Stone Age cooking, hunting, and even sarto-rial practices were transformed as European goods began circulating among the tribes. A nascent "middleman" economy emerged in which eastern tribes ferried pelts and European goods between inland fur-producing tribes and European traders on the coast. During this time, Europeans only intermittently penetrated the interior or attempted to establish permanent settlements there.[41]

Beginning in 1534, Jacques Cartier and a crew of Frenchmen from Brit-tany traveled among the Iroquois on the St. Lawrence River. Cartier re-turned in 1541, and a commission appointed him Lord of Nurembega. Technically, he was the sole possessor of all the land in present-day Maine, New Brunswick, and Nova Scotia—in fact, Cartier is credited with giving Canada its name, the apparent result of his misunderstanding of an Iro-quois word for ample fields of corn. But Cartier's ventures were not prof-itable, and in the spring of 1542, he returned to France permanently.[42]

Despite their success in Central and South America, as well as in the Caribbean, Spanish efforts to found colonies on the North Atlantic coast of Florida were quite unsuccessful until the founding of St. Augustine in the 1560s, and even then they were hardly lucrative compared to the flourishing Spanish Empire to the south. Spain's primary interest in Florida was to repel the French, who had commissioned a fort on the nearby St. John's River.

None of the settlements of either New France or New Spain were intended to revolve around subsistence agriculture. Commerce—chiefly trafficking between eastern natives and western Europeans—was the focal point of colonial affairs throughout the sixteenth and early seventeenth centuries. Fur traffic provided occasional income for European fishermen until the early seventeenth century, when the French returned to the mission of exploring, and exploiting, the North American interior. The Dutch colonies along the Hudson River and the early Puritan communities of New England were also active in the early fur trade.

The emerging economy of New France marked the earliest origins of Canadian statecraft (British involvement was still a long way off). Given all the perils of living in an extreme northern climate such as Quebec's, it is indeed remarkable that unacclimated Europeans could build viable settlements along the St. Lawrence seaway. Of course, indigenous peoples had been doing exactly that for generations; the difference was the degree to which they were already accustomed to living in such climes. New France almost did not survive; not due to a failure in adapting to the environment, but because of poor political decisions on the part of its leader, Samuel de Champlain.

New France

French interest in North America began in earnest in 1603 when, under the reign of Henry IV, the Companie de la Nouvelle France was granted a monopoly over all trade, mining, and fishing in the region of Acadia (modern-day Nova Scotia). Such monopolies were a common legal privilege granted by European sovereigns to entrepreneurs who were interested in overseas trade; however, as we have seen, this basic "company" form took on several different manifestations in the New World.

The Companie de la Nouvelle France, led by Pierre du Gua, Sieur de Monts, was comprised of a group of La Rochelle merchants who were experienced in the American coastal trade. De Monts took with him to Acadia a young lieutenant named Samuel de Champlain. Both their original settlement on St. Croix Island in the Bay of Fundy and their subsequent settlement at Port Royal (now Annapolis Royal) on the north coast of Nova Scotia were deemed failures, and de Monts lost his monopoly charter in 1607.

Champlain remained undaunted, however. He anticipated the potential of the fur trade along the St. Lawrence River and built a trading post in 1608 at a place where the river narrowed and was fronted by tall bluffs, thus providing good natural defense by land and sea. That post, named Quebec, eventually became the capital of New France, with Champlain as its governor.[43]

Champlain's goals were twofold and largely emblematic of the subsequent colonial regime in New France: first, Champlain sought to capitalize on Europe's increasing demand for fur items, especially hats, made out of precious North American beaver; and second, he aimed to bring Christianity to the natives. Religious indoctrination and economic exchange were intimately wedded in this scheme. This contrasts with the Spanish approach of enslaving natives in order to "save" them, while seizing their assets.

The French marriage of religion and trade worked relatively well for a while. French missionaries traveled throughout the region and helped maintain the traders' friendly relations with the resident natives. At the same time, the missionaries benefited from the traders' willingness to provide natives with desirable European goods. Trois-Rivières was founded after this fashion in 1634, as was Montreal in 1642. Traders built forts at these mission sites, thus expanding French control of the area. Nevertheless, Champlain's efforts to secure fur-trading contacts among inland tribes soon brought forth several new and less-welcome challenges: forestalling competition from other French and Dutch trading outfits and helping "friendly" natives fight native rivals.

Economic self-organization was a perpetual problem in New France. Though the king of France sought to charter only a small number of exclusive fur trading companies in the New World, there was no legal infrastructure in place to enforce such a system. Illegal trading was common, and such competition could be ruinous to everyone involved. Europeans had scant bargaining power with their native counterparts, a position that was worsened by the presence of other nearby European trade outfits. The high cost of transporting European goods to trade sites meant that traders could not afford to bargain with the natives—anything that was not sold had to be transported back home or abandoned. Moreover, competition was building in the south from other European sources: Dutch merchants at Fort Orange (present-day Albany) had started inducing Iroquois tribesmen to divert furs south.[44]

Short of men and money, New France barely remained able to defend itself. From 1629 to 1632, while England and France were (once again) at war, the city of Quebec was seized by a group of Scottish-English adventurers and held for three years. Champlain also earned the enmity of the neighboring Iroquois by participating in several Huron attacks on them. Later, in the 1640s and 1650s, long after Champlain's death, the Iroquois effectively routed the Huron and then turned on the French. In 1660, the Iroquois almost seized the city of Montreal. New France was on the brink of extinction.[45]

2

Expansion and Contraction

In 1660, the colony of New France was clearly failing. The Crown had shown little interest in developing or fortifying the colony, and competition from rival Dutch traders was taking a large bite out of profits from the fur trade. During the post-1660 period, however, the French government, under Louis XIV, took a serious interest in promoting both trade and agricultural settlement in New France.

French colonial policy had a twofold impact on the social and political development of Quebec, Canada's first bona fide settlement: On the one hand, the French ventured far deeper into the American interior than their English rivals, exploring not only the entire Great Lakes region but also the river valleys leading south from Ohio and Illinois down the Mississippi River basin. New France's expanded geographical reach was so great that by the early eighteenth century, they had encircled the British east of the Appalachians. If the French had not lost the disastrous Seven Years' War, New France might well have colonized all of northern North America.

On the other hand, the western outposts of New France were small and fragile at best. The bulk of the French population in North America remained to the east in the plains along the St. Lawrence and Ottawa rivers. For centuries, this central segment of Quebec was known for its high birthrate and healthy citizens, the happy confluence of ample cropland and reasonably good government. Flexible feudalism allowed for the peaceable, orderly distribution of riparian farmlands among elites and their tenants. Peasants were given a long leash and reasonable conditions under which to forge successful lives. Social order was maintained through careful collaboration of the Catholic Church and the local aristocracy. The outside attractions of logging, trapping, and trading provided fluid labor markets for men unwilling or unable to live in the peaceable kingdom. These two patterns—wide-ranging pursuit of western trade opportunities and a conservative approach to eastern agricultural settlement—came to characterize Canadian life, English and French, throughout much of the next two centuries.

Early settlement patterns in the British colonies were much different, and a great deal more varied, than in New France. After decades of civil war, 1660 brought a restoration of the monarchy in England. Earlier, at English regicide Oliver Cromwell's behest, Admiral William Penn (father of Pennsylvania's William Penn) had seized Jamaica and unsuccessfully tried to take the larger Spanish island of Hispaniola as well. Cromwell's successor, King Charles II, was no less interested in colonial expansion. Under his reign, English forces ousted the Dutch from New Amsterdam and renamed it New York—after Charles's brother, James, the Duke of York. A number of additional proprietary colonies were then chartered by Charles, mostly to the duke's friends and associates.

Though fur trading was originally a staple of the British colonial economy in New England, the coastal areas were soon trapped out and the western expanses were blocked by Dutch and French traders. Agriculture became a mainstay of the colonies, supplemented by fishing, light manufacturing, distilling, and trade. The people who settled in the new British colonies were far more diverse than in New France—Puritans, Anglicans, Quakers, and Catholics from Britain, plus Dutch, Swedes, and Germans from the continent—and the settlements themselves were organized along different lines. Whereas the river valleys of New France were divided into neat, skinny, riverfront plots that were granted and governed by feudal representatives of the French king, land in the various colonies of British North America was conveyed by the king to any number of private entities and was settled in a haphazard, catch-as-catch-can manner. British colonists had no qualms about purchasing land directly from tribal leaders, which further undermined the king's ability to control its distribution and settlement. Left in the hands of the settlers, land became a precious commodity to be bought, sold, squatted on, or stolen. The colonial assemblies also fought viciously over their common borders, sometimes poaching entire towns with the promise of favorable jurisdiction. Coupled, these factors greatly reduced the king's ability to supervise colonial affairs, thereby prompting a series of efforts to revoke the colonies' charters and place them under direct royal control. The British colonies were caught in a mire of confusion, corruption, and collusion.

An agonistic society emerged among the various colonies of British North America, which was quite unlike that of New France. Whereas historians of New France report no serious revolts against government during the seventeenth and early eighteenth centuries, the American colonies were rife with disagreements. These disputes were not merely matters of king versus colony but also of colony versus colony, company versus company, and settler versus settler. "American" settlers were extremely covetous of their rights and freedoms and unusually proactive in pursuing them. Civil litigation was common by the early eighteenth century, unusually so by British standards.

New France: Farmland and Hinterland

Louis XIV came of age and was crowned king of France in 1661. Working through his chief minister, Jean-Baptiste Colbert, Louis began a grand reorganization of France's imperial regime. The results for New France were mixed. On the one hand, circumstances in the St. Lawrence River valley between Quebec and Montreal were dramatically improved. A new, tripartite government was installed with emphasis on military preparedness and colonial defense. Existing settlers, unlike their counterparts in New England, were happy to welcome royal intervention and military protection. An entire regiment of French troops was sent to New France to ward off the Iroquois, and many troops were compelled to remain after their service and settle in the vulnerable territory south of Montreal. Moreover, in order to encourage population growth, Minister Colbert also sent hundreds of French orphan girls, or *filles du roi*, to New France. By 1672, the population of the colony had grown to about six thousand inhabitants, a threefold increase since 1660.

However, the attempt to rationalize French rule in the fur-trapping territories around Lake Superior and down the Mississippi River valley was fitful at best. Various strategies were employed to limit the number and extent of French contacts with fur-trading natives, but none effectively stemmed the supply of pelts. Royal efforts to limit the number of Frenchmen participating in the fur trade were almost entirely unsuccessful—at one point, even the governor of New France, Louis de Baude Comte de Frontenac, was operating his own private trading post in defiance of royal edict.

Furthermore, around that time, the French accidentally ceded control of the valuable Hudson Bay region to the English. Two French explorers, Pierre Esprit Radisson and Médart Chouart de Groseilliers, had traveled to the area under French auspices and found unprecedented supplies of beaver, but they complained of being harassed by French colonial officials looking for bribes. Out of frustration, Radisson and Groseilliers reported their discovery to the English court, which gladly welcomed them and sent an expedition to investigate. In 1670, the Hudson's Bay Company was chartered by England to exploit the Hudson Bay region to the fullest.[1]

Another important feature of French colonial policy was its disposition toward the land and its native inhabitants. Unlike the English colonists to the south, who saw the land as theirs for the taking, French policy was far more circumspect about the need to respect native claims. This was not the result of greater empathy for native rights, but the realization that it was in the best interest of French trappers and missionaries to cooperate with, rather than bully, their native hosts. According to historian Richard White, both the French and their Algonquin counterparts faced a unique situation in which cooperation and cultural synthesis were facilitated by the combination of necessity, novelty, and the general inability of leaders on either side to exert much control over their constituents. Trappers and natives alike found cohesion and coalescence to be their preferred strategy when faced with the joint challenges of hostile enemies, famine, and disease. A cultural mélange was forged on "the middle ground" of the Great Lakes region.[2]

Compared to the English, the French were surprisingly devoted to learning the customs and languages of the natives. According to Peter Kalm, a Swedish naturalist who visited New France in the summer of 1749:

> Though many nations imitate the French customs, I observed, on the contrary, that the French in Canada in many respects follow the customs of the Indians, with whom they have constant relations. They use the tobacco pipes, shoes, garters, and belts of the Indians. They follow the Indian way of waging war exactly; they mix the same things with

tobacco; they make use of the Indian bark boats and row them in the
Indian way; they wrap a square piece of cloth round their feet, instead
of stocking, and have adopted many other Indian fashions.

The French cannot be said to have had the natives' best interests at
heart, but they at least were smart enough to learn from them how to
thrive in the harsh North American environment.[3]

Unlike New England or any of the other British colonies in America,
New France was run as a military bureaucracy. Authority was clearly in
the hands of the royal governor and his intendant, or civil administrator.
At the same time, the authorities recognized the fact that New France
was underpopulated and that good government was an important incentive to keep settlers from returning to France or entering the illicit fur
trade. Settlers did not pay taxes to the government. Respect for the
Catholic Church and Québécois social and legal traditions remained
paramount. Lawyers, by contrast, were forbidden to practice in the
colony, and litigation was formally discouraged. Realizing the need to
limit the power of the seigneurs (or aristocracy) in order to bolster the
population of the colony, Jean-Baptiste Colbert, chief minister to Louis
XIV, noted, "The true way to strengthen that colony [New France] is to
cause justice to reign, to establish a good civil administration, to take
care of the settlers, to give them peace, tranquility and abundance, and
train them to defend themselves against all manner of foes, for these
things are the basis and foundation of every establishment." Historian
W. J. Eccles writes, "Unlike in England and its colonies, property was
not sacred [in New France]; it was human rights, not property rights,
that were paramount."[4]

The plains surrounding Montreal were settled by French soldiers and
peasants who were brought there to people the land and protect the
colony from the Iroquois (allies of the Dutch and the English). Settlement stuck closely to the region's lush riverbanks, which were parceled
into long seigneuries that were granted to noblemen, military officers,
and religious orders; each of these groups then rented sections of the
property in perpetuity to tenant farmers. The colony was organized
along a medieval feudal system, but rents were low and the seigneurs
obtained few if any other powers over their tenants.[5]

There were several other differences between feudalism in Old and
New France. For a time, land was readily available in New France, thus

allowing *habitant* families to grow and prosper over time. Canadian inheritance laws were similarly amenable to familial growth and prosperity. Furthermore, seigneurial rents were fixed over time, and the risk of eviction or enclosure was virtually nonexistent. From the French standpoint, the asset most needed in the colony was families who were willing to clear the vast forests of the St. Lawrence River valley and settle there. Fortunately, the settlers obliged.[6]

It is notable that the seigneurs themselves did not grow into a full-blown aristocracy in New France. According to historian Allan Greer, "The agricultural economy was too small, and the seigneurs too numerous, for an opulent landed aristocracy to emerge." The seigneurial class held little sway over common people beyond renting them arable land. "Not only had few seigneurs any interest in leading; most habitants did not want to be led," writes Richard Colebrook Harris. He adds:

> A man who could travel many miles away from the St. Lawrence colony to intercept furs did not need protection on a farm in Quebec, especially when protection might have interfered with fur trading. The new freedom was attractive to the habitants, who quickly discovered that the authorities could do little to constrict it, and this discovery reshaped the social structure. The seigneur usually collected the slight annual dues, he built a gristmill, and in a few cases he conducted a seigneurial court, but unless he was a particularly attractive personality the habitants either had very little to do with him, or treated him as one of themselves.[7]

Material conditions in seventeenth- and eighteenth-century New France were actually better for most settlers than they would have been back in France. The Québécois also became known for their good humor, laid-back demeanor, and easy relationship with authority. The king remained in charge, with his local jurisdiction divided between his own administrators and those of the church, but the Québécois rarely expressed discontent or anger with either. Land distribution was closely controlled by royal authorities, and this helped preclude excessive legal squabbles and contentious speculation regarding unclaimed property. Furthermore, there was little cause to question the king's legal jurisdiction, which was a paramount problem in the colonies of British North America. Overall, this was a fairly successful exercise in colonial rule, especially in comparison with the British-American colonies.[8]

Early American Legal Culture

After successfully attaining and protecting their charter of incorporation, the Massachusetts Puritans set about the task of pursuing profit with characteristic grace and speed. Though preliminary efforts at graphite mining, salt making, iron mongering, and textile manufacturing failed, fishing proved to be a boon. The beaver population of coastal New England had already been trapped out, but fish were abundant and easily shipped back to Europe. A bona fide North Atlantic economy began to emerge around this and other goods. Historian Bernand Bailyn notes:

> The fish trade and contact with the English trading centers served not only to supply the Puritans with an indirect form of returns but also to acquaint them with other needs of the islanders and Spaniards which they were capable of supplying. Fish was but one form of food; agricultural produce was equally desired. And on islands that lived by the wine trade, barrel staves, hoops, and all manner of timber products found excellent markets. All this, as well as fish, New England could supply, and as the fish trade progressed so too did the beginnings of commerce in provisions and lumber.

Thus was born the famous "triangle trade," in which the Caribbean and New England economies were successfully integrated with that of Great Britain.[9]

At the same time, however, the new transatlantic trade increased the influence of secularism and lucre in the Massachusetts Bay Colony. "The growing economic promise of New England was beginning to attract men intent on careers in trade who were not only strangers to New England orthodoxy, but to Puritanism itself," notes Bailyn. "There were adventurous Englishmen seeking their fortunes and they brought with them the spirit of a new age." Despite rearguard efforts by the Puritan elite, it was painfully clear that religious tolerance was good for trade, and over the decades of the mid- to late seventeenth century, Massachusetts increasingly began to resemble Britain in this respect. Among the New England merchant class, dress and manners turned ever more extravagant. Anglicans settled and openly declared their faith, and the cultural tenor of the colony turned eastward, toward London.[10]

More important is the fact that successful New England businessmen started looking to real estate as a central means of investing their wealth and cultivating elite lifestyles. One of the major changes in English law that was established under the Massachusetts Bay Company was the removal of traditional encumbrances on the purchase and sale of land. "It represented a philosophical move away from the older notion of land tenure as a bundle of rights and obligations, and toward the modern concept of absolute control. Only upon the acceptance of such legal doctrine could real property be seen and used as a commodity of exchange," writes Stephen Innes. "Under the Massachusetts System of land proprietorships within the township, land could be acquired and sold quicker and more easily than in any other colony."[11]

This should not be taken to mean that the Puritans supported anything like the laissez-faire doctrine of neoclassical economics—those who governed Massachusetts Bay strictly regulated the economic life of its inhabitants. Rather, the important fact is that the Puritans reengineered English law in ways that dramatically reconceptualized the rights and responsibilities of market actors. Laws governing inheritance and land sales were codified in ways designed to promote the commodification and sale of private property.

Bailyn characterizes the early New England land system as follows: "Seeing in real property a means of social fulfillment, a form of transferable property, and a promising object of speculation, the New England merchants bought and sold, bequeathed and inherited, mortgaged and released land in a bewildering maze of transactions." In Watertown, Massachusetts, in the late 1630s, nonresident land speculators fueled an increasingly brisk market. Bailyn continues:

> It would appear that already during the first decade of its existence the close homogeneous community, founded on a basis of mutual consent, was changing. Men who in the East Anglian woods [of England] might have spent a lifetime building up a compact farmstead accomplished the same thing in Massachusetts in a number of years. The rapid turnover in land also encouraged geographical mobility. Stimulated by the economic opportunities around them, the colonists were willing to risk relocation. All of these outcomes distinguished life in New England from that in old England.

Bailyn adds, "By 1660 they [the settlers] were so involved in the ownership of land that the least disturbance of values or titles would bring them instantly forward in defense of their rights." These two traits would

be of American political culture: extreme litigiousness and a unique obsession with property rights, particularly in the New England region,
where much of the newly "Americanized" common law was being created and disseminated. Both had wide ramifications on many important
aspects of American political development in the late eighteenth and
early nineteenth centuries.[12]

Above and beyond the issue of individual land speculation, the early
history of New England, and indeed all of the seventeenth-century American colonies, is especially marked by constant, and often bitter, jurisdictional competition between colonies. The Plymouth and Massachusetts
Bay colonies fought long and hard over their common boundary. Rhode
Island assumed its present shape only after bitter disputes over land
rights and borders with Massachusetts and Connecticut, both of which
also disputed possession of the Springfield settlement on the Connecticut
River. Connecticut and the autonomous New Haven Colony even fought
one another for jurisdiction over the north shore of Long Island Sound,
and both fought with Dutch and Swedish settlements in the distant
Delaware River valley for jurisdiction there. New York also fought a long
losing battle to claim all of Connecticut's land west of the Connecticut
River. In the north, Massachusetts and New Hampshire wrangled for decades over land between them, and both resisted Mainers' efforts to be
recognized as an independent colony.

One source of these disputes was the careless attitude of English officials toward the details of North American settlement. Premodern technology made accurate surveying a problem, but Europeans had been
working around this for centuries. In discussing the new American land
market, historian Charles Andrews comments, "One wonders if any of
the crown lawyers or chancery officials ever consulted old patents in
making out a new one, or ever studied the geography of the regions they
so easily gave away."[13]

Poorly defined boundaries were a problem, but matters were made
worse by the raw aggression of the colonists. Indeed, there is nothing
more striking about the prehistory of the United States than the effect
territorialism had on its inhabitants' lives. For such a large and relatively
underpopulated place, land was highly coveted. Early Americans were
constantly on the move, looking to acquire new land on the margins of
settlement rather than rent or share already-improved areas. The quest
for territorial expansion was most acute near colonial borders, where

claims were often unsettled and thus easily disputed. Areas like the thin strip of New York east of the Hudson River between Yonkers and Albany were rife with squatters. There was no local political authority with the power necessary to prevent such lawlessness. Landowners were obliged to take any and all measures to protect their claims, thus creating a mutually reinforcing system of apprehension, mistrust, and petty legalism.

That seventeenth-century colonies qua colonies would yearn for territory betrays a thoroughly modern sensibility in which the jurisdictional reach of a polity is as important as the profits it might bring its members. "The oligarchy which governed Massachusetts was ready, whenever opportunity offered, to annex all weak or disturbed communities which were adjacent to its boundaries, and to assume protectorates with undefined possibilities over neighboring Indians," writes Osgood. Kim writes of "the chaotic condition of nearly all the colonial boundaries," and adds, "In this early period, a boundary was whatever was claimed, occupied, and forcibly held." Corporate colonies like Connecticut and Massachusetts, in which jurisdiction was divided among township shareholders, were just as eager to expand and protect their borders as were proprietary colonies, where a single proprietor or small group would profit directly from taxes on the land. Well-organized private land companies were also rife throughout the colonies, and colonial public policy then, as now, often served the interests of its wealthiest constituents.[14]

Colonial jurisprudence was a notably haphazard affair throughout the prerevolutionary period, and the further complications of intercolonial jurisdictional competition made land claims, torts, and civil suits a three-ring circus with local elites calling the tune. This situation, particularly with regard to tax collection, political appointments, and land grants, was further exacerbated by collusion between colonial administrators and local elites.

Another issue underlying intercolonial competition was religious freedom, although not to the extent implied by New England lore. It is well known that Roger Williams left the Massachusetts Bay Colony because of religious differences with the Puritan oligarchy there, but he was not the only founder of Rhode Island. The new colony was actually a jurisdictional amalgam of several independent grants, most owned by private land companies seeking claims that offered good coastal frontage not already under colonial jurisdiction. If not for the concerted efforts of physician and preacher Dr. John Clarke, the western section of Rhode

Island would have been annexed to Connecticut at the behest of its powerful governor, John Winthrop Jr., who also happened to own shares in a major Rhode Island land trust, the Atherton Company. Connecticut disputed the border given in the 1663 Rhode Island charter for the following sixty years.[15]

Similar controversies took place throughout the colonies, pitting colonists against one another in struggles over jurisdiction. Part of the problem resulted from the fact that neither Parliament nor the Crown paid much attention to the colonies of British North America, at least not until the 1660s, when war with the Dutch and the Spanish exacerbated matters of colonial defense and transatlantic trade. In the intervening decades, the colonies had been left largely to their own devices, which were poorly suited to the task of peopling a continent. Debates, prolonged legal disputes, and even violence all too frequently erupted over issues such as taxation, political representation, and colonial defense.[16]

Here, again, corporate law played a large and fairly unprecedented role in the political development of the region: Given the ambiguity of most royal land grants in New England, extended jurisdictional battles often hinged on whether or not said colonies were in fact legally incorporated. As historian Charles Andrews describes New Haven's struggle for survival, "The lack of legal charter left her defenseless at a time when her northern neighbor, possessed of greater strength, determination, and diplomatic sagacity, was able to obtain royal privileges, which, however secured, were to serve, at least in her own mind, as a sufficient legal warrant justifying her attack on New Haven, in the interest of her own expansion in rivalry with Massachusetts."[17]

The legal basis for Connecticut's charter was itself highly suspect—documentation of its original land grant was unavailable and of dubious merit. As Andrews comments in a footnote to his extensive history of the jurisdictional battles between the New Haven and Connecticut colonies: "There is something mysterious about the boundaries inserted in the Connecticut charter, just as there is something mysterious about the issue of the charter itself."[18]

All of this must have shaped the colonists' collective experience in profound ways. Countless episodes in seventeenth-century American history revolve around competing claims to land and the tax revenues incumbent upon them. Disputes such as the one concerning Massachusetts's jurisdiction over Maine ultimately forced English ministers to get involved in the fray. In this case, inquiry into the matter led the Lords of Trade and the Privy Council to acknowledge that Massachusetts was committing all sorts of illegal acts in its capacity as a corporate colony. The hazy nature of the original charters only complicated matters. Now, alongside the changes being made to English government by William of Orange following the Glorious Revolution, colonial policy regarding British North America also demanded serious reconsideration.[19]

Fall and Rise of the Corporate Ideal in New England

Neither of King William's predecessors, Charles II nor his brother James II, showed much promise as leaders of England's Protestant establishment—both had demonstrably Catholic leanings and a special knack for inspiring fear and loathing in the Protestant population. Nor were they particularly successful in dealing with Parliament, now emboldened by its actions against the Crown before and during the interregnum. Ultimately, and rather unwittingly, their actions led to the creation of representative government and religious freedom in England, as well as to the resurrection and rationalization of British overseas trade policy.

Ever since the Stuart Restoration, Charles II had sought to rein in Puritan influence in both England and America. Richard Nicolls was dispatched in 1664 to seize New Netherland, which he did, and to bring the wayward New England Puritans into line, a task he did not accomplish; the Puritans were able to ignore such threats. "Beginning about 1670, and more especially after 1675," notes Labaree, "the English authorities seem for the first time to have made a serious study of political conditions in the colonies." In 1678, the English attorney general recommended that the Massachusetts Bay charter be revoked, and though this was not achieved until later, it was the beginning of the end of the corporate commonwealth.[20]

In 1683, Attorney General Thomas Jones filed a writ of *quo warranto* against the Massachusetts Bay Company, declaring that it had exceeded the powers granted it in its corporate charter. The company hired a London barrister, Robert Humphreys, to serve as its attorney and instructed him to delay action as long as possible. By effectively showing that the company's court date had come and gone before word of the writ ever reached them, Massachusetts managed to dodge one bullet.

A new attorney general, Sir Robert Sawyer, reverted to a different legal tactic, *scire facias*, which allowed him to press action against the corporation even if they failed to acknowledge the charges. This time it worked. The Massachusetts Bay Company charter was revoked on October 13, 1684. Two years later, *quo warranto* writs also were issued against the Rhode Island and Connecticut corporations. In a famous episode now memorialized by a US Mint commemorative quarter, the people of Connecticut resisted a British effort to seize their charter by hiding it in a white oak tree—the "charter oak." Notice had been served: colonial intransigence would no longer be tolerated, particularly in New England, where it had been most pronounced.[21]

Colonial affairs remained relatively calm for a few years. New Englanders were still reeling from King Philip's War (1675–1676), a brutal conflict in which several local tribes rose up against the Puritans and nearly extinguished them. Skirmishes with local natives were quite common, and in this case, losses on both sides were enormous. Early New Englanders were extremely fierce fighters, hostile to natives and French Canadians alike. In order to bolster the colonies' collective defenses, the governments of Massachusetts, Plymouth, New Hampshire, Maine, and later Rhode Island, Connecticut, East and West New Jersey, and New York were temporarily merged under a single royal government—which was, rather ironically, modeled after that of New France—called the Dominion of New England.[22]

James II was deposed in 1688, thus beginning a new era of religious toleration and parliamentary supremacy in England. Nonetheless, for several years after the ascension of William and Mary, the exact legal status of the colonies remained unclear. Colonial advocates in London, such as William Penn and Increase Mather, petitioned furiously for colonial rights and privileges, while the colonists themselves remained ignorant of their fate. News of English affairs was slow to reach the colonies, and rumors of a French invasion of America were rife. At various points during the late 1680s, the royal governor of New England, Sir Edmund Andros, was himself unsure of his institutional mandate. The people of British North America were increasingly edgy; they wanted good government and reliable protection from marauding natives and Frenchmen, neither of which seemed in the offing.

Matters came to a head on the morning of April 18, 1689, when hundreds of militiamen gathered in Boston, jailed the royal governor and appointed a fifteen-man "Council of Safety" to take over government affairs. They appointed a prominent Massachusetts politician, Simon Bradstreet, as council president and issued a "Declaration of the Gentlemen, Merchants, and Inhabitants of Boston and the Country Adjacent," which deposed the royal governor, Edmund Andros, denounced a suspected "popish plot," and declared the rights of the Massachusetts Bay Colony under its original charter to be in effect once again. Bradstreet also sent a letter to King William saying that the people of Massachusetts were merely following his brave example in combating tyranny and blasphemy, thus expressing their continued loyalty to the Crown.[23]

In London, the circumstances of the Boston revolt remained unclear, and a new policy regime for the colonies had yet to take form. To make matters worse, the Boston situation triggered a more violent revolution in the neighboring colony of New York. Long since disaffected by the disorganized state of their colonial government, a group of colonial militiamen seized Fort James on Manhattan Island. They claimed that the colonial administration was plotting a Catholic invasion of the colony, and the rebel leader, Jacob Leisler, cast popish accusations far and wide. Governor Andros's deputy, Captain Francis Nicholson, fled the colony, as did many of the landed elite. Leisler and the rebels created a Committee of Safety and organized resistance to French and Indian raids on the colony. To justify his usurpation of authority, Leisler misappropriated a letter from the new king, William III. While the king's letter appointed but did not actually name a new lieutenant governor, Leisler nevertheless claimed that the appointment was his.

In the presence of active Indian threats to the colony and the absence of clear leadership to counter them, Leisler had some justification for exploiting ambiguities in the king's instructions and declaring himself worthy of "preserving the peace and administering the laws of our said Province in New York." This was a life-or-death matter. The colony needed to be organized for self-defense and there was no one clearly charged with the task. "The question was not self-government as against autocratic royal authority, but who would hold office in New York under the aegis of the Protestant monarchy of England," writes Sosin. Leisler assumed the mantle of authority in the absence of compelling alternatives. Though the sympathies of the colonists toward Leisler were mixed, he retained control of the colony for thirteen months, all the while gaining the approbation and cooperation of the Massachusetts,

Connecticut, and Rhode Island colonies. Eventually, however, sentiment turned against him and a royal detachment arrived to install a new royal governor. In the meantime, a great deal of mayhem and bloodshed had occurred as a result of this jurisdictional dispute.[24]

The Boston and New York revolts reflect a larger trend that emerged in the American colonies in the century prior to the Revolutionary War. While the colonists recognized the legal authority of the Crown over the colonies, they were increasingly discontent with the manner in which it was exercised. The English colonial authorities at Whitehall were insistent that the colonists recognize English sovereignty, which they were only too willing to do. However, the colonists were also angered by the fact that England was not actually helping them survive and prosper in their new home. These failures occurred largely because there was no comprehensive plan for administering the colonies, nor even a consistent sense of who had jurisdiction over what land and to what extent. Instead, the colonies were subject to ambling shifts in governance, repeated disputes over land rights and colonial jurisdiction, a persistent lack of Crown military resources that could have been mustered to defend the colonists from predacious natives, and an escalating regime of imperial trade restrictions and taxes.

Since the colonies were organized in various ways—one of the central problems of British administration in North America—myriad issues and concerns evolved. In the corporate colonies of New England, royal efforts to revoke and/or renegotiate the terms of colonial charters ignited controversy and conflict. The Massachusetts Bay Company officially lost its corporate charter in 1684. For several years thereafter, Massachusetts literally existed in legal limbo, as did all subsidiary corporations associated with it. Though it was well within the Crown's rights to revoke these charters, the colonists regarded them as sacrosanct, and they were deeply offended by efforts to amend legal privileges that they had already been granted.

Massachusetts received the official seal of England in 1691, thus reestablishing its legal right to exist, though with the added proviso that the king could now appoint a royal governor to oversee colonial affairs in the region. In addition, all laws passed by the colonial legislature would be subject to a royal veto within three years of passage. These changes to the original corporate charter were obviously a blow to the colonists—Increase Mather wrote at length about his struggles to preserve the charter, as well as his eventual realization that further resistance might simply goad the king to do worse.[25]

Because the colony's corporate charter had been revoked, the corporate status of Massachusetts's prized seminary, Harvard College, also stood in legal limbo. The college's charter had been nullified by the revocation of the Massachusetts Bay Company charter, and it had yet to be reinstated.

In May 1692, shortly after his return to Massachusetts, Mather attempted to draft a new charter creating a Harvard College corporation of ten men with virtually unlimited control over the affairs of the college. In July 1696, word arrived from England that the 1692 charter was disallowed because it did not provide the Crown the right to "visit" the college (that is, oversee its affairs). Mather volunteered to return to England once again, this time to procure a royal charter (as opposed to royal assent to a charter issued by the colonial legislature). The members of the Massachusetts General Court realized, however, that they would be powerless to amend a royal charter, whereas an indigenous charter, "even if accepted by the Crown, could be altered or repealed by the provincial legislature at any time." This urged Mather to draft a new charter for submission to the colonial legislature, which resulted in the short-lived Harvard charter of 1697. It, too, failed to receive royal assent, owing largely to the fact that it reserved the right of "visitation" not to the Crown but to the governor and council of the colony.[26]

The king was determined to retain his traditional control over English-chartered corporations. The Harvard College charter issue remained unresolved until 1707, when the Massachusetts General Court simply declared that the 1650 charter had never been repealed or annulled, thus reinstating it. Historian Richard Hofstadter refers to this compromise as an "admission of the hitherto uncertain right of the [Massachusetts] General Court to charter a college without sanction from the Crown." The legal standing of the college remained ambiguous until after the American Revolution, when the Massachusetts state legislature promptly took action to confirm the college's charter.[27]

It should be noted that the "illegal" incorporation of Harvard College is relevant to the political development of the Massachusetts Bay Colony in more ways than one: The college was meant to create an ample supply of human and social capital in the colony, and was thus an important social project to the Puritans. It resonated, too, with the settlers' general sensitivity to issues of contract and title. In addition, a fair percentage of the colony's leading doctors, lawyers, preachers, teachers, politicians, and businessmen were Harvard graduates. Many elite seventeenth-century New Englanders thus saw the fate of the college as part and parcel of the long-term health of their colonies, and they likely passed such concerns on to their children, especially those who attended Harvard (and Yale, which was founded by Harvard alumni). Their ideas about charter rights later traveled with them across the country, as New Englanders started migrating westward in search of open land.

The legal power to grant corporations remained ambiguous throughout the colonies before independence. Except in cases where such powers were explicitly granted, says Davis, "The colonial assemblies which undertook to create corporations were forced to rely upon an implied power so to act, and the question whether this implication was justified remained somewhat unsettled throughout nearly the entire colonial period." According to political scientist Harry Cushing, "The indefiniteness and incompleteness of the provincial charter, either as an instrument of government or as a guarantee of rights, had either directly occasioned or plainly made possible conflicts of opinion and of authority, the continuance of which threatened in no uncertain way the destruction of the system which it embodied."[28]

Following the colonial reorganization of the 1680s, colonial acts of incorporation tended to add language that was designed to express deference to the Crown, such as "praying his most sacred Majesty that it may be enacted." Some colonial legislatures even made a concerted effort to hide incorporation acts in language that avoided specific reference to the term. The founders of Yale College—all Harvard alumni—took this route after noting the extensive difficulties that Harvard faced in achieving incorporation. "The Connecticut clerics faced a dilemma," writes Hofstadter. "To get a charter from the legislature was to risk the total dissolution of the college, as the charter might readily be voided by the Crown if the college received unfavorable attention; but to seek a royal charter was to run the risk, as the Massachusetts men had learned, of inviting royal and Episcopal interference." Instead, continues Hofstadter:

> Yale's founders decided to solve this problem as best they could by getting a charter from the colonial legislature and by masquerading their college under the most trivial guise, hoping that English indifference to

or ignorance of colonial affairs would leave it unmolested. Hence they called it not a "college" but by the more modest title "collegiate school"; hence they call its head not the president, as at Harvard, but the "rector."

"Not knowing what to doe for fear of overdoing," wrote Judge Samuel Sewall and Isaac Addington, two men selected by the trustees of Yale to oversee its legal construction under Connecticut law, "We on purpose, gave the Academie as low a Name as we could that it might better stand in wind and wether; nor daring to incorporate it, lest it should be served with a Writt of Quo-Warranto." Unlike Massachusetts and Rhode Island, Connecticut seemed reluctant to use its powers of incorporation, or at least to publicize it. "When Yale College sought a charter from Connecticut in 1701, the bill prepared was purposely shorn, as far as possible, of any expressions indicating that it was what it was meant to be."[29]

Yale had to wait forty-four years, until 1745, before it was officially incorporated. Eleazar Wheelock, founder of Dartmouth College, originally sought a similar grant from Connecticut. In his own words, Dartmouth was denied a charter by the governor and council "upon the ground that their action would not be valid if ratified in England . . . and that a corporation within a corporation might be troublesome as Yale College had sometimes been." Dartmouth was eventually founded by royal charter in New Hampshire, where the royal governor had clearer authority to create and oversee university corporations.[30]

"Similar caution dictated the general policy of all the colonial legislatures in matters of this description," writes historian Simeon Baldwin, adding that the colleges of William and Mary and Columbia sought royal instead of colonial charters, "not caring to venture on so doubtful a title." Princeton, Rutgers, and the University of Pennsylvania were all chartered by their respective royal governors, but these charters were issued in colonies where neither the colony's legal status nor its legal right to issue corporate charters was hotly contested. The issue of incorporation was most on the minds of citizens in Massachusetts, Connecticut, and Rhode Island, where such matters had never entirely been resolved. English legal historian Frederic Maitland actually singles them as out as "three colonies which were exceptionally important on account of their antiquity and activity," by which he refers specifically to the controversies that arose as a result of their ambiguous corporate charters.[31]

Why did incorporation matter so much to New Englanders when institutions like Harvard and Yale managed to function for so long without it? Why not simply operate as unincorporated entities, as the vast majority of private businesses did at the time? The answer actually reveals much about American legal development: Under their original, common law conception, corporations had powers that ordinary individuals and groups did not. For nonprofit institutions like Harvard, the ability to put property in trust meant that the college's holdings were protected from its founders' heirs. Incorporation was also helpful for ventures that required investment capital, though the modern concept of "limited liability" emerged only later. As William Smith, a New York lawyer, wrote in a 1767 letter:

> This [incorporation] is the only way to render the project permanent, to secure wisdom and council equal to the work, to defend it against opposition, and to encourage future donations. . . . I shall [only] add that a charter is more necessary for such an institution in this country than it can be in England. An incorporated body will not only acquire rights maintainable by law in the courts of justice, but command the favor of the government, who without that sanction, may at such distance from the crown oppress the undertaking a thousand ways and utterly destroy it.[32]

In other words, Smith, and presumably others, viewed the corporation as a form of protection from the state that was granted by the state itself. This conception has since become a hallmark of American law: Corporations are seen as legally sacrosanct entities endowed by the state with special powers meant to protect them from undue incursion by the state. New Englanders viewed the corporation as a desirable form of legal protection for a wide variety of civic endeavors, from building turnpikes and churches to establishing colleges and colonies. This unique view of the legal relationship between the state and civil society evolved in New England as a result of conflicts over said relationship.

Following the creation of the new republic, New England state legislatures initiated a revolution in Anglo-American corporate law: They officially transformed incorporation from a rare and special royal privilege to something accessible to anyone who could afford the fees. This new notion of *freedom of incorporation* took several decades to develop, but even immediately after the American Revolution, New England legislators were unusually willing to grant charters for private purposes.[33]

It is important to note that the early American legislatures did not tamper much with the common law definition of corporate power; the seminal issue was who had the right to allocate such powers. As debate with England over the rights and duties of the colonies grew in the eighteenth century, colonial legislators generally became more wary of exerting their right to charter corporations at will. In turn, the newly confirmed US state legislatures launched a chartering frenzy after the Revolution. "By contrast to English and Continental experience," say Oscar and Mary Handlin, "the less advanced economy of the United States produced almost 350 business corporations between 1783 and 1801." Towns and other nonprofit, public corporations also proliferated (for example, charities, churches, and public-service corporations such as waterworks and turnpikes), thus making incorporation a cornerstone of American political, social, and economic life. Handlin and Handlin note that Massachusetts's legislative efforts to both encourage and control corporate enterprise "repeated the experience of the former mother country two centuries earlier. The Commonwealth consciously strove to direct the existing corporate bodies and to establish, in fact as well as in law, its authority over them." In discussing Massachusetts's corporate boom, historian Pauline Maier comments, "The peculiar readiness of Massachusetts to create corporations after Independence reflects the state's long familiarity with the corporate form," and she adds, "If there is a key to the corporation's popularity, it must lie in the history of New England and particularly of Massachusetts."[34]

Noblesse Oblige: The Proprietary Colonies

No one in seventeenth-century England was more aware of the dangers of colonial intransigence than King James II, who succeeded his brother, Charles II, in 1685. As Duke of York, James had been extremely active in British colonial affairs. Having received a grant of the newly acquired Dutch territory around the Hudson River, James kept "New York" for himself and (somewhat recklessly) deeded most of modern-day New Jersey, Pennsylvania, and Delaware to others. James was also party to the charters for the Bahamas, the Carolinas, the Royal African Company, and the Hudson's Bay Company.[35]

Charles II and James II were responsible for the bulk of England's eighteenth-century land grants in North America. One vitally important feature of the early British North American colonial system is that it was not conceived as a system. Separate colonies were chartered in a piecemeal fashion, often without regard for the actual means by which they would be governed. Perhaps the recklessness with which the Stuart kings gave away Crown lands in British North America reflected their own perilous experience as heirs to the office of their executed father. More likely, the Stuarts were struck by the emerging prosperity of New England, Virginia, and Barbados and were scared by the rapidly expanding French presence in New France, the Illinois country, the Mississippi River valley, and the Gulf Coast. Sponsoring North American colonization thus forwarded three Stuart goals: (1) refilling the royal coffers through aggressive mercantilist trade; (2) bolstering the holdings of the Stuart dynasty itself; and (3) putting an effective halt to French, Spanish, and Dutch colonial expansion in the North Atlantic and Caribbean.

From the beginning, English regulation and taxation of colonial goods was a source of conflict between not only the king and the colonies but between colonial elites and ordinary settlers. In order to pay for a series of increasingly expensive wars with the French, Dutch, and Spanish, the English government looked to the colonies as a cash cow. Thus, the colonies were required to ship all of their goods on English ships to English ports, regardless of their final destination. Duties could thereby be collected on American goods, whether or not they were intended for English consumers. The more pressure the Crown put on the colonies to obey the dictates of mercantilism, however, the more incentive the colonists had to evade such measures. For example, during the Culpepper Rebellion of 1677, the customs collector for North Carolina was actually deposed and imprisoned by a group of settlers (led by John Culpepper) who were angry about recent crackdowns on illegal trade. It was not uncommon for early Americans to presume the right to cheat on taxes and skirt the law.[36]

Another highly controversial feature of the British colonial system under the Stuarts was the nature of colonial rule itself. Since all unclaimed land in British North America technically belonged to the king, he could dispose of it however he chose. Land grants to private corporations were the norm in the New England colonies, but much of the rest of early America was granted by the king to individual proprietors. Granting North American frontier land was a virtually costless way for the king to repay debts and/or reward peers while at the same time providing de facto governance for open lands on the North American frontier.

New York, East and West (New) Jersey, Pennsylvania (including latter-day Delaware), Maryland, and the Carolinas were all founded as proprietary colonies. In all but Maryland, the colonists were given some stake in the political affairs of the colony through the election of a general assembly meant to rule in conjunction with the governor and his council. Unfortunately, the powers of those assemblies were generally unclear, as were those of the proprietors and their designated representatives. This led to myriad conflicts in which proprietary and antiproprietary parties waged war—sometimes literally—over issues such as land grants, quitrents (taxes paid by landholders to the proprietors), suffrage, and organized religion. Appeals could be made to the Privy Council in England, but this process was not only terribly inefficient but also predisposed to favor the proprietors' interests, given their personal connections to those in charge of colonial affairs at Whitehall.[37]

"It is difficult to imagine a more unfit body for the administration of a colony than were these proprietors," writes historian Charles Andrews, speaking specifically of the Carolinas, where eight men shared the proprietorship of the then undivided colony:

> Invested with supreme authority as rulers and landlords, they were chiefly interested in the profits of their proprietorships, and when they found that they could not protect the colony by means of the revenues arising out of their quit-rents and were faced with the necessity of advancing money from the revenues of their estates in England, they were willing to give up their rights and surrender their charter to the crown.[38]

Maryland was, until 1691, the private feudal domain of the Calvert family. George Calvert, later Lord Baltimore, had been a frequent and early investor in colonial schemes, from Virginia to Newfoundland, and he used his friendly relationship with King Charles I to request a North American charter of his own, which he received in 1632. Drawing on the medieval English practice of granting private "palatinates" to nobles—a "palatinate" was originally conceived as an absolute land grant intended to install loyal subjects on the contested borderlands between England, Scotland, and Wales—the Maryland charter made Calvert "an absolute lord, with complete control over administration, defense, and the upkeep of his province," writes Andrews. The Maryland charter completely shielded

Calvert (and his heirs) from royal intervention or appeal. This served the Calverts well, as their charter was repeatedly questioned from within by unhappy settlers and from without by agents of English trade policy.[39]

Lord Baltimore himself was an English convert to Catholicism. Though he and his heirs were strong proponents of religious freedom (for Christians), their proprietorship was severely challenged by Puritan settlers who were entrenched in the eastern part of Chesapeake Bay. The Calverts also evoked substantial opposition from their colonists by reducing the size of the Lower House of Assembly and by raising the property qualifications for suffrage. Under the Calvert regime, Maryland colonists actually had fewer legal rights than they would have had in England. They regularly complained about this, as did settlers in other proprietary colonies. In fact, American colonists in proprietary colonies frequently revolted against their overlords in pursuit of better, more democratic governance.[40]

The Calverts' political jurisdiction over Maryland was eventually challenged by a group of insurgents that called themselves the "Protestant Association," who seized the capital city of St. Mary's, and asked the Lords of Trade to make Maryland a royal province. The complaints of these Maryland colonists say a great deal about the political ordeals and aspirations of the age: "They wanted the king to take the Maryland government into his own hands," writes Andrews, "appointing Protestant governors and ministers, swearing and ruling the people according to the custom of England, and regulating taxation and the export duties not in the interests of a few but for the benefit of all." In other words, the colonists wanted law and order under an efficient, legitimate Protestant imperial regime devoted primarily to the exercise of intercontinental trade. They opposed the careless, offhand rule of the proprietors, who were inclined to regard the colony as a personal profit center rather than as home to ambitious British settlers.[41]

Because trade officials had been considering such action themselves for at least a decade, and given the Calverts' lax enforcement of trade regulations and tariffs in the region, there was finally momentum for change. Ultimately, the legal bases for all the American proprietorships, except that of Pennsylvania, were modified to substitute royal government for personal rule. In Maryland, as elsewhere, the Calvert family retained ownership of the colony's land, and thus the right to collect rent from its inhabitants, but a royal governor was inserted into the colony as a sort of imperial overseer. The new royal governor's authority, however, was never particularly clear or well respected.

Like Lord Baltimore's Maryland, Pennsylvania, another proprietary colony, was founded with religious issues in mind. William Penn, the proverbial Moses of the Quakers, was the son of a rich and powerful English naval commander and confidante of the Duke of York. His primary religious aim for Pennsylvania was not Quakerism but simply freedom of religion. Although the younger Penn's aspirations as a colonist were partially motivated by his experiences as a devout but oft-persecuted Quaker, he also stood to profit greatly from ownership of a large share of prime North American frontier land. His access to a proprietary charter was largely the result of his intimate connections at court, as well as a large debt owed his father by the Crown for funds leant the Royal Navy.

Penn ultimately spent less than four years in his colony; he recruited settlers by advertising its virtues far and wide. Pennsylvania became home to a wide array of Finns, Swedes, Dutch, Germans, Irish, Welsh, and English. A Quaker oligarchy did, however, retain political control over the assembly, thus exacerbating the political problems already present there.[42]

The circumstances of Pennsylvania's charter are unique for three reasons, all of which had important consequences for the later history of the colony: First, the charter was received at a time when the British imperial administration was in the midst of consolidating its control over the North American colonies. Thus, it is surprising, if not illogical, that Penn would have been granted proprietary control over a territory when the Lords of Trade were simultaneously *revoking* proprietary and corporate charters elsewhere in the colonies. For this, Penn probably had to thank both his close family connections to the Stuart dynasty and the Stuarts' sympathy for religious freedom, particularly that which battled against Anglican hegemony.[43]

A second, and related, feature of the Pennsylvania charter is that, although proprietary in name, it bestowed upon Penn and his heirs less jurisdictional power than had earlier proprietary grants, such as those issued in Maryland and New York. Though Penn was sympathetic to the cause of colonial self-government and endorsed the creation of a representative general assembly elected by the freemen of the colony, he was often troubled by the lengths to which settlers resisted his own authority. Jurisdictional battles between the assembly and the governor, as well as between proprietary and antiproprietary factions in the colony, continued unabated through the American Revolution and beyond. Limitations written into Penn's charter concerning royal oversight of the colony also proved irksome. "As compared with Baltimore's charter, which was wholly proprietary," writes Charles Andrews, "that of Penn was in a sense half royal, though in a manner wholly different from the half royal provisions of the Massachusetts charter of 1691." Unlike Massachusetts, in which a royal governor competed with a general assembly for jurisdiction, Pennsylvania retained a governor and governing council appointed by the proprietors, as well as an assembly elected by freeholders. Nonetheless, the Pennsylvania charter granted Parliament and the Lords of Trade unusually strong oversight and veto power over Pennsylvanian affairs. The jurisdictional ambiguity in the Pennsylvania polity was thus threefold: authority was divided between the Crown, the proprietors, and the taxpayers of Pennsylvania. Ambiguities in the wording of the charter gave rise to many subsequent conflicts over trade regulations, taxation, and the power of the general assembly.[44]

A third feature of the Penn charter was its reckless delineation of the actual boundaries of the colony. Penn's charter granted him lands that had already been claimed by both the Duke of York and Lord Baltimore. It is difficult to explain this overlap except to say that such carelessness and inconsistency were common in early American colonial charters. One important piece of land under dispute constitutes modern-day Delaware. It had originally been settled by the Swedes and Dutch and, though sparsely populated, was considered extremely valuable because of its position at the mouth of the Delaware River. Penn rightly feared that without control of the river, his colony might be cut off from access to the Atlantic Ocean. The Duke of York thus agreed to lease Delaware to Penn in 1682, though the proprietors of Maryland continued to contest the deed until the 1760s, when the famous Mason-Dixon Line was surveyed as part of an inter-colonial settlement. Though Penn intended for Delaware to be governed as part of Pennsylvania, an agreement was struck in the early 1700s that allowed Delaware to convene its own legislature. Delaware thereafter considered itself a royal province, though it was technically still ruled by the governor of Pennsylvania. As noted by Andrews, "The new colony, which had not even a name during colonial times, was unique in that its right to exist rested on no charter from the crown. It was never obliged to send its laws to England and its affairs very rarely came to the knowledge of the authorities there."[45]

Some noteworthy efforts were made to create workable constitutions for the proprietary colonies. Before John Locke became a noted philosopher, he wrote a prospective constitution for South Carolina at the behest of Lord Ashley, 1st Earl of Shaftesbury, who was a friend from his Oxford days. (Locke also met, and probably tutored, William Penn at Oxford.) But Locke's 1669 draft constitution for South Carolina was judged to be overly long and complex and was adapted only in a dramatically modified version, reduced from 120 paragraphs to a mere 41. (Later in his career, Locke was also influential in the reorganization of the British Board of Trade.) Ultimately, however, the Carolina assembly refused to accept either the long or short form of Locke's constitution, thus leading to a thirty-year standoff in which no clear jurisdictional doctrine was recognized in the colony. According to Andrews, "Thus for more than thirty years these Constitutions were a disturbing factor in the life of the colonists, and the determination of the proprietors to enforce them and the unwillingness of the assembly to accept them made it difficult for anyone, either in or out of office, to know just what were the laws they were expected to obey." Landholders and tenants of small properties were most adversely affected, notes Andrews:

> The grumbling among the poorer planters was the louder because of the uncertain tenure of their land, for which no patents had been granted; because of the demand for quit-rents, which they feared might be increased at any time; because of the occasional escheats and lapses that were enforced for failure to pay or to seat in due time; and especially because of the prosperity of those who reaped special advantages from office holding.

In sum, "The very system laid down by the proprietors only served to confuse and to irritate the colonists, because it was hopelessly intricate and wholly at variance with the simplicities of their plantation life."[46]

As a whole, then, the American colonists had their first taste of rebellion long before the Revolution. Eighteenth-century Americans did not want self-government so much as a clearer relationship with authority. Despite resentment of taxation and trade regulation, royal government was generally preferred to the authority of reckless intermediaries who lacked clear jurisdiction. It was only during the Revolution that colonists really began to grapple with the idea of separating from the Crown. As late as 1754, for example, American political leaders were forging plans for unification of British North American lands under a single royal government.

In the meantime, colonial authority was developing along much different lines in the various colonies, depending on their legal status, economy, and manner of administration. Having existed for so long without strong government or corporate mandate to form cohesive communities, the southern colonies evolved into quasi-feudal, patriarchal societies in which individual landowners were largely left to their own devices. This was made possible, or perhaps necessary, in part because of the absence of major rivers to connect the southern hinterlands with the coasts. Cities developed along the Atlantic seaboard, but the interior remained a largely unconnected expanse of individual farms and plantations. Tobacco emerged early on as a reliable, easily cured staple crop and allowed landowners to create large commercial farms far from ports. Cotton followed, accentuating the isolated plantation agrarianism of the emerging American South.[47]

The sociolegal life of the southern colonies evolved around the personal authority of local landowners. The emerging American ideal of sacrosanct private property rights took a unique form here, different than the corporate ideal that was developing in the American Northeast. In the South, slaves—both African and Native American—were regarded as personal property over which their owners had total command. Law enforcement was the unofficial responsibility of local gentry, with the ownership of land being tantamount to political authority. Little effort was made to form a professional court system in these colonies, and the practice of law for profit was banned in some. Nor was much attention paid to the establishment of formal penal codes and correctional institutions. Individual plantation owners thus held private jurisdiction over most matters of law and order.[48]

These differences had a lasting legacy on the political development of the South in juxtaposition to the North. For example, according to one comparative historian of crime and justice in eighteenth- and nineteenth-century Massachusetts and South Carolina:

> Massachusetts consistently sought to bolster the role of formal authority by strengthening its courts, establishing police, and curbing extralegal violence. In South Carolina, however, plantation aristocrats mocked court laws, took their quarrels to the dueling field instead of

the courthouse, belatedly established police, supported permanent vigilante organizations, and actually encouraged citizens to find extralegal accommodations rather than increase strife through lawsuits.[49]

In the postcolonial South, legislatures saw little need to interfere in the lives of the landowning aristocracy, who were in turn expected to maintain law and order within their own precincts. There was little perceived need for intermediary organizations like courts and corporations, and it was not considered necessary to question the rights of slaveholders to own other persons.

Problems on the Emerging American Frontier

If violence against the state is to be taken as an indication of adverse sentiment, then it is vitally important to identify the major causes of American dissent in the emerging zones of settlement—that is, the frontier. The experience of Virginia is especially revealing in this regard, as it was not only the first British colony in North America but also the first "royal" colony. The weaknesses inherent in the Virginian system foreshadow the experience of the other British colonies, most of which came under similar forms of royal control in the eighteenth century.

Colonial Virginia held vast expanses of western frontier land, including parts of modern-day West Virginia, Ohio, and North Carolina. It was there, far from the seats of colonial power, that settlers really began to test the limits of colonial jurisdiction. Frontier families needed protection from natives, legal tools for acquisition and title to land, and political representation in the colonial legislative process. Given the colonies' weak administrative capacity and ambiguous jurisdiction, their colonial governments were often unable, or simply unwilling, to meet the needs of frontier communities. This became a focal point of controversy by the mid-eighteenth century.

One catalyst of political controversy on the western frontier was vacillation on the part of royal governors with regard to their proper jurisdiction. Amid the uncertainty of the English Civil War, for example, various sections of Virginia were granted, then usurped, and then regranted to noblemen who were loyal to the king. One such grant, made in the spring of 1669, revoked a 1649 grant of the "northern neck" of Virginia (today the region just south of Washington DC, between the Potomac and Rappahannock rivers) and reissued it to four loyal subjects, the object being to assure its settlement. The problem was that this new grant ignored preexisting grants that had been issued between 1661 and 1669. Such snafus were common in the American colonies. In this case, conflict was avoided; the new grantees resigned their charter without upsetting the inhabitants of northern Virginia.[50]

In February 1672, Charles II indicated that he wished to grant the title to *all* of Virginia to two noblemen for a term of thirty-one years. Writes Osgood, "They were to have all lands, receive all rents, and exercise all jurisdictions which had arisen or existed under any grant which had been previously made. They were to receive all arrears of rents and profits which had accrued since 1669." Furthermore, "no mention whatever was made of the government already existing in Virginia, or of the planters there and their vested rights," thus denying the legitimacy of the existing government. The House of Burgesses, Virginia's legislative assembly, immediately protested. Ultimately, the two noblemen in question, Lords Arlington and Culpeper agreed to give up their claims to everything except the income from property taxes and foreclosures. However, the issue of jurisdiction surely loomed large in the minds of ordinary Virginians. The governor of Virginia, John Berkeley, reported having to quell at least two tax revolts in the colony in a single year. Matters came to a head in 1676, when the murder of a few white settlers by local natives ignited a full-scale civil war—Bacon's Rebellion.[51]

One issue underlying Bacon's Rebellion was the colonial government's perceived inability to protect its own constituents. Governor Berkeley insisted on keeping all available military resources in a defensive posture, and he assigned militia to small forts posted around the Virginia tidewater region. Up-country settlers thus felt insufficiently protected, and in Charles City County, local men took up arms in self-defense under the leadership of Nathaniel Bacon, a young landowner with legal training. Bacon led an army of some three hundred men into war against local native tribes despite Governor Berkeley's fervent protests. In essence, Bacon was questioning the governor's jurisdiction over frontier defense policy. He also accused Berkeley of unjustly taxing Virginians and using the money for patronage and personal gain while ignoring the most pressing needs of the colony.[52]

In turn, Governor Berkeley accused Bacon of treason, though Bacon justified his actions as the only available means of self-defense. Bacon died suddenly in October 1676, and the insurrection died with him, but at least thirty-seven of Bacon's coconspirators were executed first. Berkeley was never able to regain the colonists' trust; in 1677, he had to be forcibly removed from office by a three-man commission sent from England to relieve him of duty.[53]

An older generation of historians talked frequently about the "frontier mentality" of eighteenth- and nineteenth-century Americans, but it now appears that it was not the dangers of the "frontier" that made early Americans unique so much as their frustration with frontier government. They wanted, and sometimes demanded, a more transparent, accountable relationship with those appointed to rule over them. In other words, the political culture of the early American frontier revolved as much around issues of jurisdiction as the rigors of Indian killing and lawlessness.[54]

Similar complaints fomented violent conflict in colonial New York, Massachusetts, Virginia, and Maryland. Frontier settlers seemed to presume *both* the right to go west unfettered by government regulation *and* the right to government protection from whatever dangers might await them there. These sentiments resonated and grew over the next three hundred years, helping give rise to a political culture in which popular attitudes toward government vacillate between dependency and despair. In contrast with the orderly, peaceful settlements of New France, British Americans were extremely demanding of government—and equally disdainful of its mandates. Their view of government remains with us today: invisible, organic, all-powerful, and yet totally submissive to the whims of the people.

Americans created the frontier; it did not create them. In so doing, they not only eviscerated a continent and its inhabitants but also formed a political culture unlike anywhere else in the world.

3

Two Turning Points

Prior to the onset of the Seven Years' War, it would have been reasonable to predict the political confederation of all of British North America. Leading statesmen from many of the colonies did.

In June and July 1754, a group of representatives from all but the southernmost colonies convened at Albany to discuss two issues of major importance to the future of British North America. One topic was the need to permanently unify the colonies, thus erecting some semblance of consistency and oversight in governmental affairs. The popularity of this notion among Anglo-American colonists was betrayed only by their distrust of one another—no colony was willing to risk ceding power to any other, let alone to a tertiary body governed from afar.

The second, more pressing matter that brought the delegates to the Albany Congress was the state of relations with the Native American population of upstate New York, particularly the Mohawks, who for decades had proved a reliable and fierce ally in the British struggle against New France. The Mohawks, part of the powerful Iroquois Confederacy, held territory that was vital to the long-term survival of the English colonists of New York and New England—the contested borderland with New France in upstate New York and the Great Lakes region.[1]

Known for both their skill in combat and their diplomacy, the Iroquois were coveted by all the European settlements in the region. Massachusetts wanted the Mohawks to resettle near Stockbridge, where they might fortify the defense of the colony's western border. Pennsylvania and Virginia sought Mohawk help resisting recent French incursions into the Ohio Valley. Pennsylvania was also locked in competition with Connecticut—both claimed jurisdiction over the Susquehanna River valley—and it was felt that an alliance with the Mohawks might be of value in their quest for jurisdiction there.

The French were sometimes successful in inducing Iroquois bands to move north and/or temporarily ally with them against the English. France's grand strategy was to encircle the British colonies with a chain of riverside garrisons that connected Montreal, Detroit, Illinois, and the Mississippi River valley. Nonetheless, Franco-English clashes most often occurred in the American colonies, rather than in New France, thus sparing French Canadians the dangers of domestic combat. French Canadians were often reluctant to fight in the service of the Crown; native warriors and professional soldiers did a great deal of the fighting for them. In contrast, warfare was an all-too-common experience for ordinary settlers in the American colonies. Three major wars and the perpetual threat of violence took a heavy toll on the lives, spirits, and pocketbooks of American colonists.[2]

Population growth in the British colonies was, at the time, creating excess demand for arable land, thus increasing the tension between neighboring colonies over jurisdiction. Borderlands passed back and forth between rival colonies, and squatters were aggressively filling the gaps. Land speculators and absentee landlords filled the courts with competing claims for land. In 1750, for example, a notorious land speculator named David Ingersoll hatched a plan to turn leaseholders in Livingston Manor, an estate near Albany, New York, against their landlord, Robert Livingston Jr. Ingersoll's efforts were part of a larger effort to reclaim land held by several old New York families who legally governed them as private quasi-feudal estates. Ingersoll claimed that this land was not under New York jurisdiction but was under the authority of Massachusetts, and the complicated legal proceedings that ensued were held in Boston, several hundred miles away. Massachusetts supported the claim because it felt that its neighboring colonies were perpetually chipping away at its borders.[3]

In describing the depth of this problem, historian Sung Bok Kim writes, "In the mid-eighteenth century, disputes over rival claims to lands reached epidemic proportions, and almost every 'landed property' appeared to be in a 'precarious situation.'" Kim also observes that:

The practice of extending one's land beyond the supposedly granted acreage was a common vice among landowners and even townships. The colonists in general had no moral compunctions about "taking in a little of King George's ground" wherever they could find it. Innumerable boundary and claim disputes thus litter the minutes of colonial equity courts. . . . Most of the large landowners spent a good part of their lives in court and were extremely nervous over the security of their estates.[4]

Fault does not lie with the settlers alone. Local natives sometimes participated in "illegal" land deals and suspicious litigation. Given the ambiguous terms of most land deals, particularly those between whites and natives, existing titles could easily be disputed in court. "Landjobbers and squatters sought out the Indian proprietors to vouch for fraudulent land deals perpetrated by whites, and pored over old, dusty patents, deeds, and other land papers to find any title irregularities and defects," writes Kim. Hendrick, the Mohawks' chief, was known to sell parcels of land held by other tribes. At the Albany Congress of 1754, he made deals with both sides in the competition to claim Pennsylvania's Susquehanna River valley.[5]

Such actions were typical of the age. According to one historian, "In this new country there was no other problem which loomed so large and which so constantly engaged the settlers' attention. Whether a schism was brewing, a project being launched to convert Indians, a grant of lands to be exploited, or a frame of government to be drawn, a spate of discussion on the matter of organization was sure to ensue." In jurisdictional terms, one might describe this new "political consciousness" as the result of insufficient legal clarity with respect to the acquisition and possession of private property. Jurisdictional confusion created conflict by way of legal opportunism, obfuscation, and double-dealing.[6]

Benjamin Franklin, Pennsylvanian printer, public servant, and newspaperman, could not solve the land problem, but he did have an innovative solution to the French and Indian threat. One aim of the colonial representatives at the Albany Congress of 1754 was to forge a plan for mutual defense in light of renewed French aggression. Settling matters with the disgruntled Iroquois was one tactic, but the bigger concern was gaining commitments from each of the colonies to supply money and manpower in case of war. Up to that point, there had been little agreement, and even less cooperation, over proper military strategy vis-à-vis the French.

In the weeks just prior to the Albany Congress, Franklin had written a series of what he called "Short Hints toward a Scheme for Uniting the Northern Colonies," in which he proposed what later became known as the "Albany Plan," a surprisingly simple scheme whereby the separate colonies would agree to join under a single government. A Grand Council would be composed of representatives from each of the colonies and be empowered to collect revenues, prepare for and wage war, and forge a uniform policy with respect to Indian affairs.

Franklin firmly believed that the greatest danger to British America was not the French, the natives, or the wilderness, but instead the continued disunion among the colonies. In fact, the famous "Join or Die" drawing in which a snake is cut into pieces—each representing a section of the Union—was originally published in Franklin's *Pennsylvania Gazette* on May 9, 1754, along with commentary comparing "the present disunited State of the British Colonies" with that of the French, who were "under one Direction, with one Council, and one Purse." At that time, the newspaper industry relied heavily on plagiarism for most of its content, and Franklin's "snake" was subsequently published throughout the colonies.[7]

Though he later became known as one of the intellectual forces behind the American Revolution, an earlier preoccupation of Franklin's was the creation of a single British nation in North America—one that was unified culturally, politically, and militarily under the aegis of king and Parliament. In a prescient essay called "Observations Concerning the Increase of Mankind," Franklin predicted that the bulk of Englishmen would one day live in North America, peopling its vast territories with Britons, and thus creating a transatlantic dominion of unique strength and scope. Franklin's commitment to cultural unification is also evident in his calls to exclude slaves, Indians, Germans, and all other non-Britons from this union. The key to Franklin's plan was governmental centralization, whereby the interests of the various colonies might be sorted and resolved through the apparatus of a national congress, or Grand Council, and administered by an American governor general paid by the Crown.[8]

The subsequent debates at the Albany Congress over Franklin's scheme tell us a great deal about the principle dilemmas that confronted colonial union. "Four questions in particular concerned them," writes historian Timothy Shannon. "Would the colonies form one general union or divide themselves into two or more smaller [regional] unions? Would the union be enacted by Parliament or by the colonial assemblies? How would the intercolonial government be funded? And how would constitutional powers be divided in this new intercolonial body?"[9]

In each case, the prevailing issue was jurisdictional autonomy: Could the colonies be urged to delegate some of their governmental authority to a higher power? Franklin was a staunch advocate of parliamentary control, which would thus decrease the autonomy of the colonies. At that time, the key problem underlying colonial disunion was the fact that each colony had a unique and independent relationship with the Crown. In "proprietary colonies" such as Pennsylvania, single families held near total control over colonial affairs. In "royal colonies," by contrast, the king maintained sovereignty through the office of governor and council—this was the case in Virginia, New York, and New Hampshire, for example. In "corporate colonies" such as Rhode Island and Connecticut, however, the inhabitants themselves held collective autonomy over their affairs. These disparities, coupled with the fact that the colonies were in constant competition with one another for jurisdiction over borderlands and unclaimed frontier land, created great obstacles to coordinated action, let alone union under a single government.[10]

The delegates of the Albany Congress decided in favor of Franklin's Albany Plan, but no further progress was made once the proposal was sent back to the colonies for consideration. It is worth noting that Franklin had hoped to see the delegates institute this measure without further debate, thus bypassing the colonial assemblies altogether. For better or worse—arguably worse—the colonial assemblies balked at the notion of ceding their autonomy to a larger colonial body.[11]

In London, the plan received scant consideration as well. The British were primarily concerned with military matters at this point—that same summer, a small group of Virginia militiamen under the leadership of young George Washington was roundly defeated by the French in the Ohio Valley.

The Seven Years' War

Contrasting systems of landownership and property law explain a good deal of the differences in the civic and legal behavior of eighteenth-century Anglo-American and French-Canadian settlers. In Europe, land was largely controlled by hereditary clans of noblemen. Estates changed hands through marriage, sale, and royal prerogative, but the rules of the game not only kept outsiders at arm's length but also kept the courts and legislatures out of the land business as much as possible. In French Canada, an open frontier might have evolved into a speculative system similar to that in the Anglo-American colonies, but royal control prevented this from happening. Arable land close to the major waterways of New France was doled out in a manner resembling that of Old France. Rents were minimal and land division was orderly. Property west of the province remained wild and largely uninhabited by settlers, with the exception of trappers, traders, and missionaries licensed by the royal government. None of this held true in the British colonies.

The quest of British Americans for new land was a precipitating factor behind the Seven Year's War. The beginning of the war centered on control of the Ohio Valley, which was key to commanding the "American" Midwest. The first Anglo-American troops to enter the war were Virginians. Historian Guy Frégault notes that when the time came for action in Ohio, the Virginians insisted that they be the first and only colonial force sent to intervene. But why were the Virginians the first to enter the fray when Maryland, Pennsylvania, and the Carolinas were, according to Frégault, "all favorably situated for access to the Ohio country and all animated by the same ambitions as Virginia"? One reason was because the Virginians knew that preemptive action would grant them exclusive rights to any unclaimed property in Ohio. Washington was one such Virginian profiteer, and he capitalized on his youth, daring, and expertise as a land surveyor in volunteering for the dangerous but potentially profitable venture of leading militiamen into battle against the French.[12]

If before-market land prices were not enough incentive for Virginians to go to war, the pending arrival of British troops and engineers was. The order to dispatch General Braddock's troops via Virginia guaranteed that any roads built to the Ohio Valley would not only provide a direct route between the two but would also get this all-important infrastructural task done at British expense. So ardent were the Virginians that they protested General Braddock's original order to march to Ohio via Maryland. Unfortunately for Braddock, the "losers" in this struggle—Maryland, Pennsylvania, and the Carolinas—responded by dragging their feet in the war effort for the next several years. Calls for troops, revenue, and tactical coordination were so often ignored that intercolonial strife might well be blamed for the calamitous defeats the British suffered throughout the war's early years. Maryland sat out the Seven Years' War entirely.[13]

Public opinion in New France was largely against the war—most Québécois had adequate farmland and little interest in territorial expansion. They also opposed military conscription of any kind, and, having been largely spared native violence, they were against agitating their tribal neighbors unnecessarily. Nevertheless, the leaders of New France pushed the colony toward war. They sacked British-allied tribal villages, invaded the Ohio Valley, and built forts there. Until the 1750s, French policy had generally avoided open conflict with the British—the French often engaged native allies to attack Anglo-American settlements in their stead. But, in pursuit of both the good favor of the home government and the economic plunders of war, a new cadre of leaders dragged the colonists of New France into conflict. France and England were engaged in a larger, intercontinental, multinational struggle—perhaps the first ever "world war"—and the North American theater became a key site of the conflict.[14]

The North American portion of the war proved to be a poorly organized, protracted affair. Colonists on both sides were asked to provide support for continental armies while also manning and supplying their own militias. Colonial militias, in turn, tended to be disorderly and independent, and they frequently chafed the officers sent to oversee them. It seems also that Britain sent many of its worst generals to North America to arbitrate, and later execute, its affairs. On the French side, Acadian resistance fighters are said to have adopted the native practice of collecting scalps as evidence of successful raids on British war parties. In Quebec, amid the campaign to dominate the St. Lawrence River valley, British general James Wolfe wrote a colleague, "I own it would give me pleasure to see the Canadian vermin sacked and pillaged and justly repaid their unheard-of-cruelty," and, indeed, Wolfe ordered countless French-Canadian villages burned, farms plundered, and the city of Quebec bombed to rubble. Another British general, James Murray, subsequently complained that "the plundering kind of war which had been carried on this last campaign had so debauched the soldiers that there was no putting a stop to these [disorders] without very severe punishment."[15]

In Nova Scotia, the invading British army literally deported thousands of "Acadian" French Catholics, thus creating a huge vacuum in this otherwise fertile region. In *Letters from an American Farmer,* Franco-American

J. Hector St. John de Crévecoeur interrupts an ode to the democratic brilliance of the Americas to note the bleak prospects of Nova Scotia: "The power of the Crown in conjunction with the musketos [*sic*] has prevented men from settling there," he notes. "Yet some parts of it flourished once, and it contained a mild, harmless set of people [the Acadians]. But for the fault of a few leaders, the whole was banished." Many Acadians wound up in Louisiana, where they transplanted their culture and evolved into the people referred to today as Cajuns—in fact, "Cajun" is a derivative of the word "Acadian."[16]

Undoubtedly, it was not British tactical superiority that led to victory, but commercial, naval, and demographic dominance. The population of the British colonies in America was between ten and twenty times greater than that of New France at the outset of the war, and the American colonists had more to lose, given the importance of overseas trade to the Anglo-American economy. The new port town of Halifax, built by the British in 1749 to counter the large French garrison at Louisburg on the eastern end of Nova Scotia, afforded the British naval supremacy. Both countries nearly bankrupted themselves paying for the war, but England's ample supply of credit and healthy commercial markets gave it far more leeway than France, whose finances were already in shambles.[17]

The home government in France increasingly lost interest in the struggle as their forces lost ground in the Ohio Valley, Lake Ontario, and Cape Breton Island, where the French stronghold of Louisbourg finally fell. There were protracted attempts by the French to transfer the epicenter of the conflict to Europe—extensive plans for an invasion of Great Britain were even drafted—but England refused to take the bait and pressed the North American struggle to a rapid conclusion. However, adjudicating the peace was another matter.[18]

Aftermath of One War, Prelude to Another

As with most wars, the division of territory following the 1763 Treaty of Paris involved a great deal of horse trading. Britain, the victor, had a difficult choice to make: it could seize the prosperous Franco-Caribbean sugar island of Guadeloupe, or lay claim to thousands of miles of Franco-Canadian wilderness, plus a handful of small mercantile cities. The French were willing to part with one or the other, but not both. The British had every reason to opt for Guadeloupe; the volume of trade between England and the Caribbean was much greater than that of the fur trade in eastern Canada, and Quebec was already populated by sixty-five thousand French Catholics, a formidable obstacle for English administrators. However, ceding Canada to the French was tantamount to inviting France back into the continental picture, geopolitically speaking. The British chose Quebec; the French kept Guadeloupe.

Though peace negotiations between the French and English governments were bitter and protracted, the Quebec/Guadeloupe trade was settled rather quickly. The French were eager to part with Quebec. The governors of New France had never really succeeded in bringing the fur industry under their control, and though the agricultural settlement of the St. Lawrence Valley had been successful, it never generated much revenue for the Crown. The British, however, realized that Quebec might be valuable as an import market, and they had faith that the fur trade held much untapped revenue.[19]

British officials underestimated the potential difficulties of governing Quebec, but they were remarkably successful at it, nonetheless. Rabid anti-Catholicism had long been English policy in Great Britain, but the administration looked upon French Canada differently. For example, British law prohibited Catholics from voting and holding elected office in Britain, but French Canadians were soon granted both privileges. Perhaps this discrepancy resulted from the fact that French Canadians were not in any way connected to the English, unlike Irish Catholics— England's cruelty toward the Irish did not stop. Though many Anglo-Americans felt that policies should be enacted to force French Canadians to convert to Protestantism, a conciliatory policy was enacted. The Quebec Act of 1774 marked a new legal regime for French Canada.

Some have argued that the Quebec Act was passed in direct response to the rush of events in the American colonies, though clearly this is not the case. Legislation for the administration of Canada had been in the works for more than a decade. British members of Parliament realized that it was in their best interest to placate French Canadians in the advent of war, but this was never their primary motivation. Instead, the Quebec Act appears to have been the product of a series of measured assessments about the best way to govern Canada. Knowing that the *Québécois* would resist efforts to deny them religious freedom, the British guaranteed the existence of the Catholic Church in Quebec. The Quebec Act also gained the loyalty of the *Canadien* seigneurs by legally acknowledging the province's long-standing feudal system. With respect to the actual governance of the province, two further concessions were of equal importance: Though the colony would be officially ruled by an English governor, an advisory council would be appointed consisting of both Protestant and Catholic representatives. Realizing that *Canadiens* would be unfamiliar with—and probably hostile to—English common law, the Quebec Act also maintained French legal practice in most matters pertaining to civil law. A number of French-Catholic magistrates were also appointed to officiate over local trials.[20]

The passage of the Quebec Act is particularly remarkable in light of Britain's failure to achieve similar success governing the Catholic population of another new acquisition—East Florida. The British had received this latter territory in exchange for the return of Havana, which they had seized during the Seven Years' War. However, before British magistrates even had time to arrive in St. Augustine, most of East Florida's Spanish population left for Cuba. Arrangements had been made to sell all of their land to a group of American investors represented by John Gordon of Charleston, South Carolina, which did not please the Spanish in the least. Gordon's Florida purchase, and the Spanish exodus that succeeded it, greatly angered British officials, who now faced the difficult prospect of repopulating Florida. Various private investors offered to initiate large-scale agricultural ventures that would pay for the settlement of Bermudians, Greeks, Italians, and Minorcans, as well as flotsam picked from the streets and poorhouses of London. But such plans stalled in the face of Indian problems, land disputes (John Gordon and his group battled for more than ten years to gain compensation for the annulment of their extensive Florida holdings), lack of a natural ocean harbor, and unsuccessful land speculation (most grants expired if land was not settled within a preset number of years). By 1771, when the population of British East Florida was first enumerated, only 288 whites and 900 Negroes were counted in the province, none of them, presumably, Catholics of Spanish dissent. This is a testament to the fact that the British foreign office was not uniformly successful in annexing North American territories. The Florida debacle was a result of its inability to provide clear protection of property rights among the existing Spanish population. In contrast, England's success in Quebec reflects unusual sensitivity to the need for legal, as well as cultural, continuity in an annexed land.[21]

By ensuring the continuance of French-Canadian traditions of land tenure, seigneurialism, religious organization, and civil law, the English left the bedrock of Québécois society intact. At the same time, space was made in the economic and political life of the colony for a new class of British merchants and entrepreneurs. This new Anglo-Canadian elite provided the Crown with a buffer population of loyal journalists, politicians, and financial and business leaders. Scots, especially, seemed to prosper there. The fur trade had by this time become a more complicated, capital-intensive industry than it was in the early days. This created remarkable business opportunities for immigrants with good contacts and a high tolerance for risk. Wholesale manufactured goods, as well as banking, insurance, and shipping and ladling services all grew with this new anglophone bourgeoisie. Montreal began a long period of rapid, bustling, bicultural growth.[22]

Following the Anglo-French merger of 1760, Canada was a profoundly business-oriented, libertarian, laissez-faire merchant state. A major difference between it and the emerging American economy, however, was the degree to which entrepreneurs were constrained by law in the pursuit of profit. Canadians were granted only very limited access to the privileges of incorporation, for example, and monopoly rights were seriously enforced under the English regime. Moreover, while corruption was common in anglophone Canada, there was a sense of orderliness about it—a healthy respect for law and authority and the traditions of imperial Britain, particularly in relation to land grants and sales. The character of the Canadian jurisdictional landscape clearly contrasts with those in the proto-American states.

The American Colonies between the Wars

Anglo-Americans turned a corner in their political consciousness during the decade after the Seven Years' War. The issues underlying the coming revolution are extremely telling. Irreconcilable jurisdictional disputes were at the heart of the impasse.

The attitude of Anglo-Americans toward the Crown was evident in their reaction to two new tax laws: one designed to pay off British war debts through increased taxation on rum and Madeira wine (the American Duties Act of 1764), the other requiring payment of a tax on paper goods (the Stamp Act of 1765). Opposition to the rum tax was tepid at best, though evasion was rampant. The Stamp Act, in contrast, roused considerable anger throughout the colonies. The reason behind these different reactions was that the Duties Act on liquor was a tariff on trade, something colonists were long accustomed to paying, whereas the Stamp Act was a tax on consumption—there was no importing or exporting involved.

While the colonists recognized the Crown's right to regulate trade, they felt that only the colonial legislatures had the right to submit them to other forms of taxation. To the colonists, the Stamp Act thus represented a new kind of tax, the legality of which was debated even by British officials. At the same time, the leading proponents of noncompliance with the new consumption tax were outspokenly loyal to the king; it was only his attempt to expand the Crown's power that was cause for alarm.[23]

Americans and Englishmen hotly debated the technical details of Parliament's jurisdiction over the colonies—there were legal grounds to support both sides of the argument. Some argued, quite cogently, that consumption taxes were legal but not customary, a distinction that drew on the common law notion that legal actions that had never been utilized were illegitimate despite their formal permissibility. Nevertheless, "What America was constitutionally compelled to defend, the British could not constitutionally concede," writes Reid. "The difference might be a mere abstraction of law, but once stated, civil war was inescapable." In 1778, Parliament ultimately relinquished its right to tax "any of the Colonies, Provinces, and Plantations in North America," but by then it was far too late.[24]

In New York, a vicious tax battle developed between an overly ambitious lieutenant governor, Cadwallader Colden, and the Hudson Valley's landed gentry. Colden supported royal control over the colony; in opposition, local elites concocted elaborate arguments about the proper jurisdiction of government—they argued that Parliament could not tax the colonists, and maintained that only the colonists could tax themselves. The Americans were wrong, however. With the exception of Maryland, whose charter contained a clause protecting it from royal taxation, the colonies *were* constitutionally subject to parliamentary taxation of this nature.

In Pennsylvania, a different, though related, set of issues came to the fore. The colony had long been governed by a proprietary party linked to the Penn family, but by the end of the Seven Years' War, a so-called antiproprietary party was close to winning from Parliament a new royal charter, thus negating Penn's original proprietary rights. Soon thereafter, the antiproprietary party received a huge setback when a vigilante group calling itself the Paxton Boys began denouncing the antiproprietary party's soft stance on colonial defense. They began killing local Conestoga Indians to prove their point. During the winter of 1764, some five hundred Paxton affiliates threatened to march into Philadelphia and restore the assembly to proprietary party dominance. Ben Franklin, one of the colony's leading antiproprietarists, actually lost his seat in the assembly around this time, and he, along with Richard Jackson, was sent to London to help plead for royal intervention. Franklin himself aspired to be the colony's first royal governor, and he wrote prolifically at this time about the possibilities for English national hegemony over the colonies. Little did Franklin know that his mission to London would turn from a quest for royal intervention to one for American independence.[25]

Franklin's popularity, and the acceptability of his pro-British sentiments are a testament to the tenor of the times up through the beginning of the Revolutionary War. Americans were still a long way from questioning the authority of the king over the colonies. In fact, many colonists actually wanted more royal oversight. Despite the unpopularity of the Stamp Act of 1765, for example, the repeal of the onerous bill was celebrated with public celebrations and unveilings of memorials to their kind and prudent king (George III). "Thus every year till after the bloodshed at Lexington and Concord there were expressions by Americans of loyalty to the King," writes Dunbar. Even the cantankerous Samuel Adams expressed his "unspotted loyalty" to and reliance on the "wisdom and goodness of his present Majesty" in a Boxing Day editorial in the *Boston Gazette*.[26]

Colonial representatives complained not about taxation, but about "taxation without representation." Allowing any outside polity to dictate terms was considered a threat to each colony's political autonomy. In the meantime, each of the colonies also faced the challenges of civil unrest, economic depression, and political discontent. Massachusetts merchants continued smuggling goods in defiance of British trade law. Connecticut farmers usurped thousands of acres of land in proto-Vermont—then in northeastern New York—rioted, and looted politicians' homes in opposition to both the British authorities and the Albany *patroons* who owned much of the previously unsettled land. Since there was no intercolonial forum in which to hash out such disputes, the controversy only escalated over time. Each colony became a center of serious political dissent, and the prevalence of armed detachments was a natural impetus to violence. Well before the colonists began battling the British, they were fighting one another.[27]

Land disputes were a common source of violence. In the as yet unborn province of Maine (which remained under the jurisdiction of Massachusetts until 1820), settlers began organizing to defend their land from the absentee landlords who had been granted titles there by King Charles I nearly 150 years earlier. Historian Alan Taylor notes, "Mid-Maine's conflict was part of a national pattern of backcountry resistance. From the mid-eighteenth century to the mid-nineteenth century in at least ten other areas, yeomen seeking free or cheap access to wilderness land confronted gentlemen who had exploited their political connections to secure large land grants." The "great proprietors" sought protection from the Massachusetts courts, while the settlers formed armed bands. The Maine conflict lasted for several decades, erupting periodically into communal violence. Called "white Indians" in reference to their faux-Indian costumes and reported savagery, the rebels were described by one 1808 observer, Lemuel Paine, as follows:

> The most prominent feature in their character is a violent and implacable hatred to the law. . . . The sheriff of the county and his officers they have marked out and doomed as victims for sacrifice and the hated name of execution is to terrify them no more. They declare the profession of law must come down, that lawyers must be extirpated and their officers prostrated with the dust.[28]

In the royal province of South Carolina, a different set of issues fomented a similar set of outcomes—jurisdictional contention, violence, and popular discontent. South Carolinians' experience of the Seven Years' War revolved largely around bloody conflict with the neighboring Cherokees. Settlement of the colony's hinterland was thus extremely limited until 1761, when the Cherokees were finally driven west. The area was quickly settled thereafter, but the plantation-owning class of the low counties still dominated the colonial assembly. Prospering townships along the new frontier were flagrantly denied seats in the provincial assembly until 1776. They also lacked courts, sheriffs, and the normal appendages of civil government. Given the region's sparse population density, this ordinarily might not have been much of a problem, but disputes persisted nonetheless. Backcountry landowners found themselves plagued by bandits, brigands, and freeloaders, and because the law required all matters of justice to be referred back to Charleston, victims had little legal recourse. After an unusually heavy spate of kidnapping and robbery in the summer of 1767, backcountry property owners turned in frustration to vigilantism. They drafted formal rules of order, signed oaths of loyalty, and took to calling themselves "Regulators." On October 19, 1767, the *South Carolina Gazette* noted, "peaceable inhabitants . . . in a kind of desperation . . . have formed associations, to expell [sic] the villains from wherever they can get at them, and to do themselves justice in a summary way." When the governor asked the assembly to pass legislation suppressing the Regulators, his request fell on deaf ears. Soon, the Regulators were waging open warfare on outlaws, vagrants, and paupers. Technically, they were acting in open defiance of British authority. The Regulators were South Carolina's chief junta for several years following the Seven Years' War.[29]

Similar movements—often calling themselves "Regulator" movements—appeared in upstate New York and western Massachusetts, Connecticut, Vermont, South Carolina, Pennsylvania, Maine, and Virginia. In North Carolina, a Regulator movement arose in protest against land speculation and a corrupt legal system designed to favor speculators and their lawyers. It is important to note that none of these vigilante movements appears to have had any intention of overthrowing or subverting colonial government. What they wanted was local autonomy, along with local representation in their provincial assembly. The term "regulator" actually goes back to eighteenth-century England, where it was used to refer to men who sought greater control over their elected representatives to Parliament. They demanded courthouses and jails and workhouses. American Regulators desired the institutional means to enforce law and order in their communities and they wanted such institutions to be directly accountable to them, not to coastal elites. A number of these complaints foreshadow long-term tropes in American political discourse, such as the Regulators' desire to seek government protection from those who prey on the industrious; calls to limit the influence of lawyers in colonial affairs; and equivocation over the proper spheres of state and local government. In the eyes of the rebels, the imperial government was not doing its job and thus deserved the threat of replacement. In the final analysis, however, it was *more, not less,* government that they sought.[30]

French Canada between the Wars

Like many things historical, the American Revolution looks one way in its domestic context and another when considered in a comparative light. One fascinating and relatively obscure question about the Revolution is why Canadians did not take part. Certainly, French Catholics could have found cause to resist their British conquerors. Moreover, Nova Scotians (by then) were largely former New Englanders and oppressed Acadians, and they too might have been swayed by arguments for independence. In fact, American revolutionary leaders tried diligently to bring both Quebecers and Nova Scotians into the fold, hoping to split the British forces and overwhelm them from within. Understanding why this did not happen sheds important light on the causes and consequences of the Revolution itself.

After 1760, when the British military seized the St. Lawrence River valley from the French, the principal political concern of French Canadians was freedom of religion and trade. Beaver was still big business, and Canadian timber, flax, hemp, and cod had made serious inroads into European markets. French Canadians were appeased by the Quebec Act of 1774, which granted them freedom of religion, representative government, and maintenance of the French legal code for regulation of provincial affairs. It also granted Catholics the legal right to serve as officers of the court, something denied them in England until 1829. The new British entrepreneurs of Quebec were in the minority, and though they successfully blocked pro-French legislation for more than a decade after the Seven Years' War, they were ultimately unable to block this policy favoring Québécois autonomy. Nor could they complain about the generous profits they were making as a result of continued British protectionism.[31]

Meanwhile, the new post-1760 territorial regime in Canada was far different than that in the thirteen colonies farther south. Very few government charters were granted for settlement in western Canada prior to independence in 1867. Nor was there much interest among the

French-Canadian population in moving beyond the confines of the St. Lawrence River valley. (The source of Quebec's slow economic growth throughout the eighteenth and early nineteenth centuries is a subject of great contention among Canadian historians to this day.) The land west of Kingston, where the St. Lawrence River meets Lake Ontario, was thus left largely unsettled by Canadians. Similarly, the Maritime Provinces, now relieved of the bulk of their Acadian population, presented a great deal of valuable, unclaimed real estate along its ample rivers and seacoast. Land claims were clear and relatively uncontroversial, and settlers felt duly but not overly protected by the government. Thus, prerevolutionary Canadians never had cause to be overly concerned about jurisdictional clarity or legal equality. (The one major exception is New Brunswick, which became a separate colony from Nova Scotia at the demand of American loyalists who settled there after the Revolution.) The Crown granted each region enough autonomy, and backed it up with sufficient force to prevent intracolonial conflict. Where controversy did arise, it was generally settled in favor of self-government and colonists' rights.[32]

This citizen-oriented disposition might seem surprising in light of the fact that Canada remained under the royal mantle, but conditions in the American colonies were actually much more conducive to territorialism and jurisdictional overreach. The entire American West (that is, everything west of the Appalachians) stood in a state of suspended development following the Proclamation of 1763, which forbid Anglo-American settlement west of the Appalachians (and under which New France was renamed Quebec). The Quebec Act of 1774 aggravated matters by granting the formerly "off limits" land between the Ohio and upper Mississippi rivers to Quebec, thus putting the interests of Montreal fur traders above those of American traders, settlers, and land speculators.

The primary British argument for capping American expansion was the need to keep the peace with neighboring native tribes. The secondary argument, still in effect despite the conquest of New France, was national security—or what to do about the long-standing French trapping communities active between the Appalachians and the Mississippi and throughout the Great Lakes region. The British felt that these lands would be better administered under the new Quebec government than under the rival American colonies, immersed as they were in perpetual conflict. Thus, Quebec's territory grew while America remained bottled up east of the Appalachians. Some Americans took these actions as provocation for political protest.[33]

Matters were complicated by the fact that the American colonial charters granted them unrealistically large tracts of land—many of their original charters encompassed all of the land along a parallel tract between the Atlantic and Pacific oceans. The colonial authorities lacked the military and administrative power to govern such large expanses. Land speculators like George Washington and squatters like Ethan Allen continued to acquire and settle valuable frontier land, often without clear legal title. This naturally perpetuated the atmosphere of violence and litigiousness that was extant in the American colonies in the period up to, during, and directly after the Revolution. In other words, by the 1770s, the Americans had a long tradition of resistance to authority. Nonetheless, most were dragged into a war they never wanted or thought they could win.

The American War of Independence had many causes, but the jurisdictional issue deserves special mention for its salience in shaping the course of American political development in the postrevolutionary era.

4

The Birth Pangs of Nationalism

Fear of religious persecution was a major part of the American political imagination from the very onset of colonization. It is a little-known fact, for example, that religion—or more accurately, delusions about pending religious persecution—played an unusually large role in one of America's most seminal experiences: the Revolutionary War.

Though the war's causes were multiple and varied, American revolutionary sentiment was brought to a head by the colonists' fear of a French-Canadian invasion. While it was hardly plausible that George III, the Protestant king of England, would have led such an invasion, England's good-faith efforts to appease its new subjects in French Canada were perceived by many Americans as a "Popish" conspiracy against the Protestant colonies to the south.

The Quebec Act of 1774 was designed to forestall a crisis in the French-Catholic territory seized by the British in the Seven Years' War. By the act, the British allowed French Canadians to retain most of the religious and legal institutions by which they had been governed for the past century and a half. The measure itself was not without controversy. In Parliament, influential statesmen such as William Pitt the Elder warned of the dangers of French emancipation. The bill, Pitt told the House of Lords, was "at variance with all the safe-guards and barriers against the return of Popery and of popish influence." Pitt also (correctly) predicted that the act would "lose the hearts of all his Majesty's American subjects." Leading statesmen throughout the American colonies also issued fearful polemics. Samuel Adams, Alexander Hamilton, John Jay, Richard Henry Lee, John Dickinson, and John and Abigail Adams all wrote of the dangers of "popery" to the north. They openly accused the king of England of aspiring to become the pope of Canada. They apparently feared his designs on America, as well. Indeed, Samuel Adams had earlier commented in the *Boston Gazette*, "I did verily believe, and I do so still, that much more is to be dreaded from the growth of Popery in America, than from the Stamp Acts or any other Acts destructive of civil rights." Reverend Samuel Langdon, president of Harvard College, connected the Quebec Act to the "popish schemes of men who would gladly restore the Stuarts and inaugurate a new era of despotism." British administrators and Catholic clergy were burned in effigy during "Pope Day" celebrations in various cities. Rumors circulated that guns and munitions were being sent from England to Roman Catholics throughout the colonies. Newspapers as far south as Georgia and South Carolina bemoaned the introduction of "Popish principles and French law" in Quebec.[1]

American critics also pointed out flaws with the Quebec Act itself. Some argued that if the British authorities could legally make Catholicism the state religion of Quebec, then religious freedom was surely in jeopardy everywhere—an argument that was instrumental in the subsequent detachment of church and state in many of the new American states. Other critics highlighted the fact that the act denied French Canadians the traditional English right to trial by jury and habeas corpus, perhaps another portent of forthcoming restrictions in the American colonies. The British designers of the bill countered that this was only done because French Canadians had no experience with, and thus no knowledge of how to live under, said common law institutions. Nor did French Canadians seem to mind. They responded favorably to British attempts to respect their religious and legal heritage. During the American Revolution, in fact, French Canadians largely rejected American pleas to join them in war against the British.

The American Articles of Confederation (mistakenly) anticipated a Quebecois secession and included them in the proposed union. A congressional delegation was sent to Montreal, led by Benjamin Franklin and a Catholic bishop, but met with no success. In the winter of 1775–1776, a makeshift invasion of Quebec was launched. Americans occupied Montreal and Quebec City only briefly, and though they did find some local support, they left astonished at their general failure to win *Canadien* hearts and minds.

In a sense, then, the British gambit worked: By granting *Canadiens* unprecedented religious and legal freedom, the British gained their loyalty, or at least heightened their ambivalence toward the American revolutionaries. The provincial government provided them just the right amount of direction—not so much as to threaten traditional Québécois social institutions, but not so little as to foment social disorder. "The Quebec Act enabled non-English people to become part of the [British] empire without losing their identity, their religion, or their voice in government," says historian Robert Hatch.[2]

American efforts to bring Nova Scotia, Jamaica, and Bermuda into the revolution were similarly rebuffed, an important detail in the wider question of the war's origins. Jamaican and Bermudan colonists were extremely reliant on British trade, and they also relied on the British military for backup in case of a slave rebellion. Nova Scotians, however, might well have been persuaded to revolt. Halifax and Boston were a short sail from one another and were in regular contact via the brisk North Atlantic triangle trade. Most of Nova Scotia's population at the time was made up of former New Englanders and French Acadians, neither of whom had any great love for the British. However, given the presence of a major British garrison in Halifax and the promise of lucrative timber contracts with the British navy, "the most urgent desire of these hard-pressed settlers was to be left alone." Besides a few minor displays of support for the revolutionary cause, Nova Scotians largely sat out the war; they chose safety and stability over self-government. Nova Scotia suffered from few of the problems inherent in the government of the American colonies, and they were content to remain under British jurisdiction.[3]

British efforts to appease *Canadiens* had unanticipated effects on American colonists, most of whom were still resolutely opposed to war with England prior to the passage of the Quebec Act of 1774. According to Hatch, "There was hardly an American colony that was not incensed by the Quebec Act," and he notes:

> The religious issue was foremost in people's thinking. Virginia warned of a French and Indian attack motivated by religious fanaticism, South Carolina of a war between French Catholics and English Protestants, Georgia of a plot by the king's ministers to browbeat his "ancient, Protestant and loyal subjects." New England meetinghouses rocked with fulminations against the Quebec Act and the Catholic Church. . . . The

Pope was vilified as "a false prophet," the Church as the "great whore of Babylon." The divine warned of "the flood of the dragon that has poured forth to the northward in the Quebec Bill for the establishment of Popery."[4]

Thus was the initial impulse for American freedom coupled with an almost irrational fear of religious combat. British despotism was a concern for the early republicans, but it was notably veiled in the guise of ancient fears. This makes particular sense in light of the fact that, owing to poor management of relations with the indigenous people of the region, New Englanders had been fighting, and dying, at the hands of Native Americans throughout the seventeenth and eighteenth centuries. The Anglo-French alliance in Quebec revived their fears of guerrilla war and religious conspiracy. From this viewpoint, it also seems reasonable to assume that the Massachusetts militiamen who skirmished with British troops at Lexington and Concord had no idea their actions would lead to continental war. Occasional skirmishes were a regular feature of life in colonial New England.

Nonetheless, many factors prompted the Revolutionary War besides the Quebec Act of 1774. One of the revolutionaries' main objectives at the beginning of the war was to clarify the jurisdictional makeup of their relationship with England. They also sought to rectify the fact that colonists had fewer rights and freedoms than their counterparts in England. Total independence was not yet on their minds. The cornerstone of contention was ambiguity regarding government jurisdiction over tariffs, duties, taxes, and civil law. They respected British law and British jurisdiction over the colonies; they merely objected to the deceptions and violations of authority. "Thinking imperially," writes historian Peter Onuf, "Revolutionary Americans had first thought of themselves as Britons, with all the cultural baggage and national pride that that identification entailed."[5]

Interestingly, early revolutionaries also exploited loopholes in English law to hamstring the very military sent to subdue them: Since English officers would be tried by American juries for any unlawful use of force, they were exceedingly wary to exercise their power. They instructed their troops *not* to engage Americans until a local magistrate could first certify "sufficient cause." In numerous cases, therefore, British soldiers stood by while riotous mobs harried Loyalist Americans. " 'Last night we had a most outrageous riot,' Colonel William Dalrymple wrote his commander in chief from Boston, 'the populace laid hole [*sic*] of a man said to be an informer and mounted him in a Cart besmeared with tar and feathers.' " As noted by John Philip Reid, "Dalrymple was shocked by the affair and had adequate time to act"; nonetheless, Dalrymple and his men did nothing because they were wary of overstepping their authority. Says Reid, "John Alden summed up the times when he wrote, 'More than one Boston merchant was forced to sign the nonimportation agreements under the very nose of the British army.' " We learn two important things from these episodes: first, the British army was debilitated by the ambiguities of its military jurisdiction and, second, Loyalist Americans were thereby forced into submission by revolutionary zealots.[6]

Remember, first and foremost, that American commitment to the revolutionary cause before, during, and after the war was mixed at best. Many Americans were dubious of revolutionary ideology or merely fearful of the consequences of unprecedented war with the world's greatest military power; support for and participation in the revolution was generally lackluster. Washington and his officers were perpetually in need of men and supplies, and the patriot army was rife with deserters. Public support was sporadic. One of Congress's appointed representatives in Europe, Silas Deane, actually turned Tory for money. "During the Revolutionary War perhaps half as many Americans were in arms for the King, at one time or another, as fought on the side of the Congress," notes William H. Nelson.[7]

Nevertheless, draconian measures were taken to punish Loyalists, plunder their property, and exile them from places where they might be of support to the British. Most colonies enacted loyalty tests, the failure of which was punished with removal of voting and officeholding privileges. Land owned by Loyalists, and suspected Loyalists, was seized by provisional state governments and sold at profit. When the Continental Congress declared a national day of "fasting and humiliation and prayer" in July 1775, local Committees of Safety went on the lookout for clergymen and parishioners who failed to take part. At one point, the entire population of Queen's County, New York, was declared a community in exile. By writ of Congress, "All trade and intercourse with them was to cease. None of them were permitted to travel or abide in any part of the United States. No attorney could defend them in any action at law." Their offense: "They had avowed 'an unmanly design of remaining inactive spectators of the . . . contest' and it was reasonable 'that those who refused to defend their country should be excluded from its protection.' "[8]

It is difficult to ascertain the motivations of the typical American Tory, but the prevalence of Tory sentiment, coupled with those of neutrals, undecideds, and appeasement-minded Whigs, must be considered in evaluating the revolutionary moment. Prior to the outbreak of hostilities at Lexington and Concord (April 19, 1775), the representatives of the various colonies were reluctant to follow in the footsteps of Massachusetts. The consensus among colonial delegates in Philadelphia was to seek peace with the British on terms favorable to American shipping, farming, and commercial interests. As in many modern-day wars, a significant percentage of revolutionary-era Americans were dragged into a military conflict that they would rather have avoided.

In the early years of the Revolution, a primary target of opposition was the executive in each colony, as represented by the royal governors. Though the governors' powers were only vaguely defined under law, they had long since established themselves as the principal arbiters of patronage and tax collection in the royal colonies. According to Gordon Wood:

> Since the provincial governors, and ultimately the distant authority of the English Crown, were the principal source of power and prestige in the society—of preferment and office, of contracts and favors, of support for Anglican orthodoxy, and even of standards of social and cultural refinement—they inevitably had become the focal points for both aspiration and dissatisfaction among the colonists.

Their ability to overrule and/or ignore colonial assemblies and courts was also a common source of controversy. Thus, the greater part of the conflict was not over the possession of power, but over its proper enforcement—a classic question of jurisdictional law.[9]

As it stands, the American revolutionaries barely won their war with Great Britain. They relied on unconventional tactics and homeland advantage, as well as the eventual assistance of the nearly bankrupt French government. As the costs of the war mounted, Britons became increasingly wary of the engagement. Trade with the colonies could continue apace, with or without independence, and relinquishment would save the empire the escalating cost of occupying the better part of a continent. In many ways, this was a landmark event, a first in the long history of British decolonization. Similar motives would lead Britain to "free" Canada a half century later.

Who Should Govern the New United States?

Having won the war, the leaders of the "first new nation" faced an even bigger problem—how to govern it.

Despite the prevalence of revolutionary doctrine regarding the importance of democratic representation and equality under law, the founders were wary of the idea of welcoming the common man into the political arena. They remained, for the most part, firm in their conviction that elites (that is, property owners) were most suited to lead the people. They advocated retention of colonial suffrage and officeholding restrictions in order to preserve the influence of the few over the many. And while it is true that the founders consciously broke with English precedent in defining elites not by their provenance but by their proven ability to think and lead the country, the fact that they regarded property ownership as evidence of these capacities mitigates the tenor of their supposed egalitarianism.[10]

Even Thomas Jefferson, the reputed founder of American populism, was a vocal supporter of oligarchy. By Wood's account, "Experience had taught him, he told Edmund Pendleton in August 1776, 'that a choice by the people themselves is not generally distinguished for it's [sic] wisdom. This first secretion from them is generally crude and heterogeneous.'" In order to guarantee that American legislative leaders would be shielded from the whims of the public, Jefferson advocated an electoral system in which Virginia senators would be elected by the Virginia House of Delegates for nine-year terms, or perhaps, "to an appointment for life, or to any thing rather than a mere creation by and dependance [sic] on the people." This mimicked almost perfectly the English belief that the political affairs of the new nation should remain firmly in the hands of local elites.[11]

The problem remained, however, of how to justify such a system amid repeated calls for popular representation in government. The British parliament had claimed authority to govern the colonies by right of the fact that the colonists were "virtually represented" in the British legislature—the colonies sent no representatives to Parliament, but the government was charged with representing their best interests, at least in theory. A system of oligarchic rule in the new American states would thus represent a new iteration of the old form—virtual, rather than real representation. Some effort needed to be made to acknowledge the revolutionaries' own complaints about virtual representation under the Crown. A compromise would have to be struck between total democracy and outright plutocracy.

In response, the Continental Congress turned to what they called "mixed government," or a divided system of overlapping popular and elite institutions that might thus "avoid the two extremes implicit in republicanism," writes Wood. In the words of one *New Jersey Gazette* article from May 1779:

> "The one [extreme] is, that noble birth, or wealth and riches, should be considered as an hereditary title to the government of the republic . . . the other extreme is, that the government be managed by the promiscuous multitude of the community," who, "though honest, yet from many natural defects, are generally in the execution of government, violent, changeable, and liable to many fatal errors."

Legislative power would thus be divided between the rich and middling. Poor, propertyless Americans would still be denied direct representation or suffrage.[12]

This is not to say that everyone supported such a system. Radical democrats like Thomas Paine and Samuel Adams complained about its practical and ideological shortcomings. Nonetheless, notes Wood:

> The cries up and down the continent in 1776 for a simple [that is, popularly elected] legislature were generally intermittent and isolated, and were easily smothered by the Americans' overwhelming preoccupation with the balanced mechanism. However attractive Paine's call for independence and republicanism was in 1776, he was surely not speaking common American sense with his proposals for the simple form the new governments should take. Paine may have been a very keen writer, said John Adams; but he was also "very ignorant of the Science of Government."[13]

The problem remained to find suitable justification for the break with England. Why replace one system of "virtual representation" with another? Here, the Founding Fathers turned to one of the defining features of the American experience up to that time—*contract law*. Colonial Americans were unusually ensconced in the law, and they highly valued its role as a strategic weapon in the conduct of human affairs. Americans had been struggling against the constraints of English common law since at least the formation of the Massachusetts Bay Company.

"Everyone in the eighteenth century knew that the English had justified their Glorious Revolution by a violation of the assumed contract [between king and country] by James II," notes Wood. "And by 1776 Americans had in a like way come to describe their Revolution as resulting from a similar break in 'the original contract between king and people.'" This demanded an obvious amount of double-talk. "The King by withdrawing his protection and levying war upon us, has discharged us of our allegiance, and of all obligations to obedience," declared one pamphleteer, "for protection and subjection are mutual, and cannot subsist a-part [sic]." In a similar vein, the Continental Congress approved the violation of land treaties with native tribes on the ground that such tribes had violated their implicit contract with the colonies by fighting on behalf of the English king.[14]

This reliance on the language of contracts and retractable agreements also motivated the founders' desire to create a supralegal document upon which all American claims to self-government might be referred—a constitution. The English system ran without similar regard to contract; Parliament created the law as it saw fit, referring often to tradition and customary usage. The American Constitution, on the other hand, was designed to be the ultimate social contract; it would lay out, *in writing,* the fundamental expectations of American political life, a contract between the American people and their progeny that could be ratified and amended only by extralegislative means (thus putting it above ordinary statutory law). "Under the changing exigencies of their polemics and politics," notes Wood, "Americans needed some new contractual analogy to explain their evolving relationships among themselves and with the state." The Constitution would serve as such a contract—written confirmation of the rights and title that colonial Americans had come to value so dearly.[15]

Unfortunately, the notion of government by contract unleashed a flurry of "para-governmental" organizations throughout the colonies: If government was reconceived as a tacit agreement between citizens, then citizens could, and did, forge such agreements of their own accord. Following a skirmish with New York law officers, for example, Ethan Allen and his Green Mountain Boys denounced New York's jurisdictional claims over Vermont. Allen himself arrested and banished several new justices of the peace commissioned by New York. Charged with usurping the courts' authority, Allen asserted that he and the Green Mountain Boys [had] formed extralegal organizations because New York "*obliged us to it.*" (Emphasis in original.) The [Vermont] Grants settlers denied New York's right to pass laws without their approval and created committees of safety to legitimate their actions and their expulsion of New York's officials.

New Yorker John Jay commented in response to the Vermont secession, "We have unquestionably more territory than we can govern."[16]

The effort to construct a new American political system reached a turning point of sorts with Shays' Rebellion. In June 1787, George Washington wrote to the Marquis de Lafayette that he was coming out of retirement and reentering politics because he "could not resist the call to a convention of the States which is to determine whether we are to have a Government of respectability under which life, liberty, and property will be secured to us, or are to submit to one which may be the result of chance or the moment, springing perhaps from anarchy and confusion, and dictated perhaps by some aspiring demagogue." Washington was referring directly to the threat Daniel Shays and his backwoods army of western Massachusetts farmers presented to the nation. The Shaysites were moved to rebellion because wealthy Bostonians were profiteering in promissory notes issued by the state government during the war, thus bilking backcountry farmers and merchants out of hard-earned money owed them by the state. There were similar farm revolts elsewhere around the country; in some sense, they were the result of rural Americans taking the promises of the revolution too literally. What good was "democratic" government, asked the rebels, if it did not protect *their* interests?[17]

The frequency and virulence of such uprisings terrified the founders. According to Wood, some conservatives actually believed at the time that "the Shaysites were fomented by those who wanted to demonstrate the absurdity of republicanism." Benjamin Franklin said [in May 1789], " 'We have been guarding against an evil that old States are most liable to, *excess of power* in the rulers, but our present danger seems to be *defect of obedience* in the subjects." According to Wood, "The early state constitutions had rendered government too feeble."[18]

Washington's proposed solution was to form a professional, standing army to combat the rebels. In lieu of this, which was a practical and ideological impossibility, the founders redoubled their efforts to draft a national constitution that would more deftly outline the powers of government vis-à-vis the citizenry. Those at the Constitutional Convention were therefore faced with the problem of erecting a government that would simultaneously be representative, fair, and orderly. "Believing with Washington that virtue had 'in great degree taken its departure from our land' and was not to be easily restored, the Federalists hoped to create an entirely new and original sort of republican government—a republic which did not require a virtuous people for its sustenance."[19]

Such problems were exacerbated by the absence of a coherent plan for union following the war's end. "For all of their talk of choosing between 'a sovereign state, or a number of confederated sovereign states,' few in 1776 conceived of the thirteen states' [sic] becoming a single republic, one community with one pervasive public interest." The Continental Congress continued to debate issues related to war debts and land disputes, but the larger issue of self-governance was tabled and left to the individual states. "Congressional power, which had been substantial during the war years, now began precipitously to disintegrate, and delegates increasingly complained of the difficulty of gathering even a quorum. By the middle eighties Congress had virtually ceased trying to govern."[20]

Amid the swirl of regeneration and the departing fog of war, the issue of representative government came back to the fore. Debate over the best means of harnessing the energy of the people within the apparatus of republican government became the primary issue underlying the Constitutional Convention. Federalists argued that the drama of the 1780s gave lie to the dangers of populism. In a flurry of editorials addressed to those framing the Constitution, the dangers of democracy were outlined, among them its tendency to elevate unqualified men to office, reward avarice, and drown the people in false promises and inordinate power. Instead, the Federalists suggested a series of jurisdictional reforms that would restrict legislative, as well as executive, authority; foster continental union; and guarantee election of the "best" men.[21]

Anti-Federalists, in response, accused the Federalists of seeking to restore oligarchic rule. In Wood's words, they believed that "moral regeneration of America's character, rather than any legalistic manipulation of the constitutions of government, was the proper remedy for America's problems." The Anti-Federalists hoped to defeat the Federalists by urging the states to reject the Constitution. They argued that the Constitution was invalid because it subjected the people to two sovereigns—the state and national governments. They also demanded that the Constitution be ratified, or rejected, by the state assemblies, which were generally antithetical to, or at least skeptical of, the usurpation of their powers.[22]

In response, the Federalists made a rhetorical move that marks American politics to this day: They argued that there was no conflict of dual sovereignty because sovereignty exists *not* with the state or national legislatures but ultimately *with the people.* "The people" could distribute power across rival jurisdictions however they saw fit. The Federalists thereby got around the ratification issue by arguing that the Constitution was an emanation of popular will, and thus required acceptance not by the state legislatures but only by the people themselves. Constitutional plebiscites could thereby be held in each state, conveniently bypassing the legislatures. In effect, says Wood, "The Americans had taken the people out of the government altogether. . . . Or from a different point of view the Americans could now argue that the people participated in all branches of the government and not merely in their houses of representatives." Wood adds, "This image of a social contract formed by isolated and hostile individuals was now the only contractual metaphor that comprehended American social reality."[23]

It is difficult to overestimate the poignancy of these statements in describing the unique character of American politics. The particular experiences of American political leaders before, during, and immediately after the Revolution led them to construct an idea of the nation focused on the sanctity of contract, private property, and the inviolability of individual rights and freedoms. Theirs was not a Rousseauian social contract binding sympathetic hearts and minds, but a businesslike exchange of (contractual) promises. Though the founders would later promote novel ideas concerning basic human rights, their original concern was finding a way to guarantee ratification of the Constitution, thus clearing the jurisdictional hurdle of state consent to union. Seen this way, even the Bill of Rights can be seen as a political stopgap rather than a bold-faced celebration of the human spirit. "For were it not for Madison," writes historian Jack Rakove, "a bill of rights might never have been added to the Constitution. . . . Nearly all Madison's colleagues in Congress thought the entire subject could be deferred until the new government was safely operating, by which point the desire for a bill of rights might well have evaporated." Employing their keen legal minds, many Federalists feared that enumerating rights might bring unanticipated problems if other rights were unintentionally omitted. (Litigants might ask if such omissions were intentional or merely accidental.) Thus, the illustrious Bill of Rights was nearly quashed, an apt reflection of the founders' preoccupation with the need for protection from unforeseen legal loopholes, claims, and counterclaims.[24]

Another significant legal development at the time concerns freedom of religion and the division of church and state. One of the most contentious issues in America following the war was how to maintain civic virtue, the essence of democracy. Many believed that doing so required maintenance of Christian worship, and therefore Christian congregations. But the main vehicle for achieving this in most colonies had previously been collection of mandatory church taxes in support of a single "establishment" church—the Church of England in most colonies; the Congregationalist Church in others. During the revolution, notes Buckley, prominent members of the Anglican clergy "strongly rejected the concept that with political changes should come an equality for all religious groups." The presence of establishment churches traditionally left members of "dissenting" faiths in the unhappy position of paying to support churches to which they did not belong. One Virginian referred to these assessments in a 1777 pamphlet as a "badge of slavery . . . spiritual slavery." Moreover, in many colonies, dissenters faced severe restrictions in their political and civil affairs. Only Anglican ministers could sanctify marriages, for example, and voting was often restricted as well.[25]

Following independence, the separate states tackled this cumbersome issue in a variety of ways. One question revolved around the states' presumed need to require all residents to pay taxes in support of Christian worship, whether exclusively to the Anglican Church or to the church of one's choice. Some states rejected the church tax altogether, whereas others debated the tax's parameters. Freedom of religion was generally construed as toleration of dissenting Christian views, coupled with the continued obligation to contribute to, if not actually participate in, the religious activities of *a* Christian congregation. Nonetheless, state jurisdiction over religion was a hotly contested, and by no means settled, affair. Only much later did federal doctrine evolve regarding the substantive meaning of the separation of church and state—for example, prohibiting the use of government funds in support of religion.

Incorporation also became a cornerstone of debate in many state legislatures, for it was seen as a key way for congregations to accumulate and preserve church assets and private property. South Carolina attempted to appease the state's many religious factions by making it easy for religious congregations to seek charters—at least thirty-six such charters were issued between 1783 and 1790, including charters for Presbyterian, Baptist, Methodist, Lutheran, "French Protestant," and Roman Catholic churches. Pennsylvania, Maryland, New York, and New Jersey went further, passing "general incorporation" laws that permitted religious societies to incorporate without special permission from the legislature. In an attempt to keep the peace while maintaining state control over organized religion, the General Court of Massachusetts mandated that church tax exemptions only be granted to dissenters who could prove that they were members of *incorporated* (non-Anglican) congregations.[26]

Virginia, meanwhile, took a very different approach: When the Virginia assembly proposed incorporating the Church of England to secure its continued financial security, Presbyterians protested, arguing that the Church of Scotland deserved the same privileges as the Episcopal Church. The Presbyterians also cogently argued that the existing plan to incorporate the Church of England legally empowered Anglican clergy but not their constituents, thus alienating the laity from their congregational assets. Baptists were also vigorously opposed to the plan. Ultimately, the act incorporating the Episcopal Church in Virginia was repealed by the legislature, as was the idea of issuing mandatory tax assessments on all residents for the support of religious observance.[27]

Incorporation was viewed by many Virginians at the time as an intrusion of government into civil society, and the state legislature subsequently eschewed incorporation of any religious group. As historian Thomas E. Buckley notes, this settlement was supported by Evangelical Christians *not* because it would limit the influence of churches on civil society, but because it would weaken the influence of the rival Episcopal Church: "The concept that religious belief and practice were totally beyond the ken of the state was never fully accepted by the soon-to-be dominant religious bodies of Presbyterians, Baptists, and Methodists. . . . They did not envision or desire a secular state but the salvation of a Christian America through the Gospel message." By assuring that the Episcopal Church would no longer benefit from state financial support, they merely sought to level the playing field for their own endeavors; "for their work required no [tax] assessment; revivals and itinerancy sufficed," says Buckley. Evangelicals wanted the church "separated from the state precisely so that it might freely influence society and permeate it with the Gospel message." Nevertheless, continues Buckley, "Even as the evangelicals protested against the assessment and incorporation bills, their petitions expressed a desire for the members of the Assembly to 'recommend religion' by the quality of their lives and pass laws to 'Punish the Vices and Immoralities of the times.'" This justified the passage of state laws that banned activities deemed immoral by Christians—such as working on Sundays—despite the supposed separation of church and state. On this, dissenters and Anglicans could agree. "They [both] expected that government, in caring for the general welfare, would institutionalize certain Christian norms and values."[28]

Though the bedrock beliefs underlying this plan prevailed, Virginia's strategy of promoting religious freedom by *prohibiting* the incorporation of religious groups was an unusual and ultimately short-lived position. Over time, the general practice in all the American states was to nurture religious freedom by *promoting* the incorporation of religious groups. Although the idea that incorporation provided the states with a means of controlling religious activity within their jurisdiction eventually lapsed, the practice of liberally offering religious groups the rights and privileges of incorporation continued to expand. Incorporation became a shell within which the resources of even the most specious religious pursuits could be protected from taxation and government regulation. The prevailing system in the contemporary United States employs the corporate organizational form as a state-mandated way to promote religious activity while stripping the states of the regulatory power originally envisioned in incorporation doctrine.

Thus enabled, religious groups, sects, and denominations thrived in the United States. In Canada, by contrast, the European tradition of strong church-state relations remained in place. With the tacit support of the English colonial authorities, the Catholic Church of Quebec continued to grow, though jurisdictional disputes between it and Rome were common. The Churches of England, Scotland, and Rome all retained the benefit of state support. Opposition to this system was common, however, especially in areas where "dissenting" Christians predominated. The "establishment" Protestant churches in Ontario and the Maritimes suffered from constant competition, particularly by itinerant American ministers accustomed to preaching for their supper and speaking in the language of unschooled backcountry folk.

Antiestablishment opposition continued to fester in Canada through the 1830s, largely because of the generous land grants given to the Church of England but denied (most) other denominations. Its reliance on land, instead of taxes, for financial support was also a bane to the Anglican establishment, as land prices faltered throughout much of this period. The Anglicans' reluctance to accept ministers not trained in England also made recruitment difficult for the Episcopal clergy. In both Catholic and Protestant communities, moreover, the persistence of establishment churches focused public ire against them. "It is because the church is protected by the State, and has the character of an Establishment, that the leaders of the popular party make her an object of their present attack," wrote one observer of Upper Canadian politics in the 1820s. In some respects, Canadians also seemed to take pleasure in irking the authorities with their impenitent behavior, particularly in Quebec, where the Catholic Church governed hand in hand with the civil authorities. "The French-Canadian capacity to enjoy life resulted too frequently in debauchery," writes historian John S. Moir. "The feasts of patron saints became so often the occasion and the excuse for unbridled revelry that the bishop suppressed most religious holidays." Prostitution also flourished in Quebec. The province had long been known as a place where revelry, gambling, and sexual license were openly tolerated (though not necessarily legal). The presence of a state church did not seem to help tame the morals of its people; if anything, it inflamed their passions.[29]

It is ironic, then, that American debate over state support of religion and the subsequent decision to ban it actually increased the political power and social diffusion of American religious groups, whereas in Canada, state support for religious activity ultimately weakened their hold on Canadian society. Canadians today are generally less devout and less observant than their American counterparts, and Canadian politics are virtually devoid of religious issues, in contrast to their great frequency in American political discourse.[30]

The Tory Exodus—Beginnings of the "Continental Divide"?

As mentioned earlier, support for the republican cause in the thirteen colonies was far from unanimous. Neutrals and Loyalists alike opposed the war. Following the conclusion of hostilities, these colonists faced a difficult choice: either side with the English and leave the country, or accept American republican values and remain—presumably a rational choice between two rival political-ideological systems.

Many scholars—most notably, sociologist Seymour Martin Lipset— have framed this juncture as the starting point for historical accounts of political differences between the United States and Canada. Through their choices, Lipset argues, the colonists set in motion contrasting legacies of national political development. However, this scenario is not very realistic—conceptually, factually, or otherwise.[31]

For one thing, these arguments fail to account for the fact that many abiding Loyalists *remained* in the United States, thus watering down the ideological roots of American republicanism. It is hard to glean from historical records what proportion of Loyalists chose to stay rather than flee the United States, but at least one count guesses that at least twice as many stayed as left. Other figures place the number far higher. If, according to some estimates, one-fifth of the American population (or five hundred thousand persons) were Loyalists, and between sixty and one hundred thousand Loyalists left America during or directly after the war, then as many as seven-eighths of the Tory population stayed behind. Remaining in the United States was not difficult; most states required only that individuals suspected of Toryism sign an oath declaring their new-found loyalty to the republican cause. Though Loyalists faced serious danger in the American colonies during the war, there is little evidence that Tory sympathizers encountered significant problems afterward. In the interim, Tory-leaning cities such as Savannah, Charleston, Newport, and New York served as temporary safe havens.[32]

Some Loyalists *did* choose to emigrate, however, and their history does indeed constitute a key part of Canada's national origins. Following the English victory in the Seven Years' War and the subsequent expulsion of many of its Acadian residents, Nova Scotia was relatively uninhabited. At the same time, the English were looking for ways to promote English language, customs, and religion in Canada. Faced with the problem of accommodating thousands of desperate, often demanding

American Loyalist refugees, the British offered them large land grants in Nova Scotia instead of welcoming them back to England. (Some grants were also made in Upper and Lower Canada—modern-day Ontario and Quebec—though this tended to occur later, after the recolonization of Nova Scotia.) In order to sweeten the deal, qualified Loyalists were offered the hereditary honor of having the title "United Empire Loyalist" appended to their names.

In 1783, some thirty-two thousand Loyalist refugees arrived in Nova Scotia, nearly double the existing population of the province. What no one anticipated, however, was how difficult it would be for them to adjust to the stark deprivations of Nova Scotia, or "Nova Scarcity" as many took to calling it. According to Brebner, some found conditions so bad that they returned to the United States "on the gamble that time would have tempered the hostility which had driven them forth." Those who stayed grumbled and complained about the niggardly manner in which their loyalty had been rewarded.[33]

The existing population of Nova Scotia was made up of about seventeen thousand French Acadians and ex-New Englanders. Both groups had elected to stay out of the Revolution owing to their hardscrabble lives and dependence on the British sea trade. The *arriviste* Loyalists were notably suspicious of, and sometimes quite condescending to, their "neutral" hosts. Hoping to avoid intermingling as much as possible, the majority of the Loyalists took up residence in the relatively unpopulated St. John River valley. Many Acadians living there moved upstream to avoid conflict with their haughty new neighbors.

In 1784, only a year into their "exile," the United Empire Loyalists successfully demanded that the Crown grant them political autonomy in the new province of New Brunswick, thus cleaving themselves from Nova Scotia. The Loyalists wanted to manage their own affairs without the inconvenience of having to accommodate the locals. Jurisdiction was thus a major concern even for those who fled the American experiment. They demanded and received not only provincial autonomy but also permission to create a semblance of representative government in the form of a House of Assembly. Despite granting the Loyalists their own province and some trappings of democracy, however, the English authorities retained a tight grip on the levers of government.[34]

Sir Guy Carleton, governor of the new province, submitted to the Loyalists' calls for representative government, but he was careful, as he

explains, to bolster "the executive powers of Government [to] discoun-
tenance it's [*sic*] leaning too much on the popular part of the Constitution." In a letter to the British secretary of state, Carleton also noted that
he was "anxious to finish every thing respecting the organization of the
Province that properly belonged to the Prerogative *before* a meeting of
Representatives chosen by the people, convinced that they will be most
usefully employed in adapting the Laws to the Government already
formed." Carleton was supported in this by his council, leading Loyalists who themselves believed that, contrary to American practice, it was
the duty of the executive to initiate political decisions and the obligation
of the legislature merely to ratify them. The Loyalists thus gained democracy, but only of a limited sort; the governor and his self-appointed
council were the de facto leaders of New Brunswick, as they were in all
of the Canadian provinces until the 1840s, when the power of the lower
assemblies was bolstered by the British authorities.[35]

Recognizing the potential for land disputes in a province with old and
new settlers living side by side, Governor Carleton ordered that existing
claims be registered within three months or be forfeited, thus avoiding
legal entanglements stemming from overlapping titles. Condon writes:

> Carleton and his Council also began the important task of conciliating
> the old French- and English-speaking inhabitants of the province . . .
> who naturally felt a great deal of hostility towards the Loyalist hordes
> who had disrupted their settlements and oftentimes forced them to
> abandon their homes. The new government moved quickly to win the
> allegiance of these people by offering to compensate them for any
> losses caused by the Loyalist influx and to give them new land grants
> under the same favorable conditions accorded to the Loyalists.

As commander in chief of British forces in 1783, Carleton also negotiated
for the transportation to Nova Scotia of former slaves who had been freed
by the British in return for fighting alongside them. Once transported to
Canada, however, many freed slaves encountered further legal and civic
discrimination and left for Sierra Leone, where a private company had
been chartered by the Crown to settle black Loyalists in Africa.[36]

The New Brunswick Loyalists did not get everything they sought in
self-government—most believed, with their American counterparts, that
British governance had failed the colonies—but they received enough to
successfully take up the reins from Carleton and steer the colony toward

a century of intense growth and prosperity based largely on providing timber, and later ships, to the British navy and the global sea trade.

Returning to the larger issue of the "Tory exodus," we have at least two good reasons to question the historical accuracy of the "rational choice" depiction of the ideological origins of US/Canadian differences: First, the vast majority of Loyalist sympathizers appear to have remained in the United States, thus "contaminating" the stock of pure American ideologists; second, the New Brunswick Loyalists themselves sought many of the same political rights and freedoms as the Americans, the crucial difference being the way in which those preferences were realized in institutional form. By this account, we might also expect significant differences in the political ideologies of New Brunswick and Nova Scotia, the former a bastion of Loyalism at the conclusion of the Revolution, the latter a province of politically uncommitted fisherman and farmers. Instead, the two provinces appear largely to have developed rather similarly, together with the other components of the so-called Maritime Provinces.

Also striking is the fact that, following the War of Independence, thousands of would-be Canadians and Americans crossed and recrossed the border with great alacrity, most apparently choosing to do so for economic rather than ideological reasons. In fact, contemporary Canadian historians refer to the post-1784 generation of American emigrants to Upper Canada (modern-day Ontario) as "late loyalists," a term which derives from the fact that, in Brebner's words, "some of the [postrevolutionary war] emigrants to Canada saw no harm in posing as loyalists in order to secure special land grants." Upper Canada thus began to fill with land-hungry Americans who were frustrated with the high prices and corruption of the Northwest Territory's land grant system. According to John Barlet Brebner::

> In spite of the Revolution, there was little or none of the modern sense of nationality among these loose-footed Americans. They remembered their European home in a clannish way if they were recent immigrants, or the colony or state which they or their parents had sprung from if they were older North Americans, but the quality, accessibility, and price of new lands were more important to them than the flag that waved over them.

"By 1812," Brebner concludes, "eight out of ten inhabitants of Upper Canada [that is, Ontario] were of American birth or descent and only a quarter of these were [bona fide] loyalists."[37]

As Fred Landon's account of early American immigration into Western Ontario notes, "The Loyalist element was scarcely noticeable amidst the diversity of people who came in to take up land or engage in trade. Travelers who visited both sides of the boundary waters saw little difference between the two peoples." In fact, "Upper Canada was essentially an American community under British law and British forms of government down to the period of the war with the United States"—the War of 1812.[38]

In sum, there is ample cause to reject the notion that Loyalist emigration from the United States to Canada is a sufficient explanation for the ensuing political differences between the United States and Canada. Loyalists made up only a small percentage of the total anglophone population of Canada after the Revolutionary War. Some self-proclaimed Loyalists returned to the United States after a short, unhappy exile; and many Americans emigrated to Canada (and vice versa) for primarily economic reasons. Therefore, we must look beyond the notion of initial differences in "national character" and instead study the trajectory of political and legal development in both countries in order to account for their subsequent ideological differences.

From Sea to Shining Sea?

One of the primary outcomes of the American Revolution was uncertainty about what to do with the great expanses of land that was not yet incorporated into the new United States. Though the British reneged on their postwar promise to remove troops from the southern Great Lakes region, the land between the Mississippi River and the Appalachian range was almost entirely unsettled north of the Mississippi Delta. American settlement west of the Appalachians had been legally prohibited since the British Proclamation of 1763.[39]

According to historian Thomas Perkins Abernethy:

> If the British government had adhered to its policy, inaugurated in 1754, of giving a thousand acres to every actual settler on the frontier, "[Instead] the West would have filled up rapidly with men who needed no other inducement. . . . The wavering, changing colonial policy of England and the unwise legislation of the new States resulted in most of the Western lands falling into the hands of a few speculators. . . . They with their spurious grants and dubious titles, the settlers and

their "tomahawk" rights, their squatters' rights, their military and trea-sury warrants soon covered the West with layer after layer of com-peting claims, which overlapped the land like shingles on a roof. This was later to present an almost hopeless snarl for the courts to unravel. But nothing could now stay the restless, land-hungry pioneer. He was definitely on his way to the Pacific.[40]

The war's end brought the American states together in an unprece-dented new fashion. No one was quite sure how to govern this new fed-eration of states, nor was it clear where one state ended and another began. Survey lines were fuzzy at best, and states and speculators held a dizzying array of overlapping claims, both in near-Appalachia and be-yond. Several colonial charters, such as those for Virginia, Pennsylvania, and the Carolinas, literally granted them all the territory along a straight east-west plane from one ocean to the other. Matters were complicated by the fact that many of the nation's leading politicians, planters, and busi-nessmen held stakes in private land companies. George Washington, for instance, owned valuable shares in what Congress later deemed the "Vir-ginia Military District," land appointed for redemption by veterans like Washington who, in 1796, offered for sale three tracts approximating three thousand acres (a significant plot) on the Little Miami River (a very desirable location). Earlier, Washington had expanded his own holdings in the region by buying up veterans' land grants at fire-sale prices, as well as by using substitute buyers to evade laws that limited the size of indi-vidual holdings.[41]

Private land companies representing tidewater elites owned shares in wide tracts of frontier land. The land companies' claims were often of dubious legality, given the fact that they had been granted by separate colonial regimes. Native rights and overlapping jurisdictions left the field open to perpetual litigation and political lobbying. For example, the Maryland delegates lobbied Congress for a western land policy that would nationalize all western territories *except* those granted before the war, thereby protecting the interests of the Illinois-Wabash Land Com-pany, in which Maryland's governor, Thomas Johnson, ex-governor William Paca, and a number of other important Marylanders were share-holders. Their suggested policy would have blocked many rival land companies from claiming more recent acquisitions while protecting the interests of Maryland's elite investors. If passed, "there would indeed have been very little land left to be used for the common benefit."[42]

In the aftermath of war, there was still little agreement about which colony should foot the bill for protecting the western territories and who had jurisdiction over their military policy. Several districts demanded that they be granted statehood, further complicating the interests of speculators, congressmen, and settlers. Settlers in disputed territories capitalized on this jurisdictional ambiguity by avoiding taxes and military service. Currency depreciation throughout the colonies added to the chaos, driving up land prices to the benefit of absentee landlords and lien holders.[43]

Entire areas remained a jurisdictional no-man's-land, such as the border between Pennsylvania and Virginia, where neither state had been able to assert its claim over the other. Several years passed without resolution. Rather than fight over the West indefinitely, all the states struck a compromise in the winter of 1783–1784 by agreeing to *nationalize* all of the American-held territory west of the Appalachians, thus precluding further controversy *and* granting Congress valuable revenue with which to repay veterans, bondholders, and currency speculators.

This decision is surprising in light of the founders' fear of national political power and the states' long history of mutual suspicion and infighting. An important feature of this deal was that it imposed a temporary moratorium on legal claims within the new territories, thus halting the furious race to "get there first." Conflicting claims still needed to be settled—wealthy speculators from the East held claims to many minor fiefdoms in both the "Old Northwest" (Ohio, Illinois, Indiana, and parts of Michigan) and the "Old Southwest" (Kentucky and Tennessee)—but it at least brought some resolution to a potentially dangerous dispute between the states.[44]

The prospect of congressional reorganization of the western territories created a tremendous political opportunity for new land speculators. Kentucky's push for separation from Virginia was more than a quest for self-government, for example; it was a bold-faced attempt to negate land claims made under Virginia legislation. In fact, a number of Kentucky's leading political figures conspired to align Kentucky with Spain rather than the United States in order to protect preexisting land claims, as well as to guarantee access to the profitable Mississippi River trade. As Abernethy explains:

> Legal claims were fastened upon the choicest tracts before settlers
> began to arrive in appreciable numbers, and most of the newcomers

found it necessary to purchase land from the speculators who had preceded them. . . . Thus it was obvious that the Bluegrass country was
never a poor man's frontier, despite the fact that Daniel Boone was its
first famous citizen." ". . . Contrary to the popular conception that
those who pushed the frontier westward were uncouth, uneducated
but picturesque figures such as Daniel Boone, most of them were men
of position and good education. . . . They had important Eastern connections, and their influence in Virginia politics was of first-rate importance. Leadership on this frontier was at least as restricted as it was
in the older communities. The men who held the offices also fastened
their claim on the land.

Local government in the territory quickly took on the character of an
"inside job": "Most of the Bluegrass leaders were speculators on their
own account," continues Abernethy, "and some were lawyers who represented still more important absentee speculators like Robert Morris,
the great merchant of Philadelphia, who in 1796 advertised six hundred
thousand acres of Kentucky land for sale. . . . As for the rank and file of
planters and yeomen, there were few who were secure in the titles to
their lands, and few who had confidence in their leaders." Many, in fact,
"lived on lands to which they had no titles at all."[45]

Kentucky is now known for the fact that it was the first state in the
Union to grant manhood suffrage, in 1792. "This, however, was hardly
such a radical step as it might seem," objects Abernethy, "for land claims
in Kentucky overlapped each other like shingles on a roof and titles
were so subject to controversy that it would have been impossible to determine who were the freeholders [that is, eligible voters]." Furthermore, he notes, "the governor and the Senate were to be chosen by an
electoral college, and judges and justices of the peace, as well as most
other officials, were to be appointed by the governor." This later became
the norm in most of the new American states: while tipping their hats to
popular democracy, local elites held the highest offices by internal fiat.[46]

By one estimate, approximately two-thirds of the adult white male
population of Kentucky did *not* own land as of 1792. Most settlers lacked
the skills, the money, or even the basic literacy to survey land and process
land claims. Instead, note Harrison and Klotter, "land jobbers who had
no intention of becoming farmers hurried about the District acquiring
claims using the names of friends. At least twenty-one individuals and
companies acquired grants in excess of one hundred thousand acres."

Lawyers and land speculators thus bilked ordinary settlers of a great deal of Kentucky's rich farmland. Writing with regard to the new territory of Kentucky, Judge Caleb Wallace told James Madison, "I wish I could say as much to vindicate the character of our Land Jobbers. This Business has been attended with much villainy in other parts, Here [sic] it is reduced to a system, and to take advantage of the Ignorance or of the Poverty of a neighbor is almost grown into reputation; which must multiply litigation and produce aversions that will not quickly subside." Throughout the territories, rival land speculators attempted to use litigation and political pressure to vanquish disputed claims. Even after the creation of district courts in the Kentucky territories, legal appeals had to be taken to far-off Richmond for arbitration. The access that speculators had to legal aid was undoubtedly a key resource in winning legal battles with ordinary settlers.[47]

Individual state governments also faced unanticipated problems. Settlers in the disputed territories often refused to recognize the legitimacy of the state jurisdictions that claimed them. Violence sometimes ensued between settlers and state authorities, and recalcitrance with regard to state law was commonplace. As historian Peter Onuf says:

> Confusion about the status of the western lands encouraged settlers to defy state authority and plan their own new states. The effect in every case was to strengthen the position of the actual settlers in defending their interests. The states had limited coercive resources, and the United States collectively were unwilling and unable to deploy their might to secure state boundaries or put down new state movements, particularly when the rights of different claimants remained undetermined. Settlers therefore had leverage over states that claimed them as citizens. It was in their power to nullify state authority and, as the Connecticut River towns [in Vermont] demonstrated, to survive unconnected to any state at all. Consequently, settlers in these areas were able to bargain, more or less effectively, for confirmation of their property rights, military protection, and the benefits of civil government—all at considerable expense to the claiming states.

The states thus found it incumbent upon themselves to elevate the notion of statehood beyond its original purview. New states were not to be regarded as autonomous, autochthonous entities, but as legal fictions created by Congress. In the wake of this decision, a curious triangular relationship developed (unintentionally) between citizens, the states, and the nation. Though the states claimed preeminent legal status under American federalism, the federal government represented the territories. People who lived on federal land thus became a special category of citizen without committed representation at any level. Neither the states nor the nation were directly connected to territorial residents via the electoral system, and neither was in a position to devote much time to territorial affairs.[48]

The administrative capacities of the new territorial authorities were abysmally weak, not only because of the "newness" of the territorial governments but also because Congress had failed to clarify what they were expected to do. Territorial governors were notoriously disrespected, underpaid, and uninterested in the finer points of effective administration. Conflicts of interest were rampant, and the spoils system of American state and local government found firm footing in the legal anarchy of the new territories. In contrast, Canada's jurisdictional doctrine openly acknowledged the limitations it had placed on popular sovereignty but made up for them with competent, consistent administration. The American system tended to both hide and exacerbate such problems; reform was hampered by the fact that the problems of the system were not inherently addressed in its founding documents.

In hindsight, it appears that the founders—Jefferson and the Republicans in particular—left so much unsaid about the future governance of the American West because they thought such problems would rectify themselves in due time. The Republic was conceived by thirteen already well-established states with recognized governments and burgeoning economies. The founders' primary concern with respect to the territories was how best to partition them in order to maintain the existing sectional balance in Congress.

Even the issue of founding a national capital stretched on for years. Anti-Federalists like John Adams and George Mason argued that an autonomous federal seat would constitute an "exclusive jurisdiction" above the law. Like the Vatican City, they admonished, residents of an American federal city might muster their own troops (that is, a de facto federal army), expropriate state revenues, and even provide fugitives safe haven from state law enforcement. Furthermore, no region of the country wanted to see a national capital established where it might disproportionately benefit other regions. Philadelphians and Manhattanites fought bitterly over the location of the national government's temporary home, while land speculators promoted alternative sites on the Hudson, Delaware, Susquehanna, and Potomac rivers. The Potomac River concern would likely not have won if George Washington had not been on their side. Washington's family had held land along the Potomac for several generations, and Washington himself lobbied hard for removal of Congress to a new site on and around that property. He and his fellow Virginians played rival state representatives against each other until, close to the point of exhaustion, northern interests agreed to a southern capital in exchange for southern concession to the nationalization of state war debts.[49]

Having successfully forced the issue, Washington personally took charge of the Potomac River development. He started by appointing fellow members of his Potomac Navigation Company to the three-member commission assigned to oversee the project—Washington himself was president of the Potomac Company until 1789. He also supervised much of the surveying and planning of the new capital. Washington owned almost 1,200 acres along Four Mile Run and his ward, George Washington Custis, owned the 950-acre plantation that later became Arlington National Cemetery. Substantial evidence exists that Washington redrew the boundaries of the District of Columbia to encompass his property holdings. According to historian Thomas Slaughter, such behavior was not uncommon during Washington's presidency: "His mixture of public and private affairs included solicitation of a customs collector's aid in selling some tobacco and wheat, an attempt to convince the commissioners of the District of Columbia to purchase rocks from his quarry, and the enlistment of a U.S. Senator to sell land in western Pennsylvania."[50]

Supporters of an autonomous capital city continually pointed out the dangers of leaving it within any state's jurisdiction. Congress was equally cognizant of the problems it might have if it resided in any of the states. In June 1783, a group of Pennsylvania soldiers from the Continental army marched on the building where Congress was meeting (the Pennsylvania State House) in order to lobby the state government on the issue of overdue pay. The troops were not protesting Congress, but the threat to Congress of getting embroiled in state politics was duly noted by representatives.[51]

Federalists leveraged this issue in stumping for a national capital free from state affairs and autonomous in its territorial domain, exactly the position that so frightened the Anti-Federalists. In turn, a permanent new federal jurisdiction was created without the same rights as the states. "The District of Columbia has no inherent right of statehood," notes Alpheus H. Snow. "The political rights are only such as Congress shall grant of its mere will, as a 'privilege' or 'indulgence.'" In effect, then, Congress was doing exactly what it had opposed the British for doing—creating dependent jurisdictions without clear plans for their governance or support.[52]

The fate of Washington DC epitomizes many of the dangers of creating new sub-national polities without giving proper thought to its consequences. Many of the city's current problems stem from the fact that it lacks a full-blown government—it is a rump jurisdiction scarcely capable of promoting its own local interests. Though Anti-Federalists feared that the District would come to dominate the national economy to the detriment of the states, the city has never come close to realizing this potential. Politically, Congress has jurisdiction over the District, despite the fact that members of Congress are accountable only to voters in their home districts. Moreover, without the financial and jurisdictional support of a state government, the District is unable to maintain the kinds of public works and social service programs that would preserve its commercial competitiveness with other regions. More to the point, however, is the general failure of the founders to think through the implications of this jurisdictional arrangement. What should it mean for land to be under congressional jurisdiction?

The founders' lack of clarity with respect to jurisdiction over the nation's capital carried over into the frontier, where the issue of turning "territories" into "states" loomed large. Postwar territories like Kentucky and Ohio were desperate to establish exclusive jurisdiction over their own domains. Existing states holding valid claims in the West were equally reluctant to give them up. The passage of the Northwest Ordinance of 1787 was thus vital to the survival of the new nation; it created a legal framework for governing the West, though it was also noticeably shortsighted. In the words of historian Peter Onuf:

> Ambiguous and sometimes contradictory concepts of statehood reflected, and in turn contributed to, the low level of political integration actually achieved in the new American states. The establishment of legitimate authority constitutes a dilemma for any new regime. In America, state succession doctrine helped minimize the initial shock of

the transition from colony to state, but it also contributed to the conceptual confusion that impeded the consolidation of state authority.[53]

Thomas Jefferson was one of the leading proponents of westward expansion, and his thoughts on the nature of state succession are essential to understanding the institutionalization of American exceptionalism. Jefferson was not only an avid proponent of states' rights but also a firm believer in the proto-Tocquevillian notion of self-government based on communal goodwill. In his *Notes on the State of Virginia*, Jefferson mulled over the challenges of American democracy with reference to his rather fanciful account of Virginia's native population: Where native communities remained small and based their livelihood on agriculture, observed Jefferson, they enjoyed "the circumstance of their having never submitted themselves to any laws, any coercive power, any shadow of government. Their only controls are their manners, and that moral sense of right and wrong, which, like the sense of tasting and feeling, in every man makes a part of his nature." He believed that these communities had achieved the very embodiment of organic self-organization, a model for American settlement on the western frontier. In contrast, Jefferson argued, native communities perished when exposed to the depredations of the law and the market. From this he concluded that commercial cities evoked selfishness, disunion, and even treason in citizens, and that the future of the nation lay in small, rural agrarian communities with minimal laws and maximal self-government. Small communities of yeoman farmers would aspire not only to peaceful cohabitation but also to collective engagement as long as they were not subjected to the corrupting influences of law and commerce.[54]

In turn, Jefferson believed that new communities in the American West would grow organically, evolving political and legal institutions as needed. He proposed a strong role for national government as surveyor of new lands, but hoped to leave the rest of the settlement process to the settlers themselves. The drafters of the Northwest Ordinance thus gave little thought to the bureaucratic, legal organization of the territories.

In addition to leaving territorial governors a weak mandate to govern, another major problem with this vision of state formation was that it assumed a sort of primeval Eden in the West that hardly represented reality. Squatters, speculators, lawyers, land companies, and political entrepreneurs were prevalent in even the most scarcely populated territories. This rendered Jefferson's "republican" model of autochthonous communities obsolete.

Jefferson's vision also overlooked the fact that the new states were nothing like their predecessors in legal standing: The old states had gained autonomy through exploitation of their original English charters, whereas the new states could only become legal jurisdictions with the permission of Congress. Under the Northwest Ordinance of 1787, all territories would remain under congressional jurisdiction until they reached a population size of sixty thousand inhabitants. This meant that Congress would have to assume a role greater than that of arbiter between the states; it was formally charged with the administration of the territories and their eventual transformation into states. Unfortunately, Congress had no such (preexisting) power, nor did it have the will to exert it, since its members were primarily concerned with the interests of their respective states.[55]

Therefore, from the perspective of the state representatives, the issue of creating new states devolved primarily into a struggle over the existing balance of power in Congress. Representatives from New England and the Mid-Atlantic states opposed admission of new states from the West because of the potential threat presented to Atlantic business interests by the Mississippi River trade. Representatives from southern states were desperate to see slaveholding extended to new states, thus bolstering the proslavery lobby in Congress. It is rather remarkable, then, that any agreement was reached in Congress at all.

·One unintended effect of this compromise was the early politicization of the territories—knowing that admission to the union would tip the balance of national politics one way or the other, party leaders flooded the territories with political operatives in anticipation of statehood. This only contributed to the spoils and corruption implicit in the race for territorial land and mineral rights. In a sense, then, Jefferson's organic vision of state formation fostered the very ills he most sought to avoid—the premature commercialization and politicization of the frontier. These decisions had lasting repercussions on American political development.[56]

In Canada, meanwhile, British authorities also were restructuring the jurisdictional apparatus of the provinces. Under the Constitutional Act of 1791, British colonial administrators acknowledged the lessons of the American revolt and tried to put Canada on better political footing. Their aim was to partition Canada into several smaller provinces in order to render each as governable as possible. They also wanted to fore-stall Canadian defection to the United States by instituting representative government in each province, but with important restrictions that were designed to avoid the jurisdictional conflicts endemic in the American colonies before the war.

Historical judgment on the success of these measures is mixed: The Canadian economy flourished in the bosom of British protectionism, but it also benefited unwittingly from British wars with America and France. The people of Canada remained relatively docile throughout the period, but military concerns about a possible "French Revolution" in Quebec led to repressive measures that inflamed Anglo-French relations. In Upper Canada, moreover, a small cadre of British entrepreneurs came to dominate politics under an alliance referred to as the "Family Compact." The members of the Compact often sought justification for their oligarchic, collusionist tactics in anti-American rhetoric. Indeed, another major Anglo-American military conflict lay just over the horizon.

5

Nationhood Begins, and Almost Ends

Governor Arthur St. Clair formally declared the Northwest Territory a legitimate legal entity—a "body politic," so to speak—on July 15, 1788, at Fort Harmar, near present-day Marietta, Ohio. St. Clair had arrived from Philadelphia six days earlier on a twelve-oar barge and was greeted by local military officials and "a goodly group of citizens" donning "their best clothes." According to the legal authority granted him by the Northwest Ordinance of 1787, Governor St. Clair's new territory was created by Congress to provide the federal government a means of claiming the land. Although the "state" of Ohio did not yet exist, there was a blueprint for its birth, and St. Clair was its designated midwife.[1]

Legal fictions such as this—states, territories, municipalities, and so forth—are inordinately important to the process of statecraft; they allow governments to partition authority over places, things, duties, and powers. They played an especially important role in the political development of the United States and Canada, both nation-states that have been expanding territorially and jurisdictionally for much of their history.[2]

In many ways, Governor St. Clair was typical of the men responsible for the political development of the early Canadian and American frontiers. A Scot by birth, St. Clair had originally ventured to North America as part of a British military garrison during the Seven Years' War (1756–1763). He later married into a prominent Boston family and, having long been stationed in western Pennsylvania, he decided to take the side of America in the Revolution, and enlisted just in time to join the American retreat from Quebec in 1776. A large percentage of the original settlers in Governor St. Clair's Ohio territory were Revolutionary War veterans who claimed public lands that were granted them as remuneration for service. St. Clair later moved the seat of the territorial government from Fort Harmar further west to Fort Washington, where he renamed the surrounding town Cincinnati in honor of the Society of the Cincinnati, a hereditary social club created by veteran officers of the Revolutionary War.[3]

At the moment of Governor St. Clair's territorial proclamation, the United States itself was barely born. The individual states were still wrestling with the responsibilities of self-government, as well as trying to forge a viable confederation. The nation's capital was not yet built and, despite St. Clair's mandate, much of the Northwest Territory was still under British control. Formal jurisdictional boundaries were not settled there until 1794, eleven years after the Peace of Paris. Meanwhile, Spanish troops patrolled the Mississippi River valley to the west. Discontented settlers occasionally threatened to decamp to Spanish territory across the Mississippi River if their needs were not met by the American territorial government.[4]

Numerous native groups remained ready to hold the line against European incursion. Skirmishes were common; massacres occurred from time to time. In 1791, Governor St. Clair led his militia into an Indian ambush so severe that he was summoned by Congress for investigation and, although he was exonerated, his name was never fully cleared of the whiff of incompetence.

However, it is arguable that St. Clair's performance suffered in more ways than one. Because territorial governors were poorly paid, and also because their homes, businesses, and social lives lay elsewhere, St. Clair and his successors tended to spend more than half of their time "out of state," thus leaving actual administration of the territories to underlings. For example, while St. Clair was serving as governor of the Northwest Territory, he actually ran for governor of Pennsylvania where, for better or worse, he polled less than 10 percent of the vote. Dejected, St. Clair returned to his post, though he continued to spend much of his time in Pennsylvania. Such absentee leadership became a hallmark of executive office in the American territories.[5]

Admittedly, St. Clair had a weak mandate to rule: The US attorney general was the de facto supervisor of the territorial governors, who received few if any instructions from him on how to govern. Moreover, their commissions did not come from the attorney general but from

Congress, which was too preoccupied with the balance of power between pro- and antislave states to attend to the details of territorial administration.

In order to provide a legal framework for the Northwest Territory, Governor St. Clair commissioned three judges whom, along with himself, would serve as the territory's de facto legislature. The exact nature of those powers, however, remained unclear, and numerous conflicts ensued between St. Clair and the justices over the proper construction of a legal code for the territory. In fact, the exact reach of the courts' legislative powers remained a point of contention in Ohio through the 1800s resulting in several attempts to impeach and restrict state jurists. According to historian Jack Eblen, "As a result of the cautiousness, if not outright incompetence, of most district-stage legislators . . . the law developed haphazardly and was never adequate. Moreover, the laws were often unenforceable or irrelevant, either because of their nature or because of their unavailability to local authorities." The legal code remained an uncertain patchwork until 1799, when a legislative assembly was convened with power to initiate its own measures. This reformed legal code later became the basis for the state codes of Ohio, Indiana, and Illinois.[6]

Another major legal problem in the territories was the question of who actually had title to the land. Native claims notwithstanding, various states held title to western lands and sought jurisdiction over them. Despite the founders' fear of national government, the Northwest Ordinance of 1787 was a multistate compromise whereby the states' western claims were "nationalized," or moved from state to federal jurisdiction. The federal government then began liberally dispersing this land to the nation's underpaid, largely disgruntled war veterans. Such use of the public lands was a hallmark of early American public administration.

Nonetheless, despite Republican aspirations to people the West with small family farms, land speculators and private land companies supplanted individual placeholders in most areas by buying plots in bulk and reselling them at a premium. In fact, St. Clair's territorial government was preceded by the powerful Ohio Company, a land corporation created by Revolutionary War officers who hoped to reap huge profits by speculating in western land. Two of the three judges selected to help St. Clair run the territorial government, Samuel Holden Parsons and James Mitchell Varnum, were officers of the Ohio Company, and their counterpart, John

Cleves Symmes, "did not actively take up his work for some time," thus accentuating the power of the company. Such corporate concerns— private land trusts and, later, railroad and mining corporations—were the controlling factions in many of the western territories before they became states.[7]

Beginning with the Northwest Ordinance of 1787, the new United States began assembling a de facto empire among its western territories. Seen in light of the long colonial period that preceded the Revolution, the subsequent trajectories of American and Canadian political development both reveal new lessons and require new perspectives on the North American nation-building process.

The Political Construction of English Canada

On July 8, 1792, almost exactly four years after Governor St. Clair's proclamation of American jurisdiction over the Northwest Territory, John Graves Simcoe addressed a tiny British garrison on the northern shore of Lake Ontario (present-day Kingston, Ontario), took the oath of office as lieutenant governor of the new Province of Upper Canada, and bestowed upon it a constitution that he described as "the most excellent that was ever bestowed upon a colony."[8]

Like St. Clair, Simcoe was not a native-born American; he was a British military officer. Though not old enough to have served in the Seven Years' War, Simcoe earned great distinction in the Revolutionary War as commander of American Loyalist troops (that is, American volunteers trained and deployed by the British to combat the "rebel" army). A large number of Loyalist American troops chose to settle in Canada after the war. Simcoe himself returned from a postwar hiatus in England upon receiving a commission to serve as the administrative head of "Upper Canada," a new jurisdiction carved out of greater Quebec.[9]

But why were these British solders interested in moving to Upper Canada when the temperate weather and robust economy of Great Britain beckoned? Firsthand accounts of life in early Ontario are quite favorable: Property was readily available; it was so easily acquired, in fact, that land prices failed to increase much, despite expectations to the contrary. In addition, although Ontario's harsh winter weather was obviously inconvenient, it caused the rivers and swamps to freeze, thus opening the province's otherwise muddy, unpaved paths and "Indian trails" for transit. The long winter thus provided farm families an unprecedented opportunity to travel the province, visit relatives, haul in supplies, and rest from the hard labor of summer. Many English, Scottish, Irish, and American immigrants wrote home boasting of Ontario's fertile land, plentiful food, and healthy living.[10]

Violence with native tribes was extremely rare in western Canada, whereas it was exceedingly common all along the American frontier. British military and colonial officials, like the French before them, had long since learned the value of cooperating with native people. Since the primary goals of British officials in Upper Canada were fur trading and holding the line against American incursion, it suited them to respect native land claims. In some cases, such as that of the Six Nations tribe led by Mohawk Joseph Brant, native groups formerly inhabiting American lands were offered "reserves" in Upper Canada as part of military alliances. There was certainly enough land to go around—Simcoe and his successors spent a great deal of time pondering how they could get Upper Canada settled more quickly and efficiently—and, more important, there was a cohesive, provincewide legal-institutional infrastructure in place to issue, certify, and oversee mortgages and land claims.

Downstream, the province of Lower Canada now encompassed well-developed settlements at Montreal and Quebec City, as well as the expanding Anglo-American districts near the Vermont/New Hampshire border and the long-standing French-Canadian communities along Quebec's major rivers. In contrast, Upper Canada was as yet unpopulated except for a smattering of military garrisons, trade encampments, and native villages. Outside of the garrison towns of Kingston and Niagara, as historian Jane Errington comments, "There was certainly no visible sign that the backwoods of Upper Canada was British." Lieutenant Governor Simcoe felt it was his job to give Upper Canada a properly British cultural and political life.[11]

Simcoe and his successors faced several obstacles. In the 1790s, thousands of Americans began arriving in Upper Canada in search of inexpensive land. The American frontier still faced fierce native resistance, and land in the East had become untenably expensive. While upstate New York and western Pennsylvania also experienced land booms in the immediate postwar period, the advance presence of American land companies in that area had already elevated prices. As a result, many westward settlers simply continued their journey into the newly founded province of Upper Canada, where generous plots could be had for the mere price of signing an oath of loyalty to the Crown. New settlers came in especially large numbers from New England and southern New York, thus inflecting Upper Canada with a distinctly "Yankee" tinge. With them came itinerant Methodist and Baptist preachers, who quickly outnumbered their Anglican counterparts. In 1797, in fact, Anglicans were estimated to comprise not more than one-fifteenth of Upper Canada's population. Archdeacon John Strachan said with regard to the subsequent influence of American religious denominations in Upper Canada, "It is manifest that the colonial government neither has, nor can have, any other control over them, or prevent them from gradually rendering a large portion of the population, by their influence and instructions, hostile to our institutions, both civil and religious." And, indeed, Strachan was correct: Upper Canadians were strongly influenced by American civil, religious, economic, and political models. The ruling elite had numerous devices to resist such incursions—they controlled the judicial, legislative, and executive branches of government—but the presence of Americans along with their institutions and ideals were nonetheless an important presence in Upper Canada in the early nineteenth century. Any pretense that the early people of Ontario were tried-and-true Britons is betrayed by the influence of American people, practices, and politics in the immediate postbellum period.[12]

Lieutenant Governor Simcoe's main problem at the time was not attracting settlers so much as regulating their impact on the prospective culture of the new province: Simcoe and the province's Tory elite aspired to build a proper English society in Ontario, and they saw the Americans as a threat. Upper Canada also had the uniquely inauspicious distinction of being the only British colony of the era without an ocean port, thus limiting its access to both British imports and customs duties. In fact, the government of Upper Canada was beholden to Lower Canada for a portion of the imperial customs duties collected at Montreal, a dependent relationship that made the Upper Canadians uncomfortable. Simcoe's fears were exacerbated by the fact that much of Upper Canadian commerce passed through New York State and Vermont rather than Lower Canada, and that American currency, as well as American-made goods, dominated the local economy. There were literally dozens of places where goods could be shipped, carried, and smuggled into the United States, thus limiting Canada's control of its international border.

For a brief period between the first and second Anglo-American Wars (1783–1812), many things seemed to favor Canada in the bid to lure and retain settlers. In addition to free or inexpensive land, another lure of Upper Canada was the fact that the Canadians were generally on good terms with resident natives—Lieutenant Governor Simcoe entertained many natives in his makeshift quarters along Lake Ontario. Simcoe and his successors also worked diligently to avoid taxing residents while channeling as much Crown money as possible into the infrastructural development of the province. Though winters were tough and the existing settlements were rugged, Upper Canadians benefited from the ease with which they could travel downstream to the thriving cities of Montreal and Quebec, where the governor in chief, the French *seigneurs,* and a cadre of fiercely ambitious Scottish entrepreneurs lived in luxury. Intragovernmental communication was thus fairly decent, and western outposts were easily provisioned each spring by boats traveling the Great Lakes and the St. Lawrence. In fact, life in Upper Canada could be downright civilized at times: As Simcoe's wife, Elizabeth, wrote in a letter home to England, "There are as many feathers, flowers, and gauze dresses at our balls (which are every fortnight) as at Honiton Assembly [the Simcoe's home in Devon, England]." During the summer of 1792, His Royal Highness Prince Edward came for a tour of the garrison at Fort Niagara on the far western edge of Lake Ontario.[13]

Nonetheless, even after the British and American governments resolved their disputes over borderlands and Revolutionary War remunerations, the burgeoning towns of Upper Canada more closely resembled military garrisons than farmlands. The British (rightly) feared further conflict with the Americans. This brought large infusions of British capital into the province, but it also preoccupied a government with limited administrative capacity and financial wherewithal.

Lower Canada (Quebec): The Shifting Fortunes of French-Catholic Canada

Relations between the provinces of Upper and Lower Canada (modern-day Ontario and Quebec) were sometimes rocky despite the presence of a governor in chief and the ease of transit throughout most of the region. Overall, however, French Canadians were relatively content with English rule through the early 1790s, having been granted religious freedom, French civil law, and limited self-government by the Quebec Act of 1774. For a time, there was a so-called bourgeois alliance between leading British and French citizens in Lower Canada, and many *Canadiens* even seemed eager to adopt the English language and customs. "On a pastoral visit," notes Quebec historian Michel Brunet, "Bishop Briand had noted the happiness of his flock: 'Everything here [in Montreal] seems very quiet to me, and since leaving Quebec I do not recall having heard a single expression of discontent with the government. The people and in general everyone strike me as being as satisfied as if they had never known any other.'" Long-term troubles loomed over the horizon, given the difficulties that *Canadien* merchants faced importing French goods and/or receiving credit from Anglo-American importers, but, according to most sources, there was relative calm in former New France.[14]

At or around the dawn of the nineteenth century, the fortunes of Quebec's French-Catholic population began to wane relative to their new anglophone neighbors. Economically, Quebec remained almost frozen in time, preserving seventeenth-century farming and feudal land tenure practices that limited the economic power of *Canadiens* relative to their new anglophone counterparts. Those same anglophones also assured for themselves a disproportionate number of political and administrative posts in the province, and the French fur-trapping industry was gradually supplanted by Anglo-American competition. Intense loyalty to the locally dominant Catholic Church also helped preserve the conservative agrarianism of *Canadien* feudalism.[15]

Politically, affairs between Anglo- and French Canadians soured in the late 1790s, when rumors started circulating that the Americans were plotting with the French to invade Quebec. The Brits' "garrison mentality" toward the French increased, as did their legal control over the province. Before long, French Canadians were protesting British rule and cultivating *la survivance,* or the idea that the distinct culture and language of Quebec deserved special protection from British intrusion. For a brief spell during the second Anglo-American War (the War of 1812, in American parlance), James Craig, the lieutenant governor of Lower Canada, imposed martial law, arrested numerous *Canadien* journalists, and suspended habeas corpus, all measures that were generally avoided in Upper Canada, where political repression was limited to action against known defectors and treasonous aliens. Craig's French-

Canadian subjects felt unduly harassed, and Franco-English relations in Canada were never the same again.[16]

One ongoing source of tension and debate in Lower Canada was the exact relationship between English and French law in the colony. Though the Quebec Act of 1774 had specified parameters for the maintenance of French civil law in the colony, the exact parameters of civil and common law jurisdiction remained unclear until the 1860s, when a committee of jurists was formed to officially "codify" Quebec's legal system. Until that time, law in Quebec remained a hodgepodge of legal customs that combined aspects of the medieval *Coutume de Paris* with modern English law. Lord Durham, whose formal investigation of conditions in Canada prompted Britain's eventual move to make Canada independent, described the legal system of Lower Canada as "a mass of incoherent and conflicting laws, part French, part English, and with the line between each very confusedly drawn." Questions of law were decided by independent, mostly British judges, which antagonized both French and British representatives in the provincial legislature. Moreover, seigneurial, civil law customs regarding land tenure, taxation, and sales remained in place despite the objections of a new bourgeoisie eager to buy, sell, and develop land at will. One particularly troublesome appendage of New France's land law was the issuance of "secret hypothecs," or illicit but binding mortgages on land that created a hidden minefield of property liens threatening anyone who wanted to make a purchase or sale.

That the bourgeoisie of Quebec comprised both French and English speakers is a fair indicator of the social climate of postconquest Quebec: class was generally a stronger arbiter of political affiliation than language, religion, or culture. This might explain why anglophone merchants were willing to support francophone efforts to retain major portions of French civil law in Quebec law. Conversely, the province's small cadre of francophone merchants supported the maintenance of English language and commercial law in the province. Both were opposed by the *ancien regime* of New France: the clergy and those holding ancestral titles to feudal land, both of whom fiercely opposed efforts to "modernize" (that is, codify and rejuvenate) medieval French legal customs in the province. The legal culture of Quebec was thus held hostage by partisan rivalries for nearly a century (1774–1866). This proved to be a burden on the economy of Lower Canada throughout the early nineteenth century because medieval restrictions on land development and general uncertainty concerning property rights hampered the ability of entrepreneurs to build mills and dams, railroads, canals, and factories.[17]

Resolution of the issue, as achieved in 1866, is typical of politics in early nineteenth-century Lower Canada: Though codification was achieved in most European nation-states through public, political negotiations, the process was held behind closed doors in Quebec, where leading lawyers and jurists hammered out a system that would accommodate as many interests as possible. Though feudalism was formally abolished in the province, the informal apparatus whereby land was attached to powerful families and managed in accordance with the hierarchical principles of medieval France was left intact. The new mercantile elite were at the same time granted important concessions that would make it easier to buy, sell, and develop land. The Catholic orders, in the meantime, protected their extensive landholdings in the province while assuring the institutionalization of traditional social values under Quebec law—for example, married women actually *lost* rights and freedoms under the new order. Though interpretations vary, it appears that this new system essentially preserved the hierarchical social system of New France while bringing the province's commercial law up to speed with the imperatives of nascent capitalism.[18]

In this respect, it is worth examining the contrasting case of Louisiana, where civil and common law traditions were resolved to different ends. When the United States took formal control over this former Franco-Spanish territory following the landmark Louisiana Purchase of 1803, the province's legal system was in shambles. Until 1812, when the territory became a state, "Louisiana still hovered in a jurisdictional limbo," writes Mark Fernandez. "It was neither a common law nor a civil law jurisdiction but something in between, and confusion reigned, confounding efforts to render justice to a litigious citizenry." Though there were some notable political battles between the American and *ancien* factions in Louisiana, legal accommodation was reached in a much less antagonist manner than in Quebec. This is partly because American administrators in Louisiana, unlike their British counterparts in Quebec, made no pretense of "preserving" French or Spanish linguistic, cultural, or legal traditions. Creoles were expected to be able to conduct themselves in English and to adapt to American customs and laws. However, in line with common law dedication to the preservation of custom, jurists also upheld many local laws and practices from the

Franco-Spanish era, thus easing the transition to a thoroughly American legal culture in Louisiana.[19]

By strictly controlling standards and admission to the Louisiana bar, jurists guaranteed the eventual "Americanization" of legal practice while avoiding long-term squabbles over cultural patrimony and jurisdictional dominance so typical of Quebec. Under the guidance of particularly open-minded Supreme Court officials, "Louisiana attracted a competent pool of jurists trained in both the Anglo-American and civilian [that is, civil law] traditions," writes legal historian Mark Fernandez. "Far from being well-intentioned boobs who mingled traditions . . . Louisiana's judges and lawyers moved easily within both systems and adopted measures from each that ensured the traditions most important to the state's residents and most applicable to the American tradition of justice." Though other historians have sought to present the Americanization of Louisiana law as a fraught, controversial process, Fernandez notes that "the features of private law preserved in Louisiana became the model for similar code-sponsored legislation throughout the American South and West." By keeping issues of ethnicity and language separate from those regarding rule of law, Louisiana officials managed a less-contentious transition to common law than their Canadian counterparts. As historian Fernand Ouellet explains, efforts in Quebec to create provincial registry offices in order to facilitate land sales "seemed to the political leaders of French Canada to be a campaign to abolish French civil law. It was nothing of the sort, but the fear was there." After a failed Francophone rebellion in 1837–1838, the connection between Quebecois nationalism and French law began to fade, but the issue of jurisdictional compromise remained.[20]

Whereas Louisiana made a (relatively) smooth transition to American law, Quebec became mired in jurisdictional squabbling between its francophone and anglophone populations. In hindsight, it appears that the British administrators in Canada got some things very right and some things rather wrong, as did their American counterparts. These tendencies only magnified as both nations continued to spread west, accessioning new territories along the way.

Americanizing Ontario?

American settlers had been barred from settling the territory west of Pittsburgh until the late 1780s, and Upper Canada contained little more than a large Iroquois reserve and a few British garrison towns at that time. This paucity of western settlers, coupled with the complexities of myriad native regimes, made the midwestern "frontier" a legal *tabula rasa*, at least as far as the settlers were concerned: land claims, property rights, and jurisdictional landmarks were there for the taking.

Like Governor St. Clair in Ohio, Lieutenant Governor Simcoe had few resources and a weak mandate in Upper Canada. Given continuing tensions with the Americans, Simcoe, like St. Clair, was concerned first and foremost with maintaining the districts' military defenses. War remained a distinct possibility between America, England, and France throughout this period, and all three, plus neighboring Spain, coveted the rich lands west of the Appalachians. Furthermore, like St. Clair, Simcoe dedicated a great deal of time to administering and overseeing land grants to new settlers, many of whom were entitled to public land as remuneration for military service. The similarities, however, end there.

Despite the objections of French settlers, Simcoe phased out slavery in Upper Canada, whereas St. Clair defended it in the Northwest Territory.[21] Simcoe, unlike St. Clair, immediately established an elected legislative assembly and allowed individual towns to establish modest local self-government, neither of which was afforded St. Clair's American subjects. Jurisdictionally speaking, Simcoe had both a clearer mandate and a shorter leash. As lieutenant governor, he was closely supervised by Lord Dorchester, the captain general and governor in chief of both Upper and Lower Canada, and Dorchester was himself accountable to government ministers at Whitehall, England. Landon sun sums up the difference between these two nascent provincial governments as follows: "Compared with the unceasing activity of Simcoe in Upper Canada and the highly paternal attitude which he assumed towards this province and the people under his jurisdiction, there was a more casual character about the administration of the Northwest Territory under St. Clair."[22]

This simple observation actually says a lot about the political trajectory of these two new territories. On the American frontier, Congress, Governor St. Clair, local lawyers, and the territorial legislature struggled to determine the proper structure and form of territorial law. St. Clair's aide, Secretary Winthrop Sargent, personally issued legal decrees in outlying regions such as Vincennes, Mackinaw, and Detroit, where vast tangles of British, French, and native jurisdiction had yet to be unwound. Sargent was often rebuked for not consulting St. Clair before acting, though in many cases, his only alternative was to do nothing. St. Clair challenged the legality of many of these decrees and repeatedly insisted that the Ordinance of 1787 required that territorial law mimic existing state laws. At the same time, however, St. Clair challenged federal orders to collect excise taxes from residents of the territories, arguing that they were not represented in Congress at the time of the tax decree, nor were the territories so named in said decrees. After several years of legal limbo, the statutes of the territory were finally overhauled. "Maxwell's Code" of 1795, named after the Cincinnati printer charged with their publication, closely mirrored the state code of Pennsylvania, though additional laws were "lifted" from Massachusetts, New Jersey, Virginia, and New York code.[23]

This temporary lack of effective state control created a wide-open playing field for anyone tough enough to carve and defend a niche in the American Midwest. Land claims, having been issued by rival French, British, and American jurisdictions, were a mess; a perfect opportunity for speculators and squatters. Though proxy governments existed in some areas of the new American frontier, there was little or no control along its outer perimeter, where daring prospectors might take their chances in the hope of securing valuable claims against future land prices. The federal government also did next to nothing to stop illegal raids on Spanish, British, and French holdings in the Midwest, the Deep South, "Down East" (that is, Maine), and in the Pacific Northwest. The frontier itself expanded so rapidly that growth continued unrestrained for several decades.[24]

By contrast, in Lower Canada and the Atlantic provinces, well-settled seigneuries offered little room for new settlement, though fishing and lumbering opportunities remained aplenty. Britain technically held all of Canada, but most of the region west of Upper Canada was currently "promised" to the powerful Hudson's Bay and North West companies, and extensive plots of the northern Great Lakes had been granted to displaced native tribes that had sided with the Crown in the American Revolution. There was still ample frontier land available around the eastern Great Lakes and northeast up through the Ottawa River, but the reins were held tightly by the military regime that was imposed upon the new colony to regulate settlement.

Because of the vast amount of land that was open to settlement in Upper Canada and the general absence of legal jurisdictional precedents for its administration, there was a huge potential for patronage and corruption. It would be disingenuous to say that we know exactly how much land-related corruption occurred on either side of the border, let alone how these rates might compare with those in other nations; nevertheless, it appears that the *nature* of the corruption was indeed quite different in the American "Old Northwest" from that in British "Upper Canada."

The legal history of early Ontarian settlement patterns is profound in its complexity. Literally an entire province—one at least the size of all New England—was "granted" by the Crown in a brief stint of thirty years, 1783 to 1815; an instant in old colonial terms. (New England, which was largely settled between 1620 and 1750, took more than four times as long.) What occurred is best viewed as a sort of high-stakes, government-run land auction, with "connections" serving as the price of entry for most, if not all, major beneficiaries.

Because English authorities insisted on controlling western settlement from the top down, there were both opportunities and obstacles to efficient administration. Furthermore, because these same authorities were determined to protect the territory from American incursion, they faced further challenges in deciding who did and did not "belong" there. Government officials were thus left to deliberate who was a "British North American"—and therefore entitled to generous land grants—and who was merely an expatriate American looking for inexpensive land. How should "loyalty" be measured?

Those in charge faced a range of other challenging questions, such as whether land was best granted in individual, farm-sized plots or in large, township-sized plots, thus encouraging speculators to subdivide and sell parcels on their own. If township plots were acceptable (and they largely were, though policy vacillated greatly on this account), then what kinds of rents should promoters be able to extract from their tenants? Who should pay for and maintain roads and bridges? How could the collection of rents and taxes be guaranteed, especially given the scarcity of specie in the province? How could landholding natives be protected from unscrupulous neighbors and business partners?

Lillian F. Gates discusses the resolution of these and many other dilemmas in *Land Policies of Upper Canada*. While documenting in astonishing detail the smallest policy debates from year to year and district to district, her wider purview clearly demonstrates the sensitivity and attention paid such affairs by ordinary government officials, from the lieutenant governor of the province to the attorney general, the Executive and Legislative Councils, the assembly, the governor-general, and the colonial office itself (all the way back in England). English officials took their responsibility to allocate provincial lands quite seriously, though not always to the best effect. Upper Canada's highly bureaucratic land grant system likely slowed the pace of development in the province— unlike western America's fast-paced, highly speculative public land market, western Canada's was highly regulated and relatively resistant to "land jobbing" and squatting—but it also promoted order, equality, and respect for property rights and the law.[25]

The early settlement of Upper Canada was a distinctly top-down process, directed from above by the sometimes quarrelsome British ministries of military and colonial affairs. Beneath them stood two communities of politically active settlers: ultra-Loyalists, many of whom held lucrative appointive offices in the colonial administration; and so-called radicals or republican reformers, who held a strong but rarely dominant position in the colonial legislature. Though it left much to be desired from fiscal and administrative standpoints, the practice of granting land to settlers through government-backed mortgages made acquisition accessible and affordable. More controversial, especially to "radicals," was the decision to reserve ample portions of the public land for the benefit of the Anglican Church, a practice that helped foment outright but ultimately short-lived rebellion in Upper Canada in the late 1830s.[26]

Canadian "radicals" were deemed so because of their supposed pro-American leanings, and indeed they did sometimes rise to the defense of politically disempowered American settlers in the province. More generally, their aim was not "Americanization," however, but institutionalization of the same political system as England's: the restraint of executive power by a legislative assembly elected through limited suffrage; curbs on government patronage and corruption; and extension of democratic governance to the county and township levels. Says Gates, "They were opposed by persons like [Lieutenant Governor] Simcoe or D. W. Smith, whose background was military, not colonial, and who feared that the following of American precedents would lead ultimately to the breaking of the Imperial tie." At issue was a spectrum of quintessential jurisdictional concerns, from control over the government purse to authority and accountability in the issuance of Crown lands.[27]

One key, though likely not inevitable, outcome of these debates was the ascendance of a well-organized Tory oligarchy in Upper Canada—the "Family Compact," so named because of the frequency with which their offspring (supposedly) intermarried, thus solidifying their control over the political and economic fortunes of the province. This small cadre of Anglican lawyers, politicians, and entrepreneurs controlled the provincial legislature, the courts, and most of the province's capital-intensive business operations. Though not formally organized as a political party, members of the Compact were markedly Loyalist, mostly Anglican, and naturally opposed to American influence in the province. John Beverley Robinson is an interesting case in point: Born to a prominent Virginian family of Loyalist sympathies, Robinson was brought to the province by his father in 1792. He used family connections to build a promising law firm, serve as colonial emissary to England, and hold for decades the office of attorney general for the province, a position that entitled him to collect large fees, as well as serve as informal speaker of the colonial assembly. There was no mandate on separation of powers under this system; in fact, collusion between the executive, legislative, and judicial branches seemed to be encouraged under the political structure of the regime. From his estate in York (later named Toronto), Robinson became one of the richest and most politically powerful men in the province.

In the 1810s, a barnstorming Scot named Robert Gourlay took up the cause of ordinary Canadians, thus reigniting debate about the role of Americans in the province and about jurisdictional control of the provincial government's revenue streams. Gourlay was a brilliant pamphleteer, and he made ceaseless trips around Ontario accusing the Family Compact of corruption and Whitehall of neglect.

The province was still largely rural at the time, and ordinary stakeholders had more land than cash. When Gourlay sent questionnaires to townships asking for information on the health of the province and its many new settlers, he received a firestorm of criticism regarding public land policies, particularly the fact that government township plots typically "reserved" two-sevenths of town land for the Crown and clergy, which remained vacant in anticipation of future revenue through its sale. Large portions of remaining land were also granted to absentee landlords, mostly members of the provincial elite. Unsettled land was not taxed, thus allowing large landowners to amass huge tax-free holdings. Moreover, the end of continental warfare in Europe and America caused a deep depression in commodity prices, and Canadian farmers were at the mercy of British trade policy. This had the combined effect of maintaining an oversupply of unsettled land and an undersupply of taxable land in the province, thus leaving small farmers to pick up much of the tab, as Gourlay pointed out.[28]

Though Gourlay was resolutely pro-British in his cultural affinities, he believed that only America could lift Upper Canada above its problems. He disparaged America's messy politics but idolized its brisk economy. He argued that American settlers would bring much-needed human and financial capital to the province—exactly the thing Tories feared most. Americans, Gourlay maintained, would also help stimulate the local economy by buying and establishing homesteads. Land prices would improve, thus increasing tax flows and thereby infrastructure, education, and public works.

Gourlay's message found a willing audience in the outlying districts of Ontario, where most settlers were either American or intensely pragmatic about their "national identity." Because they feared American influence and also because of their personal hatred for Gourlay, the British authorities in the province decided they had to act to rid themselves of this libelous Scot who was determined to undermine the Tory order of Upper Canada. The way they accomplished this reveals several important characteristics of English-Canadian legal culture at the time:

When the Family Compact tired of Gourlay and tried to silence him, they did so by taking him to court, rather than simply arresting and/or executing him. They relied on a law drafted to limit the presence of treasonous Americans in the province: "The Alien and Sedition Act of 1804 provided that any person suspected of promoting sedition who had not been an inhabitant of the province for six months, or who had not taken the oath of allegiance, might be arrested on the warrant of certain specified authorities." In other words, Gourlay's case did not revolve around the extent to which his words and deeds were treasonous, but on exactly how long he had resided in the province. The contrast with early American legal culture here is subtle but important: Whereas ordinary Americans were wont to take one another to court to settle civil disputes, the English-Canadian courts, though equally active, were more a tool of the ruling elite, who used the intricacies of English common law to hamstring political opponents and supposed enemies of the state. Canadian jurists could serve in the legislative and executive branches, and court appointments were firmly controlled by the colonial executive. Memories of the bloody French Revolution served as a pretext for political repression in English Canada.[29]

Gourlay was ordered to leave the province by January 1, 1819, but he instead "applied for a writ of *Habeas Corpus*," arguing before the court that "the act did not apply to him because he *had* resided more than six months in the province prior to his arrest." Nonetheless, Gourlay lost the case—he never stood a chance given the Family Compact's control over the province's judicial system. "In accordance with the court's order," writes Gates, "Gourlay left the province within twenty-four hours after the conclusion of his trial, and returned to England where for years he continually and unsuccessfully petitioned the House of Commons, sometimes urging an inquiry into his own affairs, sometimes into the affairs of the province." He also spent a good amount of time in the United States, where he published an account of his persecution entitled *The Banished Briton*. "After the Union of 1841," writes W. Stewart Wallace, "his case was taken up by the Canadian parliament, and his arrest and sentence were pronounced 'illegal, unconstitutional, and without possibility of excuse and palliation.'"[30]

Having expelled Gourlay, the Tories continued their campaign against American influence in the province. They relied on the courts and anti-sedition law to harass and, in some cases, silence several other propagandists. One military veteran was deprived of his pension after saluting a public performance of "Yankee Doodle," and another group of veterans were denied land grants because they attended a convention that was called by the infamous Gourlay. "One of the most striking features of the persecution to which the Reformers were subjected was its pettiness," notes Wallace. The most famous (and perhaps most vituperative) of the "reform" agitators, William Lyon Mackenzie, actually succeeded in gaining remuneration after his printing press was destroyed by a pro-government group, though this was an aberration. The Family Compact generally kept a firm hand on dissenters like Mackenzie, who later led a short-lived rebellion against the provincial government.[31]

Land values in Upper Canada remained perpetually low, owing to the government's inability to wean itself from granting large new tracts for patronage and revenue purposes. This hurt everyone but new settlers. As a result, Upper Canada developed a large population of poor but landed farm families who were opposed to, and sometimes angered by, the profligate policies and cultural arrogance of the ruling elite. Wallace notes:

> An English traveller [*sic*] who visited Upper Canada in 1819 wrote: "I was surprised to find much discontent prevailing among the poorer settlers in Upper Canada. I could not always understand the grounds of their complaint, but they seemed to consider Mr. Gourlay as having wel [*sic*] explained them . . . his pamphlets . . . certainly appear to have spoken the sentiments of the poorer settlers, whose cause he had abetted against the more powerful land-holders, land-surveyors, and government agents."

These settlers, mostly Americans and Scots, eventually helped unseat the Family Compact and institute "responsible government," or electoral democracy, in Upper Canada. At the time, however, rigorous land law and aggressive law enforcement kept rural Ontario at peace, thus allowing its economy to expand at a slow and steady pace.[32]

Nonviolent authoritarian government seems to have served as a useful, short-term buffer against the growing pains of Canadian territorial expansion. Rebellions were few in number and minor in scope. Slavery was banned outright. Violence was rare, both between settlers and between whites and natives. The law, though obviously corrupt, was respected and reformed over time. Conditions could not have been more different in the American West. First, however, we need to assess the effects of the last major war fought between Americans and Canadians.

Forging National Identity in Northern North America

The looming threat of "Americanism" was a predominant focus of identity politics in Upper Canada after the American Revolution. The province was literally flooded with Americans after the war—one colonist estimated in 1810 that 60 percent of Upper Canada's white population was comprised of "non-Loyalist" American expatriates. Since these new Americans were generally more familiar with living and working on the frontier than their British counterparts, their farming and settlement practices came to dominate Upper Canadian life. Furthermore, local newspapers received the bulk of their information from New York papers, thus influencing the opinions of Canadian readers, many of whom were effusive in their respect for their "Yankee" neighbors. "It was said by many [Upper Canadian] teachers," adds Glazebrook, "that the books they were obliged to use in common schools were not only written from an American point of view but hardly mentioned British North America. In some districts teachers objected that the whole atmosphere was American, that even the children's voices were affected."[33]

Matters were complicated by the fact that, at the time, most settlers in the region refused to recognize the US/Canadian border despite repeated American efforts to the contrary. Prior to the opening of the Erie Canal in 1825, the easiest way for many northern American farmers to market their goods was to send them north to Montreal, rather than south to Boston, Hartford, and New York. DeWitt Clinton, then governor of New York, recognized this fact in his decision not only to lobby for construction of the Erie Canal but also to assure that its western terminus *not* link to Lake Ontario, which might encourage transit of American goods north to Montreal instead of east to the Hudson River and on to Manhattan.

Residents of northern New England and southern Lower Canada, as well as western New York and Upper Canada, generally cultivated a sense of unity around their joint economic interests. These attachments were so strong that the Jefferson administration's efforts to wage a trade war with Britain, beginning in 1806, were fiercely resisted by northern American farmers, traders, and even customs officials. Smugglers built roads, false-bottomed boats, and secret alliances whereby America's trade embargo of Britain could be undermined. In a letter to Jefferson, Ezekiel Hill complained, "Smuggling is carried on from Lewiston [Maine] to Canada to a considerable extent, and disgusting and humiliating as the practice is to every feeling that is American, it is almost publicly transacted as any common avocation."[34]

Because the border between Canada and the United States was extensive and largely unguarded, New York and Vermont remained prime conduits for the illegal transport of made goods, livestock, and other agricultural products. Coastal New Englanders also found many ways to take advantage of their proximity to Canadian, as well as British, markets. The Maine coast quickly became a liminal trade zone for timber merchants, fishermen, and smugglers looking to get export products around British trade barriers. Inland, Lake Champlain and the Richelieu River became another conduit for smugglers. Many Americans began settling in Quebec's eastern townships, an anglophone area of Lower Canada south of Montreal.

"An American-provincial borderland emerged after 1783 built around proximity, personal contacts arising from family ties, back-and-forth frontier migration, a broadly shared culture, similar institutions, and a network of growing economic links," notes historian Reginald Stuart. "They formed over time a genuine borderland where local loyalties based on human relations, survival, and self-interest often transcended allegiance to a distant national government." Following the resurrection of an American trade war with Britain, these local ties only became closer. "Jefferson proclaimed an insurrection in the Champlain Valley," notes Stuart, for example, "but town meetings in Vermont defied him. Customs officers, judges, juries, all increasingly condoned smuggling. Often the goods seized in evidence vanished from federal storerooms. Desperate collectors hired thugs as enforcers who used their new immunity to help employees smuggle on the side. Enforcement was hopeless." The embargo itself became a major liability for Republicans as the United States and Britain moved toward war—a war that New Englanders vigorously protested.[35]

What developed from all this was a cultural dynamic that most people will recognize in English Canada to this day: An unhealthy preoccupation with the United States, coupled with an intense synergy between peoples "sprung from the same stock, speaking the same language, governed by the same laws, ruled by the same customs, assimilated by the same manners and connected in a thousand ways, by the endearing ties of relationships."[36] The prevailing sentiment among Upper Canadians was thus one of affinity with *both* Great Britain and the United States. Officially, they remained a British jurisdiction, but culturally they were North Americans, bound to their neighbors to the south. Many, in fact, probably felt more connected to America than they did to their French-Canadian neighbors to the east, another legacy that has lasted, in ebbs and flows, to this day.[37]

At the same time, however, Upper Canada was in a unique situation with regard to the British Empire: Not only was its population largely comprised of current and former British subjects, but its territory stood at a crucial junction between the French-majority province of Lower Canada and the ever-menacing United States. In return, the British government regarded Upper Canada as a military dependency and funneled large amounts of capital into the province in support of projects such as military pensions, road improvements, and canal-building schemes. A great deal of new territory in the province was thereby "opened" by means of British-funded infrastructure schemes, the funding for which was justified as necessary to prepare the colony for war with the United States. (The latter-day national capital, Ottawa, was actually built at the terminus of one such project, the Rideau Canal.) Overall, the British government is estimated to have spent at least as much money in Ontario as did the provincial government.[38]

Despite the attentions of the British imperial government, the Tory elite still had good reason to fear for their future. An American army had invaded Quebec during the Revolutionary War, and there were rumors of another invasion, which in fact came true during the pending War of 1812, when significant numbers of American expatriates joined the marauding American army in its quest to annex Upper Canada. Given the uncertainty of French-Canadian loyalties and the huge distance that separated Upper Canada from the Maritimes, this new British-American frontier was vulnerable indeed. The fact that it was demographically, economically, and culturally dominated by Americans only made matters worse, for the Tory elite firmly believed that the new American settlers were ready and willing to betray the province to the United States.[39]

These fears were partly realized in 1812, when war broke out between the United States and Britain. Though many former Americans fought fiercely for their new homeland, the Tories never again rested easy with so many "republicans" in their midst. In the late 1810s and early 1820s, several efforts were made in the provincial legislature to expel settlers who were not born "British subjects." At the same time, however, a new, pro-American, Populist political faction began to emerge in Ontario and challenge the Tory elite. After 1828, when the naturalization of American expatriates was formerly made law, tensions between the Tories and the reformers only increased. Much of the debate centered around the role of American settlers and American ideas in the future of the province.

South of the border, American national identity also was altered dramatically by the War of 1812. American "war hawks" like Kentucky congressman Henry Clay lobbied fiercely for American conquest of Canada, the pursuit of which ended in several failed "invasions" of Quebec and southwestern Ontario, culminating in the ill-conceived burning of Toronto (then named York), which motivated British retaliation on Washington the following year. Despite the large number of Americans and increasingly discontented French Catholics in Canada,

American hopes for "Canadian" allies were dashed yet again. Domestic support for the war was itself far from unanimous: the Federalist New England states avidly protested the war and its effect on international trade, while state militias throughout the Northeast refused orders to march on Canada, arguing that they were not obliged to serve outside of the country.

The war itself was waged over issues that only affected small percentages of the population: namely, the British impressment of American sailors, which the British admiralty justified by saying that they were simply seizing British navy deserters, and the alleged British endorsement of native aggression in the American Midwest. (Though the British did support some native violence against Americans, the natives had more than ample cause to resist American expansion themselves.) American shipping had been in distress since at least 1807, when President Jefferson declared a total embargo on *all* American exports, and though the smuggling trade still thrived—for example, British forces in Canada were often fed American beef smuggled from Vermont and New York—American ships increasingly ran the risk of capture by English and French ships of war. Americans briefly considered a declaration of war against *both* England and France—the French, too, were in the practice of seizing American ships suspected of trading in British ports. Interestingly, New Englanders sought the resurrection of North Atlantic shipping not through war but through peace, thus pleading for free trade with Britain despite their earlier tradition of rebelliousness and anti-English sentiment. New Englanders' resistance to the war was so fierce, in fact, that the Federalist Party was entirely discredited after a plot to secede from the union came to light. Absent a viable opposition party, American politics changed dramatically.[40]

During the war itself, "war hawks"—primarily western politicians eager to conquer Canada and crush native resistance to westward expansion—sought to deflect antiwar sentiment by promising easy victory over the British, who, they argued, were still preoccupied by transcontinental war against the armies of Napoleon. "The conquest of Canada is in your power," preached Henry Clay in 1810. "I trust that I shall not be deemed presumptuous when I state that I verily believe that the militia of Kentucky are alone competent to place Montreal and Upper Canada at your feet." By war's end, however, fewer military victories than near catastrophes—the burning of Washington DC, for example, and the last-ditch stand at Fort McHenry—helped bolster a sense of national purpose and collective identity among the people of the United States. Albert Gallatin, secretary of treasury from 1801 to 1814 and erstwhile diplomat commented, "The war has renewed and reinstated the national feelings and character which the Revolution had given, and which were daily lessened. The people now have more general objects of attachment with which their pride and political opinions are connected. They are more Americans; they feel and act more as a nation; and I hope that the permanency of the Union is thereby secured."[41]

Interestingly, however, the lack of a unified Canadian resistance, as well as their lack of national identity per se, helped focus patriotic Americans' ire against Great Britain rather than Canada. Americans blamed Britain, not its Canadian colonists. This proved to be an important part of the pending peace between the United States and Canada in the centuries to come. For the next several decades, a primary component of British foreign policy regarding its colonial possessions in northern North America was fear of American invasion. Rather than choosing to bolster Canada's defenses, however, Britain decided to weaken Canada's ties to the motherland, thus leaving Canada to fend for itself, which is exactly what was achieved in 1867, when the Canadian colonies were united as an independent dominion. The only reason this policy stood a chance of success was the fact that Americans did not appear to harbor much animosity toward Canadians; it was the "British" they sought to remove from the continent. A brokered decision to ban warships from the Great Lakes also contributed to the "demilitarization" of the US/Canadian border. Rarely would the United States and Canada come close to blows again, despite their early history of invasion, hostility, and mutual suspicion.[42]

Besides solidifying American national identity, the War of 1812 also expanded America's control over Spanish territory along the Gulf Coast in Florida and native holdings in the southern Great Lakes region. It seems reasonable to argue that America's commitment to fighting natives for their land became *national* policy around this time. In the absence of clear jurisdiction or enforcement, explorers and settlers had already staked numerous claims to sections of heretofore forbidden native land west of the Appalachians. American frontiersmen were especially aggressive about encroaching on native lands in the jurisdictional "neverlands" of Kentucky and Tennessee, both of which were principally but not practically under the jurisdiction of Virginia and North Carolina until the mid-1790s. Since neither British nor American officials could bar such encroachments, American adventurers fended for themselves with the knowledge that any protected claims would likely be reified *post hoc* by whichever government ended up in charge. This pattern continued apace in the early nineteenth century, particularly in the Creek lands negotiated for American settlement by General Andrew Jackson following the War of 1812, when a land boom rapidly transformed the social and political landscape of the Deep South. The prevailing sense that Spaniards and natives could be bullied off their land by sustained aggression was enhanced by the success of Americans who did exactly this.[43]

In Canada, the impact of the war was threefold: first, it convinced the British colonial office that it was not cost-effective to use British forces to defend Canada, thus catalyzing a long period of introspection whereby the decision to grant Canada its independence was eventually made; second, the war aggravated tensions between Tory elites and Republican settlers in Upper Canada, thereby fomenting political unrest that eventually resulted in political concessions to those seeking more "open," democratic government at the provincial level; and third, British fears of French rebellion in Lower Canada sparked tension and resentment among a French-Catholic population otherwise disposed to accept British rule. All three factors came to a head in the abortive rebellions of 1837–1838, when small groups of rebels in both Upper and Lower Canada took up arms against the Crown. Though neither rebellion amounted to much in military terms, both signaled the beginning of the end of British colonial rule. In all three cases, moreover, the national and provincial identities we now associate with English and French Canada first came to bear—the former in opposition to American incursion, and the latter in response to Anglo-Canadian repression. Though there was ample precedent for both identity movements, it should be noted that these foremost markers of Canadian political culture only came into being after several centuries of settlement. Now, both English and French Canadians sought to control their own destinies; they sought new jurisdictional niches for the exercise of legislative and judicial autonomy. The slow pace of these movements in Canada contrasts sharply with the tumultuous, haphazard, and largely directionless pace of American political development.

6

Federalism Suborned

The Louisiana Purchase of 1803, an event celebrated in most histories of the American West, was actually a simple, though sizable, extension of the Northwest Ordinance of 1787. Moreover, the purchase and the ordinance shared in common many features of the original American colonial landscape. Like America's new territorial regime, the patents for the colonies were extremely haphazard: central coordination existed in theory but not in practice, and boundaries were vague and wildly unrealistic. Individual grants were large, but often their legitimacy was uncertain. The colonial governments, like the territorial governments after them, were often unsure of their actual powers and privileges.

Recall that it was Anglo-American colonial policy that limited white settlement in the West as much as possible: "Policy makers in Whitehall resented the desultory, rambling, disorganized absorption of the western lands," writes Rohrbough. "It flouted royal authority and upset the Indians." Though the British lacked the means to stop such incursions, their native allies were a fearsome deterrent. However, even this did not stop a steady trickle of settlement in the "middle ground" west of the Appalachians. "By 1775," writes Everett Dick, "in defiance of the Proclamation of 1763, there were between 25,000 and 30,000 persons beyond the Appalachians in the Fort Pitt district." Individual settlers, large land companies, and absentee landlords competed for a foothold in the rich land of the new frontier.[1]

Everywhere they went, American "pioneers" were generally unmindful of existing land law—oftentimes defying it outright—thus putting settlers and absentee landlords at odds. According to historian Everett Dick, this was a consistent theme in early American history:

> From early colonial times until the latter part of the nineteenth century the indifference of frontiersmen to the property rights of the great land-holders and the government was a real problem. In New England, New York, and especially in Pennsylvania the immigrant paid no attention to the landlord's demands, and the Virginia frontiersman regarded the king's land as lightly as Robin Hood regarded His Majesty's deer.[2]

The settlement of the Province of Ontario (called both Upper Canada and Canada West prior to confederation) was rather orderly and tame by contrast. Though the Anglo-Canadian courts were often involved in set-tling rival land disputes, the central complaint of settlers was the lack of representative government in the Canadas. In the postrevolutionary American West, it was often not clear who the relevant government even was. Kentucky was cleaved out of Virginia against Virginia's wishes, and Tennessee out of North Carolina in similar fashion. Various state gov-ernments, including those of Pennsylvania, Virginia, and New York all claimed jurisdiction over portions of the Ohio Valley. Settlers, lawyers, and politicians freely used jurisdictional discrepancies to their advan-tage. This was not a matter of character but of opportunity, the chance to profit from the uncertainties and prevarications of property law.

Squatters were a particularly unmanageable problem throughout the frontier. The tangled, underfunded federal land system seemed to encourage illegal tenancy. Federal land surveys were perpetually be-hind schedule, thus delaying land auctions, and large corporate con-cerns were always on the ready to outbid individual farmers for desir-able plots. The holders of small claims thus found themselves in a position where they would more likely benefit from simply picking a piece of land and farming it than from trying to purchase the title legally. In addition, a haphazard, perpetually underfunded land ad-ministration system made recording claims dicey, time-consuming, and expensive. Farmers with small properties sometimes banded to-gether into "claim clubs" to protect themselves from speculators and claim jumpers, but the average farmer simply settled on a plot and hoped for the best.[3]

The prevailing legal culture on the American frontier held that law was malleable, government avoidable, and force paramount. Founding father Benjamin Rush described the prototypical late eighteenth-century American pioneer as follows: "Above all, he revolts against the operation of laws. He cannot bear to surrender up a single natural right for all the benefits of government."[4]

More surprising is the degree to which the conditions established under the Northwest Ordinance of 1787 contravened the lessons and ideology of the American Revolution. Benjamin Rush was not alone in viewing the white settlers of trans-Appalachia as lawless ruffians; Thomas Jefferson viewed them as something less than "tractable people." Richard Henry Lee describes them in a 1787 letter to George Washington as an "uninformed, and perhaps licentious people." The Republican dream of a virtuous hinterland was betrayed by reality—the trans-Appalachian frontier was a reckless tumbledown and the Deep South was a primitive free-for-all.[5]

The founders drafted a plan to guide the "territories" to statehood—the Northwest Ordinance of 1787—but it never functioned very well. It was built around Jefferson's belief that the political institutions needed for Republican self-government on the frontier would naturally evolve over many generations. Jefferson brokered the single biggest acquisition of American territory to date, the Louisiana Purchase, but he did not anticipate the rush to settlement that occurred thereafter. There was no time, nor legal basis, for grassroots political development under this plan. Under the ordinance, territories were deemed "ready" for statehood when their raw population reached sixty thousand inhabitants, this having been deemed the proper threshold for political "maturity." However, no provisions were made to adjudge each territory's actual institutional preparation for statehood. For a window of about fifty years—from Vermont's irregular entry into statehood in 1791 to the slave-expansion acquisitions of the 1840s and 1850s—territories became states at will, most scarcely ready for the privilege.

Nevertheless, Congress could deny candidates for statehood on any grounds: Texas and, later, Utah were both kept at arm's length for considerable periods. Moreover, statehood was not the political destiny of all American territorial acquisitions: native reservations remained in jurisdictional limbo; Caribbean islands were held as rump states; and Central American polities were infiltrated by American paramilitary organizations. These were all instances of state formation on the cheap.

In the territories, according to the ordinance, all land belonged to Congress until it was deeded, in parcels, back to the territories. During the first of three mandatory stages of jurisdictional evolution, settlers were governed by a federally appointed governor and three jurists. At this stage, the territories had *no* representation in Congress, the same body that held them under its jurisdiction. As described by historian Richard White, "The Federal government controlled the governments of the territories and withheld from their citizens rights and privileges held by American citizens elsewhere."[6]

It is hard to imagine a starker violation of the revolutionary ideal. The territories were literally being governed as American imperial dependencies, the exact form of political jurisdiction that Americans had revolted against just a decade earlier. Historian Jack Eblen notes, "The Ordinance [of 1787] cannot be viewed as innovative or progressive in any basic sense, even in the provision for statehood; on the contrary, its system of colonial [that is, territorial] government was decidedly more authoritarian than that of the British."[7]

Under the second stage of territorial government, settlers were allowed to elect a legislative assembly, but the congressionally appointed governor still maintained an outright veto over all legislative acts. Though each territory could send one elected representative to Congress, those representatives were denied congressional votes, thus severely limiting their influence in Washington. The territories were granted local courts and federal marshals to run them, but their jurisdiction was also severely limited. Before 1805, cases decided before the territorial courts were actually barred from appeal to the US Supreme Court. After 1805, only cases directly pertaining to federal jurisdiction were permitted before the highest court in the land. Eblen adds:

> The jurisdiction of territorial courts was never fully clarified because the constitutional status of the contiguous territories themselves was always ambiguous. The only certainty was that, because the territories were extensions of the national sovereignty and not sovereignties in themselves, suits could not be brought against them— that is, lacking full independence, a territory could not be a defendant.

"On the other hand," Eblen cautions, "even if someone had wanted to test a law during the district [second territorial] stage, there was little future in trying, because he would necessarily end up testing it before the men who had written it."[8]

The Public Lands and the (Haphazard) Growth of American Federal Government

Common wisdom among political scientists today suggests that the real growth of the American federal government occurred during and just after the Civil War, when a huge scheme to provide pensions for Civil War veterans was hijacked by Republican Party politicians looking to win electoral support through federal largesse.[9] However, pensions for war veterans were already a big-ticket item in the eighteenth century, when militiamen were offered free parcels of land as remuneration for service in the Seven Years' War and the Revolutionary War. The public lands were the postrevolutionary federal government's first serious source of revenue. The money from the sale of these lands was used to compensate veterans and to repay the national debt.[10]

The public lands were placed under the stewardship of the Treasury Department in 1789. (The modern-day Department of the Interior was not created until 1849.) Though the secretary of state was officially in charge of governance in the territories, Treasury was responsible for surveying the land, auctioning it for sale, and recording sales and transfers of title. The Land Law of 1796 also made the secretary of the Treasury responsible for advertising and recording all sales of public (that is, federal) lands. Millions of dollars passed through the hands of the Treasury Department in this way; it was the early federal government's golden goose.[11]

The Treasury's task was Herculean, given the enormous tracts of open land and the huge distances separating them from Washington. Oliver Wolcott, secretary of the Treasury after Alexander Hamilton, was a career bureaucrat, one of the first ever in American service, and he took his job quite seriously. Though Wolcott and his successors devised numerous ways to supervise and streamline the land grant enterprise, they never quite mastered it. Meanwhile, Congress relied heavily on the revenues from public land sales. Treasury kept the wheels turning while the wagon mostly went awry. Most of those involved with the public land system seemed to prefer it that way. A sloppy, chaotic system created ample space for buyers, sellers, and administrators to feed at the public trough.[12]

Though the Treasury Department experimented with a number of different organizational innovations designed to rationalize the land auction business, one chief obstacle they faced was the insistence of Republicans that the federal government remain as small as possible. As secretary of the Treasury under several Republican presidents, Albert Gallatin "intended that the land business should be conducted in accordance with strict Republican principles of administration—that is to say, with a minimum of staff and the smallest expense possible." Under the original scheme, land officers did not receive a regular salary but collected fees for services rendered. Though this system was quickly abandoned, salaries for all but surveyors were still kept unusually low. This lack of administrative capacity, coupled with the legal tangles associated with disorderly land settlement patterns, made the job of the General Land Office virtually impossible.[13]

The American public land market heated up after the War of 1812, but most of the emblematic trends in American frontier settlement were in place well before the Louisiana Purchase of 1803. One such feature, made all the more prominent in comparative perspective, was frequent violence between American "pioneers" and native tribes. The eighteenth-century "middle ground" between whites and natives was threatened by the federalization of the West under the Northwest Ordinance of 1787 and shattered by the Louisiana Purchase. Violence between white settlers and Indian bands became exceedingly common. Fighting with local natives was so fierce in early Illinois, for example, that the pace of settlement lagged greatly until the 1830s.[14]

We should not overlook the fact that nothing like this occurred in Upper Canada. Canadian *Métis*, or mixed-blood natives, rebelled later in the century, but the early nineteenth-century Canadian frontier was generally free of white-on-native violence. Relations remained peaceful largely because of British policies designed to accommodate rather than antagonize indigenous peoples. Though there was occasional violence in the provinces, the provincial governments generally forestalled it by acting as intermediaries between land-seeking whites and landholding natives. The British also strategically used native intermediaries like Mohawk chief Joseph Brant to serve as brokers. While it would be unfair to say that Canada's aboriginal peoples were treated well or justly, it appears that everyone concerned was at least spared the perpetual open conflict that was such a lasting feature of the American experience.[15]

In the face of everyday violence with natives and regular legal battles with creditors, speculators, and tax collectors, American settlers nurtured a political culture that was lasting and distinct. Though the federal government fought diligently to discourage squatting—federal troops

were occasionally sent to evict squatter settlements, and an array of an-
tisquatter laws were passed—there already existed a long and historically unique tradition in America of so-called preemption rights, or legal
entitlement either to buy squat land or to receive payment for "improvements" (for example, buildings and clearings) upon eviction. Such
rights had no precedent in English land law. Nonetheless, illegal tenancy
became the norm throughout the American territories, a tradition that
had been passed down through the generations. The end result was an
emerging culture in which a deep sense of personal entitlement was
coupled with an abiding fear of government and enmity toward Native
Americans.[16]

Squatters sometimes banded together in peaceful ways to block the sale
of "their" land, but they just as often resorted to violence. In the Alabama-
Mississippi region, squatters participated in a vicious war with local Creek
Indians in 1813, an uprising in which Andrew Jackson first became famous as a military commander. Those same squatters later threatened to
wage war on veterans with legitimate land claims. As surveyor Thomas
Freeman noted in an 1815 missive, officials charged with auctioning these
lands should expect trouble from "intruders who threaten with assassina-
tion, any person who will dare to bid for the lands they, those Intruders,
occupy."[17]

Many squatters believed that the government owed them something
for settling the frontier, and any effort to evict them was perceived as a
violation of their God-given rights. According to Dick, squatters "argued
that their living on government land was a benefit to the nation in that,
by braving the dangers from the savage Indians, they set up a buffer that
protected the East; that by improving the land on which they settled,
they made the surrounding land more valuable; and that by taming the
wilderness, making homes, and utilizing the natural resources, they
made the nation richer." In 1816, John McLean, then a congressman
from Ohio, wrote Secretary of State James Monroe an impassioned plea
for squatters' rights:

> They have fought, and some of them have bled, in defense of their
> homes. Does policy require that the arm of the Government should be
> lifted against them? Shall they, with their Wives and Children, at an in-
> clement season of the year, by military force, be driven from their pos-
> sessions? This, to them will be more terrible, than the whoop of the re-
> morseless enemy, with which they have so lately been accustomed. In

the hour of attack, their bravery secured them from savage destruction. Shall their government, now, visit them with more certain ruin.[18]

At the same time, several related characteristics of the public land system promoted quick and possibly even efficient settlement patterns. For example, economic historians laud early American land companies for stimulating the land market by providing free advertising and easy credit. Because the system for registering and purchasing tracts was fairly malleable, businessmen could also buy and sell vast amounts of land with ease. The adoption of "freedom of incorporation" rules in western states facilitated the creation of much-needed banks and mortgage brokers in the region. However, collusion, bribery, and deception were also common. In the immediate postrevolutionary period, notes Rohrbough, "men appointed from the East to administer the public domain acquired the habit of investment in the public lands soon after crossing the mountains." For example, the secretary of the Northwest Territory, Winthrop Sargent, was a key partner in the Ohio Company, a private concern created to buy and then resell public land at a profit. "The territorial judges were likewise interested in land speculation," adds Rohrbough. "John Cleves Symmes was chief of a great land enterprise and a territorial judge. Rufus Putnam was the Ohio Company's representative, was nominated a territorial judge in 1790, and moved to the even more sensitive post of surveyor general in 1796. Judge George Turner, the third territorial judge, was also involved in land speculation." Most government surveyors were also speculators.[19]

Measures were later enacted to bar federal agents from buying and selling public land for personal gain, but there were countless ways they could still profit from the land trade. According to Everett Dick, land officers could and did use third parties as brokers in illegal deals. In Eau Claire, Wisconsin, in the 1860s and 1870s, for example, "moneyed interests" employed a mole in the local land office to track and purchase for them the choicest plots in the area. Some land officers also issued "personal mortgages" to buyers using the government's money. Because many purchases were intended to be made with government-issued "land scrip"—promissory notes issued to war veterans—land officers also participated in the vast secondary market for these notes. Land officers were indicted for embezzlement, graft, and assessment of illegal charges and fees.[20]

Moreover, there was little that honest land officers could do to stop corruption. According to Everett Dick, for example, In 1824:

> Robert Clark, the register at Monroe, Michigan, attempted to stop timber depredations on government land, but the people called him officious, charging that there was no law authorizing him to stop such trespassing. . . . Even when the land officers reported illegal auction proceedings to the Commissioner at Washington, as likely as not that worthy would not support them in the face of opposition from congressmen who wished to woo their constituents and win reelection.

"After the Civil War," Dick adds, "fraud was so general, so little deprecated on the frontier, and the officers so few in number that the Commissioner was like a man fighting a prairie fire with its brands flying ahead and setting many little fires. While an agent was prosecuting one violation, a score of new ones was occurring."[21]

Of long-term significance is the fact that the corruption of federal land law was also extended to areas such as mineral, water, timber, and drilling rights, where federal regulation was sorely needed in order to protect and secure just distribution of precious resources. Contemporary American antipathy toward such regulation and the federal government's lackluster commitment to natural resource preservation are indirect products of the system's earlier abuse. Notes Rohrbough:

> For the settler, the planter, the squatter, and the speculator alike, land always belonged to those who were there. These individuals accepted the hazards of competing against one another for profits from the public lands, but they did not accept the right of the government to be unreasonably stringent or exacting about the conditions or terms under which lands should be distributed. Untrammeled individualism and competition without interference from the government were the accepted standards on the frontier.[22]

A sense of unwitting optimism about the future was another feature of the new American frontier. Land booms quickly swept up everyone in their path. A dramatic rise in cotton prices, coupled with the defeat of local natives after the War of 1812, caused a speculative bubble of epic proportions in the Mississippi-Alabama area, where the largest and most notorious slave plantations of the New South were erected. There is little evidence that early nineteenth-century Americans saw this new, rapacious plantation economy as anything but normal.[23]

Though the overextension of credit in already overheated markets prompted the frontier economy to suffer several extreme declines, little was done to incorporate legal and/or financial devices that might prevent them in the future. Iowa, for example, experienced a classic boom-bust cycle in the 1850s, despite the fact that the farmers and creditors involved had every reason to know better. "It is amazing how completely our citizens were filled with the desire of sudden riches," noted one journalist in the *Charles City Intelligencer:*

> Credit was easily had—eastern citizens flooded the country—imaginary towns sprung up everywhere—lands were fictitiously high—usury was unscrupulously asked and willingly promised—farms were neglected—debts were left to run on unasked about, goods and groceries bought on credit, land alone selling for ready money at exorbitant rates. In short, every one [sic] was a professed speculator. . . . Then followed the wrecks of fortunes and the crash of business. It was natural—it could not have been otherwise.[24]

Following a dramatic downturn in the economy, settlers, entrepreneurs, and local politicians invariably joined together in calling for government assistance. They blamed Congress for lending them too much money, selling them too much land, and not keeping a close enough eye on the banking or public land businesses. This became another lasting feature of American political culture, particularly in the western states: a love-hate relationship with the federal government centered on a tug of war between states' rights and federal jurisdiction over public lands.

"Westerners were united in their demand that the federal government should donate to the states the land within their boundaries," writes historian Paul Gates. "This demand was never attained in full but it was achieved in part through a piece-meal system of securing special grants for education, canals, river improvements, and the drainage of swamp lands." The federal-state fiscal relationship was never routinized, but instead remained a random system of favors and one-off grants. At the same time, the nascent chaos of the West contributed greatly to the growth of federal government via its arbitrary but growing system of public surveys, land grants, and military occupations of native lands. "The [ever-expanding] American West, more than any other section of the United States, is a creation not so much of individual or local efforts, but of federal efforts," writes Richard White:

> Except during the Civil War, most nineteenth-century Americans had little direct experience with federal influence over their daily lives. Westerners were the great exception. Westerners usually regarded federal government much as they would regard a particularly scratchy wool shirt in winter. It was all that was keeping them warm, but it still irritated them. Westerners, unlike southerners, never actually tried to remove the source of irritation; they were content with complaining. . . . This federal supervision and maintenance of order was, of course, supposed to be temporary; the central state was supposed to wither, but instead it expanded.

Along with the pending federal war against Southern secession, this primed the pump for a vast expansion of federal power across the nation; but, notes White, "in the West, this process had begun earlier. This head start added momentum to the larger national trend of bureaucratization and made the impact of the federal government on the West in the twentieth century even greater than it had been in the nineteenth."[25]

According to historian James McPherson, "From 1815 to 1850 the population of the region west of the Appalachians grew nearly three times as fast as the original thirteen states." Malcolm Rohrbough adds, "Land was the nation's most sought-after commodity in the first half of the republic, and the effort of men to acquire it was one of the dominant forces of the period." Says McPherson, "During that era, a new state entered the Union on the average of every three years." The rapid addition of territories and states played directly into the sectional balance of power in Congress. By the time territories became states, the national parties tended to be firmly entrenched therein. Moreover, by the Civil War, so-called new states made up 50 percent of the nation's population and nearly half the seats in Congress. This dramatically altered the balance of federal-state power, particularly after 1828, when the "New South" elected its first president, Andrew Jackson.[26]

A Colony within a Corporation: The Canadian Frontier, by Contrast

While there were challenges and difficulties aplenty on the early nineteenth-century Canadian frontier, the general tenor of land politics was quite different there than in the United States: settlers in Western

Ontario remained extremely respectful of government, and the distribution of public lands remained firmly under the royal government's control.

The disbursement of public lands was probably too efficient for its own good in some respects; so many claims were granted that land prices stayed perpetually low, to the dissatisfaction of absentee landlords and tax collectors. Between 1826 and 1838, notes Gates, "The Crown disposed of forty times as much land by grant as by sale, exclusive of the sale to the Canada Company," a small, unsuccessful, and vastly unpopular private land concern. Holders of small claims had no problems finding adequate, raw but fertile plots in Ontario's ample woods. Squatting, violence, and litigation were all rare.

In contrast to the American system, whereby the public lands were governed, and thus disbursed, by the Treasury Department for maximum revenue, the public lands of Upper Canada were managed by the Colonial Office and assisted by a commissioner of Crown lands. Though corruption and mismanagement were endemic to both systems, the general notion prevailed in Canada that public lands were part of the public trust, a key part of the colonial project of Upper Canada, as opposed to a fungible resource available to the highest bidder. Whereas American settlers guides of the mid-nineteenth century include copious lists of legal representatives, Canadian guides like *The British-American Guide-Book for 1859* list Crown land agents and clear, unambiguous instructions for acquiring public land at inexpensive prices.[27]

Also unique to the British North American West is the degree to which two privately held corporations—the Hudson's Bay Company (HBC) and the North West Company (NWC)—held such firm jurisdiction over such huge expanses of land. These corporations exerted remarkable discipline over their officers and employees. Annual shipments of supplies and mail kept far-off posts connected to the firms' headquarters in London and Montreal. Legal infractions were largely settled within the firms. Jurisdiction itself was held in place by local "factories," company forts dedicated to trade with local natives. The factories were steadfast bureaucracies crafted for high-stakes trade in a deadly climate.[28]

An even more important dimension of the Canadian frontier at this time was the strict limits placed on westward migration. The fur trade relied on maintenance of friendly ties with native tribes who were willing to exchange furs for weapons, manufactured goods, and alcohol. It was therefore in the trade companies' interest to limit the presence of "white" settlers in their territory to all but those engaged in company business. The HBC's corporate charter literally gave it commercial jurisdiction over millions of miles of frontier, nearly one-twelfth of the earth's land surface at its greatest extent. The HBC assiduously protected this land from encroachment by would-be farmers and land speculators. Though the agents of the HBC were never quite as willing to intermingle with native peoples as their French counterparts, a lively "middle ground" emerged in the territories that comprised northern Ontario, northern Manitoba, the Northwest Territory, and later, after a successful merger with the rival North West Company, the Canadian Rockies west to the Pacific.[29]

It is easy to imagine the ramifications that HBC policy had on the development of western Canada. Due to a combination of tradition, tolerance, and commercial self-interest (on both sides), a large native-white mestizo population calling themselves *Métis* (French for "mixed") emerged as cultural intermediaries between whites and natives. Though there were other mixed-blood populations in the region—only those of French and aboriginal lineage were originally considered *Métis*, though the scope of the term has since expanded—the *Métis* were strongly allied with the NWC, for whom they hunted and prepared buffalo meat for convoys that ferried furs and merchandise back and forth from Montreal. In the process of "opening" the Canadian Midwest to settlement, the *Métis* gained a degree of political standing and territorial enfranchisement unmatched by their mixed blood counterparts in the United States. The *Métis* were, and continue to be, a vocal, recognized minority in Canada.[30]

The absence of officials representing the British royal government in western Canada is truly exceptional. The HBC was chartered in 1670, and by 1821, the company became the sole corporate possessor of an absolutely amazing expanse of resource-rich, settler-free land. Its jurisdiction was near total, which makes it even more remarkable that it *ceded* all that land back to the Dominion of Canada in 1870. Having benefited from centuries of corporate privilege, the HBC peaceably redeemed its land for cash and an assured presence in Canadian merchandising. There were no protracted lawsuits, lobbying campaigns, or legislative showdowns over the turnover. This mirrors exactly the way a privately held corporation was meant to function under royal English purview.

The Red River settlement marked a major challenge to corporate jurisdiction in the Canadian West. This settlement, near the present-day city of Winnipeg, was the work of Thomas Douglas, 5th Earl of Selkirk. Lord Selkirk was a major shareholder in the HBC, and he was also an enterprising philanthropist; earlier, he had paid groups of displaced Scots to emigrate to Prince Edward Island and Upper Canada. He wanted to do the same in "Rupert's Land," the jurisdiction held by the HBC around the shores of Hudson's Bay.

Selkirk sorely underestimated the obstacles in his path. This land was not government land; it was company property. Despite Selkirk's controlling interest in the HBC, company officers strongly opposed the Red River settlement; they viewed it as an unwelcome intrusion on trade lands. Selkirk ultimately sold the idea to the company only by promising to use the settlement to provide food and manpower for the HBC's vast inland empire.[31]

The NWC was also vehemently opposed to the settlement idea. Selkirk's colony not only gave the HBC a leg up in the race to control the western fur trade, but it encroached on the jurisdictional settlement reached between the rival companies through the Canadian Jurisdiction Act of 1803. This measure, initiated after a spate of violence between company employees, formally granted the Crown's representatives the power to appoint justices of the peace in the far western trading zones. It also informally allowed the companies to settle "minor" matters among themselves, thus protecting their legal autonomy in the region. Since the Selkirk colony would be governed according to British law, it represented the leading edge of legal rationalization in the West. Selkirk's colony thus "threatened to destroy the structure of legality which the Canadian Jurisdiction Act of 1803 had provided for the country of the West, and of which the North West Company had habitually made use to further the aim of eliminating its rival."[32]

Upon arrival, Selkirk's band of colonists received only begrudging help from their compatriots in the HBC trade outposts. "The [Hudson's Bay] Company had pledged support to the settlement," writes Jean Murray Cole, "but some of the most influential of the Company's officers . . . actively opposed the whole idea." After an arduous journey into the interior, Selkirk's band was also taunted by neighboring NWC representatives. Duncan Cameron, the NWC officer in charge of the area, hatched a plan to harass Selkirk's settlers so they would leave the territory. Again, his goal was not to seize the land as his own (as one might have expected in the American context) but to block any agricultural settlement and make life as difficult for the HBC as possible. As one of the partners in the NWC, Simon McGillivray, put it, "It will require some time, and I fear cause much expense to us all as well as to himself, before he [Selkirk] is driven to abandon the project, and yet he must be driven to abandon it, for his success would strike at the very existence of our trade."[33]

Remember that there was as yet no provincial or territorial government anywhere west of Upper Canada—the frontier was literally under corporate jurisdiction with only the frailest appendages of legal accountability or state-supervised rule of law.

A veritable siege ensued at the Selkirk colony. From 1814 to 1817, marauding bands of *Métis* and NWC employees regularly harassed members of the nascent Red River settlement, raiding homes and caches, slaughtering livestock, and threatening to murder any family that did not leave the colony immediately. When this did not work, the Northwesters also began offering free transportation and land to Red River colonists who were willing to decamp to Upper Canada. A mercenary army of local *Métis* was hired to intimidate Selkirk's settlers. The local station chief, the aforementioned Duncan Cameron, posed in uniform as a royal military officer and had settlers (illegally) arrested. Soon, Red River colonists started leaving in droves, tempted or intimidated into accepting the offer of better prospects in the East.

On June 14, 1815, Archibald McDonald, a man appointed by Lord Selkirk to personally steward the collapsing colony, wrote in his journal with palpable desperation: "The state of affairs this evening is miserable. . . . Our horses have been stolen and shot with arrows, our pigs worried by dogs, our cattle slaughtered, and part of our cultivated fields still without seed in the ground. The lives of the few families we have under our protection have been threatened . . . all this at the instigation of the N. W. [North West Company] proprietors."[34]

The following June, the conflict reached its climax: At a cluster of trees known as Seven Oaks, a band of *Métis*, commanded by officers of the NWC, attacked, killed, and mutilated the corpses of twenty men from the Red River Colony. The so-called Seven Oaks Massacre prompted Selkirk to organize retaliation against the NWC's Fort William, which led to a "series of law suits in Canadian and British courts, where each side charged the other with unlawful settlement." Selkirk himself was harassed in court back in England for debts incurred in relation to the colony, and he died a few years later, penniless and ensnared in the legal quagmire laid for him by representatives of the NWC. The Red River settlement slowly developed into the city of Winnipeg, the first and only major population center in the Canadian "Midwest" through independence, when the tiny province of Manitoba was created as Canada's lone jurisdiction between Ontario and British Columbia.[35]

The salient point here is not that the Canadian frontier was sometimes lawless and violent, but that the monopolistic British fur-trading corporations there were able, with the complicity of the Canadian colonial government, to resist even legitimate plans to plant agricultural settlements in the ample lands of the Canadian plains. No substantial "Euro-American" settlement occurred west of Upper Canada until the 1870s, with the exception of Vancouver Island and bits of the British Columbia coast.

Thus, settlement patterns were not only more orderly and constrained in Canada's "near west" (Ontario), but there was virtually no settlement beyond the trading posts in the Canadian "far west" (Rupert's Land and beyond). The United States, by contrast, spanned almost its entire portion of the continent by then. In the Canadian case, this gradualism appears to have benefited native aboriginals, *Métis,* and ultimately the white settlers who migrated there after confederation.

American Sectionalism and the Demise of States' Rights

Occasionally, events happen that dramatically reshape a nation's trajectory. Though a variety of factors fomented Southern secession, the outbreak of the Civil War remains a largely unforeseen fracture in the American national narrative. The Civil War split a nation that was otherwise growing quickly and coming into its own. The founding ideology of the nation was suddenly turned on its head—a nation founded firmly on the principle of state's rights was now waging a war to defend federal supremacy. Northern states had threatened secession on numerous occasions before, and New Englanders had largely sat out the War of 1812 in opposition to federal policy; nevertheless, secession from the Union was now deemed treasonous despite the founders' insistence on protecting states' rights and limiting federal power.[36]

This is not to say that President Lincoln was unwarranted in his actions—slavery was increasingly unsustainable on moral, economic and geopolitical grounds. The manner and means used in realigning the Republic were nonetheless unprecedented *and* illegal under American federal law. Though Andrew Jackson had initiated the rise of the "imperial presidency" and John Adams had encroached on First Amendment rights with the "Alien and Sedition acts of 1798," Lincoln's administration broke new ground in expanding and entrenching federal power vis-à-vis states and citizens. He suspended free speech rights and habeas corpus in early wartime Maryland, and his original requests for troops and military engagement were done without congressional authorization—all actions repeated by future presidents.[37]

Arguably, economic interests and jurisdictional competition were the real catalysts of the American Civil War. The cultural logic behind it was highly suspect, as many contemporaries noted. In justifying military maneuvers against the South, President Lincoln tacked and jibbed, pronouncing that he was for racial segregation but against slavery, for states' rights but against secession, seemingly contradicting himself at every turn. At one point, he even declared, "The Union is older than any of the States and, in fact, it created them as States." Lincoln's Southern rivals were no less guilty of sophistry. This was not a war over civil rights or personal freedom so much as one over state power and property rights.[38]

It is surprising, indeed, that the United States would come apart at a time when, economically and geographically, it had never been more interlinked. The first half of the nineteenth century brought unprecedented advances in American transportation infrastructure, as well as in commercial and industrial enterprise. Intersectional political parties, too, had successfully managed to broker meaningful alliances between Northern and Southern voters. The advent of the steamship and the railroad, coupled with a canal-building boom and a general interest in lending money for infrastructural development (itself primed by "freedom of incorporation" statutes that allowed for the easy creation of chartered banks and transportation and finance companies) dramatically lowered the cost of shipping goods from Southern plantations to coastal entrepôts such as New York, Boston, Baltimore, and New Orleans. The South remained a largely rural-agrarian society, however, while the North and Midwest had rapidly growing cities and booming factories. Of added importance is the fact that the South lagged behind the North in the erection of modern transportation networks that linked cities and towns with the rural hinterlands around them. Southern cotton and other agricultural products were primarily carried by northern and European railroads and shipping lines. These peculiarities of the Southern economy are both significant and difficult to explain.[39]

Recall, again, that the Southern land boom of the early nineteenth century created the preconditions for large-scale, slave-based plantation agriculture in the Deep South, a system that thrived as world cotton prices skyrocketed. Slavery itself, however, was not unique to the American South. Slaveholding was popular in the Northern states through the late eighteenth century—in fact, as late as 1770, there were more slaves in New York State than in Georgia—and slavery was still legal in the British and French Empires at this time, as well. Prior to emancipation, several features of American slaveholding were nonetheless distinctive: First, American plantations were often much smaller than their Caribbean counterparts. "Only about one-fourth of the South's heads of families in 1860 owned any slaves at all," notes Thomas, "and of these an estimated 60 percent owned no more than five." French and British plantations were usually quite large, leaving the white population vastly outnumbered, whereas whites were rarely a minority in the American South.[40]

In turn, a very high percentage of American slaves were born into bondage in the United States, as opposed to being captured and/or sold into bondage, as was often the case elsewhere. Combined, these factors made for a relatively docile slave population in the United States, which resembled a permanent underclass more or less integrated into the fabric of Southern society, as opposed to a transient population of violently oppressed workers whose individual lives were of little or no value to their owners. In other words, slavery was more enmeshed in Southern life than it was in other slaveholding societies. Most slaves had been born in the South, born into slavery, and were considered functioning members of white homesteads.[41]

Even more important is the fact that in the United States, slaves were generally denied the right to buy their own freedom. In world historical terms, the absence of manumission makes American slaveholding quite unique. Besides eliminating any opportunity that slaves might have had to work their way out of bondage, it also meant that there was no viable way for American slaveholders to realize equity in their slaves other than by selling them to other slaveholders. Following the end of legal slave importation to the United States in 1807, slaves themselves became a valuable commodity in the Southern economy, thus turning "slaving" itself into an industry. Manumission would have allowed slaveholders to gradually turn their investments into cash, as occurred elsewhere. Absent manumission, some three billion dollars worth of slave equity was trapped within the Southern American economy, equity that slaveholders were understandably loath to forfeit.[42]

One can therefore comprehend, in the abstract, why Southern slaveholders were so willing to fight to the death to protect their property. Property rights had long been a paramount ideal of American legal culture. Several landmark Supreme Court decisions, beginning with *Prigg v. Pennsylvania* (1842), justified not only the legality of slaveholding but the obligation of officials in "free" states to support the institution of slavery by helping to return escaped slaves to their rightful owners. By extension, *Prigg* and the subsequent *Dred Scott* decision (1857) implied that no state could truly ban slavery, since slaveholders had the unconditional right to travel to and presumably reside in free states *with their slaves*. All state and federal officials were legally required to help slaveholders retain their property—escaped slaves. By extending the jurisdiction of slaveholding societies into that of nonslaveholding societies, the courts thus fomented a nearly irreconcilable conflict.[43]

During the 1840s and 1850s, escaped slaves became increasingly successful at gaining safe passage to the North. Though the federal courts backed Southerners in their quest to retrieve escaped slaves, such jurisdiction was not transferable to Canada, whose black population grew rapidly. "Most of the communities along the border served, at one time or another, as terminals for the underground railroad. Fugitive slaves crossed the border from Detroit, Cleveland, and Buffalo, from upper New York and Vermont. They crossed the Great Lakes in open boats to land at the tiny ports of Canada West or trekked north into the Maritime Provinces." Though accurate figures are hard to come by, it is estimated that there were about sixty thousand "Negroes" throughout Canada by the start of the Civil War, twenty thousand of which had arrived in the decade after the passage of the fugitive slave law. The prototype for the eponymous character in *Uncle Tom's Cabin*, Reverend Josiah Henson was himself a former slave who had escaped to Canada in 1830.[44]

At the same time, a dearth of federal marshals and stubborn local juries made enforcement of the fugitive slave law extremely difficult.

Southerners opted instead to spend large sums of money on civilian slave patrols that were organized to catch runaways. This was consistent with one of the longer-term trends in Southern legal culture, "development of rule by men instead of law and institutions." As Confederate historian Emory Thomas says, "Paradoxically, while Southerners depended on legal absolutes in Congress to preserve slavery, law on slave plantations was essentially what planters said it was."[45]

Ironically, however, secession only promised to make things worse for Southern slaveholders. To get beyond the reach of fugitive slave law, runaways would only have to travel north of the Mason-Dixon Line, rather than go all the way to Canada (assuming Congress would have revoked the law following Southern secession). The secessionists were seemingly undeterred by this not-so-subtle point of law. By the 1850s, abolitionist violence and an increasingly vocal, well-distributed abolitionist news media stoked the Southerners' sense of degradation and fear.

The progression from tacit to rabid support for slaveholders' rights was gradual and reactive in much of the South. Writes Thomas:

> During the middle third of the nineteenth century, Southerners began to close their minds to alternatives to their "way of life"; they celebrated and sanctified the status quo and prepared to defend and extend it against threats real or imagined. . . . Questions about the Southern way of life became moral questions, and compromises of the Southern life style became concessions of virtue and righteousness. . . . The cause was Janus-faced: it stood *for* a distinctive Southern life style and *against* the Yankee alternative. Indeed, it is often difficult to determine for any given time whether love of things Southern or hatred of things Northern was the dominant motive force. . . . In this process, interests and institutions became ideals and goals."[46]

The publication of *Uncle Tom's Cabin* in 1852 substantially increased public pressure on the South. Here, indeed, a cultural artifact played a major role in the final march to war. In fact, upon meeting Harriet Beecher Stowe, Lincoln himself remarked, "So you're the little woman who wrote the book that made this great war." At the same time, the mutability of culture is again demonstrated in the fact that one of the book's greatest legacies—the term "Uncle Tom"—bears none of the pejorative connotations in the original text that it has today. "Dramatized versions of *Uncle Tom's Cabin* quickly reached the stage," writes James

McPherson. "At first these plays expressed the novel's themes and augmented its antislavery message. As time went on, however, 'Tom Shows' lost much of their antislavery content and became minstrel-show parodies." Regardless, domestic and foreign opposition to slavery mounted rapidly in the 1850s, giving even nonslaveholding Southerners a reason to dig in their heels.[47]

Another key factor fomenting civil war was the Republican Party's proposal to dramatically increase tariffs on imported goods, a tax hike that would disproportionately hurt the South and its export-oriented agricultural economy. Tariffs had long been an issue of dispute between the industrial North and the agrarian South, but further economic specialization had dramatically upped the stakes for both sides. Higher tariffs on imported goods, such as those proposed in the Republican Party platform of 1860 (and subsequently in the Morrill Tariff of 1861) threatened to increase the cost of living for all Southerners.[48]

In addition, the western frontier continued to provide a locus for conflict over slavery, states' rights, and federal jurisdiction. The legality of slaveholding in the territories, and the subsequent admission of those territories as states, provided a running battleground between abolitionists and slavers. Here, the preexisting liabilities of American territorial government exacerbated tensions over slavery. In Kansas, for example, the institutional weakness of the territorial government led several territorial governors to quit in frustration over the lack of resources and manpower necessary to prevent sectional violence. Governor John Geary kept law and order briefly—his prior post had been mayor of San Francisco, a notably "lawless" town—but even he soon became exasperated and resigned. There was insufficient police power in Kansas to quell sectarian violence. Jurisdictional ambiguity also added a dimension of complexity to the conflict. At one point, beginning in 1856, Kansas was simultaneously governed by two different territorial governments: one in Lecompton, run by a proslavery legislature (elected by sham polls), and another in Topeka that represented the majority, antislavery settler population. Neither government recognized the legitimacy of the other. Though both sides were notoriously well armed, the fact that the Pierce administration was unable, or simply unwilling, to keep the peace takes us further toward explaining the prevalence of violence in "bloody Kansas."[49]

Moreover, tensions over the tenor of western settlement were exacerbated by numerous civilian attempts to annex Spanish land in the Caribbean and Central America, especially after the successful Mexican-American War. These so-called filibusters—the word stems from the Spanish *filibustero* for buccaneer and the old Dutch *vrijbuite* for "freebooter," or pirate—were unsanctioned raids on foreign territory, most often Spanish-American lands, though several filibusters targeted Canada as well. (Around the same time, the term was employed to describe a legislative delaying tactic occasionally used in Congress.) The presumed goal of these filibuster invasions was to add would-be slave states to federal jurisdiction. The federal government never authorized any such raids, but federal efforts to prevent filibusters were often halfhearted. Filibusters and other paramilitary schemes were a convenient, covert means for Washington to conduct geopolitical strategy. This has been a hallmark of American diplomacy ever since. Such extragovernmental military actions fit nicely with the emerging American belief in "manifest destiny"—Americans' God-given right to take control of all of North America by any means necessary.

Federal troops were sent to intercept illegal filibustering parties in a few select cases, but their actions were limited by questions of jurisdiction: Technically, federal armed forces had no mandate to act against American civilians—British soldiers had faced similar fears in policing colonial rebels in the Revolutionary era. Though the Neutrality Act of 1818 formally prohibited unsanctioned military action against foreign jurisdictions, American military personnel remained fearful that they would be deemed liable for their actions. "Federal officials not only had to infiltrate covert operations," notes Robert May, "but also had to counter the filibusters' pretense of remaining in technical compliance with the law." In the great American tradition of upholding the letter of the law while violating its spirit, "filibustering leaders studied the Neutrality Law looking for potential loopholes, and often found them. William Walker," perhaps America's most notorious filibuster, "boasted to one confidant, 'I know the Act of 1818 pretty thoroughly and do not intend to violate its provisions.'" According to May, "Federal intervention, as a result, faltered in a morass of legal, jurisdictional, and procedural restrictions governing the circumstances under which arrests could be made." Walker's repeated raids on Nicaragua, coupled with efforts by others to conquer Cuba, tendered a lasting hostility toward the United States in Latin America.[50]

Another important institutional legacy of the Civil War is the founders' belief that civilian militias—as opposed to a standing, professional army—provided the safest, best means of national defense. At the onset of hostilities in early 1861, US federal forces were marginal at best. Several Southern states might have sat out the war altogether if not for Lincoln's original need to call up the state militias—this order forced several state legislatures, particularly those in "neutral" Upper South states, to get off the fence and either comply with Lincoln's order or openly defy it. For example, Virginia clearly would have preferred to avoid war, but its legislature ultimately decided it could not justify sending its state militia into war against fellow Southerners. Lincoln forced their hand. At the outset of the Civil War, the federal army was only sixteen-thousand-men strong, and though Lincoln was eventually able to muster hundreds of thousands of militiamen and recruits for war, training and commanding those troops proved difficult indeed. Had there been a stronger, better trained, and better deployed federal army in place in 1861, South Carolina might never have led the South into war in the first place. The prevalence of civilian militias also helps explain why the South had prepared ample munitions and manpower. Despite having only 10 percent of the white population of the United States and 5 percent of its industrial capacity, the Confederacy successfully fought federal forces to a standstill before finally succumbing.[51]

These last observations illustrate yet again the ephemeral nature of political culture: Much of the South, particularly the "Upper South," was ambivalent about the long-term sustainability of American slavery and thus willing to compromise with abolitionists on the issue. Similarly, if Lincoln had decided to ask Congress for permission to muster against secession, as he was required to do by law, his request might well have been denied, thus forcing a peaceful resolution upon both sides. Public opinion in the North varied widely up to and during the war—many Northern abolitionists believed that emancipated slaves would never be fitting members of American society and therefore originally proposed shipping them to Africa. Draft riots occurred in the North during the war, and antiabolition riots took place in several cities prior to the war. Reading the history of what led up to the war itself, one is struck by the sophistry of opinion leaders on both sides of the issue.

Slavery itself, notes historian Eric Foner, "could not have existed without a host of legal and coercive measures designed to define the status of the black laborer and prevent the emergence of competing modes of social organization." In Canada, for example, "By the beginning of the nineteenth century, practically all Negroes in the provinces had been freed because their owners could not depend on the courts to recognize such property rights." The British Parliament formally freed all slaves in its colonies in 1833, but slavery was already defunct in Canada by then. Without jurisdictional support for slavery, in other words, slavery itself would likely have disappeared of its own accord, cultural preferences notwithstanding. Slavery would gradually have bankrupted itself, though the social costs of collective emancipation might still have been crippling. Economic historians have debated endlessly the economic "efficiency" of early nineteenth-century American plantation agriculture, but there is little doubt that new technology eventually would have swept away large-scale slavery. Instead, jurisdictional conflict hardened collective identities and solidified white Southern resistance to racial and sectional integration.[52]

The American South exited the war a remnant of its former self. Already lagging the Northern economy before the war, the devastated South was left in shambles. Moreover, many Southern whites continued to harbor the notion that they had never really lost the war, a sentiment that was exacerbated by subsequent federal efforts to force racial integration and legal reform on the South. "Reconstruction" was short-lived, and it left in its wake a groundswell of resentment, race pride, and messianic religiosity intent on reviving the fortunes of the "Old South."[53]

One noteworthy outcome of the Civil War was the reinstitutionalization of American gun culture. Following the war, ethnic and trade-based volunteer militias were extremely popular. In the South, posses and lynch mobs remained common and were usually overlooked, if not tacitly sponsored, by the authorities. Factory and mine owners also exploited the Second Amendment to justify hiring private armies like the infamous Pinkerton guards to police their facilities and put down strikes. The legality of such actions was adjudicated unevenly; courts could (and did) limit the ability of labor unions and leftist political organizations to create militias comparable to those deployed by capitalists and racists. In all of the above cases, the state actively ceded its monopoly over the legitimate means of violence, a jurisdictional elision with serious consequences for American civic and political development. The American labor movement, to name but one example, might have evolved in a much different direction if not for the private armies afforded its bosses.[54]

Despite the poor performance of militiamen in the Civil War, the United States once again shrunk its standing army after the war. In order to bolster the nation's civilian military aptitude, a group of former Union army officers formed the National Rifle Association (NRA) in 1871. The group had strong backing from the start. *New York Sun* publisher William Conant Church helped pay for it, and New York State governor John T. Hoffman was a vocal supporter. Their first project was construction of a large, high-tech shooting range at Creedmore, Long Island. Training Americans to shoot was seen as a key to national defense, and the NRA received ample government support. Most of its officers were retired military men, and the majority of its members for the remainder of the nineteenth century were National Guardsmen. By 1878, the NRA's Board of Directors included representatives from all the major institutions of the federal army. American jurisdictional law—stemming from the Second Amendment, as well as basic states' rights doctrine— guaranteed citizens the right to arm themselves, but in this instance, the US government was actually *encouraging* it. The NRA never acted in a military capacity, but government support for paramilitary organizations have a long history in American military policy. Government subsidies for private paramilitary organizations are legal still, and they are not likely to stop anytime soon, as seen by the use of private mercenary armies in modern-day American military campaigns.[55]

The key point here is not that Americans of the post–Civil War era were suddenly well armed, which they were, but that they retained and *expanded* legal protection for gun owners vis-à-vis the state. Canadians are actually quite fond of guns, but gun ownership is limited to weapons for hunting and sport. Moreover, Canada historically has no comparable tradition of independent militias and paramilitary organizations. An active belief that citizens have the right to form private armies seems uniquely American, at least to the extent that such behavior is encouraged by government.

Last Gasp: The Idea of Continental Union

The American Civil War was also an epochal event for Canadians, though it is not currently a part of their collective memory per se. Americans and their armies represented a genuine threat to Canada at the time. "Manifest Destiny" justified American continental expansion, and the military strength of the United States was unparalleled in the hemisphere, as demonstrated in earlier aggression against its southern neighbor, Mexico. Great Britain, Canada's colonial overseer, had the ability but not the desire to fight the United States over the fate of Northern North America. Britain needed American wheat. It had military worries of its own in Europe and Asia, and it had already broken most of its paternalistic bonds with Canada—plans were long in the works for the political emancipation of British North America. What British officials did *not* want, however, was to cede land to the United States, a military rival in its own right. In the 1840s, Britain and the United States had nearly come to blows over disputed territory in the Pacific Northwest—thus the slogan, "Fifty-Four Forty or Fight!"—and maintaining Canadian autonomy was an important priority. What Britain did in response was to try and bolster Canadian nationalism, thus forestalling the possibility that its citizens might willingly seek union with the United States.

Strategically speaking, Ontario was Canada's most vulnerable point. The Great Lakes provided many potential places for an American invasion. British military planners knew they would have to relinquish Ontario immediately in the event of continental war. So, they pulled their forces back to Quebec and waited, sensing that the Americans would also wait, thinking that there was enough pro-American sentiment in Canada to bring it into the Union without force. "That Canada West could be had by conquest was evident, and perhaps as long as this were so the Americans would be content to wait for the Canadas to join the Union willingly," says historian Robin Winks. Nonetheless, the threat of Britain coming to Canada's defense also helped keep American generals at bay. Both sides knew that another Anglo-American war would be costly.[56]

Britain's strategy was actually quite brilliant. It simultaneously brokered a lasting truce with the United States and preserved Canadian national autonomy. By the late nineteenth century, something akin to geopolitical symbiosis was achieved: Canada remained intact, with America as an abiding military ally. This suited the United States, because Canada now served as a military buffer against possible invasion from the North, an ally against possible invasion of the Southern United States or either coast, *and* a key partner in trade. In turn, Canada could rely on America to provide most of its national defense—the United States would never tolerate an invasion of Canada by anyone but itself.

Canada thus saved public revenue, and the United States earned a trust-worthy, pliable neighbor. The two are now the world's most active trade partners. Coexistence is well entrenched; it is a very successful peace.

In the fall of 1861, however, tensions between the United States and Canada temporarily boiled over. Given a long history of jurisdictional tension on the high seas—the War of 1812, for example, was prompted by American ire over British ship searching—another conflict was likely.

The so-called Trent Affair was started when an American naval officer stopped the British mail steamer, *Trent,* and removed two Confederate envoys, arguing that they were being carried illegally. Conservative Canadian newspapers like the *Toronto Leader* and the *Fredericton Head Quarters* incited Canadians to arms. The *Christian Watchman* of Saint John, New Brunswick, editorialized: "A war now would forever deliver us from all fear of our dangerous neighbour, and elevate us to a position of importance and influence."[57]

The Lincoln administration backed off and released the two Confederate envoys soon thereafter, wisely choosing to fight "one war at a time." A long legacy of economic exchange helped mitigate the geopolitical currents pushing the United States, Canada, and Great Britain toward war. In the 1840s, Great Britain had formally renounced protectionism as the basis of its overseas trade policy. The British negotiated a free trade agreement with the United States that opened American markets to Canadian timber and agricultural products in exchange for allowing American vessels into Canadian fisheries. Manufactured goods, however, were exempted from the Reciprocity Act (1854), part of a long history of variegated trade between the United States and Canada. Nonetheless, the United States had begun accepting Canada as a distinct, friendly twin. The American and Canadian economies were by then so well integrated that, for example, Pennsylvania *exported* coal to Ontario (Canada West) while New England *imported* coal from Nova Scotia. Population centers along the US/Canadian border also fostered close cultural and demographic ties. The United States dropped the Reciprocity Act soon after the Civil War, but the border remained more or less "open" to population transfer and bilateral trade.[58]

Nonetheless, Britain remained fearful that Canada would willingly become part of the United States. In turn, its ministers correctly deduced that Canadian nationalism (and thus anti-Americanism) could be stoked in the provinces by granting Canadians self-government under a constitutional monarchy. Britain offered the "Dominion of Canada" sovereignty in 1867. Nationalism would protect her from the United States better than the British military, Whitehall concluded.[59]

Prior to this, during the American Civil War, Canadians fully expected an American invasion, if not outright war between Britain and the United States. Extra troops were sent from England, and fortifications were built in strategic points along the US-Canadian border. By the spring of 1862, Great Britain had eighteen thousand troops stationed in Canada, largely in Quebec, where invasion from New York, Vermont, or Maine was possible. Ontario, considered largely indefensible, was left open to American invasion.[60]

Interestingly, Canadians themselves showed little inclination for self-defense, at least with respect to probable American conquest. Robin Winks reports that in March 1862, "The British House of Commons passed a resolution to the effect that colonies 'exercising the rights of self-government ought to undertake the main responsibility of providing for their own internal order and security.' But Canadians were to continue to show that they considered defense to be largely the duty of the mother country and not their own." Ontario's largely pro-American population might have even welcomed an invading American army.[61]

In the Canadian West, meanwhile, the Red River Colony faced a jurisdictional crossroads of its own: Though this territory was still nominally part of British North America prior to Canadian independence, it had no representative government, nor was it even an official colonial "province." Instead, as you will recall, Selkirk's colony remained a jurisdictional island in western Canada surrounded by the HBC, an intrusion still resented by the company. Because a large percentage of the fifteen thousand settlers now inhabiting the Red River District either came from America or had traveled through it en route to western Canada, there was mounting sentiment there in favor of annexation to the United States, too. "Many Americans and Britishers felt that, except for the symbol of British authority in the British and Hudson's Bay Company's flags that flew over Fort Garry, they were a part of the United States," writes historian Robin Winks. Trade goods were generally shipped from the Red River to eastern Canada via American canals, rivers, and railroads. Though the Americans made no specific offers of sovereignty, most in the Red River settlement believed that annexation would bring them greater political autonomy than currently available under British rule.[62]

Even farther west, in the Puget Sound area, Americans, Anglo-Canadians, and Hudson's Bay Company employees lingered in an oft-disputed zone of jurisdictional uncertainty. Several treaties, and a few violent skirmishes, brought peace and order to the region, but many Canadians and British foreign officers still believed that the United States might soon look to annex this territory in full.[63]

Ultimately, about fifty thousand Canadians—including between thirty-five and forty thousand French Canadians—served in the Union army during the Civil War, though it is difficult to determine how many did so for economic as opposed to ideological reasons. (Immigration to the United States from Canada was common in this period, and immigrants could sometimes receive payment for taking the place of American draft dodgers.) Impressment "and other unprincipled activities of professional recruiting agents on both sides of the border" also brought Canadians into American military service despite the protests of the British ambassador in Washington.[64]

Meanwhile, wartime Canada came to resemble a sort of nineteenth-century Casablanca, serving as a neutral entrepôt for Union and Confederate purchasing agents, diplomats, and spies. According to Winks, "Southern emissaries on their way to Europe, dispatch-bearers returning from the continent's capitals, escaped Confederate soldiers, Northern observers, draft-dodgers, disgruntled Peace Democrats, and even the women spies necessary to all such cloak-and-dagger scenes met in urban centers of the provinces." A clandestine route connected Wilmington to Halifax via Bermuda and the Bahamas (both British jurisdictions). A vibrant cross-border smuggling trade thrived despite Union efforts to stop it.[65]

The exact nature of Canada's participation in the Civil War explains several features of its political development: First, it foreshadows Canada's contemporary obsession with the United States. Because the economies, societies, and polities of the two nations were integrated to such a large degree, the impact of war in one was bound to be felt in the other. This was partly a matter of timing, notes Winks: "The age of personal journalism was one of lively reading, and circulations were growing during the war years, partially due to the desire for war news. In 1861," he adds:

the major [Canadian] dailies averaged 42 columns of American news space and 6 columns of editorial opinion on American issues per week in an average of 228 columns of total newspaper space. . . . Although frequently in error, the news was at least as accurate as that which appeared in Northern newspapers and possibly more so, since the time required for transmission of it also permitted corrections on overhasty dispatches.

Canadians were, and still are, extremely well apprised of American affairs.[66]

A second telling feature of this period in Canadian history is the general population's reluctance to fight or even muster for active military duty. Whereas the British had expected American colonists to defend themselves against Indians and Frenchmen, they had exercised jurisdiction differently over the subsequently acquired Canadian territories. Professional British soldiers and sailors were generally charged with defending the Canadian colonies, and local militias knew that they could rely on them in the event of war. Britain, having mustered the bulk of men and munitions for the Revolutionary War and the War of 1812, was expected by most Canadians to continue to meet their military needs.

A third important point, perhaps the most important one for our purposes, abides in the jurisdictional backdrop to the war. In essence, Southern secession put the map of northern North America in flux. The United States suddenly found itself divided in two, with numerous outlying territories in limbo. Canada, moreover, lay on the brink between autonomy, continued British colonial rule, and American annexation. (Canada never seriously considered joining the Confederacy.) In addition, given the frequency of filibustering and guerrilla raids throughout North America, the borders separating the Union, the Confederacy, and British North America remained important for unusual reasons.

During the fall of 1864, a posse of young Kentuckians arrived in St. Albans, Vermont, from Canada. Their intention was to rob all of the town's banks and steal off with money for the Confederate army. Bennett Young, one of the robbers, stood in the town square on the day of the raid and brashly announced, "In the name of the Confederate States, I take possession of St. Albans!" The townspeople were notably suspicious. This was an (unusual) act of war, which was made, according to Young, in retaliation for General Sherman's "march to the sea."

American posses went after the Kentuckians, chasing Young and his companions into Canada, and thereby launching a jurisdictional endgame already well-known to both sides from earlier conflicts: the Confederate "raid" was deemed a provocation to the United States, but this did not justify American incursion into Canadian space, even if it appeared that Canadian law officers had allowed the robbers to escape. In other words, British jurisdiction had been violated by the United States and thus Britain had cause to start a "diplomatic incident" if it so wished. The Confederacy had found a legal excuse to try and coax Great Britain into the war.[67]

Britain's envoys demurred, saying the St. Albans raid was not sufficient provocation for war. British neutrality held, thus squelching the South's last best chance for survival. Nonetheless, the St. Albans raid did provoke the United States to try yet again to attain better control over its border with Canada. In 1864, it was decreed that all persons wishing to enter the United States from foreign territory would henceforth be required to show passports. "A passport system applied to the Canadian-American frontier could never be anything but a means for showing displeasure," notes Winks, "for it manifestly was ineffective." Knowing this, American officials nonetheless inaugurated what continues to be a florid tradition of jurisdictional "combat" regarding the joint US/Canadian border: Having removed military engagement as a strategic tool, the respective sides can "wage war" by limiting passage of people and goods across the border—or by simply threatening to. Even passage of the North American Free Trade Agreement (1993) has not ended US/Canadian disputes over tariffs and border crossing.[68]

The first half of the nineteenth century thus set many political precedents for the United States and Canada: contrasting patterns of continental expansion; different military traditions; and much different relationships between local and extralocal authority. The United States nearly tore itself apart over the issues of states' rights and personal freedom; Canada was not yet even a nation. The second half of the century saw them diverge even further.

7

Completing the Journey West

The story of Canadian independence, like many episodes in Canadian history, is both more varied and less dramatic than its American counterpart. Canadian independence took more than three decades from conception to execution; longer, if one considers the first gasps of mitigated autonomy granted in the Quebec Act of 1774. Though Canadians did wage violence from time to time in the name of independence, their decades-long quest for national autonomy was mostly peaceful and largely bureaucratic. If Americans won their freedom in the swamps of New Jersey, one might say that Canadians negotiated theirs over drinks, in a warm boardroom, somewhere very cold. The process took decades of political maneuvering, a noteworthy contrast to America's radical "break" with the Crown.

Truth be told, the British "let go" of Canada more than Canada "grasped" for freedom. There was no concerted Canadian movement for independence, though small numbers of Canadian "radicals" occasionally threatened to carry the provinces into confederation with the United States. Nor was Britain reluctant to see Canada become autonomous, provided it did not, in fact, join the United States. Canada carried with it several long-term burdens from the perspective of the Crown: trade protection, military protection, and bureaucratic administrative support were all owed the provinces at a minimum. There was little to be gained in return, as long as Britain could maintain a privileged position in Canada's import and export markets. Britain's military obligations to Canada would likely remain, with or without Canadian independence. And it was perceived that Britain's sustained imperial presence in Canada only increased its likelihood of being dragged into war against the United States. Canadian independence was thus primarily a bookkeeping question for the British government: Given inescapable obligations to the British North American provinces, where would Canada-related debt best be garnered—on England's books or on Canada's, under a new national government, perhaps in a new federal capital somewhere between Quebec and Ontario? Britain continued to contribute to Canada's coffers until at least the First World War, but it began relinquishing the reins of power in the middle of the nineteenth century, culminating in Canada's formal re-creation as an independent "dominion" in 1867.

Dragging the various jurisdictions of British North America into confederation took a curious blend of rhetorical artistry and legislative logrolling. One proto-Canadian province, Newfoundland, refused to join altogether. In the United States, the federal government waged transcontinental war against similarly recalcitrant states. If history is any indication, Canadians simply are not much for wars of "independence," though they (and especially Quebecers) talk a good game. In this, legendary sociologist Seymour Martin Lipset was correct: Canada is a land of "counter-revolution," or, more properly put, antirevolution, whereas America is a land of revolution (as are most modern nation-states—something Lipset failed to notice).

The prevailing ethos of Canadian political culture, then and now, seems to be something that might best be called "optimistic fatalism," or a forthright belief in the will of the people tempered by deep distrust in their baser political instincts. "To Canadians 'happiness' was too much to hope for from any government," says historian S. F. Wise.[1]

Wise adds:

> However much the fortunes of nineteenth-century [Canadian] radicalism have attracted the interest and sympathy of later historians, the Canadian radical tradition is so episodic in character that it may scarcely be said to have existed. . . . The real puzzle in the history of Canadians ideas about the United States is why the bulk of Canadians, standing on the very threshold of liberty, were so *little* susceptible to American institutions, a seeming contradiction of nature, environment, and proximity.[2]

Recall, again, that in the earlier nineteenth century, Ontario's population was largely American, as were many of its predominant religious and social institutions. This was especially true in southern Ontario, where Canada was growing the fastest. After the War of 1812, however, and especially by the 1840s and 1850s, Americans largely stopped emigrating to Ontario and Britons, particularly poor Scotch-Irish and Irish Catholics, began arriving in their stead. This helped "Anglicize" anglophone Canada and subtly changed the political temper of the province. Canadian religious and cultural institutions turned east, adopting English-style institutions instead of American. Canada's "dissenting" sects—primarily Methodists and Baptists—reunited with their British counterparts in the mid-nineteenth century, and this had the incumbent effect of tempering their theological goals and congregational styles relative to their American, especially Southern American, counterparts. Despite being vastly outnumbered by "barnstorming" American Baptists and Methodists, the Anglican Church maintained deep roots in Ontario society. A substantial portion of every royal land grant was "reserved" for the church's profit. Anglicans and Anglican sympathizers also held most of the prominent positions in the provincial government, which showed favoritism toward the Church of England and its affiliated social and educational pursuits.[3]

Note that there is no legal separation of church and state in Canada. In the mid-nineteenth century, Anglicans founded important new educational institutions in Ontario, including the University of Toronto (originally King's College) and Upper Canada College, a private secondary school modeled after Britain's elite "public" schools. The business, financial, legal, and scientific elite of Ontario also tended mostly to be Anglican or Presbyterian. Ethno-national "Loyalist" organizations like the Orangemen—anti-Catholic Ulster Irish who regularly organized parades and demonstrations in the name of "fraternal brotherhood"— also appeared and grew in Canada around this time.[4]

With the education, civic, and religious systems of Canada West (Ontario) firmly tethered to England rather than to the United States, and with the Catholic population of Canada East (Quebec) grasped tightly by the state-sponsored clergy, American notions of "rebellion" and "democracy" lost some of their allure. Many of Canada's new settlers were fleeing worse conditions in Europe—famine, epidemic disease, and economic turmoil—and they were only too happy to simply have a plot of land and enough food to support and raise a family, colonial "oppression" notwithstanding. It was a hard life but a good one, at least in the eyes of the thousands who immigrated to Canada from the British Isles between 1830 and 1850.[5]

Nonetheless, a well-known, potentially very successful Scottish rabble-rouser named William Lyon Mackenzie threatened the ruling "Family Compact" in Ontario with provincewide rebellion in 1837. Mackenzie had charisma, American backing, and a keen rhetorical sensibility. Trained as a newspaper reporter, editor, and printer, Mackenzie's pen was so feared that the authorities once dumped his printing press in a river to try and silence him. But only a few hundred rebels mustered with Mackenzie on the appointed day in 1837, and they were quickly routed by English troops and Loyalist militia. To many Canadians, it seems, Mackenzie's anti-English "rebellion" looked only like another excuse for American interference, if not outright invasion. This perception was supported by the actions of a small band of American filibusters, the Hunter Patriots, who fought British forces and Loyalist militia for nearly a week in a small town on the Canadian side of the St. Lawrence River. According to the lieutenant governor of Upper Canada at the time, Sir Francis Bond Head, "The people of Upper Canada preferred the freedom of monarchy to the tyranny of democracy." Though his account of Canadians' political sentiments is biased in the extreme, Head was successful in rallying the majority of the province around the Loyalist cause.[6]

Atlantic Canadians also showed little interest in rebellion. Shipbuilding was one of the more innovative—and profitable—new industries in the Maritimes throughout the nineteenth century. Maintaining ties to Britain was vital for the Maritime shipbuilding, shipping, and fishing industries, and the large British garrison at Halifax provided additional jobs and security in the region. The collapse of wooden shipbuilding and the nascent decline of the North Atlantic fisheries subsequently devastated the economy of Atlantic Canada, which is, a century and a half later, still one of the poorest regions of Canada.

French Canadians, however, were more ready to fight, and they, like Mackenzie's Ontario rebels, were also well versed in the ideology of American republicanism and rebellion. A radical bloc of French Canadians had been calling for electoral reform in Lower Canada for some time—a movement that was also supported by some British Canadians in Quebec. After decades of legislative debate and delay, a frustrated minority of so-called *Patriote* rebels took up arms against the Crown. Though the revolt was quickly put down, it immediately preceded, and helped foment the Mackenzie revolt in Upper Canada. For a brief moment, radicals throughout Canada saw an opportunity for change—again, not independence, but democratic reform under English auspices. Nonetheless, support for rebellion was never overwhelming. The revolts of 1837–1838 were easily defeated and never garnered much local support or momentum. They resulted in some democratic reforms in Canada, but also the decision to make a more concerted effort to assimilate French Canadians into the British-Canadian fold.[7]

Historians debate the nature of early nineteenth-century Quebecois nationalism at length, but most seem to agree that it was in the best interests of the peasantry, as well as the clergy and seigneurs, to sustain British rule in Quebec. Ethnic nationalism continued to stir and brew in the province, but it did not reach anything like its contemporary fervor until the First World War.[8]

Preliminary Steps to Canadian Confederation

In the decades leading up to confederation, the British authorities experimented with several alternative forms of colonial administration. In 1841, in order to streamline administration and diminish the French presence in Canadian politics, the English imperial government merged Ontario and Quebec into a single province, the United Canadas. In addition to being a last-ditch effort to assimilate French Canadians into British or at least anglophone society, the merger was a plain power grab. Canada East and Canada West were granted equal seats in the new provincial Parliament—even though Canada West's population was much smaller. (Later, when Canada West surpassed Canada East in population, Ontario politicians turned against the formula that had previously benefited them, hypocritically calling for "Rep. by Pop" after earlier opposing it.) As part of the merger of the Canadas, Ontario's elite "Family Compact" allied with Quebec's "Chateau Clique" in order to dominate Canadian politics. As noted by historian Ian Radforth: "The triumph of counter-revolution in the wake of the rebellions [1837–1838] had eliminated democratic and republican alternatives, while the rebellions themselves had alerted [Loyalist] conservatives to the need for administrative and other reforms that would strengthen their hold and permit various proposals and means for advancing reforms."[9]

Despite the new alliance of Ontario and Quebec elites, Canadian politics gradually became more democratic, changes that politicians referred to as "responsible government" in order to differentiate it from American-style republicanism. Under the harness of a series of unusually competent governor-generals, patronage and elitism were diminished in the United Canadas, as were factional tensions between French- and English-Canadian politicians. By the late 1840s, Canadian Parliament functioned more or less like English Parliament, with an executive council (the prime minister and his cabinet) nominated from the ranks of the dominant party in the legislative assembly (the House of Commons). Though voting rights were still fairly restricted in the United Canadas, the voice of those who could vote had tangible influence on the political affairs of the province. The executive also gained more power, and competitive political parties began to form in Canada for the first time.[10]

Nevertheless, this new merger-plan government did fail in one important respect: it continued to recognize many jurisdictional divisions between the former provinces of Upper and Lower Canada, thus perpetuating ethnic strife between French and English Canada. For example, from 1841 to the mid-1860s, the seat of provincial government rotated every four years between Toronto and Montreal. Two parallel civil services were carried over from the preunification era. Two prime ministers were also appointed, one from each half of the United Canadas. Political parties thus tended to focus on one or the other half of the population at the expense of the whole. Fiscal negotiations, political appointments, and judicial proceedings were still conducted as if Canada East and West were separate provinces.[11]

On the plus side, provincial governments under Lords Sydenham, Elgin, and Grey vastly improved their administrative capacity, efficiency, and competence. Lord Durham, author of the 1839 report that began a period of intense, English-led political reform, wisely noted that the overlapping jurisdictions of "colonial" and imperial governmental agencies created enumerable problems: "Unity of command" became Lord Sydenham's rallying cry, a well-timed pursuit that had the effect of putting more governmental power in the hands of Canadian bureaucrats, rather than in the control of party hacks. At the same time, Lord Durham's recommendations led in part to the quasi-unification of the Canadas in 1841. Durham favored subtle Anglicization of Canada's francophone population, and his not-so-subtle plans to undermine francophone rights have proven a lasting source of discontent in French Canada. Quebec had the first professional police force in North America (1837) and, though her courts and legal system were surprisingly well run, there was an element of ethnopolitical repression in them. As one "stipendiary" magistrate noted of Quebec in 1839: "I cannot however report that the tranquility which exists is the result of any alteration of the political opinions of the People [of Lower Canada]. . . . I attribute the present tranquility of the district to the presence of the Rural Police; to the fact that no illegal meeting can be held without their knowledge . . . and to the immediate assistance of a military force if required."[12]

Though colonial government was far from efficient prior to confederation, the fact that most of the Canada's population remained bottled up in the East lessened some of the burdens of provincial administration. Well-worn land and sea routes connected Ontario, Quebec, and the Maritimes, and there was as yet little government business in the West. The direct accountability of each province to the Crown via its respective lieutenant governor also facilitated administrative rationality and reform. Under the stewardship of Lord Sydenham in the 1840s, the Canadas made great strides in political economy and public administration in response to domestic growth and the challenges of Britain's new imperial-industrial, laissez-faire system.[13]

The fact that Canada was partitioned into fewer subnational jurisdictions (provinces and territories) than the United States meant that Canadian administrators could attain bureaucratic "economies of scale" that were not attainable south of the border. The power of the Canadian subnational government was further enhanced through the common law tradition of limiting the presence and power of municipal corporations, thus centralizing most functions of local government in the offices of the provincial authorities. In the United States, by contrast, state governments had both greater autonomy from federal government and less control over municipal governments in their midst, thus expanding and complicating the matrix of interlocking jurisdictions that required coordination and control.[14]

It is essential to note, however, that while Canada's preconfederation jurisdictional landscape promoted governance that was relatively "better" than the American system, the conditions under which the Canadian provinces were unified put noteworthy strains on the long-term viability of confederation. The United States was founded as a merger of equals, with controversial issues like suffrage and slavery left for the states to decide. Canadian confederation, in contrast, was a top-down process initiated by the royal government and opposed by many Canadians. The respective provincial legislatures had to be coerced into joining, often with outright bribes.

For example, the Maritime Provinces were extremely reluctant to join the confederation. Nova Scotia adamantly resisted until it was promised fiscal subsidies and infrastructural development. Prince Edward Island was brought in a few years later, in 1873, along with similar incentives. Notably, Newfoundland chose to stay *out* of confederation until 1949, and the decision was particularly controversial even then. Having failed to culturally "assimilate" French Canadians, greater Canada accommodated itself to Quebec's sometimes strident demands for provincial autonomy. Federal subsidies—including enormous grants for construction of a domestic transcontinental railroad—were crucial in getting all of the provinces to agree to confederation. Up to that point, most of Canada's trade goods were being carried to market via American ships and railroads.

Taking into consideration that one of the earliest actions of the US federal government was the nationalization of millions of acres of land formerly claimed by the states, Ottawa's generosity toward the provinces is worthy of note. It is also an important harbinger of Canada's pending jurisdictional makeup with respect to state-federal relations. Forged in a system of "compound monarchy," the federal and provincial governments maintained independent relationships with the Crown. "The Crown [thus] endowed the provinces with unlimited potential for action," notes David Smith, "a reservoir of power which, when exercised in the absence of a common national denominator, heightened the distinctive characteristics of each province evident since its founding." The American system would never be so formally mindful of states' rights.[15]

The Confederation Conundrum: Dominion's Early Years

Canada's first prime minister, John A. Macdonald, aspired to create the strongest possible central government for the new confederation. Having noted the conflict caused by America's system of states' rights, he saw centralization as the key to successful federalism. Unfortunately for Macdonald, there were many in Canada's provinces who disagreed, particularly supporters of the Liberal Party, which was strong in Canada's largest province, Ontario. Elected in 1867, one month after the creation of the dominion, Macdonald's Conservative Party government stayed in power until 1873, when they were ousted following allegations of waste, delay, and corruption in building the Canadian Pacific Railway, British Columbia's oft-promised link to the East. Ottawa's debts to the provinces threatened to hamstring the new federal government. British Columbia's legislative assembly voted several times for secession in its first decade as a Canadian province. Several other provinces also threatened to break their ties to the new confederation.[16]

Alexander MacKenzie, a penny-pinching Liberal, took the reins of power after Macdonald. Under MacKenzie, a domestic Supreme Court was established, thus bolstering the autonomy of Canada's justice system. MacKenzie's minister of justice, Edward Blake, also had the governor-general's "instructions" changed in order to limit Britain's power over Canadian domestic affairs. Canada was achieving a measured degree of jurisdictional autonomy from the Crown, one agency at a time. However, the Judicial Committee of the [English] Privy Council (JCPC) maintained veto power over Canadian public law; the Supreme Court of Canada still was not the nation's final court of appeal.[17]

Macdonald's Conservatives were reelected in 1878, and they remained in power until 1896. These were difficult years for Canada's ruling party despite their continued electoral support. Immigration from the British Isles waned in the later nineteenth century, supplemented by large outflows of native Canadians to the United States; both contributed to a decline in economic prosperity and proconfederation sentiment in Canada. The Canadian economy faltered despite intensive investments in railroads and protectionist legislation. The strength and flexibility of the American economy was simply too strong for Canadian competition, especially given the slow pace of growth in Canada's once-celebrated "Midwest." Moreover, throughout this period, the provinces continued to chafe against the mantle of federal power, causing it to slowly relinquish the centralized control so carefully crafted by Macdonald at confederation. A landmark Interprovincial Conference was held in Quebec City in 1887 to bring provincial premiers together to discuss plans for strengthening provincial autonomy.[18]

When Macdonald died, in 1891, the Conservatives lost their motive force. Until then, the provinces had only toyed with the principles of provincial rights and, in a few cases, outright secession. In 1896, a landmark election brought a new political coalition to the fore under the Quebec Liberal Wilfrid Laurier. Laurier, a loyal Catholic, made a strong and precedent-setting move when he opposed an act intended by Parliament to protect French-language schools in Manitoba, a province whose francophone population had dwindled in the years since its creation. Though Laurier was sympathetic to those who argued that the Manitoba Act of 1870 protected the linguistic rights of ethnic minorities in the new province, he was also a fervent supporter of provincial rights; in this case, such rights were being threatened by national "remedial" legislation overturning a provincial mandate regarding Manitoba's schools. Laurier argued that Manitoba had the right to close its French-language schools if it wished to do so.

Laurier's gambit proved to have a lasting effect on the balance of power in the confederation: Instead of alienating Canada's Catholics, Laurier was actively supported by a coalition of provincial rights supporters from Ontario and the West, accompanied by compromise-minded Québécois who liked the idea of a French Catholic leading Parliament, even if he represented the anticlerical, mostly English Liberal Party. "Laurier had taken his stand squarely on the well-established Liberal principle of provincial rights," writes J. M. S. Careless. "The Dominion should not interfere in education, a field which by the British North America Act (1867) belonged to the provinces. . . . He also made clear that, while a faithful Catholic, he was not ready to accept the Church's orders in political matters. On this stand he swept the election of 1896 for the Liberals."[19]

Laurier accepted a relatively weak role for Canada's executive branch, mainly keeping peace between French and English Canadians while leaving responsibility for policy making to Parliament, and especially the separate provincial governments. This remained a mainstay of Liberal electoral strategy for the next century. The nearly unshakeable majority governments of Prime Ministers William Lyon Mackenzie King and Pierre Trudeau were based on exactly this formula: appease French Canadians while vigorously opposing separatism; bolster Canadian nationalism; and stay out of the way of the provinces.

Constitutional limits on the power of Canadian federal government, coupled with perpetual tension between French and English Canada, also helped force the federal government to cede many important policy matters to the provinces. The Judicial Committee of the Privy Council (JCPC), Canada's court of last resort until 1949, repeatedly decided cases that favored provincial over federal government in jurisdictional questions. According to Simeon and Robinson, "The first step was the recognition that provincial governments were as sovereign as the federal government in their respective areas of exclusive jurisdiction. In *Hodge v. the Queen* (1883), the Privy Council endorsed the view that provincial governments were not subordinate to, but coordinate with, the Dominion." The JCPC preserved Ottawa's right to override provincial legislation in some cases, but the federal government was progressively less inclined to use this power over time. Simeon and Robinson note that by the 1880s and 1890s, "organized political support for a centralist vision [of Canadian government] simply did not exist."[20]

The centralist formula proposed by Macdonald for the new dominion had largely come undone by its third decade. Despite the Conservatives' best efforts to cultivate nationalist sentiment and centralized government, relatively minor articles in the British North America Act (1867) protecting provincial rights became the cornerstone of Canadian national politics. Each province supported the others in resisting federal incursion while generously sharing the proceeds of federal revenue. Though antifederal sentiment at times threatened to boil over into outright secessionism, the continued presence of powerful Québécois Liberals in Ottawa helped keep the dominion's largest "outlier" in line while preserving legal precedents valuable to the rest of the provinces. Perhaps the ultimate irony here is that Ontario, Canada's most populous province, remained largely complicit in this effort despite the fact that its taxpayers ended up footing the bill for the rest of the provinces. The same is now true in Alberta, contemporary Canada's richest province and also one of its most ardent supporters of provincial rights. This, one might argue, is the "catch-22" of Canadian federalism—in endorsing provincial separatism, Canada's richer provinces tacitly accept the burden of keeping poor-province voters happy through federal subsidies and income redistribution plans.

In the United States, by contrast, a larger number of subnational jurisdictions (fifty states), coupled with a lack of party discipline in Congress and an uneven tradition of state-federal administrative coordination, means that each state is left to fight for one-off federal disbursements on its own. What Americans call "pork barrel projects" are an ordinary function of federal party politics in Canada, the difference being the permanence of Canadian subsidies, as well as the rhetoric used to support them. For example, no governor in America would request federal outlays in the name of states rights, as do poor-province Canadian premiers (for example, Maritimers and Manitobans). Federal assistance to states under the American system is justified instead via the aligned specters of nationalism, patriotism, and the commonweal. Canadians have never been so comfortable with the rhetoric of nationalism, particularly when the subject is the delegation of government revenue and jurisdictional authority.

Jurisdictional Opportunism: The American West

In the context of the long nineteenth century, the ability of central governments to monitor and control affairs in faraway territories was limited at best. Nonetheless, conditions on the American and Canadian frontiers presented quite different challenges. Until 1870, western Canada was largely governed by the Hudson's Bay Company (HBC), a private corporation charted by the Crown in 1670. In the American territories, by contrast, there was far from a single governing authority, if any at all.

In the prairies along the Red River, for example, American traders competed with the HBC by smuggling alcohol and trade goods across the border and trading it for pelts, something the HBC was forbidden to do by its charter. Despite fervent efforts to prevent Canadian *Métis* from trading with these firms, the HBC lacked the resources to police all of their territory. Moreover, the *Métis* made the powerful argument, in a petition to the Queen, that they themselves had never consented to the HBC charter and were thus not subject to its proposed restrictions on their trading activities. Since the American trade system was virtually unregulated at this time, there was little the HBC could do but try to keep Americans out, a monumental task for which they frequently relied on government assistance.[21]

British troops were sent to defend the Red River settlement for a brief spell in the 1840s, in response to President Polk's aggressive attempts to regain contested northern territory for the United States. The costs of maintaining these troops ultimately proved too high for the Crown, however, and following their departure, the situation of the HBC rapidly deteriorated. "By 1856," writes historian Alvin Gluek Jr., "Simpson [head of HBC operations] regarded the Red River trading situation with unmitigated pessimism. He could see that his Company's *charter* was 'almost a nullity . . . set at nought by the Americans and their Half-breed allies.' "²²

The American presence on the Red River also stimulated the rapid growth of Minnesota. Founded as a US territory in 1849, Minnesota grew from 6,000 inhabitants in 1850 to more than 172,000 in 1860. Absent a single trade monopoly, independent companies competed for trade with local native bands. St. Paul, located at the juncture of the Mississippi, Minnesota, and St. Croix rivers, thrived as a shipping depot for American *and* Canadian goods entering and exiting the Red River area. This was a development of great concern to Canadians.²³

West of Minnesota, the Dakotas and Montana offered Americans further opportunities for profit and adventure. Though early explorers felt that the semiarid bottomland of the Dakotas would not be particularly amenable to American methods of farming, a few enterprising soldiers stationed there intuited its potential. Captain John Blair Smith Todd, an army officer stationed on the Missouri in the mid-1850s, epitomized the forces at work on the midwestern American frontier: Todd was Mary Todd Lincoln's cousin, a "presidential" relation he successfully used to influence the location of the Dakotas' capital near his lands on the Missouri River, as George Washington had done before him on the Potomac. Todd resigned his military post in 1856 and founded a private trade company with a St. Louis businessman, Daniel Marsh Frost. Todd and Frost not only secured licenses to trade with local natives but also began buying large blocks of land along the South Dakota-Nebraska border. According to historian Harold Lamar, "Both Frost and Todd spent the winter of 1858–59 in Washington as lobbyists for the creation of a new territory, which by common consent was already called Dakota." Lamar continues:

> By 1855, a new attitude toward the value of the Upper Missouri Plains region was developing, an attitude due not so much to the actual pressure of agricultural settlers or to the decline of the fur trade as to the pressure and the interest of the land speculators and the railroad expansionist. . . . The entire region lying within the Big Sioux, Red, and Missouri Rivers—an area as large as the state of Illinois—was left without any government. . . . With settlers pouring in and with a dozen township companies . . . anxious for territorial government to legalize their actions, some sort of territorial organization was imperative. The stakes were so large by 1859, an observer reported, that unclaimed land was already difficult to find along the Missouri.²⁴

In addition, knowing that federal money would follow the declaration of territorial government, Todd and many others sought patronage positions in the new territory's political ranks. Notes Lamar:

> There is evidence that the expectation of political office brought many of the earliest and most able settlers to Yankton [Todd and Frost's main land speculation site] and to other settlements on the Missouri River . . . Such evidence suggests that a large number of Dakota frontiersmen thought of the federal government not only as a paternalistic provider of land and governmental organization but also as a subsidizing agency which furnished needed development funds in the form of offices, Indian and army supply orders, and post and land office positions. In short, many frontiersmen joined the vanguard of settlement to profit from the "business of government," and for that reason they thought of economic security in political terms.

In the meantime, conditions at Yankton were so primitive that Dakota's first governor spent his first six months in office sharing a room with the attorney general in the town's lone hotel.[25]

A dynamic contrast should be evident between the nascent settlement of the American Upper Midwest and its neighboring Canadian territories. While commerce was a focal point of both frontiers, particularly through government-subsidized efforts to distribute land and appease local natives, the organization of such efforts was vastly different. In contrast to the top-down, government-sanctioned Canadian approach, Minnesota and the Dakotas were open to myriad small and virtually unregulated trading firms and land companies. Relations with natives were plagued by treachery, aggression, and illegal alcohol sales on the American side of the border, and competition for valid land claims became a question of timing, aggression, and legal sleight of hand. Federal support was viewed opportunistically in the American West, a handout for settlers rather than a regulating force for law and order.

Historian Everett Dick describes the jurisdictional explosion on the American plains frontier as "chain store" township building. Using America's now ubiquitous "freedom of incorporation" doctrine to organize and spread private land companies, the territories were settled fast and furiously, with an advance party of lawyers, speculators, politicians, and financiers leading the way. The Dakota Company, based in the new town of Sioux City, not only sought to procure and create townships on rivers throughout the state but also asked the Minnesota legislature to certify such claims and erect county borders on terms favorable to the company. Settlers viewed local government as a tool for long-term economic and political success, a system in which the spoils would go to those first able to create a government. This was the case for the settlers of Sioux Falls, who, in the fall of 1858, decided to form a territorial legislature without federal permission. Quips Lamar:

> On October 4, fifty of the citizens of Sioux Falls split into parties of three or four and traveled over the countryside near the settlement. Every few miles each party would halt, take a drink of whiskey, establish a voting precinct, and then proceed to vote several times themselves by putting the names of all their relatives or friends on the ballots. After a reasonable number of fictitious voters had cast their ballots, the party would travel to the next polling place and repeat the process.

Though the legality of Dakota's subsequent "squatter assembly" was never officially recognized, such efforts were not uncommon on the frontier. Hurly-burly economics and business-friendly local governments gave the US frontier a very different sort of economy than Canada's at the time.[26]

Every Man His Own Lawyer: Private Property and the American Dream

There is no better example of western American political and economic development than frontier California, once a sleepy Mexican hinterland transformed almost overnight into a bastion of legal aggression, political chicanery, and get-rich-quick optimism. Before the gold rush of 1849, few Anglos were attracted to California, most preferring the rich, well-watered farmlands of Washington and Oregon. The gold rush changed everything.

For a brief spell of years, California held the gravitational pulse of North American opportunity and promise. Thousands flooded California in 1849 from as near as Baja and as far as Europe, looking to "strike it rich" in the goldfields. The gold rush catapulted Northern California's economy past those of Washington State and Oregon.

Much has been written about the rugged conditions and hardy collectivism of California's early mining camps. Having just acquired California from the Spanish, the American government took several years to put a territorial government in place to oversee the thousands of prospectors arriving there daily. "Since Congress adjourned in 1848 without providing a territorial government for California (because of disputes over slavery in the newly acquired territories), there was no civil government until California's admission as a state in 1850," writes Andrew Morriss. Federal mining law was not adapted to America's new mining boom until 1866, a decade and a half after the original gold rush. The only legal authorities in California at the beginning of the gold rush were military outpost commanders "who so feared their troops' desertion to the mines that they rarely allowed soldiers outside the post walls," Notes Morris. Given the situation, miners themselves established rudimentary legal institutions governing land claims and frontier justice. Having come to California almost solely for the purpose of making money, property rights were their central concern. Informal rules that governed claims and titles, profits and theft were enacted through ad hoc meetings among miners with abutting claims. "The emergence of an explicit property-rights contract occurred not once but 500 times," writes John Umbeck. "And the length of time in which this took place was not centuries but days."[27]

The success of such collaborative mechanisms of American self-government has been the object of much interest to scholars, particularly those of libertarian sympathies who wish to find evidence of successful entrepreneurship and law and order on the American frontier *in the absence of* formal government. Late nineteenth-century historian Charles Howard Shinn went so far as to trace the origins of American mine camp meetings to medieval Germanic *folkmoots*, thus evoking the sturdy, independent, but always pragmatic character of western America's Anglo-Saxon roots.[28]

In truth, however, the origin of the miners' most important legal precepts were Spanish-American mineral rights laws brought to California by the first wave of prospectors, who arrived from Mexico and South America before Yankees and Europeans could make the three- to six-month voyage to California from the East Coast. Though each mining community in California met to enact its own informal mining codes, there was a surprising amount of uniformity among them; they had a common origin in Spanish civil law, specifically the Royal Spanish Code of 1783. One of the great ironies of Californian legal history is thus that the so-called Teutonic libertarianism of the early Anglo mining camps was actually based on the ham-fisted appropriation of Spanish land law, as brought there by early prospectors from Mexico, Central and South America. The existence of similarly self-governed—though arguably more orderly—mining communities in Canada is also often overlooked.[29]

Origins notwithstanding, California mining law was something distinctly new and different in the global common law community. Under English common law, an absentee landlord would be entitled to the usufruct of subsurface minerals found on his land, even if someone else (for example, a tenant) had invested the time and money to find and extract them. In California, by contrast, miners benefited from a new conception of mineral law that recognized the efforts of those who struck "pay dirt," even if it was on land they did not own or even have legal permission to mine. "Finders, keepers" would be an apt summary of this new version of mining law, especially in contrast to English precedent. Requirements for maintaining claim over said plots were also eased in order to permit prospectors to travel, quit, return, and work several plots simultaneously.

Because water was a key element of placer mining, water rights also became a key source of American legal innovation. Californians departed from the English "riparian rights" tradition whereby water rights were allocated to abutters according to the amount of shoreline they owned. Under the new "prior appropriation" doctrine, water rights were regarded as a commodity distinct from land. Access to water rights could thus be bought and sold irrespective of landownership. In cases where there was not enough water to go around, those holding the oldest claims were given priority. If said rights were sold, their new owner would maintain the chronological purity of the original claim.[30]

One major obstacle that confronted western miners, however, was the Hispanic *Californio* ranchers who already held claim to the land on which American fortunes were being made. In the eyes of new white settlers, the Sacramento Valley was theirs for the taking. Instead of trying to take ownership of these lands through violence, however, the Anglos used the courts to nullify existing claims to resource-rich lands; there was no time for fighting. Legal action was a much more efficient means of forcing Mexicans and Native Americans off the land.[31]

The first laws legitimizing eviction of "nonwhites" in California were passed as early as 1850, only two years after the opening of the goldfields. Several mining camps enacted their own provisions that barred foreigners that year, including the Jacksonville District's decision to prohibit persons "coming direct from a foreign country" to "locate or work any lot within the jurisdiction of this encampment." In April of that year, the new California state legislature adopted its own statute, entitled "An Act for the Better Regulation of the Mines, and the Government of Foreign Miners." It required all non-US citizens to obtain (expensive) licenses in order to work the mines. "The law," notes legal historian Raymond August, "was not vigorously or uniformly enforced, *except* against the Latin Americans and newly arriving Chinese." As August notes, "The knowledge and skills the Latin Americans brought to California's mines was the very cause of their expulsion, and the reason why they have not been recognized for their contributions to American mining law (and American law in general)."[32]

Vacating *existing* claims to the minefields was potentially a more difficult task, though the process was facilitated by Americans' long-standing familiarity with American land law and its malleability and convenience, particularly in defeating adversaries who were fluent in neither English nor American court procedures. Justice Stephen Field, of the California and later the US Supreme Court, was instrumental in institutionalizing these new standards of western American law. Field had extensive experience defeating Mexican land claims on behalf of Anglo prospectors and squatters. In *Hornsby v. United States* (77 U.S. 224, 1870), the Supreme Court bent the law to the idea that new, illegal claims could win out against those of *Californio* landlords. Morriss notes,

> It was the misfortune of the [Mexican] government to be saddled with inferior counsel in the crucial early years of the Mexican land litigation. The claimants' [that is, Americans'] lawyers also deserve credit for their clever strategy and skillful lawyering in maneuvering the courts to first consider [hearing challenges to] Mexican land claims in cases where the factual basis for the [existing] claim was relatively strong. Whatever or whoever receives the credit, the rules established in those early cases went on to provide cover for litigants like Hornsby, whose claim rested on extraordinarily weak evidence.[33]

As in colonial New England, the respective states—or rather their respective lawyers, entrepreneurs, and politicians—played fast and loose with land claims and property law. California became an active incubator for legal-cultural reform. According to Donald Meinig:

Fueled by the near absence of police and judicial authority, squatting became an endemic and often riotous problem, cursed by many persons, then and later, as "a universal abomination of the California of the 1850s." Under the special circumstances of California the clash between the two peoples and their contrasting systems was unavoidable and exceedingly difficult to mediate. The United States solution was to depend upon the courts and a special California Land Act of 1851 designed to ascertain the validity of land titles.

Most Mexicans lost their cases, and also their land. "Although some californio families persevered on at least a portion of their properties, and even enjoyed some degree of social prestige," continues Meinig, "the Hispanic society as a whole, captive within an alien social, political, legal, and linguistic imperium, was ever-more constrained, weakened, and impoverished, its lower levels reduced to peonage, vagabondage, or, in some notorious cases, banditry."[34]

The travails of territorial conquest in California dovetailed nicely with eastern legal doctrine, particularly in the thriving areas of property and corporate law. "Freedom of incorporation," New England's gift to America, was exported to California by lawyers, prospectors, and bureaucrat opportunists like Mark Twain—a Missourian who worked several claims in the West and later worked for his brother, a territorial civil servant. Twain writes of his subsequent adventures as a miner on the Comstock Lode in his usual peppery but truthful manner:

> Every one of these wildcat mines—not mines, but holes in the ground over imaginary mines—was incorporated and had handsomely engraved "stock" and the stock was salable, too. It was bought and sold with a feverish avidity in the boards every day. You could go up on the mountainside, scratch around and find a ledge (there was no lack of them), put up a "notice" with a grandiloquent name in it, start a shaft, get your stock printed, and with nothing whatever to prove that your mine was worth a straw, you could put your stock on the market and sell out for hundreds and even thousands of dollars. Every man owned "feet" in fifty different wildcat mines and considered his fortune made. Think of a city with not one solitary poor man in it!

Men like Twain—fortune-seekers in the American West—were helping to reinstitutionalize American property rights and make the most of "freedom of incorporation." At the same time, the federal government was selling millions of acres of public land throughout the West. One hand shook the other with fortune and ease.[35]

After the peak of the California gold rush, prospectors moved on to other sites in the Far West and brought with them the customs and decrees of the mining camps, thus transforming American (not just Californian) legal doctrine concerning mining law and mineral rights. Through a miracle of cultivated judicial "inattention," western states and territories largely managed to maintain autonomous jurisdiction over mineral law. Federal "noninterference" ended in 1866, but the subsequent regime only opened the door wider for corporations and private consortia. In 1872, Congress passed a now infamous law that not only granted private mining companies publicly owned lands at scandalously low prices but also largely exempted them from providing the government any compensation for the profits they extracted from it. California, and ultimately all of the Far West, was transformed by this unique cadre of amoral bureaucrats, politicians, prospectors, and their "take no prisoners" lawyers.[36]

California's legal innovations were quickly and easily diffused to other "new" states and territories. Talented lawyers like Justice Field and California railroad attorney (and later Supreme Court justice) William Stewart made millions advancing corporate land claims, railroad expansions, mineral rights, land companies, and ordinary corporate charters. Washington reciprocated by funneling vast amounts of money to West Coast law firms and Republican Party politicians.

There is a great deal to be learned from the exact circumstances under which western state constitutions were subsequently drafted. These constitutions drew liberally on existing state constitutions (New York State's was a common source) and erected the legal infrastructure around which local political-legal culture evolved. Nevada's roots are quite telling in this respect.

Nevada was then, and is now, a virtually unregulated economic opportunity zone for Californian and East Coast capitalists. William Stewart, then California's top railroad attorney, pushed for the initiation of Nevada statehood in order to end-run around anticorporate territorial justices. He then helped some of San Francisco's richest financiers procure vast mineral rights for small, under-the-radar mining companies that they knew could subsequently count on generous state subsidies, corporation-friendly politicians, and legal free reign. Nevada's so-called

Comstock Lode was granted to California corporations through legal sleight of hand, which caused a subsequent economic boom in late nineteenth-century San Francisco. Meanwhile, the scrappy miner camps of the post–forty-niner West were being transformed into bleak company towns. Bars, brothels, and hotels prospered. Corporations reigned, as did land and corporate lawyers. Mark Twain quipped about his time as aide to an assistant functionary in newfound Nevada, "The government of my country snubs honest simplicity but fondles artistic villainy, and I think I might have developed into a very capable pickpocket if I had remained in the public service a year or two." Nor were they missing ample opportunities for private profit. Noting the effects of freedom of incorporation, Twain adds, "The legislature sat sixty days and passed private toll road franchises all the time. When they adjourned it was estimated that every citizen owned about three franchises, and it was believed that unless Congress gave the territory another degree of longitude there would not be room enough to accommodate the toll roads. The ends of them were hanging over the boundary line everywhere like a fringe."[37]

Several parallel streams of legal-cultural and political-institutional development were thus hatched, nearly simultaneously, on the American frontier. Separate states largely copied extant models and innovated on the margins of statutory law, though sometimes not without major consequences. For example, extensive studies of antebellum Michigan, Indiana, and Illinois have shown that "frontiersmen borrowed a lot of English statute and common law. The frontiersmen copied old legal and institutional forms. But as would be expected, they modified these forms as time went on," notes legal historian Gordon Bakken.[38]

On those same margins, state legislatures sometimes achieved great feats of legal prescience, legalizing female suffrage, for example, and reforming marital property law. These surprisingly progressive legal innovations occurred in the West in part because it was in the interests of these new states to promote an attractive legal environment for westbound females. The early American West suffered a severe shortage of "available" women, native women having been deemed by most Americans as ineligible partners. (Interestingly, in Canada, by contrast, white prospectors routinely took native "wives" and used the ensuing family ties to forge demographic and (some degree of) cultural integration between the races.) American men in the West were socially distant from native women, and new American cities like San Francisco and Carson

City offered well-paying jobs for women who were willing to work in bars, do housework, entertain, or practice prostitution. Legal reform of marital property and suffrage laws helped induce more women to go west. Simple statutory and common law revisions that favored women's equality and legal and economic empowerment were thus born in the American West. The Eastern states only slowly followed suit.[39]

Elsewhere in the West, the political trajectory from native land to territory to state followed a pattern something like California's: For example, in Nevada's early years, major deposits of silver were uncovered in one major vein that, until about 1861, had been considered multiple veins owned by numerous prospectors. Lawyers soon got wind of the stakes and began cutting one another to pieces over the takings.[40]

According to an account by Gilman Ostrander:

> For the next three years there was an unceasing frenzy of litigation. The overlapping claims would of themselves have been sufficient to support a happy crowd of lawyers—there were 215 resident lawyers in Virginia City in 1863, in a year when the city's population dropped to less than ten thousand. . . . Once the territorial judges were installed [in 1861], all of the major mines were entangled constantly in suits, most of them brought to court on the flimsiest of pretexts simply for blackmailing purposes. Down to 1867, the first district court, in which the Comstock was located, handled 245 suits involving the dozen richest companies. The Ophir, as the first of the bonanza mines, received the brunt of the litigation with 37 cases. . . . The suit cost the defendants thousands of dollars before it was dismissed. Dozens of other companies were similarly formed on terms of the most specious legality, and they frequently received settlements out of court from the threatened mines. Lawyers naturally poured into town by the dozen. "I think I have a certain fortune ahead of me in this country," wrote one. "It is the wildest one for law that you ever heard of, indeed it is a lawyer's paradise."[41]

The discovery of gold in 1890s Alaska and Yukon territory stimulated similar booms, but never with quite the same sizzle and flair. Though the Canadian goldfields were peopled largely by American prospectors (as well as Britons and Anglo-Canadians seasoned in the American mineral extraction business), the Canadian government, and especially the Royal Canadian Mounted Police, maintained law and order and, most saliently, tried to deter the kind of legal opportunism that was so rampant in American mining districts.[42]

Interestingly, in Utah, this new legal climate was used to much different effect. The federal government, as well as thousands of ordinary Americans, had harassed Mormons to no end. After fleeing from upstate New York and various points west, the Mormons settled in and around the eastern shores of the Great Salt Lake, which was then part of Nevada territory.

As inhabitants of a US territory, the Mormons could not keep non-Mormons out, but they could use the electoral and local civil service systems to legally dominate territorial affairs, and they did this with great success. In addition to monopolizing local politics, the Mormons used the shield of "freedom of incorporation" to protect their economic power by building their own "company store," Zions Cooperative Mercantile Institution (ZCMI). Opening in 1868, ZCMI was never actually a nonprofit cooperative; it sold a miraculous $1.25 million worth of goods its first year and was (and is) a for-profit corporation committed to funneling profits back to the Mormon Church. ZCMI sold goods inexpensively, and their variety of merchandise—ZCMI is credited by some as being the nation's first "department store"—soon gave fruit to company-owned factories, as well as shoe and clothing lines. Meinig writes:

> In addition to those colonizations undertaken to provide supplies of basic goods, such as coal, iron, lead, and cotton, the church fostered the construction of woolen mills, a silk mill, a sugar mill (a famous first American attempt—a failure—to extract sugar from beets); established the *Deseret News,* the Bank of Deseret, and ZCMI, a mercantile chain store; and built roads, telegraph lines, and railroads. Some of these facilities became corporations, but their initiation was made possible by a strongly promoted policy of tithing by the church membership. Such monies also sustained the building of temples, tabernacles, and other edifices, which were often initiated as public works projects in times of labor surplus from large immigration.

More generally, the territorial government of Utah liberally used the corporate organizational form to sponsor church-based activity. According to legal historian Gordon Bakken:

> Manifestly, the corporate instrument gave the Church a Gentile [*sic*] device to work in saintly ways. The state of Deseret incorporated the Church of Jesus Christ of Latter-Day Saints with broad powers. . . . Given the secular power to operate in the marketplace, the power of

the Church was awesome. . . . Utah's legislators also provided a corporation for the gathering of the saints. They incorporated the Perpetual Emigrating Fund to maintain the immigration of saints and to carry on the work of the kingdom. Similarly other Church organizations became corporations.[43]

As territorial governor *and* church elder, Brigham Young steered much federal patronage to the Mormons. He also used a loophole in Utah's territorial charter that enabled them to operate a special, Mormon-only court system. Unfortunately, a tendency to overstep the bounds of American law repeatedly got Young in trouble. Incidents like the Mountain Meadows Massacre of 1857—when a Mormon militia slaughtered some one-hundred Arkansas migrants in cold blood—brought Utah intense federal scrutiny. Young further antagonized Washington lawmakers by proclaiming polygamy to be an *official* Mormon practice.

Given the tremendous success the Mormons were having in Utah, it is surprising that Young would risk outside interference by sanctioning bigamy. Religious zeal aside, one might take this as a sign of the confidence Young had in the territory's political autonomy. The Mormons wanted to build a *bona fide* religious state in Utah. Unlike French Canadians, who had a similarly intense relationship with their church, the Mormons were intent on *colonizing* North America. French Canadians merely wanted some measure of jurisdictional autonomy—by the nineteenth century, Quebec was a sagging, tradition-bound, church-laden society running on the fumes of French-Catholic colonial institutions.

Anticipating opposition from Washington over the bigamy question, Young tried pleading on Utah's behalf by likening the Mormons' quest for spiritual freedom to the slaveholders' quest for economic freedom. Utah's fate thus became intertwined with that of the slave states in 1856. Young's logic backfired: Republicans started campaigning on promises to "abolish the twin relics of barbarism: slavery and polygamy." President Buchanan rightly reasoned that Republicans and Democrats alike could agree on the need to "clean up" Utah, thus distracting voters from the emerging congressional crisis over slavery. "Even Stephen Douglas, whose doctrine of popular sovereignty the Mormons had adopted for their own ends, rose in Congress to denounce them as 'a pestiferous, disgusting cancer . . . alien enemies and outlaws engaging in treasonable, disgusting and bestial practices,'" notes White. The year 1856 also brought a severe winter followed by drought.[44]

"In the midst of these interconnected crises, all order began to unravel in Utah," writes White, and he adds:

> Mormon youths broke into the offices of Judge George Stiles of the territorial court and stole and destroyed court records. Rumors of murders and blood atonement exacted by the Danites, or Avenging Angels, a band of murderers who supposedly acted under the command of Brigham Young, circulated in the territory. . . . The Mormons were clearly defying federal rule in Utah, and this second band of fugitive officials declared that the Mormons were in revolt against the United States.[45]

In response, President Buchanan sent twenty-five hundred federal troops—"one-sixth of the entire U.S. Army"—to suppress what was perceived to be a territorial rebellion in Utah. Fortunately, a "Mormon War" was never actually fought—the army got delayed and had to winter in the Rockies while cooler heads in Utah convinced Young to stand down and cede jurisdictional supremacy to the federal government. Nevertheless, a military garrison was permanently installed at Camp Douglas, overlooking Salt Lake City. According to White, when Young was dismissed as governor by President Buchanan, he

> ordered a withdrawal from the Salt Lake valley and planned for resistance, but he also began to moderate his rhetoric. He no longer issued pronouncements that resembled those of the leader of an independent country. In the spring of 1858, as the army renewed its march toward Utah, Buchanan dispatched peace commissioners with an offer of amnesty. Young came to terms, but he had to accept the presence of the federal army in Utah to make sure that he observed the terms of peace.[46]

Federal repression of the Mormons became more or less official policy of the US government thereafter. This is somewhat odd in light of the fact that Utah was in every other way a model western territory, one Thomas Jefferson himself would have lauded for its collectivist agrarianism, legal minimalism, and functional collaboration between religious and civic organizations. The attack on polygamy was also a slight on the idea that the states and territories should rule themselves as they wished, free from federal oversight.

While maintaining a grip on the reins of local financial and political institutions, Young and the Mormon elders gradually ceded jurisdiction over religious and military matters to the federal government. Nevertheless, Congress delayed Utah statehood for decades, finally giving in to the territory's repeated pleas in 1896, more than fifty years after the Mormons' arrival. The lack of formal recognition of Utah's ties to Mormonism is a jurisdictional hallmark of the American territorial system. Unlike French Canada, where the church was permitted a formal presence in the political life of the province, the Mormon influence on local political life was limited to indirect electoral campaigns and intermediary associations such as Mormon colleges, charities, and business corporations. Mormons could run the state, in other words, but only as long as they did so through the cover of corporations and with due deference to Congress.[47]

Utah's experiment in autojurisdiction epitomizes the nineteenth-century American political experiment in ways that highlight its most important differences with Canada. In Canada, jurisdictional disputes were—and still are—largely settled through intergovernmental bargaining and bureaucratic reform, with a modicum of judicial oversight. The United States, in contrast, matured from a bevy of litigious but also prosperous colonies to a nation obsessed with winner-take-all competition via private corporations and the law.

Library collections deep in western Americana are filled with hard evidence on this account. H. H. Bancroft, a western writer and publisher of great renown, made most of his fortune publishing legal digests for American settlers and attorneys. In fact, law books were the most profitable part of the western American publishing industry.[48]

The 1860 "revised and enlarged" edition of *Wells' Every Man His Own Lawyer* is as revealing an artifact from the American West as one might ever hope to find. *Wells'* unself-consciously bills itself as every young American's best friend. "The utility of a volume of this character is too obvious to need commendation," reads its introduction. *Wells'* is rather specific in naming its many functions and audiences:

> The design in its preparation has been to offer the professional man, the farmer, the mechanic, and the business man, a comprehensive and reliable work, which will enable him to draw up any instrument in writing that may be required in the course of business, in a legal form; to furnish him with all such legal information as is usually called for in the various avocations of life and to make a plain, common-sense work, that every body can understand, and which will enable any man or woman to be his or her own lawyer.[49]

Wells' complete title says a great deal about the state of legal culture in the American West: *Every Man His Own Lawyer, and United States Form Book: Being a Complete Guide in All Matters of Law and Business Negotiations, for Every State in the Union. Wells'* accentuates the close relationship between law and business and the crucial role of independent mastery of applicable legal codes in successful business transactions. The very confusion *Wells'* notes concerning new and evolving legal codes in the states and territories is an additional clue. Books like *Wells'*—and the professional lawyers who might actually own it—were the key to unlocking the confusion of overlapping, haphazard state and local codes, and thus the economic opportunities embedded in that confusion. With everyone everywhere so actively engaged in practicing the law, there was substantial room for growth in the American legal services industry.

This contrasts sharply with the excessively formal practice of the law in British-Canadian jurisdictions. Guidebooks for emigrants to Canada tend not to mention potential legal problems. They describe in a straightforward, calm manner the procedures to follow in procuring public land. *A Year in Manitoba, 1880–1881* comments on Canada's unexpectedly high taxes and unusually bad roads but makes no mention of the law, legal title, or problems with either. Another guidebook, Mrs. Edward Copleston's *Canada: Why We Live in It, and Why We Like It* (1861) goes so far as to say, "The prospects of an English lawyer [in Canada] are not encouraging. Commercial employment is neither so easy to get, nor so remunerative when secured, as at home." After visiting Canada in the early twentieth century, English colonial writer Rudyard Kipling wrote, "The law in Canada exists and is administered, not as a surprise, a joke, a favour, a bribe, or a Wrestling Turk exhibition, but as an integral part of the national character—no more to be forgotten or talked about than trousers." Conditions could not have been more different in the United States. Law for Canadians was something formal and orderly that should be revered and respected; for Americans, it was an opportunity, a palimpsest, a commodity, a lark.[50]

In 1880, another gem appeared on the American "how to" book market: Henry N. Copp's *American Settlers Guide*. Copp's *Guide* pitches itself less as a do-it-yourself book than as a "read this and hope you don't get ripped off" manual. It simply and plainly explains federal and state law with respect to public and private land claims but is less forthcoming than *Wells'* in offering fill-in-the-blank forms for legal do-it-yourselfers. From this, one can infer that an increasing percentage of the paperwork and motion of American legal practice was now in the hands of professional lawyers. Copp's *Guide* is also chock-full of ads for professional law firms, many of which, not surprisingly, are deeply entrenched in public land law. Reads one such ad: "J. Vance Lewis, attorney at law . . . will pay cash for bounty land warrants, and all kinds of land scrip, railroad and other bonds, and western land. Old land claims looked up and secured for heirs and claimants." Another extols the "PACIFIC COAST LAW, LAND AND CLAIM OFFICES of Mullan & Hyde, Attorneys for Land Claimants, and Dealers in Land Warrants and Land Scrip."[51]

In addition to comprehensive listings of nearby United States Land Offices, Railroad Land Commissioners, and the like, Copp's *Guide* contains numerous advertisements for the rest of its line of books, all of similar ilk. An ad for Copp's *Public Land Laws* appeals: "If you wish to increase your practice and widen your influence; if you desire the home-seekers of the present to regard you as their protector, and the land-owners of the future to *reward you with political honors,* first subscribe for Copp's Land-Owner; and, second, purchase Copp's Public Land-Laws; then, if nature has done her share, success is certain." This was quite the model of careerism on the American frontier.[52]

Copp's *Guide* concludes with an "advice" chapter on "where to settle" aimed at easterners and European immigrants. After advising settlers to take careful note of climate in considering their plans, Copp notes that, "The surroundings, especially the state of society, have much to do with physical comfort. In a turbulent, irreligious community, where crime goes unpunished and the criminal is somewhat of a hero, a peace-loving family will be in a constant state of worry, that must eventually affect their general health." For "mental" and "moral" growth," Copp's *Guide* advises would-be settlers to "Seek a State or Territory whose officials appreciate churches and schools; where tax-payers perceive the fact that every dollar spent on education and religion is saving of two dollars on the jail and penitentiary, where newspapers are numerous and libraries have been started, and literary, temperance, and other societies are encouraged by leading citizens." Besides demonstrating the increased bureaucratization of American legal practice circa 1880, Copp's *Guide* lauds what was by then a consistent theme in American legal culture: freedom of association and the accompanying belief that there was something healthy and democratic in its practice.[53]

Matthews's [sic] *Guide for Settlers upon the Public Lands, Land Attorneys, Land Agents, Clerks of Courts, Notaries, Bankers, Brokers, and All Other Persons Interested in the Public Lands of the United States and Having Business before the District Land Offices and the Department of the Interior,* an 1889 legal digest edited by William B. Matthews, a former "assistant chief of the pre-emption division, General Land Office," seems even more confident that the private practice of law and the public administration of law were mutually self-sustaining, and thus likely to last and grow over time. Matthews outlines, for example, "the principal disabilities which operate against the emigrant or settler on the public lands"—"fraudulent, inaccurate, and imperfect surveys," as well as "the neglect or refusal of Congress for many years to authorize by adequate appropriations the necessary surveys or resurveys of the public lands," or "'private land claims,' many of them fraudulent but supported by powerful interests, of pretended ancient dates" that can never be settled or owned with confidence. In fact, the general advice that Matthews gives to emigrants is rather bleak, a noteworthy contrast to the sunny, optimistic reports of emigrants to Canadian lands. Matthews warns (as does the California Emigrant Society, from which he reprints this advice):

> Buy your tickets for passage on railroad or steamboats only at the office before starting. . . . Many of the runners who offer tickets for sale in the streets are swindlers. . . . Thieves prefer to rob emigrants. . . . Do not mention the fact that you are an emigrant to persons who have no business to know it. . . . Never carry any large sum of money. . . . Avoid those strangers who claim to be old acquaintances and whom you do not recollect. . . . Do not drink at the solicitation of strangers. . . . Advice about the purchase of land is often given with corrupt motives.

These were grim prospects, indeed.[54]

Further evidence of the unique legal culture that evolved in the American West can be found in the Dakotas, a cauldron of competing developmental forces. Among the first American settlers in the Dakotas were adventuresome New Englanders like Newton Edmunds, who went west looking to make his fortune. "Dignified and courteous, and somewhat solemn, he was perhaps a perfect example of a New England squire in western politics," says Lamar, noting that men like Edmunds brought with them crucial legal knowledge and political skills from the East:

> The result was that the transplanted New Englander, whether he was from Maine or from Indiana, brought with him some of the social and political institutions of his home state and set them up in Dakota. And although these men did not form the greater number of the Dakota population in 1861 or later, they contributed a disproportionate number of local political leaders, who in turn partly fashioned political traditions.[55]

As governor, Edmunds, a loyal Republican Party hack, faced the challenge of ruling a federal territory that was still at war with local native bands. Edged up against the southern Canadian frontier, local Sioux had proven worthy opponents for slow federal troops. The western states and territories had been competing for new settlers ever since the passage of the Homestead Act of 1862. Establishing a peaceful frontier was thus a crucial first step for the Dakota territories. Jurisdictionally, moreover, war seriously threatened the political power of the local Republican Party machine. "A large scale offensive against the Indians, the Dakotans argued, was what the Army wanted as the excuse to retain its size and its great importance in national affairs."[56]

Though suppression of natives and alienation of their land claims were in Dakotans' short-term interests, federal interference in local politics was not. The army had jurisdictional autonomy from the territorial authorities. "The local politician . . . saw the Army as an independent government agency which could not be brought under territorial control the way the Indian Bureau could," notes Lamar. The army and the Bureau of Indian Affairs were also frequently in conflict. Edmunds spent much of his time worrying about interference from federal agencies working at cross-purposes.[57]

Nonetheless, all three parties—the army, the Bureau of Indian Affairs, and the territorial government—agreed that cooperation around the issue of Native Americans was necessary. Edmunds made a name for himself by brokering this truce, which assured the continuation of valuable federal spending in the territory as well as the ultimate pacification of the natives. Though soon ousted from office in the never-ending struggle for plunder and power, Edmunds remained a dominant figure in Dakota politics for the next twenty years, ruling "from his office in the Yankton bank, which he opened after his term as governor ended."[58]

Though important contemporary scholars such as Theda Skocpol have characterized late nineteenth-century American politics as a quest to eliminate corruption from government practice, patronage politics were alive and well in the American West throughout this period. Patronage contracts were a prize possession of local, federally appointed territorial politicians. Moses Armstrong, a longtime Dakota assemblyman and a contemporary of Edmunds, wrote in doggerel prose in his glorious compilation, *Early Empire Builders of the American West:*

> *No politician yet is dead,*
> *Nor ever will be, long as Hay,*
> *And Corn, and Cordwood fill the way.*

Similarly, Enos Stutsman, an early and largely unsuccessful governor of the Dakota territories, joked: "In the great squabble for office and place . . . I have tried office and find it does not pay, and, as a mere experiment, I intend to . . . see if I cannot make an honest living!" Walter A. Burleigh, one of the rare Democrats to achieve political success in early Dakota, was a master at this game. "The personification of the ambitious, amoral, rugged individualist seeking a fortune on the frontier, Burleigh saw in politics one of the keys to power and financial success," notes Lamar. Besides working diligently to promote land sales in the territory, Burleigh worked hard to serve himself. Lamar writes of Burleigh:

> With an energy approaching fanatic zeal he had assailed doubts about the unfavorable soil and climate of Dakota. . . . Yet most of this had been done to enhance his own financial and political career. An investigator sent to observe Burleigh's conduct while the latter was an agent to the Yankton Indians at Greenwood Reservation was so impressed with the payroll padding, graft, and nepotism practiced by this able, jovial doctor who was also a lawyer that his report was written in a tone that sounded less like condemnation than respectful awe. Indeed, the investigator noted, it took a superior imagination to be able to perpetrate so many frauds at one time.[59]

Atop the pyramid of government sat the territorial delegates to Congress—Burleigh was one before being appointed governor. Though deprived of voting power, territorial delegates were responsible for directing federal largesse to the territories. Writes Lamar of Dakota politics, "The importance of the delegate's role in territorial politics is difficult to exaggerate. As the single elected representative in Washington of an entire territory, he was the clearing house for most of the territorial-federal business. Through his office flowed rivers of patronage of every sort, and if it did not flow freely, he was promptly defeated in the next election."[60]

The war-emboldened Republican Party reached deep into the American territories in the 1860s and 1870s. Native-born Americans held new immigrants at arm's length, relegating them to municipal politics while statehouse politics remained firmly "Anglo." The Dakota legislature, for example, was staffed by a surprisingly young cadre of skilled and entrepreneurial Yankees, each of whom, quips Lamar, "was first of all an opportunist, flexible in his ambitions and shifting in his loyalties," adding that:

> The average legislator was such a young and active man that the sessions often resembled a college fraternity meeting. On various occasions these frontier solons brandished pistols to get recognition from the speaker, or had drinks sent in from a nearby saloon. Of the thirteen members of the House of Representatives only six were over thirty years old and of these only two were over thirty-five.

Of these young men, "Eight of the House members claimed to be farmers, but a majority of these were actually land speculators or agents. Two were surveyors, one a lawyer, one a trader, and Waldron of Sioux Falls described himself as only a laborer though he was actually the treasurer of the Western Town Company."[61]

Still only a federal territory, Dakota's relationship to Washington was passive-aggressive and distant. The members of Dakota's first Legislative Assembly "were very conscious of the fact that they were laying the foundations of representative government in a new area of the Northwest. They likened themselves to the Pilgrims at Plymouth and to the Founding Fathers at Philadelphia." Moreover, like their forebears, the Dakota assemblymen resented outside limitations on their power:

> Hence they showed an unfailing antipathy to federal control by the governor or by other appointed officials. They voiced the traditional

frontier demand for "local" and therefore "truly democratic" self-government. Hidden beneath such phraseology was the ambition to achieve supremacy over territorial executive, legislative, and judicial powers, to ignore completely any concept of checks and balances in government, and to deny any separation between government and private enterprise.[62]

Jurisdictional ambiguity and wayward federal spending affected ordinary settlers in extraordinary ways on the frontier. In this respect, the postbellum American West was re-creating the colonial politics of seventeenth-century New England. Ostensibly, the legal culture of early New England had been transported to the Midwest and the Far West by lawyers, prospectors, speculators, and political cronies. This institutional bridge of legal practice and rank opportunism was built on hundreds of separate territorial appointments, public land schemes, corporate charters, and court battles.

Crime and Culture on the "Lawless" Frontier

Three primary facts about the American West defy common belief and frontier mythology alike. First, it appears that the average nineteenth-century white western American actually had very little to do with natives—most of the "injun-killing" was done by official representatives of the US government. Natives often spent whatever money they could put together trading with whites; otherwise there was not much cause for interaction between the two, nor was there much desire to do so. Mutual distrust, coupled with legitimate fear, kept white Americans and Native Americans apart much of the time.

A second easily debunked myth of the early American West is that gunslingers and shootouts were an everyday occurrence in barrooms and on dusty Main Streets. During the twenty-five years (1860–1885) that marked the period of greatest violence in the frontier West, "an equal number of killings occurred in New York's Hell's Kitchen, Chicago's Tenderloin, and New Orleans' Storyville," says historian Richard Erdoes. "More people were killed in New York's Civil War draft riots than in a wild and wicked Kansas helldorado in ten years." In other words, although a good deal of killing did occur in the frontier Far West, the amount was far from unprecedented. In fact, notes Erdoes, fighting was probably no more common in the West than anywhere else in nineteenth-century America, the chief difference being that western males generally spent a lot of time in saloons, gambling and drinking. Erdoes's exact description is worth repeating:

> Men died in saloons first because they foolishly followed the prevailing fashion in going around "heeled"—that is, armed—while they really did not know how to handle themselves with a gun; second, because the saloon was the place in which to get drunk—and drunken men fight; third, because the saloon was the place in which to play cards and meet bad women, and men quarreled over poker, and women, and other things in that order. . . . Poker mixed with alcohol accounted for more deaths than all other causes combined. A further reason for gun-play and knifings was the fact that the majority of shootists were Civil War veterans, and it was the most restless, adventurous, and embittered among them who moved west. Bull Run and Gettysburg were fought over and over again in western barrooms by former bluecoats and rebs full of firewater; the saloon, after all, was the most likely place for them to run into each other.

Western sheriffs are today celebrated as noble, self-sacrificing heroes fighting evil against all odds, but they too were far more fallible than legend would have it. Contemporary pistols were notoriously hard to aim and fire, and sheriffs apparently killed innocent bystanders about as often as their crime-committing foes. "The heroic gunfighter was an eastern invention," concludes Erdoes; "for the westerner he was a pain in the ass."[63]

A third myth about the frontier is a bit harder to explain given its purely academic origins. Renowned legal historian John Phillip Reid is partly responsible for a particular bit of self-congratulatory Americana: In his book, *Law for the Elephant: Property and Social Behavior on the Overland Frontier,* he asks what civic life was like on the overland trail in the mid-nineteenth-century United States. Much to his surprise—but not to mine—Reid finds that Americans were unusually, but also idiosyncratically, civil to one another amid the hardships of western passage. Absent formal law enforcement, these travelers somehow avoided massacring one another, a Hobbesian paradox if ever there was one. Without so much as an ounce of government meddling—Reid's Leviathan—these travelers not only avoided killing each other, but even limited robbery to a great extent.

Starvation was a constant threat on the overland trail. Hungry pioneers sometimes found themselves in the peculiar situation of finding someone else's cattle, water, or foodstuffs abandoned by the side of the road; or a particularly well-stocked traveler might find himself surrounded by a group of starving neighbors, as did one of Reid's subjects in Death Valley in 1849. As told through the diaries and letters of Reid's travelers, respect for private property prevailed in a surprising number of these situations. Starving travelers were reluctant to take property that belonged to others; they might well shun a greedy fellow traveler—"insistence on property rights could cause ill feeling and make one a leper"—but it is notable that Reid's pioneers never resorted to outright theft despite their obvious need and probable anger. In other words, their regard for private property could be nearly suicidal. "That one man or company had more than necessary for survival while others were starving did not mean that the surplus belonged to the needy," comments Reid. "There can be no better evidence of exclusive possession," he concludes. "If, even with those conditions, water could be personally owned and denied to others, anything could be." In an apt summation of American legal culture as a whole, Reid notes, *"It was rights, not persons, that were respected."*[64]

Why is this conclusion *not* surprising? First, because it seems consistent with the prior history of civil litigation and private property rights in American history (though pioneer Americans did not seem nearly as respectful of land claims as personal property); second, because sociologists well know that people carry legal culture around with them in their heads, acting more or less "morally" regardless of the presence of active enforcement. In other words, though law enforcement was sorely lacking on the overland trail, there was no lack of self-discipline. Reid's travelers were mostly American, plus a smattering of Britons and Germans, all of whom would have been familiar and more or less compliant with American standards of private property. It is thus no surprise that thievery was not more common on the overland trail. What is surprising, perhaps, is the sheer extent to which Americans tolerated cupidity and selfishness. A well-stocked traveler in another national-legal context might well have felt compelled to share his or her extra supplies with the less fortunate. As Reid writes elsewhere: "Nineteenth-century Anglo-Americans, it seems, were imbued with a legal culture making them more comfortable with a system producing winners and losers than with a system under which risks were less and costs were shared." This is not to say that non-Americans are comparatively kindhearted, but to note the power of group norms when it comes to defining antisocial behavior. Greed is legally defensible under American law, so Americans act more selfishly than they otherwise might. It is rights, especially property rights, that are respected—not persons.[65]

Jurisdictional Expansion: The New Canadian West

Canada began its gradual transition toward jurisdictional control of its western territories by limiting the power of the Hudson's Bay Company. British Columbia was a particular problem for the authorities, given American efforts to control the Pacific coast. The British-Canadian authorities ultimately realized that territorial settlement was a better hedge against American incursion than the HBC's corporate monopoly.

In the 1840s, the royal government had negotiated a temporary grant on Vancouver Island for the HBC, thus retaining a stopgap against American incursion in the region. However, the HBC was notified that colonization was coming and that the company's jurisdiction would eventually have to give way to Canadian territorial government. This was a natural condition of British corporate law—chartered corporations existed "at the king's pleasure" and could thus be expected to bend to the mandates of royal stewardship. A "confidential" 1848 government missive concerning the fate of the HBC's grant of land on Vancouver Island clearly states that, "The general effect of the grant therefore is that the Company hold the land, as any individual grantee might hold it, *without* any powers or authorities such as are contained in their old charter. These remain with the Crown." Furthermore, it was clearly stated that the HBC grant of land on Vancouver Island would only last ten years, at which time jurisdiction would be transferred to the colonial government. This did in fact transpire in 1859, and the orderly transfer of jurisdiction is in itself quite extraordinary: When seen in comparison with the rapacious and sometimes intransigent role of railroad corporations in the American territories, the repercussions of mid-nineteenth-century Anglo-Canadian corporate regulation on the political development of the Canadian West are indeed striking.[66]

Following the accession of the Red River settlement, the Canadian West (British Columbia, and the territories in between in 1870) steadily—but not very quickly—began filling with settlers, settlements, and enterprise zones. The Canadian federal government preserved peaceful relations with native peoples through centralized, top-down control, which is also how one might describe its territorial system. Residents of the Northwest Territory only gradually wrested self-government from Ottawa, for example. The Northwest Territory's Legislative Council only slowly expanded to include representatives from new districts, and the council itself gradually gained control over the public purse. The territory also (slowly) gained the power to incorporate businesses, as well as to fund schools and municipal public works.

Progress was measured and was not without resistance, but Ottawa ultimately retained a degree of territorial control that was then unheard of in the American West, where territorial government had been reformed after 1827 so that, in the words of historian Earl Pomeroy, "The newer form was less a unit of [federal] control than a framework for self-government." By the later nineteenth century, American territories were being created with full-blown legislative assemblies, whereas the Canadian Northwest Territory had to wait almost two decades for this elementary step toward democratic governance. Some degree of congressional representation for American territories had been a standard feature of American statecraft since 1787, while Canada's territories had to labor and fight for parliamentary representation. At the same time, however, government "control" in latter nineteenth-century American territories was "ineffective rather than either tyrannical or generously moderate," comments Pomeroy. "Normally control over the territories was designed to operate over only a fraction of governmental activities, and normally it fell far short of its purpose."[67]

In British Columbia and early Alberta, the ever-present Hudson's Bay Company, and later the North West Mounted Police, kept a handle on the "middle ground" then emerging between native and Canadian peoples. Native tribes flocked north from the United States in flight from the US Cavalry. And, as in the Ohio Valley in the eighteenth century, the incursion of American tribes into the Canadian plains fomented conflict between native bands, traders, and *Métis*. Canadian law enforcement officers—mostly British military personnel—played a large though sometimes exaggerated role in maintaining a degree of law and order unparalleled in the American West.

Canada's new prime minister, John A. Macdonald, "first began organizing a [federal] mounted police force in 1869, as part of the preparations for assuming sovereignty over the lands granted by charter to the Hudson's Bay Company," writes historian S. W. Horrall. "The Prime Minister was anxious that Canadian expansion into the Northwest should not be accompanied by the violent conflict between the Indian population and settlers which had characterized settlement in the American West."[68]

The Anglo-Canadian population of western Canada was still miniscule as of the early 1870s, and formation of the Mounties was delayed for several years. Macdonald was reluctant to send troops farther west, beyond Manitoba, as long as the threat of *Métis* rebellion remained at Red River. Nonetheless, the persistence of illegal liquor sales by independent traders (mostly from the United States), as well as violence between the American traders and Canadian natives, and the additional threat of cross-border Fenian raids (Irish-American efforts to gain British withdrawal from Ireland), finally prompted Ottawa to act. Parliamentary permission for the Mounties was easily obtained, and the 1873 bill authorizing the formation of the Mounties also included provisions for creation of territorial courts, jails, and magistrates.

Rather than adopting the model of unarmed London police, Macdonald looked to the English police force deployed in Ireland, the Irish Mounted Constabulary, as a basis for the Mounties. "They would have the advantage of military discipline," Macdonald told Parliament, "would be armed in a simple but efficient way, would use the hardy horse of the country, and by being police would be a civil force, each member of which would be a police constable, and therefore a preventive office." The decision to dress the Mounties in gleaming scarlet was a matter of pragmatism, not philosophy; American army personnel usually dressed in blue, and the Mounties had no wish to be mistaken for Americans, given recent levels of violence in the American West. Contrary to popular opinion (and American popular culture), working for the Mounties was far from glamorous. The Mounties spent much of their year in dangerous, isolated, claustrophobic winter camps, and members are not infrequently described in firsthand accounts as snarky, paranoid, and mean. Infighting in the officer corps was endemic. Desertions, demotions, and even mutinies were not uncommon in the ranks. "The government in Ottawa repaid the sacrifices and devotion to duty of the Mounted Police by reducing their already low pay and skimping on equipment, horses, and quarters."[69]

The original Mounties were mostly reassigned British army regulars. Throughout the 1870s, British detachments served close by, in Winnipeg, in order to keep an eye on the *Métis* and guard the American border. George French, the first commander of the Mounties, was recruited without significant leadership experience after three months of service in western Canada with the Royal Artillery. "Commissioner French, while frequently reminding his men that they were not soldiers, created a force 'which in every respect had more the characteristics of a first-class cavalry regiment than those of an ordinary rural police.'" One of the Mounties' primary responsibilities early on was to stamp out illegal sales of alcohol to natives; another was enforcing Canadian jurisdiction vis-à-vis the United States and overseeing the affairs of the Hudson's Bay Company. While Commissioner French spent most of his time procuring horses, weapons, and provisions, as well as training his poorly prepared men to ride, the Mounties originally received "no legal or police related training." They were a military organization, though one that was not particularly inclined toward violence or abuse of its own power.[70]

The reason for this is a matter of hindsight and speculation. Presumably, the fact that the Mounties were directly accountable to the British imperial government helped to rein in corruption and excessive violence. Historian Louis Knafla adds that police violence in western Canada was tempered by the British legal tradition of respect for local customs—"law was embodied not only in the written statutes of Parliament and judgements [sic] of the common law courts, but in the unwritten customs of the people." British civil servants in Canada also seemed remarkably earnest about their professional responsibilities, though exceptions did occur. The ongoing presence of the Hudson's Bay Company, coupled with the constant threat of violence between Americans and/or American Indians, also greatly limited the presence of prospectors and land speculators at the time (the 1870s). Outside the flourishing Red River settlement, there was only Hudson's Bay land. According to historian R. C. Maclead, "serious conflict was relatively easy to avoid where the population was sparse and an effective [commercial] monopoly existed." Royal Canadian Mounted Police (RCMP) officers saw it as their duty to educate new immigrants living in the West about Canadian legal culture. One RCMP commissioner commented in an 1893 report, "The opinion these people form of our administration of the laws on their first arrival has the greatest possible effect on their future conduct. An inability on our part to impress them with the necessity of strictly obeying our laws, will be certain to lead to heavy expenses later on in the administration of justice."[71]

The central problem for the Hudson's Bay Company remained maintaining their profit margins in the face of soft fur markets and burgeoning expenses. At this point, with the market for furs long in decline, the HBC was looking for a way to transition out of the beaver business and into merchandising and exchange. In the burgeoning city of Winnipeg, it erected a "magnificent" four-story building "to accommodate each department of their extensive trade." "This is a really grand edifice," remarked one English emigrant in 1880, "and seems likely to form a very prominent feature in this wonderful town for many years to come." The HBC's more remote outposts were becoming market towns based less on the fur trade than on provisioning local natives, *Métis,* adventurers, and prospectors. The presence of the Mounties was thus consistent with the long-term goals of the HBC. By shifting responsibility for outright jurisdictional control of the western territories to the new Canadian federal government, the HBC could unburden itself of a major liability. It also shared with the Mounties an interest in only gradually letting new settlers into the territory.[72]

Violence was not unknown on the Canadian frontier, but again, most parties shared with the Hudson's Bay Company a desire for law and order. After several fitful years under the barely competent leadership of Commissioner French, the Mounties were an established presence. They held secure outposts and regular provision routes, something the French had struggled to create *de novo*. As the selfsame English emigrant to Manitoba notes of his time in Winnipeg, "There is an efficient and vigilant police force, and the magistrate's levées [sic] attest that disorder at least is not practiced with impunity in Winnipeg." No Mounties were killed in encounters with natives, moreover, and relations were relatively peaceful. "With the arrival of the Mounted Police," writes historian Jim Wallace, "the liquor traffic was largely curtailed and white men who had exploited aboriginal peoples were dealt with firmly." A large part of this effort entailed ejecting Americans from Canada—liquor sales were only loosely regulated in the American territories, whereas licenses were required in western Canada for the possession of even just personal supplies. Ironically, the United States subsequently created much stricter alcohol licensing laws than Canada, thereby reversing the flow of illegal cross-border liquor sales.[73]

Naturally, the presence of the Mounties in western Canada changed the social dynamic of existing populations there, white and native alike. Wallace writes, "As the perception of danger waned, the *Métis* settlements . . . became more permanent and the *Métis* hunters ventured into Blackfoot hunting grounds they would previously have been afraid to enter." Competition for scarce resources—pelts, meat, and land—increased rapidly. Crimes of vengeance continued to occur among the denizens of the fur trade. Nevertheless, for a frontier area of its size and scope, settlement remained a relatively peaceful affair, especially when compared to the example of the American West. Historian Roderick Macleod attributes the success of the Mounties to their "psychological" role on the Canadian prairies: "Even if the police did not do everything they were supposed to, the government and public believed they did. . . . Their existence gave the government the confidence necessary to undertake a task that might otherwise have seemed impossible."[74]

"The Mounted Police could exercise jurisdiction over the widespread territory because of their broad powers to arrest, try and sentence offenders," adds Jim Wallace. "Initially, they were much harder on white men who ran afoul of the law. The Indians were given a period in which to become familiar with the new laws. In contrast, to the south, the United States Army, faced with divided jurisdiction and locally elected law officers who favoured white settlers, could often do little except resort to force."[75]

Over the long term, western Canadian courts exerted an unusual degree of independence from dominion law, and thus English law. This was achieved not by design—the new dominion government fully intended to subsume territorial courts to federal supervision—but because of the independence of the early western Canadian judiciary, a group that was committed to a flexible interpretation of "royal prerogative" based firmly on Blackstone's maxim that "colonists carry with them only so much of the English law as is applicable to their own situation." Western jurists thus resisted the intrusion of outside influences on the evolution of a legal system for the Canadian West. "Sovereignty was perceived more often as vested in the homestead of the western provinces than in Ottawa," writes legal historian Louis Knafla. "This perception led to the formation of strong, centrally organized provincial governments in the

West, governments in which the Crown was clearly identified with provincial institutions [as opposed to only national institutions]."[76]

In equal measure, western Canadian jurists sought to promote the sustenance of law and order by combating corporate malfeasance and lawyerly "tricks" and delays. These western judges were, like their Elizabethan counterparts, "always eager to put down a frivolous suit of faulty legal counsel," says Knafla. "Begbie [key justice in early British Columbia], for example, condemned attorneys who used 'trivialities and unfounded quibbles and objections which have long defaced the administration of criminal law." In part, they were motivated by the example of American litigiousness, or more specifically the desire to avoid it. "Prairie judges were also not hesitant to rule against the questionable activities of corporations."[77]

At the same time, western Canadians clearly shared many of the same political values as their American counterparts, specifically those regarding individual freedom and jurisdictional autonomy. For example, in expectation of the arrival of a new, Ottawa-appointed lieutenant governor prior to the creation of the Mounties, the *Métis* of the Red River settlement convened an assembly at which they drafted a tentative "List of Rights" in 1869. In addition to asking for the right of self-government, public roads and schools, and bilingual legislatures and courts, the representatives demanded "fair and full representation in the Canadian Parliament" and that "all privileges, customs, and usages existing at the time of transfer, be respected"—a rather English way of saying that all essential civil rights and freedoms should be protected. (England has no formal bill of rights, though the same rights and freedoms guaranteed Americans in their Constitution are more or less presumed in England under common law.) Historian Lewis Thomas refers to this *Métis* List of Rights as "a striking example of the mingling of American, British, and French Canadian political ideas."[78]

A number of Red River settlers were willing to fight for these rights. In 1870, under the leadership of a mentally unstable *Métis* firecracker named Louis Riel, a *Métis* army turned away the new lieutenant governor and installed a "provisional government." On December 8, 1869, Riel issued a formal declaration of jurisdictional autonomy—"often described as the Declaration of *Métis* Independence, because of its obvious similarity to the American document of 1776," writes Gerald Friesen. Riel and his men might have succeeded in gaining "independence," had they not executed a twenty-eight-year-old laborer from Ontario who had been caught fighting for the "Loyalist" opposition. British troops and Canadian militia were promptly sent to quell the rebellion, which was short-lived.[79]

The following year, Prime Minister Macdonald moved to increase federal control over the West. In order to placate the *Métis*, a tiny enclave province—Manitoba—was created, though it was not granted control over its public lands, an exception to practice in the existing provinces and a source of future controversy in the Canadian West. The *Métis* rebels were denied amnesty, and Riel lived in exile in the United States until 1885, when he returned to lead yet another unsuccessful rebellion.

In retrospect, both the United States and Canada ran their territories as subject populations without representative government or control over their own public lands. The principal difference between them seems to be that Ottawa genuinely regarded the territories as delicate projects in statecraft, whereas Washington DC largely left its territories in the lurch, exploiting and ignoring them in equal measure.

Both Canada and the United States created new Departments of Interior to oversee their territories and native populations in the early 1870s—Canada following America's lead. As Thomas writes:

> However, in so far as the supervision of a territorial government was concerned, the politics of the two departments were quite different: in the United States, control was confined within narrow limits, inspired by the philosophy that "in construing provisions for the self government of an inchoate state, under our principle of administration, every intentment [sic] is to be made in favor of the powers of the local legislature. . . ." In Canada, however, the system of close centralized control . . . was to continue—territorial autonomy having to be wrested from the federal government in piecemeal fashion. Senator Campbell, the first Minister of the Interior, expressed the prevailing Canadian philosophy when he referred to his position as "Secretary for the Colonies"—a term which was meant to imply the full measure of imperial control of dependent territory.

Furthermore, the lieutenant governor of the new province of Manitoba was expected to serve as "a paternal despot . . . governed by instructions from Head Quarters [sic]," said Prime Minister Macdonald.[80]

Neither nation's territorial governments had much in the way of administrative capacity, but the formal powers of the lieutenant governor and the formative presence of the Mounties at least lent the Canadian West an air of discipline and order. In the United States, federal control of the West was expected to wither and die as the territories grew to maturity.

The political development of these two frontiers also reflected long-standing national differences in corporate law and the perceived role of corporations in the economy. This is particularly true with respect to comparative efforts to build railroads across each country. Having long since institutionalized "freedom of incorporation" doctrine in the United States, private railroad corporations were encouraged to invest and build networks of their own. American railroads vied with one another to build competitive, financially successful lines. Though the first transcontinental route across America was backed by the federal government, the field was quickly opened to competition. The English common law sense of the corporation as a special monopoly grant had long since vanished in the United States, and with it the sense that competition should be anything but limited, however ruinous to individual firms, workers, and constituents. On the rapidly developing Rocky Mountain frontier, for example, "Corporation law was an open-ended invitation to entrepreneurs to use the form to develop the region." "The railroads brought prosperity and a marked increase in business activity, but they also imported a frenzied atmosphere."[81]

Canada's quest for a transcontinental railroad mirrored its experience with the traditional English conception of the corporation. By this time, a general suspicion of competition and a decided preference for limited monopolies prevailed. Thus, Canada chartered a single railroad, the Canadian Pacific, to build its transcontinental route, guaranteeing it a virtual monopoly over much of the ensuing business. An English settler in Manitoba in the early 1880s noted with some surprise that the terms of the Canadian Pacific Railway's contract "do seem to place an almost unlimited control of the entire railway system of the country in the hands of a single corporation, thereby creating a monopoly dangerous in the highest degree to the best interests of the country"—Britain by this time had begun revising its system of corporate monopolies. Nonetheless, though western Canadians often used American railroads to transport goods to and from eastern Canada, the construction of a transcontinental, domestic railroad was long seen as vital to Canadian national development. By the 1880s, Canadian fur and buffalo markets had been almost entirely replaced by cattle ranches that extended across the

Rocky Mountain foothills from Montana to Alberta. American railroads spanned the continent, and American transit routes remained cheaper than Canadian routes until the Canadian Pacific Railroad (CPR) finally punched through the vast Canadian interior. Prior to completion of the CPR, communications between Ottawa and Winnipeg were difficult at best: In 1871, the first telegraph connection was established via *American* lines and mail service remained only triweekly, "though it was necessarily a slow service until rail connections with Minnesota were completed in 1878," notes Thomas. "In the Territories," moreover, "a government mail service was not inaugurated until 1876 when it was arranged that Edmonton, Winnipeg, and intermediate points would be served once every three weeks."[82]

Working in tandem, in part through common board members, the CPR and the Hudson's Bay Company gained favorable terms for acquisition and sale of the new public lands of western Canada. The Winnipeg Board of Trade fought diligently to have the CPR's main western hub located there, a deal that benefited everyone except, presumably, the ordinary taxpayers of Winnipeg, who were saddled with huge debts by the effort. A monopoly clause negotiated by the CPR with the Ottawa government also blocked American railroads from competing for western Canadian freight. In addition to diminishing the long-standing economic connection between the US and Canadian prairie states, the CPR's close connection to Ottawa thereby focused much of western Canadians' ire on federal, as opposed to local, politicians: Whereas American farmers could only indirectly appeal for federal aid in regulating transportation costs, western Canadians focused from the outset on Ottawa's responsibility for their transportation woes. This created a repertoire of grievances in western Canadian provinces that remains with them to this day—opposition not to *all* forms of government paternalism (as in the United States), but to federal interference with provincial rights. Exactly such grievances underlie the creation of the two new provinces of Saskatchewan and Alberta in 1905: "Only provincial status would permit the citizens of the Northwest to make their case for improved federal grants," notes historian Gerald Friesen.[83]

Long before confederation, plans were in place to build a Canadian national railroad, and the promise thereof was a key incentive for both the western territories and the Maritime Provinces to join the new dominion. Private, independent railroads already existed throughout the

East, but the task of building a transcontinental railroad was put firmly in the hands of the federal government. By building its own railroads, Canada was shielded from the diplomatic and economic vicissitudes of American transportation policy, a system known for its combativeness and corruption. This afforded Ottawa a degree of control over the railroad industry unprecedented in the United States, where monopolies were anathema to federal antitrust policy.[84]

Nonetheless, while the CPR helped keep Canadian trade on Canadian soil, native bands were less deterred by the international border. US and Canadian officials agreed early in the 1870s that jurisdictional clarity with regard to native tribes was in the interests of both nations. Though natives did not necessarily acknowledge the existence of the US/Canadian border, their respective federal governments desperately wanted to clarify which governments were responsible for which tribes, thus facilitating domestic law enforcement and resettlement policies. In response, the Canadian government deemed native bands living within its jurisdiction permanent "clients" of the Crown—sovereignties entitled to dominion land and support in exchange for forfeiting native claims to all lands not expressly reserved for them. "Foreign" (that is, American) natives were discouraged from entering Canadian territory and not afforded such rights, thus respecting American jurisdiction over its indigenous peoples.

Generally speaking, government relations with natives were much more peaceable on the Canadian side of the border. Government assistance to "domestic" bands was adequate, if not generous. The Canadian government, like the American, supported a sometimes harsh policy of "domesticating" natives by resettling them on small reserves where, it was hoped, they would take up farming and Christianity and ultimately assimilate into Anglo-Canadian life. English-language boarding schools were built in both countries to forcibly assimilate native youth.[85]

Though both nations harbored unrealistic, unjust aspirations for their native populations, the tenor of enforcement and control varied greatly. So-called American Indians were treated quite harshly in comparative terms. In turn, American tribes sometimes sought refuge in Canada, thus forcing the Mounties to act as arbitrators. After years of persecution by the US Cavalry and a now-historic victory over Custer at Little Big Horn in the summer of 1876, a small band of Sioux fled to Canada with their chief, Sitting Bull. The Mounties did not try to "evict" the Sioux, but they did not offer them much help either. Sitting Bull's Canadian handlers spent a great deal of time and effort trying to coerce him to move the Sioux back to US jurisdiction, thus respecting prior agreements with the United States regarding native affairs. Sitting Bull waited both parties out until, abandoned by most of his followers and on the verge of starvation, he finally turned himself in. In 1881, the Mounties escorted him to the border, where he was picked up by the US Army and marched to a reservation in North Dakota. A few years later, Sitting Bull was shot to death on the reservation by Indian police summoned by Washington to monitor "suspicious" activities among the Sioux. This tactic of victory through attrition was practiced by the US Army throughout the West.

Jurisdictional conflict between rival American federal agencies only complicated matters for Native Americans: While the Bureau of Indian Affairs was trying to coax natives onto reservations by spending—sometimes lavishly—on Christian missions, farms, and schools for natives, the US Army was waging war against them. Lack of interagency coordination exacerbated existing problems with administrative capacity and mission control. Formalization of the American reservation system only gradually emerged, and then only after Anglos had picked over their land, keeping the choicest bits for themselves.[86]

Regional Development, American Style

In both Canada and the United States, the erection of transcontinental railroads was an important step in bridging the gap between the frontier and the rest of the country. Canada built its transcontinental railroad using strict, centralized federal oversight. In the United States, independent railroads competed for rights of way and public land grants. Though federal officials were well apprised of the need for a transcontinental railroad, sectional conflict tied Congress in knots over the selection of routes and contracts. Instead, Washington spent amply on several, and later numerous, private railroad contracts to "connect" the West with the already well-serviced East. Eastern financiers, engineers, and lawyers benefited most from this initial growth spurt. The South, already lagging in railroad development before the Civil War, continued its drift into disconnected isolation as a harsh but profitable agribusiness frontier. Southern textile factories procured cotton from their respective hinterlands and then ferried the final products—and most of the profits—to northeastern ports and railroad terminals in places like New York, Philadelphia, and Baltimore.[87]

In the new American West, railroad financing took on an unusually desperate character. As White writes:

> In the mid-nineteenth century, railroads confronted westerners with a frustrating paradox. Except in unusual circumstances, development would be slow and unrewarding without railroads, but until development took place, railroads could not make a profit (for they would have neither freight nor people to haul), so there was little incentive for private capitalists to build them. To escape from this dilemma, westerners looked to the government, particularly the federal government, which, they contended, should provide the aid necessary to build the railroads.

This is very elegant thinking, though it is mendicant in the extreme. At the local level, says White, "Boosters expected states, counties, and towns to provide yard and station sites, donate rights-of-way, exempt the roads from taxation, and, above all, to fund bond issues the proceeds of which would help to build the railroads. The bulk of the aid, however, came from the federal government in the form of land grants and loans." Federal aid originally went to the states for distribution, but by the 1860s, "the federal government usually made direct grants to the railroads that it intended to aid." In return, Congress mandated that "the railroads use American iron and steel for their tracks, and Congress required the railroad to carry troops and the U.S. mail at special rates," notes White. Enterprising railroad entrepreneurs like Leland Stanford and Collis Huntington leveraged this requirement by investing in timber, steel, and railroad-building companies, thus effectively paying themselves with federal money for building their own railroads. An ancillary development was the proliferation of extremely large for-profit corporations of all types on the American frontier.[88]

Railroad corporations were, perhaps, the most extensive example of organizational innovation under American law. Though corporate freedom was expanding in Canada and the British Isles, it had reached nowhere near the proportions of the American scene by the mid-nineteenth century. Having established a vast, financially "secure" railroad sector in the East—bankruptcies, mergers and acquisitions were huge in the early to mid-nineteenth-century, fueling incumbent growth in the legal and banking sectors—the American corporate business model was easily transported to the West.

The legal jurisdictional apparatus underlying the rapid growth of the American railroad industry was both fueled and complicated by its close connection to western land sales. Independent railroads received millions of acres of public land from the federal government as encouragement for westward railroad building. The railroads, in turn, had to find ways to sell all that land and promote its desirability in order to stimulate business. Not surprisingly, then, the railroads were a major sponsor of the nascent American advertising industry. European immigrants, as well as any array of East Coast prospectors and midwesterners, needed to be told of the great riches awaiting them in the West. As translocal businesses, railroads needed to find a way to advertise their lands broadly, as did steamboat lines, stage companies, express agents, express companies, and forwarding agents.[89]

"SIX MILLION SMILING ACRES," leads an ad for North Pacific Railroad lands in Copp's *American Settler's Guide,* an 1880 legal digest of federal land laws. "Nowhere in the world are farmers making so much money as on the line of the NORTHERN PACIFIC RAILROAD! . . . The great Railroad is fast SPANNING THE CONTINENT, and when it is completed land will immediately advance *two or three hundred per cent.*" Another Copp's ad pitches the "winter wheat and fruit lands" of the Illinois Central Railroad Company and notes that, "The country is rapidly settling up with a substantial class of citizens, who will soon surround themselves with every convenience, and all the comforts of civilization." A new culture of public-private land sales is notable here, though one with proximate ties to the land grant system of the early American colonies: In the lawyerly words of the Illinois Central ad, "THE TITLE TO THESE LANDS IS PERFECT."[90]

Generous federal policies regarding acquisition and payment for land, public and private, helped foster a unique legal culture in which government and private entrepreneurs worked hand in hand to promote land sales and speculation. Small towns like Wichita, Abilene, and Dodge City spent recklessly in pursuit of railroad access. The railroads, in turn, expected generous financing and tax-relief packages in exchange for linking their roads to these new locations. Custom and heritage had been completely expunged from English common law, as had its joint obsession with tradition and order. America's streams, rivers, farmlands, and mineral deposits were open for pillage. Outright theft was less common than legal manipulation and trickery, as in California, where Spanish ranchers were bilked out of their land in the courts—that is, frontier violence was more legal than physical.[91]

Via this system, a small cadre of wealthy lawyers and financiers, many from San Francisco, "captured" the Rocky Mountain West for their own profit. Political entrepreneurs also felt secure in their ability to "buy" votes. "Some thirty years after American conquest," writes Lamar of territorial New Mexico, "the privilege of the vote was still taken so lightly that corruption characterized every election. The mere party labels Republican and Democrat became caricatures in this unique situation." New Mexico was still largely occupied by Spanish-speaking, civil law–abiding Mexicans, yet American institutions were beginning to take root there. According to Lamar:

> By sheer persistence and propinquity, American ideas were insinuating themselves into the local customs. More Americans began to appear in the legislature. And down the trail from the states came such an amazing number of lawyers that soon one in every ten Americans in the territory was reputed to be a member of the bar. What was in the air? . . . How could an attorney survive in a community where even federal courts were often dismissed for lack of a docket? The answer lay in the exploitation and amortization of another old Spanish colonial custom. These shrewd and aggressive young lawyers, still stumbling over their Spanish, would build their own political and economic empire out of the tangled heritage of land grants.[92]

In addition to the legal landgrab created by tangled jurisdiction regarding pre-American titles to land, these small, dense, and often conflicted networks of elite, well-connected gentlemen became firmly ensconced in the purse strings of federal government. Senate seats were especially prized among western politicians, in part because they came at a very high but predictable price: purchase of majority support in the state legislature, which selected that state's two senators. (Direct election of senators only came later, in 1913, during the Progressives' fight to decouple money and office in Congress. In Canada, Senate seats are still honorary appointments made by the provinces.) The US Senate became a virtual "millionaires' club." Jurisdictionally speaking, the *intent* of the American system was local autonomy, but the *effect* was federalization of western politics. The impact, influence, and presence of American federal government was far more present in the West than the founders had ever imagined—or intended.

Western lawyers, entrepreneurs, and politicians cultivated a new form of American political culture firmly ensconced in, but dramatically different from, New England's colonial obsession with corporate autonomy and charter rights. Western political culture—"plutocratic populism," in Ostrander's words—combined the elitist sentiments of early republicanism with the populist elements proliferating on the mid-nineteenth-century frontier among small-time miners, land speculators, ranchers, dairymen, and farmers. This emerging western American political culture also comprised tacit support for anti-environmentalism, legal activism, and ethnocentric regionalism—western Americans sometimes acted as if the West was a totally unique place cut off from, and superior to, the rest of the United States. In fact, the West was merely the new leading edge of the "Americaniza-tion" of the common law.[93]

Federalism and the American Frontier

Having created an institutional climate in which bold-faced grabs for local power were possible, the federal government worsened matters by imposing unreasonable efficiency standards on federal offices in the West. Western alienation was thus exacerbated by a generation of Republican administrations in Washington that were determined to cut costs and increase administrative control over federal offices on the frontier. Fear of corruption, coupled with a lack of real accountability to territorial voters, promoted a haphazard federal appropriations process in which decreased spending was a singular priority in all cases, except those that benefited territorial secretaries and congressional delegates. At the same time, powerful interest groups—primarily large private corporations—"had real political power and could influence the present fortunes of the administration, while territorial citizens could not," argues historian Thomas Alexander.[94]

One of the most interesting things about the growth of American federal power on the frontier is the fact that none of it was ever supposed to happen in the first place. According to Alexander, federal agencies like the Bureau of Indian Affairs were:

> created to disappear in the process of accomplishing its task. At the same time the service was hampered by the legally equivocal condition of the reservations themselves where the Indians were not legally authorized to make even closely supervised decisions—such as leasing coal mines—which might have provided funds to promote self-sufficiency. . . . *Since*

the system was designed for impermanence, long-range planning was not contemplated.

Nonetheless, Congress bolstered its hold over the territories. "Congress might have turned the whole responsibility for the governments over to the territories, but under the pupilage theory it refused to do that," writes Alexander. "Instead it merely reaffirmed its own responsibility, then abdicated without making any provision for a successor." This, arguably, epitomizes the prevailing ethos of American democratic theory in the late nineteenth century: government should not need to exist, so when it does exist, it should be lean, cheap, and designed to achieve its own obsolescence.[95]

The Department of Interior had the third most civilian employees in the entire federal government by the turn of the century. Congress, at the same time, was completely unaccountable to citizens in the territories. Alexander refers to this as a "power vacuum" that "allowed Congress to disregard territorial needs and wishes with impunity. Political pressure forced it to appropriate money for eastern and midwestern rivers and harbor projects and for naval displays in New York, but there could be no effective political pressure applied from the territories for additional funds for land and irrigation surveys or to pay adequate salaries." Nonetheless, federal money was a huge part of the western equation. White notes:

> Particularly in the early years, government expenditures formed the lifeblood of a territory as the federal government heavily subsidized territorial economies. The direct subsidy to the territorial government was relatively small, but the government maintained military posts in the territories and spent money to fulfill treaty obligations to Indians. It built roads, provided and staffed land offices, and extended mail routes into newly settled areas. Such expenditures could be sizable. In New Mexico during the 1850s, for example, the federal cost of defending the territory was $3,000,000 a year, with over a thousand civilian workers employed at Fort Union alone. Over 8 percent of the money in circulation in New Mexico came from army expenditures. Colonel Edwin Sumner summarized the situation: "The truth is, the only resource of this country is the government money. All classes depend on it from the professional man and the trader down to beggar."[96]

"From the building of the transcontinental railroads through the Bureau of Reclamation's irrigation efforts in the West, the government provided the only alternative to total dependence on eastern or foreign capital," continues White. "As a result," he notes,

> successful western politicians have been those able to secure federal favors for significant constituents or constituencies. In the East, politicians sought to prevent federal interference with the power held by corporations; in the South, they sought to prevent federal interference with an established racial order. In the West, politicians sought federal intervention to open up Indian reservations, build railroads, and guarantee cheap and docile labor; above all they have sought to control federal land and resource policy.[97]

This unusual position helps explain the origins of one of the great ironies of western American political culture today: its fierce libertarian streak coupled with tepid collectivism and extreme respect for federal patronage and corporate interest. Comments Alexander:

> For territorial politicians, the ability to make sure that such federal expenditures kept flowing and found their way into the correct pockets depended on maintaining and strengthening one's ties to the party in power in Congress and at the same time trying to destroy the ties of a rival. Under these circumstances, territorial politics often became politics of personality as one faction or official tried to blacken the reputation of others.

"Territorial government under these conditions of patronage, factionalism, and boosterism came to sport a special adornment," continues White, "the so-called territorial rings, which were corrupt combinations of business owners and politicians. They existed to turn public expenditures into private profits." Institutionally decoupled from Congress, state and local government in the West became a particularly fertile place for financial skullduggery.[98]

It should also be noted that a surprising number of federal employees "went native" in the West, organizing illegal wars and antigovernment revolutions with tacit federal support. General John C. Frémont charged about the frontier as if it were his own personal kingdom, an American Kurtz in a Native American "heart of darkness." Men like Frémont established independent "republics" in places like California, New Mexico, and Texas. The specter of vigilantism lurked everywhere. The Texas Rangers were originally founded as an extragovernmental (that is, private, civilian) military organization devoted to the "protection" of Anglo rights on the Hispanic frontier. Lawless gangs roamed 1860s Montana, while the sheriff of one major town, Bannock, commanded his own murderous posse. Limited in their ability to remove local law enforcement from office, a vigilante movement arose in 1863 to expel Bannock's corrupt sheriff. San Francisco itself was twice overrun by vigilante armies—the San Francisco Vigilance Committee of 1856 comprised some six to eight thousand members who ruled the entire city for almost a year, jailing and lynching city dwellers at will, especially those of "foreign" extraction.[99]

Nonetheless, the federal government retained the reins of power despite efforts to undermine its jurisdiction. Federal oversight of the territories was originally conceived as a temporary measure, but

> this combination of federal control, political corruption, and dependence on federal economic support was neither temporary nor fleeting in many areas. Washington spent more than thirty years as a territory. Utah spent nearly half a century, and New Mexico was a territory for more than sixty years. The territorial era would not end in the trans-Missouri West until 1912, when New Mexico and Arizona entered the Union as states. It survived outside of the West in Alaska and Hawaii well into the twentieth century.[100]

Richard White, one of America's preeminent frontier historians, aptly communicates the nuance and ramifications of this system; his words bear repeating:

> This long territorial interlude, during which federal government dominated western government, shaped the political realities of much of the Western United States. The West lived for long periods under a system in which local political power, while considerable, always needed the approval of outside officials. Many westerners came to associate public office holders with incompetence and corruption. They resented the federal government both for its power and for its failure to use that power to help the people. They simultaneously denounced federal tyranny and clamored for increased federal expenditures in their region. This long territorial period thus left a legacy of ambivalence toward the federal government that would continue into

twentieth-century western politics. Migrants had expected to transform the West into a replica of the East. They only partially succeeded; they created a region that, while sharing the institutions of the nation, forced these institutions into new forms.[101]

We thus see the concretization of two distinct national political systems in their nineteenth-century expansion and consolidation of rule. Westward accession accentuated the features of early colonial administration, bearing witness to the institutional strengths and weaknesses of comparable federal systems. In Canada, slow growth was the cost of measured autonomy and persistent law and order. In the United States, western economies boomed, though so did opportunism, corruption, and a generally agonistic tenor of life. In both cases, the social norms of the frontier had a reciprocal effect on their federal capitals and eastern metropoles via the migration of talent, capital, and influence, thereby transforming the nations as a whole.

8

Nations Reborn

Political cultures are never so static as to reach the point of no return, nor are the people of the former British colonies of North America particularly given to inertia, stagnation, or complacency. In fact, many of the things we most associate with contemporary Canadian and American political culture were, in hindsight, barely visible well into the last century.

Despite their contemporary outlook of inclusive multiculturalism, for example, Canadians at the beginning of the twentieth century supported strong anti-immigration laws designed to minimize the presence of non-whites and non-Christians in their country. Ample welfare state programs also were anathema in Canada at that time. In the late 1930s, for instance, Canada's Parliament still insisted that poor relief and unemployment insurance were undesirable stopgaps best left to local government. One of the questions we must ask in this chapter is how the long-run trends and tendencies we have discussed thus far have constrained and enabled the short-term tacks and jibes of recent national political development.

The United States also changed enormously in the twentieth century, particularly with regard to the size and scope of its federal government. Prohibition bolstered the formation of new federal surveillance and "special" crime enforcement agencies. Vast increases were also made in federal land management and regulatory powers. And while some American social service programs grew enormously during this period—none more so than the Social Security system of pensions for the elderly, widows, and the disabled—other important programs were allowed to lapse after the trials of the Great Depression and the Second World War.

More than in any other realm, midcentury growth in the size and jurisdiction of the American federal government occurred in the defense sector. American imperial ambitions had been on the rise since the mid-nineteenth century, culminating first in the Spanish-American War of 1898, which greatly extended the international range of American political and economic interests, and then the First World War, in which vast armadas of troops and mechanized armaments were mobilized for overseas engagement. Concern over the control of America's official and unofficial protectorates was a motivating factor in both the expansion of the federal armed forces and their increasing involvement in global geopolitics.[1]

America's armed forces had been drastically cut back after the Civil War and replaced by volunteer militias and local units of the National Guard. The Militia Act of 1903 and Hays National Defense Act of 1916 helped pave the way for the use of local Guard units in foreign conflicts, thus overturning the founders' desire to limit the use of American armed forces to domestic self-defense.[2]

Despite President Wilson's fervent efforts to keep America out of World War I, rumors that the German government had approached Mexico about taking preemptive military action against the United States was considered incontrovertible support for the argument that America's jurisdictional autonomy could only be preserved through conflict. As in the War of 1812, German and British attempts to restrict the activities of "neutral" American merchant ships were seen as justification for war. Many private, nonprofit associations—such as the American Legion, the Military Training Camps Association, the Junior American Guard, and the National Society for Patriotic Education—helped push the United States toward war by sponsoring private military training camps and public propaganda on behalf of wartime mobilization.[3]

Canada faced a very different set of challenges in deciding whether or not to enter the First World War. Nearly a half century after confederation, Canadians were still legally obligated to support Great Britain in war, though the nature of those obligations had become increasingly ambiguous. Could Canada be "required" by Great Britain to supply a specific number of troops? Could she be forced to conscript an army into imperial service? And if so, how much say would Canadian generals and politicians have in making military decisions regarding their troops? Canadian forces stayed under British command, but one offshoot of Canada's otherwise successful war effort was a nasty feud between Quebec and the rest of the nation. This, in fact, began the contemporary Franco-English conflict that festers in Canada to this day.

Social and political relations between English and French Canadians in Quebec had been relatively peaceful since the *Patriote* rebellion of 1837. At the outset of the First World War, French Canadians actually rallied around the flag—the *British* flag! (Support for France, interestingly, remained tepid; Quebec was a much more religious and politically conservative place than France at the time, and Quebecers were generally quite suspicious of France's atheistic, socialist leanings.) Québécois priests and politicians lauded the commonwealth cause. The provincial government of Quebec even offered Britain four million pounds of cheese "as a freewill offering to the imperial authorities."[4]

Quebec had earned unprecedented jurisdictional autonomy under the provincial arrangements of confederation. Quebec's provincial government had jurisdiction over its churches, schools, natural resources, and tax revenues. Quebec did not have jurisdiction over defense policy, however; nor could it control events in other provinces, such as limitations put on French language instruction in Ontario schools in 1915, a policy change poorly timed to concur with the second year of the war. This about-face infuriated francophone Quebecers, as it did Ontario's francophone minority. In response to the Ontario schools controversy and related events in Manitoba, French-Canadian newspapers almost immediately began backing away from support for the war. Quebec's Nationalist Party began questioning Ottawa's war policy. French-Canadian goodwill toward the rest of Canada disappeared. Quebec nationalism had come of age.

In 1917, when Canadian military commitments demanded widespread conscription, French-Quebecers rose up in protest, rioting repeatedly in the spring and summer in cities like Montreal, Quebec, and Trois-Rivières. (There had been similar threats of anti-draft action in Quebec during the South African, or Boer War.) Serious talk of secession swept the province. Former prime minister Wilfred Laurier, "the great compromiser," saw his powerful Liberal bloc decimated by the draft issue. Later that summer, the police uncovered a secret plot to bomb the Montreal residence of English-Canadian newspaper magnate,

Hugh Graham, Lord Atholstan. Over Easter weekend in 1918, bloody antidraft riots ensued after a young French Canadian was detained by the police for not having his draft exemption papers on hand.[5]

Laurier soon convinced Quebecers to do their part in the war effort, however, and he also helped broker much-needed reforms to Canada's military recruitment system. Anticonscription riots quickly died down, and the nation turned directly to the business of war. Though it seems a bit facile to say, there is some truth to historian Elizabeth Armstrong's claim that, "The French Canadian had every intention of standing up for what he considered his just rights, but none whatsoever of turning revolutionary. The law remained the law, and the constituted authorities were there to be obeyed." The seeds of open dissent had already been sown, however. Secession was, for the first time, a bona fide political option for nationalist Quebecers.[6]

During the first few years of the war, it was entirely unclear whether the United States would remain neutral, fight with the entente (France, Russia, and the United Kingdom), or fight *against* them. International relations were fraught between the United States and all of its possible allies. In 1895, when President Cleveland put the nation on the brink of war with Britain over a border dispute in South America, War Department planners began drafting official scripts for a would-be invasion of Canada. A large tract of land in upstate New York was purchased in 1909 for military training exercises in the snowy plains just south of eastern Ontario—Fort Drum. A trade dispute between the United States and Canada in 1911 heightened tensions. Though President Taft glibly dismissed talk of violence, American forces stood at the ready.[7]

Trade relations, rather than international relations, ultimately kept the United States, Canada, and Great Britain closely allied: After 1914, when German submarines began attacking American merchant marine vessels, some carrying industrial and agricultural supplies to support the imperial war effort, American sympathies quickly turned against Germany and toward Great Britain. The United States could not afford to stop trading with Britain because of the size of its markets and its favorable terms for long-standing trade partners. But while the United States slowly geared up for war, it too suffered a serious wave of dissent.[8]

It is telling how differently draft resisters and war protesters were treated in the United States and Canada. In the United States, anticonscription rallies were met with severe, state-sanctioned violence. Both the police, the military, and private armed citizens took part. Protesters were viciously attacked, beaten, and jailed. German Americans were openly taunted and harassed. Journalists, lecturers, and labor organizers were all targeted for sedition. In Boston, notes Fleming, a peaceful labor union rally was "attacked by well-organized squads of soldiers and sailors commanded by uniformed officers. For three hours the military pursued, clubbed, kicked, and battered the paraders, often forcing them to kiss the American flag on their knees." In eastern St. Louis, white workers held riots, protesting the arrival of black migrant laborers looking for work in the city's booming factories—the rioters were responding to rumors being circulated that German agents were recruiting black revolutionaries in the American South. Whites went on killing sprees in black neighborhoods throughout St. Louis. Samuel Gompers, emperor of American labor, blamed black strike breakers for the violence. President Wilson refused to meet with a delegation from the National Association for the Advancement of Colored People (NAACP) seeking redress.[9]

American Socialist organizations were particularly hard hit during the war years. Federal persecution of suspected "reds" and Communists began in earnest. Such actions were predicated upon the jurisdictional ambiguity of American war powers. As Lincoln and Adams had done previously, the American president assumed the power to suppress "treasonous" activity in the name of national security.

In Canada, by contrast, antiwar efforts were met more peaceably and prowar sentiments were expressed more reasonably. Part of the reason for this was a jurisdictional stipulation that prosecution of suspected Communists and "dangerous" radicals in Canada had to be initiated at the provincial level, thus limiting Ottawa's ability to expand its powers under the aegis of homeland security. Nativism, too, was milder in wartime Canada than in the United States. A federal War Measures Act was passed in 1914, allowing for the detention of thousands of German and other "alien" residents—nearly nine thousand immigrants were detained in Canadian detention camps for "enemy aliens" during the war—but the overall tenor of immigration-related police action was rather tempered. In 1916, the city of Berlin, Ontario, had its name changed to Kitchener, but it was only tepidly supported by residents. In the United States, by contrast, anti-German action was exceedingly common.[10]

Freedom of the press also took a beating in the wartime United States. In West Virginia, a Socialist Party member was jailed for six months for publishing an antidraft pamphlet, a sentence later upheld by the US Supreme Court. The American system had emerged as one designed to meet dissent, especially from the Far Left, with quick and decisive force. Counterintelligence, police brutality, and arbitrary enforcement of firearms and freedom of association statutes all afforded the executive branch a free hand. Dissent from American foreign policy was, and is, a limited civil right in times of war.[11]

Legal, or quasi-legal, violence has long been a predicate of American domestic and foreign policy, and such tendencies have a tendency to grow and mutate over time. The constitutional limits placed on the war powers of sitting presidents have been repeatedly and consistently undermined. Leftists and labor unionists are still objects of intense federal scrutiny. Guns, gunplay, and civilian readiness to support nationalist militancy are mainstays of the American experience.

Corporate Culture and the Progressive Era

Private, for-profit corporations are powerful in both Canada and the United States today; nonetheless, there are persistent differences in the scale and scope of corporate power: There are not only many more corporations per capita in the United States than in Canada, but American corporations are legally granted access to, and influence over, the political process in ways not tolerated in Canada. The roots of this system began in colonial New England but were firmly entrenched in the emerging American West, where land, railroad, and mining companies had free reign over the territories and, in the face of weak federal oversight, formed unusually close ties with Washington. Notably then, the idea of reforming—that is, limiting—the power of for-profit (but not nonprofit) corporations became a key aim of the so-called progressive movement in the United States. During this same period, Canadian ire was focused more on tariffs and the banking sector, both of which directly affected the financial prospects of Canada's thriving farmers. In general, the Canadian economy was much less robust than America's at the time. Many of its largest firms were owned and financed with foreign capital, and it lacked the intense entrepreneurship of the US economy. Farming and resource extraction (timber and fish, for example) were still the mainstays of the Canadian economy.[12]

Two forms of American political behavior that were typical at this time came together to make the Progressive Era distinctive: first, a tendency to create various and sundry voluntary associations for every purpose imaginable; second, a spirit of righteous indignation toward government affairs. Thus, the US Progressive Era was awash in so-called reform clubs.

Numerous private reform organizations were founded in the 1870s and 1880s in response to widely publicized political scandals and the financial panic of 1873. By the mid-1890s, and accelerating into the 1900s and 1910s, the influence of reform clubs in American cities was widespread and their organizational forms were multiple. This was also an era when political discourse, if not political office, was increasingly dominated by "amateurs." For example, consider New York's once-influential City Reform Club, founded in 1882 by a twenty-four-year-old politician then just out of Harvard—Theodore Roosevelt. Upset by the "deplorable lack of interest in the political questions of the day among respectable, well-educated men," Roosevelt promptly sent out invitations to join a club that would help bring to office "citizens of high personal character and known capacity, who will administer their offices on business principles as opposed to party methods." Unlike most civic associations of the time, there were no formal membership requirements save a statute prohibiting admission of "politicians" to the club. Nevertheless, most who joined were prominent, native-born businessmen and professionals, many of whom were close personal friends or familial acquaintances.[13]

Describing the rise of this new form of political organization in turn-of-the-century American cities, historian Richard McCormick writes:

> Civic group organizations of all sorts began to take permanent roles pressuring, advising, and cooperating with the different agencies of New York City government, no matter which party was in office.... Tenement-house reform, health and sanitation matters, schools, utility franchises, and mass transit all drew the attention of specialized reform organizations. Some occupational groups, especially merchants, lawyers, doctors, engineers, and other professionals, also began using their economic-interest associations to inform and pressure city officials about particular matters where they had demands to make and expertise to offer. Common to these efforts were certain methods of operation: the collection of information, the reliance on experts, the establishment of close working relations with the relevant city departments, and the acquisition

of the influence that came with regularly having answers to difficult problems of municipal governance.

This new form of political mobilization is perhaps the Progressive Era's greatest legacy to the realm of American urban affairs. Many years later, after the hopes of the City Beautiful movement had faded, the influence of special-interest lobbies remained, sometimes an unprecedented weapon of the weak, much too often the irrepressible bludgeon of the strong. McCormick aptly summarizes the impact of the movement in saying: "Here were informed and aroused citizens who had found non-electoral means of permanently participating in municipal administration and of modernizing it according to their own lights."[14]

Early twentieth-century "reform" groups supported two fundamental ideas, neither of which would be seen as overly "progressive" today: The first was a firm if not prophetic belief in the power of "business principles" to set right the ship of state; so-called scientific management required scientific methods, training, and data collection. The nation's first professional schools of social work and public administration were founded in the dawning years of the new century.[15]

A second progressive ideal, one closely allied with the new "gospel of efficiency," was the belief that foreigners and working-class agitators were ignorant of this new "science" of public administration, and thus incapable of stewarding the public interest. Here again, the specter of corruption and profligacy reared its ugly head, as immigrants were blamed for all the ills of American municipal government. Nowhere was this logic more convoluted than in discussion of the rapid growth of municipal expenditure, which Good Government reformers blamed on the "Hibernian [that is, Irish-Catholic] oligarchy" while simultaneously endorsing enormous appropriations for public parks, streetcars, public buildings, and other "European" advances. Quoth E. L. Godkin, standard bearer of late-century mugwumpery, in the thinly veiled language of Spencerian Social Darwinism, "The great law which Nature seems to have prescribed for the government of the world, and the only law of human society which we are able to extract from history, is that the more intelligent and thoughtful of the race shall inherit the earth and have the best time, and that all others shall find life on the whole dull and unprofitable."[16]

One unusual aspect of the dialogue of reform displayed at the time was its obsession with "cleanliness." Reformist speeches were literally peppered with sanitary metaphors for the body politic, conveniently comparing corruption to infectious disease and political reform to a "clean sweep" of the city. In Reverend Parkhurst's *Our Fight with Tammany* (1895), for example, the author disparages "the slimy, oozy soil of Tammany Hall," claims that it had turned the city into an "open cesspool," and refers to the reform campaign as an exercise in "municipal sewerage" designed to "drain that political quagmire, and . . . get rid of the odor, the mire, and the fever germs." Similarly, William T. Stead, who helped organize Chicago's Civic Federation in the terrible winter of 1893, describes Chicago as "the *cloaca maxima* of the world," in his messianic *If Christ Came to Chicago* (1894). Plunging still further into classical allusion, Stead refers to the city's aldermen as men who have turned City Hall into an "Augean stable" in desperate need of a Herculean "revival of civic faith."[17]

Despite the progressives' interest in "efficiency" and "scientific management," their perception that naked capitalism had beached the American economy lent credence to the idea that, despite the obvious corruptibility of government officials and party operatives, the public interest was best served by *public corporations*. The call for "municipalization" generally began at the point where city rate payers found themselves paying exorbitant rates for shoddy service. The question then became; Who is more corruptible: public officials or private profiteers? THIS was an issue debated *ad nauseam* in the literature of the period.[18]

Gustavus Myers concludes in his (1900) study of the "History of Public Franchises in New York City," published in *Municipal Affairs*, a national reformist magazine, that:

> The process has been very much the same in every line. First, there was [private] competition more or less severe. Then came combination, division of territory or a working agreement. This period came to an end either through the formation of a new company, because of the large profits made, or the breaking of agreements because of internal dissatisfaction. Strenuous competition—rate wars—followed, which end in combination or agreements, and finally after one or two complete revolutions of the wheel, all interests merged into one gigantic corporation.

Rather than calling for sterner regulation of the marketplace, however, Myers calls for *greater* monopolization of city services, preferably under the aegis of local government. "Something must take the place of competition," he demands. Whereas monopolies were strictly limited on the interstate level by the Sherman Anti-Trust Act, they were (and are) actually quite prevalent at the city level.[19]

Great debate ensued across the country, pitting municipal reformists against laissez-faire advocates. In his 1903 text, *Municipal Public Works: Their Inception, Construction, and Management,* Samuel Whitney comments:

> No question relating to city government or municipal economics has in recent years been discussed with more interest and zeal on both sides than that of whether it is best for municipal corporations to own outright and operate plants for supplying public utilities. So great has been the zeal of those who have been engaged in this discussion, whether on the one side or on the other, and so exaggerated have been the statements and claims made, that the careful student is often bewildered and confused as to the real facts and the sober arguments upon the basis of which the question must in the end be answered.[20]

In some cases, municipalization was used only as a club to threaten private firms into improving service; in other cases, there was a groundswell of electoral support for public ownership of one form or another. In cities across the country, politicians began running on full- or partial-municipalization tickets, promising to rectify poor services in one or more areas by getting government involved. Mayor Hazen Pingree was elected in Detroit on such grounds, as were Tom Johnson in Cleveland and Edward Dunne, with his "Immediate Municipal Ownership" platform, in Chicago. In New York, newspaper tycoon William Randolph Hearst was nearly elected governor on a similar platform. The quarterly reform periodical *Municipal Affairs* also launched a campaign in favor of "municipal socialism" during its short life span (1896 to 1902).[21]

The debate about municipal ownership was one that was never really resolved in the American national consciousness, and there is probably as much debate and city-level variance today as there was at the turn of the century. Whether or not the progressives achieved their dream of efficient and civic-minded public utilities, the period marks a high point in deliberation over the issue. Mass transit and utility companies were as good or bad as their particular sponsors, and individual city-level decisions seemed to reflect the exigencies of backroom deal making and the vagaries of available backers and investment capital more than any singular commitment to one or the other method of regulating the economy. Political culture was, again, a highly variable, highly amorphous simulacrum of competing interests, electoral exigencies, and political-institutional constraints. Having created a sociolegal space for corporations, however, the corporate organizational form remained (and remains) a centerpiece of American political action and public policy. While opinions change about the most desirable function and form of corporations, their importance in social, political, and economic action remains sacrosanct, protected equally by the judicial, executive, and legislative branches of federal government.

A related feature of the Progressive Era in the United States was the transformation of the political party system from one based on local machines and grassroots organization to one dominated by professional party operatives and corporate fund-raising. Most famous of the innovators in this domain is Mark Hanna, who masterminded William McKinley's defeat of the charismatic Democrat-Populist William Jennings Bryan in their hotly contested 1896 presidential race. Seen in hindsight, it is ironic that Bryan, a Democrat, campaigned as a God-fearing Evangelical Christian intent on instituting the "social gospel" throughout the land and was handily defeated by a secular Republican, William McKinley. Only much later, in the 1980s and 1990s, did the American Republican Party assume the religious mantle, this time transposing it with laissez-faire economics instead of quasi-socialist populism.

Bryan ran for president several more times, but never as successfully as his 1896 bid. Though many factors contributed to his defeat, one was surely the Republican Party's innovations in big-money electoral campaigning. Under Mark Hanna's tutelage, McKinley outspent Bryan by nearly twelve to one, money raised largely from corporate concerns wanting to protect their business interests via a McKinley victory. Hanna bureaucratized the Republican National Committee and updated campaign and patronage techniques for the new age. At Hanna's urging, McKinley also used the press to push the nation into a one-sided war with Spain that resulted in the acquisition of new territories in Latin America and the Philippines. Ultimately, the rising role of corporate fund-raising and professional lobby organizations utterly transformed American politics. Canada, by contrast, has worked hard to limit the role of outside funding in political campaigns.[22]

Reform seems to come in unusually frequent waves in the United States; reformism never completely disappears, but it often wanes. Every so often, however, something cataclysmic triggers a public spate of self-loathing conveniently targeted at the one group almost everyone can turn on: the *politicos*. In the trenchant words of Lincoln Steffens, *McClure's* star muckraker:

> [For] reform with us is usually revolt, not government, and is soon over. Our people do not seek, they avoid self-rule, and "reforms" are spasmodic efforts to punish bad rulers and get somebody that will give us good government or something that will make it. A self-acting form of government is an ancient superstition. We are an inventive people, and we all think that we shall devise some day a legal machine that will turn out good government automatically.[23]

Political Activism and Labor Unionism

In line with Americans' passionate embrace of messianic political rhetoric, American workers, labor organizations, and activists have been more vocal, strident, and radical than their Canadian counterparts. Today, however, many more Canadians join and support unions than in the United States. Explaining the reason for this "switch" is yet another challenge of comparing American and Canadian political development.[24]

Bona fide labor unionism did not come into being in northern North America until the late nineteenth century, after numerous other features of Canadian and American political culture had already been put in place. In Canada, French-Catholic workers created conservative Christian unions beholden to church sentiment and averse to socialism and radicalism. In English Canada, various movements and groups came and went, many affiliated with American labor organizations. In general, Canadian workers seemed relatively uninterested in socialism or radicalism of any kind. Says Canadian labor historian H. A. Logan, "The political experiments, the radicalism, and the various panaceas which successively challenged industrial methods in the United States found no response in Canada—if perchance they were known among the workers at all. The outlook in Canada [before the 1870s] was local and divided; in fact there was no labour *movement*."[25]

Prior to the legal recognition of the right of Canadian workers to unionize in 1948, notes Kenneth Tunnell, "Government policies and legislation sided with employers, leaving workers who attempted to organize to not only engage in conflict with the employer but with a politico-legal system that was far from neutral." Nonetheless, though Canada possessed strong antilabor laws, it only weakly enforced them. Strange and Loo note, "Despite the clarity of the [Canadian] law against combinations, and the antipathy of many employers towards trade unions, few workers were actually prosecuted for criminal conspiracy in the nineteenth century." Canada also limited the power of employer associations and similar groups. Beginning in the early 1870s, note Strange and Loo, "the courts ruled that combinations of employers, like the Canadian Manufacturers' Association, were legal [only] as long as they did not unduly 'restrain' trade." In the United States, by contrast, such organizations were popular and legally protected, as were employer-led efforts to physically intimidate union organizers and "radicals." The American system validates both sides of the class divide and lets them fight to the finish.[26]

The paternalistic streak in Canadian common law, and its traditional restraints on corporate activity in general, lent the courts the power to consider what would be "fair," as well as "equitable" in the marketplace. American courts have traditionally eschewed responsibility for "fairness." Employer associations were thus given a much freer hand in the United States, where the courts were not accountable for "power disparities" and the like. American courts repeatedly overturned congressional acts aimed at promoting fair competition, collective bargaining, and safe workplace provisions. In discussing the role of the American federal courts, Robert H. Jackson says, "The final refuge of property from unwelcome legislative restrictions or burdens was the courts. Its advocates beat incessantly upon the big bass drum of the Constitution and, when that did not work, argued for an 'interpretation' of statutes which would eviscerate them." By such means, the Federal Trade Commission, the Sherman Anti-Trust Act, and various appendages of trade union and labor law were undermined through litigation. "Popular government demanded a curb on the growing financial and industrial giants," Jackson writes. "The courts put a curb on the popular will instead." American labor regulation was not formally systematized until the 1930s, and even then, suspected radicals and Communists were subject to unusually strict surveillance and suspicion. Employers also retained strong legal protections against striking workers and political protests. These legal disparities have helped quell repeated tides of radicalism and leftist political organizing in the United States.[27]

The case of socialist Eugene Debs's American Railway Union is an excellent example of the rise and fall of radical unionism in the United

States. In June 1893, Debs, former secretary-treasurer of the Brotherhood of Locomotive Firemen, resigned his office and founded the American Railway Union (ARU), a new industrial union hoping to represent all railroad employees. Prior to the formation of the ARU, railway workers had largely organized around the quasi-fraternal model espoused by the Knights of Labor—"secret fraternal societies, emphasizing primarily insurance systems to protect members and their families from the hazards of the very dangerous occupation of railroading." With the exception of the Brotherhood of Locomotive Engineers (founded in 1863), the remaining rail-related labor organizations—the Order of Railway Conductors, the Brotherhood of Locomotive Firemen, the Brotherhood of Railroad Brakemen, and the Switchmen's Mutual Association—were poorly organized, poorly subscribed, and generally unconcerned with the larger problems of American workers. This is rather surprising given the low-wage/high-risk nature of railroad work at that time, but, like some factions of the Knights of Labor, members of the railway brotherhoods considered themselves "aristocrats of labor" and espoused "bread-and-butter" unionism (that is, simple agitation for better wages and working conditions), as opposed to political agitation for widespread transformation of the American capitalist system. They sought respect, not revolution.[28]

The ARU's first major success came in the spring of 1894, when, in response to wage cuts on the Great Northern Railroad, all nine thousand employees—including engineers, conductors, switchmen, truckmen, roundhouse workers, firemen, and section hands—united in opposition and shut down all of the railway's transcontinental trains. After an eighteen-day strike, the company relented. A rush to join the ARU's ranks ensued, swelling membership at a rate of two thousand new railway workers a day. By the end of that year, the ARU was one hundred fifty thousand members strong, while the rival brotherhoods' ranks were shrinking rapidly (membership stood around ninety thousand at that point).[29]

The railroad owners were quick to react with a powerful, new "association" of their own. Founded in 1886 in response to widespread strikes that year, the General Managers' Association (GMA) was a coalition of businessmen representing twenty-four member railroads centered or terminating in Chicago, each committed to breaking strikes and suppressing wage demands through collective action. It was one of the first national employer associations and, as ARU members soon found out, it could be a powerful and coercive presence in the labor arena.[30]

A showdown occurred in Pullman, Illinois, a company town owned and operated by George Pullman, founder of the Pullman Palace Car Company. Though the Pullman Strike, or "Debs' Rebellion," eventually led to the demise of the American Railway Union and the beginning of an especially rough spell for American labor, it started as a relatively minor labor dispute over wages in arrears from the previous year. The newly organized workers formed a grievance committee to present demands for reduction in rent, an investigation and correction of shop abuses, and the restoration of wages to pre-Depression levels. Pullman refused to budge, and three members of the grievance committee were summarily laid off despite promises that no such retaliatory actions would be taken against worker representatives. Nonetheless, when workers met with officials from the ARU, they were advised to put off hasty action. Not to be deterred, four thousand Pullman workers walked off the job at noon on May 11, 1894, and a central strike committee was established. (Though not directly employed in the railway industry itself, Pullman employees had begun organizing their own branches of the American Railway Union in March 1894.)[31]

On June 26, 1894, the strike officially began. In a few days, nearly 125,000 workers across the central and western United States had joined in. Though the leaders of the railroad brotherhoods refused to participate (and actually encouraged scabs to cross picket lines), many of their members broke ranks, joined the boycott and, in some cases, actually defected to the rival ARU. Railroad workers refused to decouple Pullman cars or even operate trains containing them. By June 28, traffic out of Chicago was at a standstill, and at least eleven regional lines sat idle. This was, according to labor historian Philip Foner, "the first truly nationwide strike" in the United States.[32]

The reaction of the General Managers' Association was fast and furious. On June 29, they announced that any worker who was discharged for refusal to perform his duties would *never* again find work on *any* railroad represented by the GMA. They also had an important ace up their sleeve: Richard Olney, US attorney general. Olney was a former member of the GMA and legal counsel for the Boston & Maine Railroad. Edwin Walker, Olney's special deputy, remained an *active* employee of the GMA even while working on the case for the Justice Department. Wielding his considerable powers of office, Olney opened a federal case against the leaders of the ARU, stating that the strike was illegally interfering with the transit of federal property—the US mail. Despite the persistent objections of Illinois governor John Peter Altgeld, Olney also successfully petitioned President Cleveland to send federal troops to Chicago to enforce the injunction and quell the strikes.[33]

On July 10, 1894, a federal grand jury in Chicago returned indictments against the officers of the ARU, and Debs and several deputies were picked up and arrested. Union leaders responded by calling for a citywide strike, and they went so far as to petition American Federation of Labor (AFL) leader Samuel Gompers for help. This was the beginning of the end of the American Railway Union. Gompers, already at odds with Debs over his refusal to bring the ARU into the AFL, refused to cooperate—factionalism has always been a problem for the American labor movement. Gompers took the ARU's collapse as validation of his own conservative union ideal. In response to Debs's desperate pleas for help, the Executive Council of the AFL firmly staked their ground, a stance that predominated over American labor for the next three decades:

> We claim to be as patriotic and law-abiding as any other class of citizens, a claim substantiated by our actions in times of public need and public peril. . . . The trade union movement is one of reason, one of deliberation, and depending entirely upon the voluntary and sovereign action of its members. It is democratic in principle and action, conservative in its demands, and consistent in its efforts to secure them.

Radical labor movements occasionally surfaced again in the United States—most notably the Industrial Workers of the World (IWW, or "wobblies")—but they remained hampered by the combination of strong legal protections for employers seeking to combat union militants and strong opposition from the conservative, bread-and-butter AFL movement.[34]

The US Supreme Court subsequently issued a number of decisions barring union activity of various forms, most notably in the Debs case, in which the Sherman Anti-Trust Act was invoked to restrict workers' power to strike and boycott. "From then on," comments legal historian Lawrence Friedman, "the injunction, in the hands of a strong-minded judge, was a mighty adversary that organized labor had to reckon with. The injunction was swift, and it could be murderously inclusive—broad enough in its contours to cover a total situation, outlawing every aspect of a strike and effectively crushing it." Though many states had *prolabor* legislation on the books, particularly those requiring payment of workers in a fair and timely manner, state courts frequently threw them out on constitutional grounds.[35]

While both countries experienced extended periods of labor upheaval, one can fairly say that America's unions had largely been "tamed" by the 1890s, whereas Canada's unions were only then beginning to radicalize, culminating in the nationwide Winnipeg General Strike of 1919. Nevertheless, until the 1960s, the percentage of the nonagricultural workforce enrolled in labor unions was nearly the same in the United States and Canada. At that point, American unionization rates began to drop precipitously while Canada's unions began a period of steady increase. Many factors obviously contributed to this divergence, but two long-standing differences were clearly at play: first, the legal advantages afforded American employers vis-à-vis labor unions, which put American employers in a stronger position than Canadian managers in disputes with employees; second, the general tradition of bread-and-butter unionism in the United States, which focuses on bolstering the wages of members rather than improving the conditions of workers more generally. Over time, Canadian unions found support in increasingly union-friendly legislation and in the formation of various labor-left parties. This set the stage for growing union density in late twentieth-century Canada. In the United States, equally inhospitable conditions left unions vulnerable to hostile legislation, mainly in the Reagan era, and to employer resistance, particularly as the manufacturing base of the American economy weakened.[36]

Though these differences in union density and orientation are plainly evident today, they would have been quite difficult to predict a century ago. In addition, none of the major social programs for which Canada is now known were instituted until the 1940s. In the meantime, however, Canadian farmers achieved impressive gains in the political and economic spheres, particularly in the wheat-growing provinces of Alberta and Saskatchewan. Though radical farm movements were not uncommon in the United States—neighboring North Dakota had a series of successful reform governments in the early twentieth century, for example—American radicals were never able to break free of the existing two-party system, nor were they able to sustain political momentum long enough to leave a major imprint on state politics. A central feature of western American political development was the early infiltration of the territories by operatives of the national political parties. Third-party movements were thus difficult to sustain at the state level, dominated as the statehouses were by the nation's two major parties. This was not the case in Alberta or Saskatchewan, where both the parliamentary system and a preconfederation tradition of independent provincial parties kept the door open for movements other than the dominant Liberal and Conservative parties.

Two distinctively different third-party reform movements came to power in western Canada during the 1930s and early 1940s. The Co-operative Commonwealth Federation (CCF) was the first bona fide socialist government at the state/provincial level in northern North America. Its leaders in Saskatchewan created Canada's first state-run health insurance program in the 1940s, though "agrarian socialism" has lost some of its allure in the province in the years since. Two key factors help explain the rise of this movement in Saskatchewan: first, Saskatchewan's economy in the early twentieth century was almost entirely centered around wheat farming, which bolstered solidarity among the province's ethnically diverse population. Long before the advent of the CCF, the farmers of Saskatchewan were experimenting with quasi-socialist "wheat boards"— farmer-owned wholesale exchanges designed to benefit farmers by eliminating middlemen and stabilizing prices. Second, Canadian radicals were more deeply influenced by British than German socialism. The German socialist tradition was radical and strident; it was more common in the United States than Canada. British socialism, by contrast, was brought to Canada by its many British immigrants and was much more pragmatic. It pointed Canadian socialists in conciliatory, reformist directions rather than pitting them in a fight against the capitalist system. The rise of socialism in Saskatchewan was also facilitated by Canada's multiparty system. Third parties were, and are, quite viable in Canadian politics.[37]

Alberta's Social Credit Party grew from similar roots, but in a largely different direction. The Social Credit Party dominated provincial politics in Alberta from 1935 to 1971 and gave birth to the subsequent Reform Party movement of the 1980s and 1990s. The party was initially elected on an antibusiness, pro–worker/farmer campaign. Its founder, "Bible Bill" Aberhart, was a barnstorming Evangelical preacher with ample access to voters via his weekly radio show. One of Aberhart's bedrock policies, adopted from the fringe English "social credit" movement, was the regular issuance of government paychecks to voters, a popular policy with no real economic logic behind it except the notion that a government/business cabal (suspected, in many circles, of being a worldwide Jewish conspiracy) profited unfairly from public resources and should thus be forced to kickback money to ordinary citizens. Free money was an illusion not unappreciated by Albertan farmers. Social Credit, like the CCF in neighboring Saskatchewan, also exploited local antipathy to eastern bankers and politicians. Given the strong powers granted provinces by the British North America Act (of 1867), provincial radicals could make serious promises about independence and reform. They also had the financial muscle to follow through on some of them. Aberhart forged an electoral alliance between agrarian populists and the business sector that still dominates Alberta today.[38]

As premier, Aberhart did surprisingly little to help Depression-era workers and farmers. A minister turned politician, he switched policies erratically and seemed to have little or no grasp of the actual workings of government. After his death, in 1943, the party was taken over by more self-consciously conservative politicians, such as Ernest Manning, whose son, Preston, went on to be a founding member of the ultraconservative Reform Party. (Even conservative Canadians are fairly "left" by American standards, at least on fiscal issues. Nonetheless, most still actively oppose social policies like same-sex marriage and abortion, both of which have since been legalized in Canada over their objections.) Social Credit was gradually transformed from a party devoted to fighting the pernicious influence of business on ordinary Canadians to one integrally committed to promoting the business interests of the province. Ernest Manning was a director of the Canadian Imperial Bank of Commerce, for example, whereas Aberhart's original Social Credit platform was anchored around fear and loathing of the banking industry. Part of the reason the party was able to stay in power so long was the landfall wealth generated by the discovery of major oil reserves in the province in 1947. Historian Alwin Finkel comments, somewhat controversially, "Social Credit's social expenditures, rather than its right-wing ideology, no doubt explained the government's popularity in the post-war period."[39]

Albertan conservatism grew out of its progressive movement. American radicals were originally more "radical" than their Canadian counterparts, yet the latter has a stronger tradition of state socialism today. These contradictions are largely products of abiding national differences in the legal protections given laborers and employers; the financial advantages given special interests in campaign finance; and jurisdictional differences in the power of subnational government to fight inequality, manage unemployment, and provide a basic social safety net for ordinary workers and their families.

Prohibition, Moral Regulation, and Criminal Law

Its current reputation notwithstanding, Canada was once a country of devout Catholics and Protestants who sought strict government enforcement of Christian behavior. Birth control was available but technically illegal, and divorce was rare and hard to obtain. Criminal law remained a matter of federal jurisdiction in Canada. Law enforcement, however, was chiefly left to the cities and provinces. This gave subfederal government some, but not too much, agency in forging its own moral compass.

In the United States, by contrast, the founders thought little about moral regulation and presumed that the states would evolve their own means of defining and enforcing moral behavior. Lacking large, state-supported churches, the American states were free to define state-sponsored morality on their own terms. The federal judiciary could steer state decisions of this kind, but only when provoked to action by local actors via the federal courts—which has happened with increasing frequency in the later decades of the twentieth century.

Canada's first prime minister, John A. Macdonald, clearly saw the importance of creating a rational, workable legal system for the new confederation. In addition to streamlining and consolidating the laws of Canada's four preexisting provinces, Macdonald oversaw construction of the British Empire's first fully integrated postcolonial criminal code. "For Macdonald," note Strange and Loo, "codification was a project in nation-building, akin to building the Canadian Pacific Railway; like the railway, a criminal code would unite disparate jurisdictions." One strength of this system was its lucid resolutions limiting excessive punishment for minor crimes, thus preventing the kind of ratchet-effect that has filled America's prisons with small-time drug dealers. Moreover, rather than using the criminal law to harass homosexuals and sexually active teens, Canada's early legal reformers created strong rape and seduction laws, thus creating a landmark regime of protection for crimes against women. Indecent assault and statutory rape were made crimes, and rape itself was changed from being defined as a crime against property to being a crime against a person, thus lowering the threshold for legally proving that rape had occurred. Firearms, too, became federally regulated in Canada over time. "There is not even the possibility of suggesting a specific constitutional support for the right to bear arms" in Canada, writes one analyst.[40]

After confederation, all but Canada's short-term prisons were placed under federal control, thus standardizing penal practice and taking the provinces out of the prison-building business, a huge industry in the contemporary United States. In general, public police forces remain small in size and scope in Canada. Many provinces and cities, especially in western Canada, adopted the practice of contracting out their police needs to the Royal Canadian Mounted Police rather than building their own force. This combination of strict insistence on lawful behavior and passive restriction of police power appears to have helped Canada realize John A. Macdonald's goal of founding a nation around the principles of "peace, order, and good government."[41]

The interesting thing about Canada's law and order ethos is the pragmatism underlying it. In the case of Prohibition, Canada was committed to combating "intemperance" through a combination of police enforcement and liquor licensing. Canada curtailed the consumption of alcohol during World War I, and it formally remained illegal in most parts of the country. But, whereas the United States attempted to ban alcohol outright via amendment to the federal constitution, Canada passed modest, pragmatic local bans. Following the 1880 federal court decision in *City of Fredericton v. the Queen,* in which the city's attorney made a strong but ultimately unsuccessful case against federal jurisdiction with respect to temperance policy, the provinces gradually gained greater control over this important area of public policy. In all but Quebec, the Canadian provinces banned the *public* consumption of alcohol—bars, saloons, and such; private consumption, however, was completely legal. Another legal wrinkle limited the manufacture of alcohol, though it remained legal to manufacture for international or transprovincial export. In practical terms, then, Prohibition-era Canadians could keep drinking as long as they bought their liquor from an "importer" and consumed it "in private." Thus recognizing the ills of public drunkenness and the impossibility of banning alcohol consumption outright, the Canadian political system embraced an ethos of limited moral legislation.[42]

If you have ever wondered what makes "Canadian whiskey" different than other kinds of whiskey, the answer lies deep in the heart of *American* law. The Eighteenth Amendment to the US Constitution banned the manufacture, distribution, and sale of alcohol everywhere in the United States. This did not stop millions of small "moon-shine" operations or hundreds of bathtub manufactories from operating. One result of outright Prohibition on the liquor trade in the United States was a drastic downturn in quality. American liquor prices during Prohibition largely reflected the risk of breaking the law. The very wealthy could procure contraband liquor from the finest European distilleries; the rest drank whatever was available. Some distillers made "whiskey" and "gin" by mixing high-test grain alcohol with artificial colors and whatever additives might be cheap and palatable. Turpentine, rubbing alcohol, and even animal carcasses sometimes found their way into American spirits.[43]

The manufacture of alcohol was still legal in Canada when American Prohibition began, and American gangsters soon realized that well-made liquor could fetch astronomical prices in the United States. "Canadian whiskey" thus came to signify pure, rather than adulterated or home-made spirits. "At the primary level of distribution," writes Ernest Forbes, a historian of the Maritime liquor trade, "rum-running emerged less as a new industry than as a redeployment of the [Canadian] fisheries." According to Forbes:

> In January 1925, the *Maritime Merchant* reported that about half the Lunenberg [Nova Scotia] fishing fleet of approximately one hundred vessels was engaged in the rum trade. Many of these were leased to American syndicates at the prevailing rate of $2,500 per month. In the same year, partly as a result of more vigorous American enforcement, monthly rentals on Lunenberg schooners rose to a reported $4,000.

Those who would not participate in the rum trade, such as the Maritimes' many Evangelical Christian fishermen, often sold their boats, "initially at bargain prices, to the rum-runners, whose needs created a growing market for second-hand boats and, eventually, for new vessels from the boatyards of the region."[44]

Given its proximity to Canada, Detroit became a key link in the American liquor trade. Smugglers bought small, fast boats that could sneak over to Canadian docks via the St. Clair River, the Detroit River, Lake St. Clair, and Lake Erie. American federal agents devoted significant resources to the battle against smugglers, but ultimately, the border remained extremely porous, particularly given the high wages smugglers could get working for American gangsters.[45]

Al Capone himself traveled to Saskatchewan in 1926 to arrange a business deal with the Bronfman brothers, creators of Canada's huge Seagram's empire. The Bronfmans wisely saw the profit in liquor exporting and built enormous factories in sleepy Canadian towns near the US border. From the Bronfmans' side of the table, their business was perfectly legal; they could manufacture and sell alcohol to Americans at will, as they could to distributors in other Canadian provinces. Mobsters like Capone, Lucky Luciano, and Detroit's Purple Gang took the risk of getting the alcohol across the international border, and they also kept the profits from the enormous markups charged for "Canadian" alcohol.

In Canada, liquor licenses remained widely available, with the peculiar wrinkle that, following English tradition, tavern keeping was often seen as a charitable enterprise best left to elderly widows. During Prohibition, indigent women played an integral role in the smuggling, sale, and distribution of liquor. In Saint John, New Brunswick, for example, Mrs. Donnie Hart was arrested every year from 1916 to 1924 on bootlegging charges, but she was never sent to prison because she had three dependent children. Beginning with a British Columbia anti-Prohibition referendum in 1921, some provinces (for example, Nova Scotia) responded by passing long-awaited mothers' support bills; others (for example, New Brunswick and British Columbia) kept the business closely regulated and even built state-run liquor stores. Today, every province but Alberta operates its own liquor franchise; most retain a monopoly over retail liquor sales.[46]

This is not to say that excessive drinking is or was taken lightly; early twentieth-century Canada in many ways surpassed the United States in legislating its moral agenda. Says historian Gerald Hallowell:

> The consequence was the unique blandness of blue Toronto. . . . [O]n an Ontario Sunday in 1919 . . . it was forbidden to buy ice cream, newspapers, or a cigar; to play baseball, tennis, or golf; to fish or take a steamboat excursion. The Lord's Day Alliance carefully guarded against the breaking of the Sabbath. Horse-racing suffered from restrictions; "moving pictures" were heavily censored or prohibited; the use of tobacco was increasingly attacked.[47]

But the legal culture surrounding drinking in Canada evolved separately from the moral rhetoric of temperance reform. The legal history of temperance in the city of Moncton, New Brunswick, provides a telling example. Heavily Protestant and largely Evangelical, New Brunswick was a province rife with antiliquor sentiment. Following the passage of the Canada Temperance Act (CTA) of 1878—a federal act entitling city or county voters to legislate and enforce Prohibition within their jurisdiction—Maritime cities like Moncton quickly passed Prohibition laws. But Moncton's Prohibition regime failed miserably; intentionally so.

Moncton's courts initially got involved in a challenge to the federal Canadian Temperance Act in 1881. Only one liquor dealer in town was convicted that year of violations, and he took the city to court, exploiting a technicality in the CTA that potentially made Moncton's new Prohibition law illegal. "'It so happens,' noted the [*Moncton Daily*] *Times*, 'that no man living knows what the law is except for their Honors of the Supreme Court—and they won't tell.'" Under common law, the provincial and federal courts could make pragmatic decisions regarding commerce cases without settling important matters of law. "The legal imbroglio began to subside in 1882, the year during which the Judicial Committee of the Privy Council ruled that the CTA was *intra vires* of the Canadian Parliament [that is, legal]."[48]

Having sustained Prohibition, there was little the courts could do to mandate and oversee enforcement. The variety of subsequent failures reflects less on Canadian political development than it does on the institutional makeup, strengths, and failures of jurisdictionally divided federalist justice systems. The parallels with contemporary American experience regarding drug enforcement are striking. The city government of Moncton, realizing the enormity of the task of eradicating liquor consumption, first ceded responsibility to a private venture, the United Temperance Committee (UTC), a "legal action committee" organized by local Evangelical churches and temperance associations. A sum of $450 dollars (Canadian) was collected among the members in 1886 and granted to the city in support of Prohibition enforcement, particularly legal fees. But the UTC also struck a bargain with the city that permitted it a portion of the proceeds from liquor-related fines. Citing ever-popular fiscal reasoning, the mayor of Moncton, D. A. Duffy, proudly toted the collaboration for providing legal services to the city without, in Duffy's words, "any expense to the taxpayers, the costs being paid by private subscription." The UTC then initiated what might be called a minor reign of terror in Moncton. Paid witnesses, including children, were sent to bars to entrap liquor dealers. More reluctant witnesses were sometimes put in prison to assure their presence in court.[49]

Many liquor retailers nevertheless continued to operate under the radar, dealing only with those who could be trusted to keep quiet about the location of their business. Acadians, New Brunswick's French-Canadian population, were particularly active in the liquor trade. The local police, who reluctantly took over for the UTC in 1888, had a terrible time enforcing the law. Couturier writes, "Too few and underpaid, the police were compelled to enforce a law upon members of a group with which they had frequent dealings and with whom they often shared the same socio-economic conditions." One Moncton police chief, Ferdinand Thibodeau, was forced to resign in 1890 over his weak though well-intentioned enforcement of Prohibition. Shortly thereafter, Thibodeau became a major liquor dealer among his native Acadians.[50]

Two other organizational problems arose with respect to enforcement of Prohibition in Moncton: unpaid fines and court logjams. Fines constituted the main weapon in Moncton's punitive arsenal, but many indicted liquor law violators simply never paid their fines; they moved out of the city and/or passed the business along to friends or relatives. Repeat arrests were rare. The liquor trade thrived.

New Brunswick's courts nearly drowned under the stress of their liquor-related caseload. Violators knew they could easily tie up the courts for years, and they did so with a vengeance. According to historian Jacques Paul Couturier, close to half the liquor convictions raised in Moncton from 1886 to 1888 were appealed to the province's Supreme Court. "In the end this judicial resistance, along with the geographical mobility of the liquor community, resulted, if not in complete paralysis, then at least in a notable slowdown of the penal process."[51]

Citing the failures of the UTC regime and the UTC's own disappointment with the revenues it had generated, the city reinstitutionalized drinking as a heavily regulated industry in which liquor dealers paid regular fines in return for minimal police harassment. Arrests were replaced with fines. "From 1889," writes Jacques Paul Couturier, "the enforcement of the CTA indeed seemed less rigid, and consequently less litigious." He adds, "Between 1889 and 1896, some $16,000 worth of fines were paid to the city for CTA violations, which, on average, represented over $2,000 annually."[52]

Moncton now received 2 to 5 percent of its annual revenues from liquor-related fines, a sum that more than equaled the previous receipts from liquor licensing fees. Several members of the city council were involved in the liquor trade themselves, and a stable peace seems to have evolved:

> The liquor retailers and the town authorities seem to have reached a mutually beneficial compromise through this method of enforcement of the CTA. While the fines increased municipal revenues, they were not frequent or important enough to stifle the liquor trade. . . . In a sense the imposing of fines at more or less regular intervals simply replaced the issuing of liquor permits."

Staunch prohibitionists kept up their moral furor but had to live with compromise.[53]

The Canadian government ultimately took a sensible, and sustainable, approach to the demands of regulating alcohol, a highly addictive, inexpensive, and easily manufactured drug. Provincial and local governments were allowed to enforce the law in ways that suited their particular constituencies, thus avoiding national conflict over the tenor of liquor law. This is not to say that such matters are better decided at the local than national level but merely to point out the successes of Canada's moderate approach to moral regulation. According to Strange and Loo, "State officials . . . found that criminalizing certain kinds of immoral behavior could create as many problems as it solved. . . . Perhaps the most significant obstacle to making good was the resistance that morals laws inspired."[54]

US and Canadian Responses to the Great Depression

Piecemeal change was the operant condition of early twentieth-century Canadian politics, a slow-moving machine that quickly found its limits in the challenges of the Great Depression. By the end of the Second World War, the Canadian government emerged transformed, the birth of modern social service agencies being the chief change of the period. In the meantime, jurisdictional confusion over the proper relationship between federal and provincial authorities kept Canada hamstrung. The British Judicial Committee of the Privy Council (JCPC) was still the court of last resort, and it refused to take an active role in the issue. Deciding largely on technical issues, the JCPC overturned several efforts to steer the dominion toward a more transparent, workable federal system. "Thus every halting step in the direction of satisfying collective wants was transformed into a debate on constitutional first principles," writes James Mallory. "The courts were dragged in because of this uncertainty, and, whether composed of Canadian judges or the learned lords of the Privy Council, were torn by the same uncertainties. Their method of reasoning and the whole spirit of the common law itself contributed to the resulting stalemate, but the courts were not more confused than the people for whose constitution they acted as custodians."[55]

In turn, Canada weathered the Great Depression with few, if any, landmark new social programs. To those unfamiliar with Canadian history, this might come as a surprise given Canada's extensive social welfare system today. "The emergence of the welfare state did proceed more incrementally here," notes one Canadian scholar, "involving as it did a long series of small steps rather than dramatic, comprehensive leaps forward such as the American Social Security Act of 1935 and the consolidation of the welfare state in Britain after the Second World War." "Incremental" would, in fact, be an apt way to describe Canadian political development as a whole.[56]

In the United States, a very different type of transformation occurred, one unique in its focus on intranational jurisdiction and big-money politics. The Great Depression resulted in massive increases in the scope and size of American federal government.

Prior to 1932, the federal government was still eyed with suspicion by most Americans. As Franklin Delano Roosevelt warned while still governor of New York State: "There is a tendency and to my mind a dangerous tendency, on the part of the national government to encroach, on one excuse or another, more and more upon state supremacy." Writes James Patterson, "Few party leaders between 1919 and 1929 expected meaningful reform from the national government and fewer still called for federal aid to the needy or legislation to benefit the laboring man. Even those who pursued the quest for social justice often preferred to work on the state instead of the national level." And yet, only a few years later, Roosevelt himself masterminded vast expansion of the federal government, largely at the expense of the states.[57]

The rights of the states had long been a mainstay of American federalism. In fact, notes Patterson:

> Though judicial decisions had discouraged some reforms, states still had managed to expand their powers considerably before 1920. They

had preceded the federal government in regulating large corporations, establishing minimum labor standards, and stimulating economic development. By the 1920's state and local governments accounted for 74 percent of public spending and 67 percent of taxes. They dominated the fields of education and public welfare, and their impact on American citizens was considerably more tangible than that of Washington.

But, Patterson continues, "When Franklin Roosevelt called for broad executive power in 1933, Americans responded quickly. . . . By 1940, progressive opponents of excessive federal centralization such as [Supreme Court justice Louis] Brandeis seemed like voices from a bygone past."[58]

Ironically, and perhaps predictably, the jurisdictional vagaries and vulnerabilities of American state government provided a landmark opportunity for federal intervention during the Great Depression. Constitutionally, American states only derived jurisdiction by omission; only those powers not formally granted to national government in the Constitution could be cleaved to the states. The largest priorities of American progressives—corporate regulation, transportation policy, labor regulation, and interstate commerce—could all be readily, and constitutionally, taken over by the federal government. In Canada, by contrast, the provinces maintained much wider constitutional sway over similarly important matters, especially in the eyes of the JCPC, still Canada's court of last resort. Wealthy provinces such as Ontario and Quebec had the resources and economies to weather the Depression. Their poorer counterparts were left to scrounge for resources while their economies crumbled. Canada's prime minister from 1930 to 1935, Richard Bennett, believed that free trade and patience were all that was called for. Though the increasingly powerful CCF party repeatedly called upon Bennett to create new social programs, Quebecers remained hostile to any suggestion that federal jurisdiction should be expanded. They were equally opposed to programs that smacked of "socialism" of any kind. At the time, politics in Quebec remained quite conservative, still dominated by the Catholic Church, along with Catholic labor unions and church-based charitable organizations. Quebec's "left turn" was still a long way off.[59]

The United States responded to the Depression by implementing strong federal programs for the poor, unemployed, and indigent. Canada, by contrast, floundered. Its "poor law" system left relief to the local governments that, by this time, were singularly unable to cope with the masses of needy constituents.

When the Great Depression began in earnest, state and local governments in both countries were hit hard. American cities and states were especially unprepared, given large preexisting debts and a rapidly eroding tax base. Because the American federal government had little or no experience dispersing money to the states, the states were largely on their own in tackling the challenges of the crisis. President Hoover established a federal commission on coordinated poor relief—the President's Committee on Unemployment Relief (POUR)—but allocated no money for it. Hoover launched a smattering of federal work-relief projects, but none were large or widespread enough to have noticeable effect on the flagging economy. Furthermore, governors and mayors were not particularly anxious for federal assistance; at least not until the Depression deepened. "This 'do it ourselves' refrain sounded with remarkable frequency through 1931," notes Patterson. "The mayor of Hartford, Connecticut, insisted, 'We believe in paying our own way. It is cheaper than to bear the cost of federal bungling.'"[60]

Historically, Canada's provinces had taken a variety of approaches to poor relief. In Newfoundland, still a British colony through 1948, aid was readily available for workers and families, many of whom relied on the seasonal fishing industry for a living. Quebec depended largely on its extensive network of church-related charities, subsidizing them with government money. In Prince Edward Island, by contrast, aid could only be obtained through special legislative fiat, thus connecting poor relief and political patronage. Ontario, Manitoba, Saskatchewan, and British Columbia all employed modified relief systems in which the state distinguished between the "deserving" and "undeserving" poor in an attempt to avoid tempting eligible workers into substituting welfare for work. Nova Scotia and New Brunswick retained workhouses for aid seekers, thus tying shame and forced labor to government assistance. Each province was free to handle the issues of unemployment and mendicancy in its own manner. Stringent residency requirements were common, thus allowing mayors to deport migrants seeking aid in their jurisdiction, which they did with abandon throughout much of the Depression.[61]

Lacking the resources and the mandate to confront the miseries of the Depression head-on, several provinces created temporary "work camps" where thousands of indigent Canadian men were forcibly sent; housed in makeshift tents, cabins, and sheds; and paid only paltry wages for their labor. The camps served as breeding grounds for the grassroots organization of what eventually became a nationwide movement against conscript labor and inadequate federal relief. Activists smuggled radical newspapers into the camps and eventually whipped their members into action, culminating in a protest march that took thousands of unemployed men across the country, their ire focused on Ottawa. The 1935 March on Ottawa reached as far as Regina, Saskatchewan, which the protesters literally took by siege. The police contained the marchers but did not elicit further conflict. The people of Regina greeted the marchers with food and sympathy. A wide swathe of Canadians supported the movement.[62]

Nonetheless, lasting policy change in Canada's welfare domain did not come until well after the Depression. In the meantime, Canadian law afforded the provincial governments strong powers against suspected Communists and radicals, and throughout the Depression, the power to jail agitators was liberally used. In Quebec, the quasi-fascist Duplessis government was especially fervent in its efforts to root out communism. In 1937, the so-called Padlock Law allowed the Quebec police to close down presses that were suspected of circulating subversive literature. Though Duplessis declined to specify what exactly qualified as subversive material, thousands of newspapers, pamphlets, books, buttons, and badges were confiscated. In Alberta, too, an Accurate News and Information Act was passed to ban radical literature.[63]

Comparatively speaking, the US federal and state governments seemed to take a (surprisingly) more sympathetic stance toward the victims of the Great Depression. Once elected, President Roosevelt responded to the Depression with a vast array of hastily organized, but surprisingly efficient, federal relief programs. Most of these programs were explicitly designed to bypass the states in their funding, implementation, and administration, including among them the Civilian Conservation Corps, the National Labor Relations Board, the Agricultural Adjustment Administration, the Farm Security Administration, and the Security and Exchange Commission. The Rural Electrification and Federal Housing Administrations required only a minimum of state involvement, and the United States Housing Administration was designed to work with local governments instead of state administrations. "All these creations," notes Patterson, "involved at most token state appropriations and little change in administrative structure. Most [state] legislatures gladly complied." The Public Works Administration raised the hackles of some state legislatures, but it also was "primarily a federal-local rather than a federal-state operation" that ultimately "proved a financial boon to states unwilling or unable to appropriate substantially for public works." Roosevelt further created the National Emergency Council to help coordinate the efforts of these various new federal agencies, as well as help coordinate such actions with the states.[64]

This is not to say that all, or even most of these programs were objectively (let alone subjectively) successful—the National Emergency Council was essentially abandoned in 1935, for example, after a few lackluster years—but to point out the significance of the Roosevelt administration's efforts to expand the jurisdiction of the federal government over traditional state-level functions such as poor and unemployment relief, infrastructural development, and labor relations. One of Roosevelt's biggest victories was passage of the Social Security Act of 1935, which inaugurated the federal government's largest income redistribution program to date and legitimized the idea that the federal government had proper jurisdiction to oversee such programs. Unlike Canada, which retained provincial jurisdiction over most elements of public welfare policy, the United States now had judicial and legislative permission to centralize social insurance. A downside of this move, however, was the related fact that controversial programs such as universal health insurance legislation also became matters of national debate, around which Congress was (and is) easily deadlocked.[65]

Having aggregated so many new government programs at the federal level, Roosevelt faced the challenge of overseeing and coordinating these many agencies, often without success. The National Recovery Administration (NRA), for example, was persistently hampered by jurisdictional ambiguity and legal challenges. "Handicapped by trying to enforce so many different codes and lost in a maze of litigation," writes Patterson, "its compliance machinery was already ineffective, its constitutional future uncertain." Because the NRA required state legislative action, it could easily be stymied by resistant legislatures, and because the Supreme Court is the ultimate arbiter in American disputes over federal-state jurisdiction, it was empowered to overturn such programs, as it did with the NRA in 1935.

As in Canada, the courts were thus a major obstacle to the creation of new Depression-era social programs. The chief difference was that American opponents of the New Deal actively engaged the courts in their struggles against centralization; the Canadian courts, and especially the JCPC, were passive participants in strictly procedural disputes. This contrast is in keeping with the long-term differences between the American and Canadian common law systems. Judicial activism and politically motivated litigation were, and still are, mainstays of the American system. Traditionally, the Canadian courts and their English counterparts have been reluctant to get embroiled in political battles and policy disputes.

Throughout the 1930s, Republicans set about using the courts to stymie the Roosevelt administration. They had earlier recognized the importance of presidential power over the appointment of federal judges. According to Robert H. Jackson, President Taft "was proudest of the fact that six of the nine members of the Supreme Court, including the Chief Justice, bore his commission. 'And I have said to them,' Taft chuckled, 'Damn you, if any of you die, I'll disown you.'" The courts proved a major obstacle to Roosevelt's New Deal via their jurisdiction over federal-state power-sharing issues. In some cases, such as the Supreme Court's 1936 rejection of the 1934 Municipal Bankruptcy Act, conservative justices went so far as to reject *state* requests for federal oversight because they were violations of *states' rights*. Roosevelt got so frustrated with the courts that he waged an unsuccessful battle to expand the number of seats in the Supreme Court in order to purge it of his enemies—the Constitution does not actually stipulate how many justices should preside over the Supreme Court, thus supporting Roosevelt's attempt to increase it to as many as fifteen. So-called court packing was not new to the American scene—President Grant had attempted similar maneuvers in order to skirt a challenge to Lincoln's Legal Tender Act. Earlier, in 1866, Congress limited the Supreme Court to eight justices in order to block President Andrew Johnson from making appointments; Congress restored the Court to nine justices following Johnson's impeachment. Nonetheless, Roosevelt's unsuccessful effort to alter the size of the Supreme Court cost him dearly; it was widely viewed as an illegitimate effort to expand the jurisdiction of the executive branch.[66]

Despite Roosevelt's occasional failures, the 1930s were a landmark period of jurisdictional reconfiguration in American history, though the consequences were often unintended. According to Patterson, "An assessment of federal-state planning in the 1930's must be largely negative, but it must also recognize how little had been done in the 1920's and estimate how much less might have been done in the 1940's and 1950's without the positive example of the New Deal." Though this is an overgeneralization to be sure, Patterson hints at some wider truths when he notes that, as a result of these struggles and their unintended consequences, the "[American] states lost potential as positive agents of reform at the same time that they retained a rather negative freedom from federal dictation." As in the late nineteenth-century American West, opposition to federal intervention became a standard cultural trope in Depression-era America, especially in the South and West. Governors like Georgia's Eugene Talmadge played both sides against the other, denouncing Roosevelt's New Deal while actively benefiting from its largesse. Canadian politicians also played this game. Quebec premier Maurice Duplessis was particularly effective at criticizing Ottawa while coercing from it valuable resources.[67]

In the final analysis, Roosevelt's efforts to transform the American federal government and American political culture were only mitigated successes. Many of his most promising programs were short-lived, and many state politicians—including many Democrats—fought the New Deal to the last, as did business, professional, and patriotic groups. The forces of inertia are indeed great in any political system, especially one as large, multifaceted, and open to special interests as that of the United States. Seen at a distance, however, Roosevelt did steward a lasting transformation in American political development. "Compared to the national government," writes Patterson, "the states lost authority in the 1930's—and they have regained very little since."

The manner in which American federal government expanded during the New Deal also reflects long term trends in American political development: Of those funds allocated for federal works under the Public Works Administration (PWA), more than 45 percent spent between 1933 and 1935 were allocated to the army and navy. "This amount was larger than the total sum of money spent on nonfederal PWA projects sponsored by states, municipalities, and other public bodies," writes historian Jason Scott Smith. Big government in the twentieth-century United States has often meant federal defense spending. A related bias, if it can be called such, is evident in the NRA's predisposition to spend big money on environmental projects meant to harness the forces of nature for "progress" and profit rather than environmental preservation. From the Hoover Dam to the Tennessee Valley Authority, a federal preference for unleashing nature's productive capacities, rather than protecting it from the ravages of capitalism, was, and still is, the order of the day.[68]

While it is true that, in Patterson's words, "The New Deal produced neither federal dictation, a completely cooperative federalism, nor a new state progressivism," it did create the institutional imprint of the even more massive institutional innovations of the 1960s. Federal defense spending skyrocketed in the postwar era. The collective memories of a nationwide economic catastrophe, coupled with those of earnest federal response, also helped create a new constituency in the United States for federal activism, as well as the institutional infrastructure necessary for running large-scale, federally funded social service programs. The ideological controversies of the 1930s also helped create and reinforce rhetoric across the political spectrum; progressives were encouraged and conservatives embittered in equal measure.[69]

In Canada, an altogether different lesson was drawn from the experience of the 1930s and 1940s. Though Ottawa deigned to establish a "Little New Deal" beginning in 1935, it did comparatively little to combat the vast social misery created by the Depression. In retrospect, most Canadians seem to have realized that their counterparts in Britain and the United States had weathered the Depression in much different fashion. Following economic recovery and the Allied victory in World War II, Canadian politicians seemed determined to forge a new path. Great strides were made in expanding Canada's welfare system over the next few decades. The Canadian judicial system was also reformed in such a way that removed crucial decisions about jurisdictional affairs from British control and put them in domestic hands. With only minor help from American labor unions, Canada's reformist agitators made great strides recruiting work-camp laborers, starving farm families, and underemployed city dwellers. At the provincial level, quasi-socialist farmer-worker parties continued their rise to prominence in the prairie provinces of Alberta and Saskatchewan, a key antecedent of Canada's postwar transformation.

9

The Vagaries of National Political Development

When pundits write about "American exceptionalism," they are usually referring to the fact that the US government generally spends less on social welfare programs than its counterparts in Canada and the nations of Western Europe. Explanations for this vary, but it is generally argued that the American people themselves are hostile, or have learned to become hostile, to the idea of "socialism," or the collectivization of assets, goods, and services. Though Canada is usually not described as a "socialist" country, it is often typified as being a great deal more "socialistic" than the United States. This viewpoint underlies much of the extant scholarship on political differences between the United States and Canada, most notably in the work of social scientists Louis Hartz, Seymour Martin Lipset, and Werner Sombart.

A major problem with this "exceptionalist" version of American political development is the factual inaccuracy of the claim itself. There is a long tradition of socialist thought, propaganda, and labor and party organization in the United States. And, as noted in Chapter 8, radical leftist political movements were actually more radical and more prevalent in the United States than in Canada before the Second World War. American Marxists hardly ever won elections on Socialist Party platforms, but sympathetic politicians found reasonable and sometimes ample support in the late nineteenth and early twentieth centuries. Milwaukee, Wisconsin, for example, elected openly socialist mayors and a socialist representative to Congress, and Robert La Follette's Progressive Party continued to bear the socialist mantle into the 1920s.

Labor unionism also once stood tall in American politics, though it has since withered in the face of both internecine competition and unfavorable state and federal policies, most notably President Reagan's move to fire more than eleven thousand striking air traffic controllers in 1981. Technically, the controllers were barred from striking as government employees, but similar strikes had been permitted in the past. Reagan's move tore down what was a tacit national agreement *not* to allow employers to fire striking workers. American union participation rates have been on a steep decline ever since. By the mid-1990s, US/Canadian differences in union participation were "pervasive rather than being concentrated in specific sectors of the economy or segments of the labour force.... A Canadian worker is approximately twice as likely to be represented by a union as his/her American counterpart," concludes one report. "Much of the Canada-US unionization gap can be attributed to inter-county differences in the legal regime pertaining to unions and collective bargaining and to differences in overt management opposition to unions (itself possibly a consequence of differences in collective bargaining laws and their administration)." American state and federal law consistently favors employers over employees, thus denuding labor of the opportunity to build and coalesce as a sustaining force in American politics.[1]

This compliments a broader argument about the nature of US/Canadian differences: For a long time, American and Canadian unionization rates were about the same, thus indicating no prior national differences in public opinion or collective repertoires regarding unionization. Legal differences in the ambit given employers and employees in industrial labor relations provided an opportunity for divergence. American employers have long had the upper hand over workers and labor unions, and this became the basis for a renewed assault on labor organizations, and on workers more generally, in the 1980s and 1990s.

Another factor behind the difference in contemporary unionization rates is the generally larger size of the Canadian public sector: The aforementioned report notes: "In both countries, public sector employees are substantially more likely to be unionized than their private sector counterparts in the same industry or occupation." Far fewer Americans are employed in public sector jobs today, another important vestige of US/Canadian political differences.[2]

It is difficult to generalize about why unions survive or fail, let alone liberal parties or leftist social movements. Three elements seem crucial in the US/Canadian case: (1) party networks at the local, subnational, and national levels; (2) private interest group lobbies; and (3) campaign finance law. The latter of the three, comparative campaign finance law, is peculiarly understudied. I have found little scholarly work dedicated to this subject, despite its significance to democracy as we now know it. Some characterize the American system as one that is riven with party-based corruption, or "patronage politics." By this account, the United States is unique in its so-called courts and parties system, which is rife with logrolling, influence peddling, and electoral shenanigans. This seems an apt description of American political life, the origins of which we have traced here.[3]

Nonetheless, "patronage" of one form or another exists in all political systems; it is the "relational" heart of rational-bureaucratic modern governance. What really seems to make American patronage politics "exceptional" is the degree of influence that is *blatantly* exercised by independent private interests in the electoral and policy-making processes. Budgets get skewed and laws are bent and twisted in order to reward one particular group—generally at the expense of others. Elections themselves resemble a high-stakes poker game, each side *publicly* building a war chest with which to (attempt to) "buy" elections—albeit via media time and high-priced consultants. Most countries limit the amount of time campaigns last as well as the amount of money spent on them. This breed of American exceptionalism stems directly from the agonistic model embedded in American political relations overall—Americans are comfortable, as a nation, with heavy competition and winner-take-all gambits; law itself is the ultimate weapon in American civic combat. By contrast, "corporatist" polities, like Germany or the Netherlands, formalize the role of interest group self-seeking through organized negotiating sessions between major economic blocs—labor, finance, heavy industry, and government ministers, for example.

It is almost as if the American system were explicitly designed to enhance the role of money in politics. The haphazard structure of American federalism creates multiple points from which to influence political outcomes. Corruption on election day—from ballot tampering to all-out skullduggery—has a long and storied history in America. Political office itself is openly regarded as something fungible, a holding that can be bought and sold. Even judges and sheriffs are elected in many US districts. In part, the "openness" of the American system is a result of the

Founding Fathers' belief that individual elites could best represent the interests of constituents.[4]

In parliamentary systems like Canada's, there are fewer opportunities for independent influence peddling in the system. Unlike America's loose party system, in which each candidate runs an independent campaign and, if elected, is free to vote independently of his or her supporting party, parliamentary parties like Canada's exert greater control over candidates and members of Parliament (MPs). Individual candidates are elected less on the basis of their personal appeal, and they serve at the behest of their party once elected. Voters thus tend to consider the platforms of the party rather than the characteristics of individual nominees. Parliamentary systems make it harder for single interests to "lobby" politicians—individual MPs are highly constrained in their ability to vote independently of their party, so they have less to offer lobby groups.[5]

Permeable as it is to single interests, the rightward slant of American politics is nonetheless hard to account for. There is no a priori reason that conservative interest group lobbies and political movements should be wealthier, more active, or better resourced than their liberal counterparts. America's Machiavellian electoral system serves those with the most power in American society. Corporations, of course, are at the heart of American electoral politics, but they do not necessarily support Republicans over Democrats. Big corporations—say, tire manufacturers—create small corporations—political action committees, think tanks, and trade associations—in order to gain influence with individual politicians of all stripes.

America's disproportionately large number of legally enfranchised interest group organizations also distinguishes its political system. Take health care, for example, a policy issue around which Canadians proudly (for the most part) mark their distinctiveness from Americans. American politicians have repeatedly tried to create universal healthcare programs, and a few have nearly succeeded. The state legislatures of California and New York nearly passed health coverage bills just after World War I. President Harry Truman later proposed such a plan, as did Republican Richard Nixon. There are two reasons, jurisdictionally speaking, that there is no universal health care in the United States: (1) lobby pressure from doctors, private hospitals, private health insurers, and private mutual benefit societies; and (2) the rise of federal jurisdiction over health and welfare issues during the Great Depression. Both circumstances magnify the power of interests opposed to new health insurance legislation.[6]

Canada's national health system is not a "national" system at all; it is a patchwork of provincial programs assisted with federal money. The Canadian federal government only has responsibility for seeing that funds are more or less evenly distributed between rich and poor provinces, thus assuring that basic standards of care are maintained throughout the country. It is worth noting that many Canadian doctors protested mightily against single-payer insurance at the outset. Ultimately, however, they and related interest groups were not able to obstruct the political process to the extent that compromises could not be reached. The premier of Saskatchewan, Tommy Douglas, minimized the power of individual interests by planning the province's new insurance system via a mediated, "corporatistic" advisory committee. Relevant interests—doctors and unions, for example—were promised a place at the bargaining table, but they were forced to compromise rather than use back-channel obstructionist tactics.[7]

Single-payer health care is not unique to Canada; what is unique is its repeated *failure* in the American political arena. Given the prevalence of legal backing for privately owned businesses, churches, and philanthropies, early American health care developed along a two-track system: fee-for-service care for those who could afford it and free (that is, charitable) care for those who could not. Under this system, Americans built thousands of innovative, efficient, state-of-the-art hospitals and medical research facilities with private money; a surprising number were built by and for specific religious groups and fraternal lodges. Americans also built thousands of orphanages, old-age homes, and asylums with donated money, some of which came directly from the state. Nearly all of these charitable care organizations were built and run as private, non-profit (that is, tax-exempt) corporations.[8]

The creation of social welfare programs designed to help Americans unable to pay for private health care expanded the entire American health-care industry enormously. Medicare and Medicaid created substantial new business opportunities for health-care providers willing to treat the poor. Once the government began paying for poor Americans' health care, a great deal more money entered the system. By 1975, six out of every ten dollars spent in the United States on public assistance went to Medicaid. Whereas American doctors once volunteered their time to treat those who could not afford their services, they now began collecting fees from the government for those services. Those fees are often less than what the private market would bear, but they are billable nonetheless. Quality of care is surely better than it has ever been, and steadily improving, but one wonders how long costs can keep rising at current rates. Canadians collectively control costs by agreeing to only spend a serially negotiated amount on health care per province per year. This might be called "rationing," but so could regulations on factory emissions or fuel consumption. Americans were not predisposed to loathe "rationing"; they came to loath it because they built a different kind of social welfare system first.[9]

The Canadian provinces retain absolute discretion in deciding exactly how to spend their health-care dollars. Cities, however, are relieved of many direct burdens otherwise left to them in the United States: child care, housing assistance, and emergency medical care, to name a few. Having sustained such programs more or less continually since the 1960s, even the most politically conservative Canadians now accept the usefulness of and need for a publicly funded social safety net. There is disagreement on the margins, but this bedrock Canadian "value" now seems lasting and secure, the result of a rather haphazard policy innovation in a small midwestern province.

Since at least the New Deal—but beginning with federal benefits for veterans of the Revolutionary War through the Civil War—the US social support system has been run from the "top down." Congress, with the advice and administrative support of the president, decides what to fund and by what combination of state, federal, and local agencies, public and private. Neither the Canadian parliament nor the prime minister has anything like this power over social welfare programs. Congress, together with the White House, devises new social welfare schemes—The New Deal, for example—and forces them on cities and states, hoping but often failing to provide much-needed administrative backup or fiscal support. Absent a serious national crisis such as the Great Depression or 9/11, Congress is an unusually difficult place to craft sweeping social welfare legislation. There are simply too many parochial interests at the bargaining table. This is a major factor contributing to the difficulties of passing single-payer health insurance programs in the United States—Congress is too fraught to forge a consensus on this issue.[10]

Some large social welfare programs were passed by Congress without the specter of war or a global economic crisis, nonetheless. Congress *can* enact sweeping social legislation; however, execution of such programs is often a mess. Policy implementation is not a strength of the American government, in part because of the jurisdictional ambiguity in the American federalist system. The White House holds both too many responsibilities for federal policy implementation and too few coordinating arms that span disparate state, federal, and local agencies. Canada's parliamentary system and civil service favor efficient coordination of disparate agencies, and the jurisdictional certainty of its constitution with respect to federalism facilitates power sharing and task allocation. The social welfare infrastructure of Canada grew piecemeal, one small step at a time, with one program building on the next.[11]

Culturally speaking, it also seems relevant to note differences in the vocabulary of social policy in the United States and Canada. Americans speak in terms of "civil rights"; Canada and most of the rest of the world speak of "human rights." Ostensibly, they mean the same thing; realistically, the American system focuses less on necessities of the human condition than on the perquisites of fairness, particularly on legal remedies for past "wrongs" and injustices.[12]

Another remarkable feature of the American sociopolitical landscape relates to America's strangely unbalanced education system. "Public" secondary school education was invented in the United States, and America currently has the best-financed, most prestigious university system in the world; yet millions of young Americans receive substandard secondary education (and suffer from malnutrition and are homeless or live in poverty). America, a country long obsessed with private property, has a public primary and secondary school system that relies heavily on local property taxes for funding. This puts students from poor neighborhoods in poorly funded schools. Like its health-care system, American secondary education follows a two-track model: let everyone seek the best that they can afford; let those who cannot afford much languish.

In contrast, America's higher education system is arguably the best in the world. American colleges and universities—especially American "private" colleges—charge tuition and fees nearly as high as the median family income, admit who they want, and keep and reinvest donations and profits tax-free. American universities are wealth-seeking nonprofit corporations that rely on the perpetuation of American status anxiety for continued inelasticity of demand. (Even "state" universities in the United States are increasingly focused on "selective" admissions and are run and financed like private universities.) As a result, American higher education comprises a huge number of schools and campuses, each of which garners its own legal, financial, and human resources to fund research, teaching, and financial aid, as well as lush residential, athletic, and "activities" centers. No other country in the world has a system quite like it. Besides their opulence and the expectation that every American can and should go to college, American colleges and universities are cornerstones of the vast American sports and health-care industries. Universities rest at the heart of the American social project: open, free-form centers of idea manipulation, self-creation, and debt. The free enterprise spirit of American academe, coupled with the all-frills residential system of US colleges and universities, probably explains a lot about the things Americans are best at today: branding and advertising, movies, music, television, and an ever-more-manic cult of celebrity. Americans invented the slacker, the big-budget motion picture, the personal computer, and rock and roll.

Recall the legal struggles of Harvard College to make its way in the world, a lowly private corporation denied the right to exist by the king. Following the successful conclusion of the American Revolution, the Massachusetts General Court hastily renewed its charter. It also freely chartered other schools and seminaries, as did many of the American states in short order. Anyone with enough money to find office space and hire teachers could start a corporation of higher learning. By the mid-nineteenth century (before the land grant system of public "state" universities), hundreds had been created, many with ties to specific religious denominations. Colleges and seminaries offered innovators and ideologues two mutually reinforcing advantages: first, they provided stable, tax-free repositories for finance capital; second, they provided ample opportunity to cultivate human and social capital. This was especially advantageous for religious groups, which were sorely in need of both. Denominational colleges and seminaries bred new generations of leaders and followers, and they also conveniently served as vast corporate tax shelters.

The same logic applies to American religious organizations more generally—not just sectarian hospitals and universities, but churches themselves. While Canada force-fed its "established" churches (Anglican and Catholic) and starved the others, American state legislatures primed the pump by making the privilege and protection of incorporation a right available to any religious group. Storefront churches, city dioceses, and opulent "ministries" all grew, financially and socially, from the corporate seed. Though state laws vary, the *Catholic Encyclopedia* notes:

> It may be said that as a rule, all Catholic educational and charitable institutions throughout the United States which have attained any importance or permanence are incorporated, usually under the provisions of general statutes for the incorporation of civil corporations. . . . In many states, such as New York and Pennsylvania, legacies to religious corporations are exempt from the inheritance tax; whereas a bequest to an unincorporated body, even though religious in its purposes, would be charged with the inheritance tax. . . . *The policy of the law evidently favours the incorporation of religious societies.*

Furthermore, in the United States, churches are *automatically* recognized as tax-exempt organizations by the Internal Revenue Service (IRS). American churches are not required to apply to the IRS for tax-exempt status, although, says the IRS, "the organization may find it advantageous to obtain recognition of exemption." By contrast, the Canadian Convention of Southern Baptists notes that Canadian churches *must* register as charitable organizations with the Canada Customs and Revenue Agency (CCRA) to gain tax-exempt status, and it warns about the legal complications of applying for a corporate charter, noting that "many churches do not incorporate until they are considering purchasing property."[13]

America clearly has the world's most competitive market for religious affiliation, one that promotes innovation and change in order to cater to the wishes of would-be parishioners. In the competition for members, many American churches and sects have built astonishing numbers of private schools, charities, clubs, gymnasiums, and fraternal organizations in order to extend their reach and stay one step ahead of the competition. Built on the bedrock of corporate and religious freedom, the United States is now captive to both.[14]

A related, "exceptional" outcome of American political development is the odd marriage of social and fiscal conservatives in the Republican

Party. God and mammon have always had a fraught relationship, but before Reagan, the Republican Party scarcely concerned itself with religious issues. If anything, Democrats were inclined to preach on the hustings; they, too, were the "social gospel" party, as well as the party of the nation's burgeoning Catholic and Jewish populations. Specialists tend to agree that it was the one-two punch of New Deal secularism and Great Society civil rights legislation that divorced the Democratic Party from its southern, white supporters. Democratic presidential administrations alienated white working-class voters by abandoning the Democratic Party's traditional pro-South, anti-integrationist stance.

The current balance of power between Democrats and Republicans is not as important to note as the fact that *both* American parties are generally to the "right" of even Canada's right-wing parties. Alberta's conservative Social Credit Party, for example, supports "socialized" medicine and government subsidies for all residents. On most issues, Canada's current Conservative Party could pass for the Democratic Party in the United States.

Many third-party movements have been hatched in the United States, but one reason they perpetually fail is because of the strength of federal party organizations at the state and local levels. Party operatives can and do work to quash third-party movements proximate to their own. Owing to the decentralized nature of Canadian federalism, there is fairly little intersection between the national and provincial political parties— provincial pols rarely if ever "rise through the ranks" to national positions, and the provinces have traditionally hosted a range of successful third parties. At the same time, however, the major Canadian parties exert fairly strong control over party affiliates at the national level. Under the traditional Westminster parliamentary system, MPs vote as a bloc, as dictated by their party's leaders. In the United States, neither party exerts much control over party members. Congress has thus been a hotbed of ideological innovation, allowing the parties to be transformed from within.

Arguably, these unusual characteristics of the American party system stem in part from the way in which the western territories were formed and politicized. Political entrepreneurs were some of the first settlers in many of the territories. Because entry into statehood required congressional approval, the national parties knew that dominating the electoral scene in a new territory could be vital to their long-term role in the sectional balance of power. Territorial legislators, bureaucrats, governors, mayors, judges, and lawmen all recognized the need to curry favor with Washington, thus extending the reach of the national parties to the lowest levels of government. Under Canadian federalism, provincial self-government only gradually arose, and when it did, it retained a strong sense of autonomy from the national parties, as well as national politics as a whole.

Suffrage, Schism, and Community

American suffrage was unusually wide following the Revolution. In Canada and Western Europe, suffrage came much later than the rudimentary bureaucratization of their national governments. This, according to political scientist Samuel Huntington, explains the relative dearth of radical socialism in the United States. Would-be American "radicals" had electoral options not available to their counterparts in other countries, thus precluding the need to sustain "revolutionary" movements aimed at overturning the existing political order. Canadian suffrage was fairly limited until the twentieth century, thus allowing elite groups to dominate electoral politics. Moreover, Canada's provinces only gradually attained self-government, thereby allowing the colonial and later the dominion authorities to strictly oversee territorial affairs. The Canadian government was "bureaucratized" before it was "democratized," in Huntington's parlance—Americans "were the first to achieve widespread political participation but the last to modernize their traditional political structures." Even today, Canadian politics has a decidedly more elitist tenor—"executive federalism" in the words of Canadian political scientist Donald Smiley.[15]

Nonetheless, Huntington makes a number of missteps in trying to explain "American exceptionalism." He argues, for example, that the absence of a feudal aristocracy in the American colonies precluded the need for a strong state to displace it, as had been the case in many Western European societies. America had no ruling class to displace, and thus no need for a highly bureaucratized government to take the reins of power. Arguably, however, the early American colonies *did* have a landed aristocracy, if only a *de facto* rather *de jure* one. For example, a fair number of the early American colonies were chartered as patrimonial gifts from the Crown to its loyal servants; one—Pennsylvania—was still struggling with the legacies of proprietary rule at the time of Independence. This was not European feudalism per se, but it had many of its relevant features—land granted to specific individuals, transferable to their heirs, and governed at their discretion. In the corporate colonies of New England, furthermore, the congregationalist descendants of the Puritans inherited huge wealth and held a firm grasp on state politics until well into the nineteenth century. Rhode Island maintained its property restrictions on voting through 1842, and a hereditary class of "first families," the "Boston Brahmins," dominated Massachusetts politics and society through the nineteenth century.

Huntington's suffrage-before-bureaucratization thesis of American exceptionalism also overlooks the very grave problem of race in the United States. In the hundred years between the end of the Civil War and the passage of the Voting Rights Act of 1965, the majority of eligible African Americans were denied the right to vote. This was especially true in the South, where the majority of blacks lived until the mid-twentieth century. In Selma, Alabama, where a campaign for voting reform began in 1965, only 383 blacks were registered to vote out of a total voting-age black population of 15,000. Six percent of voting-age blacks were registered in Mississippi at that time; 19 and 32 percent in Alabama and Louisiana, respectively. Given the prevalence of literacy tests in many precincts, hundreds of thousands of eligible immigrants were denied the vote as well.[16]

In fact, one of the landmark features of American public policy until the 1960s was its tacit support for racial inequality. American government has had a major role in both maintaining and later combating the presence of America's "aristocracy" of race, to put it in Huntington's terms. The effort to deconstruct racial apartheid has been hampered by the fact that racial discrimination is treated under American law largely as a matter of grievance, rather than equality. The makeup of American civil rights law puts the onus of enforcement on the individual; that is, the complainant. Burke Marshall, head of the Civil Rights division of the Justice Department in the Kennedy and Johnson administrations, complained often of this fact: "Federal attorneys could not . . . seek injunctions to *prevent* violations of constitutional rights, unless, as in the 1957 Voting Rights Act, Congress specifically provided statutory authority. In a federal system," Marshall declared, "civil rights 'are individual and personal, to be asserted by private citizens as they choose, in court, speaking through their chosen council.'"[17]

In the face of such obstacles, the power of the Justice Department to break one hundred years of segregation and discrimination was limited. Resistance was sometimes fierce, but, notes Allen Matusow, a historian of the Great Society programs:

> Immediately upon its [the 1964 Civil Rights Act] passage, men in the South's cities and larger towns—even in bulwarks of the old order like Albany, Georgia and Birmingham, Alabama—complied with the law. Surveying the touchy problem of gas-station accommodations in twenty urban areas, a government survey in 1965 reported continuing discrimination only in Savannah and Jackson. The old ways died hardest in rural areas, where significant resistance lingered for years and where even the long arm of the Justice Department seldom reached. But the remarkable collapse of segregation in the urban South, the ease with which white waitresses learned to be polite to black patrons, the routine mixing of the races at lunch counters and theaters— all this confirmed the liberal faith that *law, at least sometimes, could help change custom.*[18]

Canadian experience clearly differs from American in the extent to which it has had to struggle with the legacy of slavery and racial discrimination. The particular limits of American civil rights law are also evident in areas where discrimination is harder to prove. For example, housing discrimination continues apace in the United States despite repeated federal attempts to provide financial incentives for the construction and maintenance of low-income, desegregated residential development. Residential segregation continues, largely through extralegal means, as do the related specters of discrimination in education, electoral districting, and police enforcement. Where there is a will, there is not always a way, or at least not a government-mandated way of creating social change.[19]

Another case—President Johnson's Community Action Program (CAP)—shows that even where there is general consensus on the need for change, change is not always successful, particularly under American federalism. CAP was inspired by the hope of American social scientists to improve the lives of America's poor by providing them the tools for self-governance. CAP funneled millions of dollars into local programs designed to help poor communities build deliberative institutions, after-school programs, and social service agencies. Much of this money was offered in support of the formation of so-called Community

Action Agencies (CAAs). Thousands of CAAs were created almost overnight—415 by June 1965, less than a year after passage of the 1964 Economic Opportunity Act, and more than 1,000 a year later. Matusow notes, in passing, that 80 percent of these were founded as "private non-profit corporations." "Elected officials took the initiative in forming most of them," he adds. The program was a massive failure. CAP funds were notoriously misused, and in some cases, new community organizations turned against the very government agencies that were funding them. "CAP, in short, increased the very fragmentation and bureaucratic rivalry it was designed to remedy."[20]

Jurisdictional confusion and a lack of clear, consistent bureaucratic oversight doomed this effort at federally sponsored community activism. Not to be deterred, however, Johnson's passion for community action has resurfaced in Washington and academe of late. With the publication in 1993 of Robert D. Putnam's *Making Democracy Work* and his subsequent work on "bowling alone," or the negative consequences of community disorganization, American social scientists have once again raised the mantle of state-funded community organizing—now technocratically referred to as "building social capital." Instead of offering organizing funds for radicals and liberal advocacy organizations, as Johnson had done, Washington now flirts with the idea of funding private, "faith-based organizations." There is now as large a literature criticizing the utility of Putnam's social capital concept as there is in support of it, though conservative support for such measures continues apace.[21]

The ascendance of the "Republican right" in the late twentieth century is rather hard to explain, historically speaking. American aggressiveness in global geopolitics, coupled with the explosive growth of its military-industrial sector, seems to have enhanced the power of conservative business leaders and political entrepreneurs in twentieth-century America. In the rise of the post–World War II American military-industrial complex, moreover, we see the reemergence of the "paranoid style" of American political thinking from the early colonial period. As in the lead-up to the Revolutionary War, when American public opinion leaders allowed consideration of pertinent economic and legal issues to be tainted by fear of "Popery" and an impending French-Canadian invasion, American politics in the 1950s and 1960s turned to apocalyptic thinking about the Communist threat to American society. For a period of four years, Senator Joseph McCarthy captivated the nation with a tizzy of conspiracy theories and political purges of the public and private sectors. Red-baiting advanced the cause of conservative politicians and industry leaders, and blackmailed the nation into the ceaseless expansion of defense spending and expensive, often futile foreign military engagements.[22]

Absent the perceived burden of leading a global war against "Communism," Canadians could better attend to the business of domestic well-being. More to the point, America's new role in global affairs was not simply a result of its size or wealth but of its historically unusual approach to international relations. Beginning with the Revolution and continuing thereafter, American political leaders proved unusually *willing* to break treaties and international agreements when it served the nation's interests. In addition, national military power was frequently supplemented by "unauthorized" private militias, from the "filibusters" of the nineteenth century to the Mujahadeen and Latin American insurgent groups of the twentieth. None of these actions are unprecedented in world affairs, but American foreign policy has come to rely on such tactics to an extent that is unparalleled. These efforts, of course, are predicated on the exertion of executive power, the presumed right of American presidents to bypass legislative oversight in the interest of national security.

Though the Militia and Hays National Defense Acts of 1903 and 1916 marked the end of American national defense based primarily on amateur, local militias, it did not end Americans' infatuation with guns or the legal protection for possession of firearms. Canadians do, in fact, own many guns, as filmmaker Michael Moore is at pains to tell us in his movie, *Bowling for Columbine*. Many Canadians are hunters; they use sport rifles in limited contexts. Handguns and automatic weapons, however, are under much better control in Canada than in the United States. Though this is partly a factor of contemporary politics—particularly the strength of the National Rifle Association in the United States—it has important antecedents not just in the American Constitution but in late nineteenth-century government-supported programs aimed at promoting gun ownership and gun-handling skills among America's population at large.[23]

In the context of the historical ground already covered, it seems highly unlikely that the vast difference in gun-related deaths between the United States and Canada is a product of some homicidal, gun-crazed collective psyche that is inculcated in people on one side of the border but not the other. And, *contra* Moore, Canadian newspaper and television reports *are* filled with stories of violence and mayhem. Theft, rape, and other forms of crime are surprisingly prominent in Canada, too; in some cases, higher than in the United States. For example, Organization for Economic Cooperation and Development (OECD) data for 2000 report slightly higher rates of "assault" and "property crime" in Canada than in the United States. The likely reason the United States has such a bad reputation for violence is surely its high murder rate—4 homicides per 100,000 people, compared to just 1 per 100,000 in Canada—as well as its unusually high incarceration rates: As of 2000, the incarceration rate in the United States was about seven times that of Canada. Both discrepancies point to the lasting effects of differences in national legal culture: namely, America's penal approach to petty crime and its strong defense of the private right to own guns.[24]

My point here is that political culture reveals itself more in the structural opportunities that create it than in the resulting sentiments, preferences, and values of citizens. If we assume that the propensity to commit a gun-related crime (suicide or homicide, for instance) is more or less randomly distributed across any population, our focus then needs to be on the *availability* of guns and opportunities to use them, rather than on the *desire* to use them per se. The result of repeated opportunities to act on this desire via easily accessible fatal weaponry is a large number of murders. New cultural norms and expectations regarding retribution, anger, and group rights are thereby created and sustained over time—violence breeds violence, in other words. Americans are not otherwise more "violent" or gang oriented than the inhabitants of comparable societies.[25]

Late Twentieth-Century American and Canadian Legal Culture

There are many instances in which endogenous legal action has had lasting effects on the way Canadians and Americans actually behave. Following the conventional English notion of "parliamentary sovereignty" over law, Canadian jurists have historically remained far less willing to make substantive proclamations on the law than their American counterparts. Americans, in general, treat law as an extremely malleable set of rules and principles. "Truth" is contestable. Let the best lawyer win. There is no bedrock of American law; it is a shifting pile of stones.

The United States is also exceptional in the degree to which it is governed as a polity in which the courts are the arena of first and last resort. Supreme Court Justice Robert Jackson referred to America's government as "the most legalistic system of government in the world with the judicial power penetrating and legal philosophy governing our whole national life." From the fits and starts of Puritan litigiousness to the bald-faced appropriation of indigenous land claims in gold rush California, America has long been on a trajectory in which the social contract is perceived as mutable, opportunistic, and highly confrontational.[26]

Canada also has turned in this direction of late, particularly since the passage of the 1982 Charter of Rights and Freedoms, which established for the first time a codified set of legal rights for all Canadians and exalted the role of the courts in adjudicating them. In the British tradition, Canadian courts were once considered weak appendages of government; dispute resolvers, not constitutional watchdogs. Prior to 1949, Canada did not even have ultimate jurisdiction over its own courts—the British Judicial Committee of the Privy Council (JCPC) had the final say in Canadian judicial appeals. More important, the Canadian legal profession lagged far behind the American bar in its size, power, and ambition. Perfect data are hard to come by, but recent figures indicate that the United States has about 3.2 lawyers per 1,000 people and Canada has only 1.95, or almost 40 percent fewer lawyers per capita. According to Graham Parker, this is especially evident in the history of Canadian legal education:

> Canadian legal education did not become academically respectable until the latter half of this [the twentieth] century. . . . Before that, the profession was trained on a part-time educational system with the emphasis on office apprenticeship. No doubt many lawyers were competent but narrow technicians, but they lacked a broad perspective on the law. In the 1960s, the law schools made the transition from trade school to instant American law school: teaching case methods, preparing case books, flirting with the social sciences and starting legal clinics. Canadian legal scholarship was poverty stricken until twenty years ago. Learned treatises did not exist. Legal texts were of the most practical variety and were often Canadianised [sic] versions of English black-letter or practitioners' manuals.

Circumstances could not have been more different in the United States, where formal legal education has a long and storied history, as does the pursuit of law as a high-status, high-income profession. The growth of the legal profession and Americans' litigious legal culture grew hand in hand.[27]

Contemporary Canadian legal scholars have been extremely concerned about the potential impact of the 1982 Charter of Rights and Freedoms on the country's legal culture. One pronounced fear, again mirroring the tendency of Canadians to see their future in America's past, concerns "judicial review" and the role of the courts in the legislative process. Canada, like Great Britain, traditionally considered Parliament the proper arena for resolution of political questions; jurists in both countries regarded the American system of judicial review as an unfair, antidemocratic restraint on the deliberative process.[28]

The case of abortion rights is especially telling in respect to the contrasting legal cultures of the United States and Canada. Abortion is now legal in both countries, but it achieved this status in notably different ways. In Canada, public opinion is far from unanimous on this issue; Canadian pro-lifers have protested the legalization of abortion, and Parliament has been repeatedly stalemated over the issue. Furthermore, the Canadians have not been spared abortion litigation, both for and against. What is different between the two countries is the perceived role of the courts in settling such disputes: In Canada, the Supreme Court has heard repeated abortion rights cases but generally refused to settle anything beyond procedural matters related to evidence and legal "standing," or the jurisdiction to bring a case before the courts. In the United States, the Supreme Court has tackled the abortion issue full-on, effectively deciding national policy on its own. American justices have the power to create law, not simply arbitrate it.

Canadian government has framed abortion as a public health issue, not a moral-legal conundrum, and it favors leaving specific decisions about abortion policy to the provinces. In fact, the original impetus for de facto legalization of abortion was initiated by the provincial government of Quebec, which unilaterally decided in 1976 to disavow federal restrictions on abortion. Given provincial power over health policy matters, this was within Quebec's jurisdiction. According to political scientist F. L. Morton:

> The policy vacuum at the federal level opened the door for innovations and initiatives at the provincial level. While criminal regulation of

abortion remained the exclusive jurisdiction of Parliament, the provinces could influence the availability of abortions through their jurisdiction over health policy. By attaching conditions to public health insurance funding of abortions and by permitting or prohibiting abortion clinics apart from hospitals, each province could influence the availability of abortion services.

In the United States, abortion remains federally protected by the courts (though recent decisions have suggested a return to allowing states to add restrictions). Abortion debate has largely subsided in Canada, whereas it remains a perpetual source of contention in the United States. American-style judicial activism leaves the door open to continued lawsuits and protests, as well as conflict over judicial nominations.[29]

The degree to which Canadian scholars and pundits bemoan the recent "judicialization of Canadian politics" reflects the existing distance between the Canadian and American legal systems. Though Canada is moving in this direction, it is still a long way from the American judicial system, which only appears to get more partisan and politically proactive over time. These contrasting trajectories highlight a larger difference in the legal cultures of Canada and the United States. "During its first 100 years," notes Morton, "the Supreme Court of Canada laboured more or less unnoticed in the wings of Canadian politics. Unlike its American counterpart, it rarely appeared on the centre stage of national politics." Though the Supreme Court of Canada has become more active in public policy debate since passage of the Charter of Rights and Freedoms, it retains a conservative sense of its place in Canadian political life. The American Supreme Court, in contrast, remains a hothouse of ideological and political strife. American voters have become increasingly conscious of the partisan nature of federal judicial appointments in casting votes for president and Congress.[30]

At the same time, Canada has intractable political problems of its own, the largest, most would agree, being Quebec separatism and preservation of the confederation. Quebec experienced a radical shift in political culture beginning in the post–World War II era and culminating in the "Quiet Revolution" of the 1960s and 1970s, when a massive secularization wave swept the province, accompanied by an exodus from Quebec's traditional farms and villages. Quebecers increasingly called for enhanced government spending, liberalized social policies, and renewed pride in francophone language and culture. The separatist movement once again gained steam. Political violence, it should be noted, was rare, with the exception of the actions of a single terrorist group, the *Front de libération du Québec* (FLQ). After the FLQ bombed the Montreal Stock Exchange in February 1969, and kidnapped and murdered a prominent nationalist politician in October 1970, Prime Minister Pierre Trudeau imposed martial law. Notably, however, this crackdown was short-lived, and separatism soon resumed a peaceful mode.[31]

In true Canadian fashion, the secession issue has been disputed primarily through political deliberation rather than litigation or violence. Representatives of each of the provinces have repeatedly met, alongside federal politicians, to find solutions to Quebec's grievances. The debate has been framed as one about the status of provincial rights. Though the Canadian Constitution was officially "repatriated" (that is, eschewed, jurisdictionally speaking, by England) in 1982, along with passage of the new Canadian Charter of Rights and Freedoms, Quebec has repeatedly failed to endorse a final, binding version of the constitution. This is troubling to many, though the tide of separatism appears to have at least temporarily subsided. What progress has been made on the constitutional issue consists of an agreement that any clear resolution in favor of secession would require serious negotiation on the part of the rest of the provinces. In other words, Quebec cannot act alone, though neither can it be prevented from seceding should it so choose.[32]

One way that nationalist advocates have mitigated support for Quebec separatism is by taking the rhetoric of francophone nationalism at face value and reframing it as support for multiculturalism of all stripes. Francophones cannot easily argue against the cultural rights of Pakistani or Chinese immigrants, let alone aboriginals or nonheterosexuals. Aggressive immigration and naturalization policies have increased the ranks of Canadians who are neither anglophone nor francophone, thus checking the efforts of French Canadians to sustain a binational framework for discussion of Canada's future. Several cities in Canada are now comprised of more foreign-born than native-born Canadians, and protection of "group rights" has become a mainstay of Canadian political culture. Gay rights, immigrant rights, and legal and political recognition for nonwhite religious and ethnic minorities are areas where Canada is fast becoming a global leader. Federal efforts to reform and solidify aboriginal rights have been another aftereffect of this trend toward widening the ambit of "group rights" beyond the traditional

Anglo-French divide. The new territory of Nunavut was created in 1999 out of the larger Northwest Territory and is governed by and for its largely Inuit population. Plans are also in train to create another Inuit province, Nunavik, out of territory in northern Quebec.[33]

It is (extremely) noteworthy that despite a weak constitution, strong provincial governments, and the perpetual threat of secession, there is no history of violent conflict between the provinces of Canada. One basis for Canadian consensualism would appear to be the legitimacy it grants secessionist claims: Overall, and in comparison with the United States, Canadian separatists seem content to rely on electoral deliberation rather than violent confrontation to assert their cause. Secession is a legitimate legal action in the Dominion of Canada, though one with consequences that no one can readily predict. Nonetheless, the very fact that separatists *can* contemplate separation without having to consider civil war may explain why they have never quite made it over the hurdle of actually "separating." Though referenda on secession continue to be hard fought and extremely close, Quebec voters have yet to ratify a full-fledged act of secession. Sovereignty is spoken of incessantly in Québécois political circles, and it has probably hurt the economy of Quebec over the past forty years, but the end result is generally more political power for the province in national affairs. The threat of secession remains an important bargaining chip for the province, maintaining its political power in the face of declining demographic and economic significance. Quebec's ability to find common cause with other provinces in the quest to limit federal power also assures that it continue to find reasons to remain at the bargaining table rather than secede. Interestingly, Quebec has also gone from being one of Canada's most politically conservative provinces to being one of its most liberal.[34]

In Ottawa today, provincial representatives do a good bit of horse-trading for their constituents, but the mandate for equalization payments and minimal federal interference in provincial affairs helps keep the peace. Albertans complain of their disproportionate contributions to Ottawa's coffers, but they are ultimately obligated by the jurisdictional rules of the game to support the poorer provinces in some measure. Quebec, meanwhile, is allowed to prevail in its quest to protect bilingualism, a self-interested game that ultimately helps protect group rights of all kinds in Canada.

This helps explain why native-born Canadians are generally more tolerant of immigrants and nonwhites than their American counterparts.

Resistance to the cultural project of nationalism—the formation of a univocal national identity—is part and parcel of Canada's vision of itself. Like the French after 1774, all manner of domestic minority groups are tolerated and protected by Canadian law today.

It is impossible to predict exactly how issues as contentious as abortion law or secession will play out in future years, but it would appear that the *style* of such debates will remain essentially the same. Canadians, long accustomed to settling difficult issues through bureaucratic debate and deference to the provinces, will likely continue on this track. The future of American politics is harder to predict, given the openness of its political system to outsider challenges and political entrepreneurs. It seems predictable, at least, that the federal courts will continue to play a paramount role in the creation of American public policy.

In general, we might describe the Canadian system as one of "negotiated politics," in contrast to the agonistic American system of "contested politics." The singular competition of each and all in American politics, law, business, and civil society is quite remarkable when seen in comparative historical terms. Its antecedents were apparent as early as the 1630s.

Conclusion

We have, probably, had too good an opinion of human nature in forming our confederation.

—George Washington (1786)

In mapping out several centuries of history over thousands of miles of territory, I have observed many inconsistencies in the things people say and do. Public opinion oscillates, voters are fickle, politicians profess one set of beliefs while abiding by another. Political identity itself is highly malleable.

Yet we persist in thinking that the political cultures of the United States and Canada are reliably, credibly different.

Seen in comparative historical perspective, the flash point issues of Canadian and American political life are starkly different—linguistic and cultural identity in Canada; religion and race in the United States, for example. So too are their political party systems skewed differently—Canada has bona fide socialist and "green" parties, as well as a fairly moderate "conservative" coalition; the United States lumps numerous ideological groups into two grand parties, both of which oscillate between mainstream and margin. The quintessential rights and freedoms of citizenship are framed and enforced differently as well—"individual rights" are the central ethos of American life, whereas "group rights" tend to prevail in Canada.

And yet, despite all this, when Canadians and American meet, they not only share a language and dialect but common moral, philosophical, aesthetic, and conversational approaches. "Foreigners" can barely tell them apart. The "memes" of Canadian and American popular culture are the same, too—put a Brit, an American, and a Canadian in a room and more than just dialect will differentiate the Brit. The rudiments of everyday life in England are much different than they are in the United States and Canada.

What happens if we add an Australian and a New Zealander into the mix, also anglophones from countries with English political roots and common law–based legal systems? The Canadian and the American will still seem most similar culturally, but the political picture will begin to blur. Canada, England, Australia, and New Zealand share a centrist-liberal political culture that puts them somewhere in between the social "welfare state" democracies of Western Europe and the extreme laissez-faire system of the United States. Though clustering schemes differ on specifics, all five are likely to agree that the United States stands alone, politically speaking.

With language and English-colonial origins factored out of the picture, the next most common explanation for Canadian and American political differences is America's size—its geopolitical might and enormous economy. But there is no a priori reason for this disparity. The United States started just as small as Australia, Canada, or New Zealand. England was the megapower of the bunch until at least 1900. The roots of the size and speed of the American economy lie in the colonial period, as do a number of its most striking political features.

Founded haphazardly and without clear legal title or administrative oversight, the American colonies grew restless with their imperial stature, broke away from the Crown, and created a country in which legal title and administrative oversight were unusually contentious. Moreover, the American law of incorporations evolved in such a way that allowed, if not encouraged, an unprecedented amount of independent entrepreneurial activity that was legally protected by and from the state. This affected not only America's market economy, but its civic sphere as well, for the corporate organizational form came to be exploited by myriad charities, churches, and private voluntary organizations in the nineteenth and twentieth centuries.

In Canada, by contrast, royal governance morphed into a new form of colonial federalism based on strong provincial governments backed by a weak but fiscally generous central authority. Law and order, established first by the Catholic Church in collaboration with the French royal government, passed into the hands of domestic forces that oversaw the slow but orderly settlement of the Canadian West. Church-state collaboration had largely withered in Canada by the late twentieth century, but the tradition of state support for health care, education, and culture has remained firmly in place. For example, Canada's national health insurance system emerged from an early institutional order in which religiously based hospitals received state support in exchange for granting admission to everyone. In the United States, a stronger divide between free and fee-for-service care provided the institutional basis for its current system.

The legal basis for political authority in the proto-American colonies was structured in a way that promoted uncertainty, conflict, and exploitation of the many by the few. Jurisdiction was a fuzzy, agonistic affair before, during, and after the struggle for independence. In Canada, by contrast, the powers of state were both more clearly laid out and more sparingly bestowed upon new territories and peoples. The authoritarian tendencies of royal government were balanced by clear delimitations of state power. Provinces were encouraged to work with one another, rather than in competition, and settlers were repeatedly reminded of the need for, and expectation of, law and order. Police in the territories actively worked to encourage civil, nonviolent behavior while respecting the parameters of individual and group freedom. Land grants in the provinces and territories were allocated and managed in an orderly, if not totally efficient, manner.

One thing that is particularly fascinating, and confusing, about law is the range of opportunities it affords social actors to challenge, defy, and exploit it. Moral legislation—such as bans on the consumption of certain intoxicants—is easily dodged, and thus difficult to enforce. Associational law, like those outlining the rights and regulation of churches and corporations, puts legal shells around private actors, thereby incentivizing behavior those same actors might not otherwise pursue. Intergovernmental law, such as those coordinating different levels of government, both constrains and enables political action. It defines the very relationships we rely on to delegate and delineate the levers of public administration. Ambiguity in the nature of such relationships—that is, jurisdictional ambiguity—can just as easily derail those relationships. For example, the US Constitution describes the role of federal government clearly but leaves the role of state governments murky. While this specificity was intended to *limit* the powers of federal government vis-à-vis the states, ambiguity concerning state powers has served to enhance federal power over the long run. In Canada, by contrast, the British North America Act of 1867 is clearer about provincial powers than federal responsibilities, thus tipping the balance the other way. Once again, this was done in the spirit of *limiting* provincial power (in this case, the possible intransigence of Quebec), but it has had the unintended effect of bolstering provincial power and weakening federal oversight thereof.

Law is a specific, highly codified and coercively enforced domain of culture. It shapes and enables individual and group behavior in ways that reflect the boundaries of modern political life—states and nations, counties and corporations. We each may agree or disagree with the tenets of the law, but it is largely the explanation we seek in asking why the political culture in one place differs from that in another. People move around and act and think for themselves, but "places"—that is, jurisdictional spaces—remain more or less the same.

If we consider national political culture to be a subset of some larger, more amorphous sphere of beliefs, practices, and preferences, then clearly the dynamics of cultural domains are not all alike. Social processes occur simultaneously on a number of levels, each with causal mechanisms and ramifications of their own. This is helpful to keep in mind when considering why the United States and Canada have converged in some domains of culture (such as sports and most forms of leisure activity) but diverged in others (namely, political culture).

It helps in this regard to consider cases where national borders—and thus macroeconomics, geopolitics, and large-scale cultural, linguistic, and demographic differences—need not factor into our thinking. Consider the case of two neighboring American states that were once quite similar but now could not be more different: Vermont and New Hampshire. Until the 1950s, Vermont and New Hampshire were two of the most resolutely Republican states in the country; they shared in common a fierce suspicion of state and federal government, taxation, social programs, and anything else that interfered with the rights and freedoms of ordinary citizens. Vermont changed radically after 1950, while New Hampshire continued to follow essentially the same course of small-town libertarianism. Not only the politics but the general cultural ethos of the states also diverged: Vermont became known as a hotbed of hippies, farmers, and artists, whereas New Hampshire maintained its reputation for rugged, outdoorsy types interested in hunting, fishing, motorcycles, and all-terrain vehicles (ATVs). Part of this is just our imagination—we "see" difference where we expect to find it—but much of it is real. Vermont and New Hampshire, like Canada and the United

States, are genuinely different places despite our (reasonable) expectation that they be quite similar.

Interestingly, in explaining the intranational divergence of Vermont and New Hampshire, a causal factor mistakenly associated with US/Canadian political differentiation gains traction: *selective migration*, or population flows based on place-based preference, such as the desire to live in a more ecologically conscious or politically liberal place. Though I have discounted the role of selective migration in the post-Revolutionary split between Canadian and American political culture—the so-called Tory Exodus—the role of self-selection is actually quite important in the case of Vermont and New Hampshire. New types of people began moving to Vermont in the 1950s, 1960s, and 1970s, solidifying social, cultural, and political transformations already under way.[1]

What is the difference between the cases of US/Canada and Vermont/New Hampshire? Migration *within* a nation is far more common than transnational migration. International borders are a major obstacle to moving, for obvious reasons. In general, people seem most likely to make choices about which country to live in or emigrate to on the basis of job prospects, preexisting family ties, language competency, and the vagaries of immigration and naturalization policy. This was certainly true with migrants to the United States and Canada. Intranational migration, however, is an entirely different matter. People ostensibly move *within* countries for a variety of reasons, and they usually do so without any state interference. Thousands of Americans moved to Vermont after 1960 because of its reputation as a beautiful, inexpensive, relatively "untouched" hinterland welcoming of artists, bohemians, students, and the like. New Hampshire's lasting reputation for low taxes and libertarian politics has recently attracted new types of Americans to migrate there as well. Thus, we see how a single causal process—selective migration—operates differently at different levels of analysis.

Emerging differences in post-9/11 Canadian and American immigration policy will likely have dramatic but highly unpredictable effects on the political culture of both nations. This, too, reflects the malleability of political culture and political development more generally. Of the two nations, America has the stronger claim to an abiding history of openness to immigrants and their various cultural heritages, yet the window of opportunity for new immigration to American is now nearly shut, as it was once before, in the period between the First World War and Vietnam. Canada, once a nation with a fairly insular view of itself and comparatively low in-migration rates, is now a world leader in welcoming new and diverse peoples to its shores. It is nearly impossible to predict how newcomers will change these societies or how these societies will change them, but it is clear that immigration will continue to be a major factor in the fate of nations.

Findings and Deliberations

The five features of US and Canadian political development are reassessed below, while contemplating future possibilities:

Economic development. Canada's economy has matured greatly in the past several decades, but it is still different than the US economy in the extent of foreign ownership and state regulation of private enterprise. Historically, the American economy gained its unique character from a combination of features: freedom of incorporation, coupled with emerging recognition of the legal autonomy of private corporations; loosely governed western territories open to "capture" by early entrepreneurs and corporate concerns, plus innovations in mineral and land law that favored commerce over preservation; and a legacy of labor law that tends to favor employers over employees. The Canadian experience was opposite that of America in these regards: strictly regulated corporations; a law-and-order, environmentally sensitive approach to western development; and labor law comparatively sensitive to the need for balance between workers' rights and economic growth.

It would seem that state involvement in Canada's economy is likely to increase in the future as a growing share of its gross domestic product (GDP) comes from industries dedicated to marketing Canada's copious supplies of oil, natural gas, timber, uranium, and hydroelectric power. Interestingly, however, environmental regulation of these industries devolves to the provinces in Canada, as opposed to the federal government in the United States. This may open the way for unique, innovative solutions in industrial policy and environmental regulation, or for dramatic disparities in interprovincial wealth and environmental degradation. In the United States, by contrast, there is no reason to believe that current trends in corporate independence, commercial corruption, union busting, or interest group political lobbying will change anytime soon. America's boom-bust cycle of economic development seems likely to continue apace.

Collectivism, social services, and voter alignment. Canada's social demo-cratic welfare system is a relatively recent innovation, though one that is built firmly on the edifice of strong provincial government and a history of paternalistic law enforcement, particularly on Canada's western fron-tiers. Though further experimentation is always a possibility at the provincial level, Canada seems unlikely to abandon its social welfare programs anytime soon. Even right-wing Canadian political parties see the provinces' single-payer health insurance systems as sacrosanct, for example. The stigma of "Americanization" only makes free market solu-tions to these problems in Canada more unlikely. Change in social ser-vices and voter alignment are likely to come at the margins of Canada's bedrock social democratic system. In the United States, by contrast, pro-gressive efforts at collectivizing risk and mobilizing left-wing voters will likely continue to surface, and will likely continue to fail. The stigma of "socialism," coupled with the power of business-minded interest groups and the entrenchment of private, for-profit social insurance schemes make such moves unlikely. Moreover, the relative weakness of American state governments makes the likelihood of serious policy innovation and/or lasting third-party movements at the state level unlikely. State-level social welfare, educational, and economic development programs exist in the United States, but even there—as with President George W. Bush's plan, "No Child Left Behind"—federal oversight looms large. The jurisdictional reach of Congress into so many aspects of American social policy makes innovation, compromise, and regional party movements far less likely than in Canada, where provincial autonomy truly makes the provinces "incubators of democracy."

Comparative federalism. Though built firmly around the doctrine of states rights, the American federal government's jurisdiction has grown relative to state jurisdiction. This began with the 1787 decision to na-tionalize all of the territory west of the Appalachians, coupled with con-gressional inaction regarding governance of said territory. An increasing tendency to engage in geopolitical maneuvering furthered federal power through the growth of civilian militias and the armed forces. Numerous American presidents exploited ambiguities in the Constitution to ex-pand executive power and the jurisdictional reach of federal govern-ment more generally. Beginning with the Quebec Act of 1774, by contrast, Canada has assiduously protected the jurisdiction of its provinces, as well as the religious and cultural rights of minority groups. Though a federal agency was charged with policing the western territories in their early years, nascent provincial governments were gradually afforded responsibility and autonomy in accord with their abilities and needs. Today, with the rising economic power of Alberta and the continuing political power of Quebec, provincial rights remain a firmament of Canadian politics. This is not likely to change anytime soon. In fact, further decentralization seems likely.

Individual and civil rights. Given the malleability of the law and the unpredictability of the courts, the future of individual and civil rights in the United States and Canada is hard to predict. What we do know is that lawyers and legal disputes played an unusually large role in early American society, and that the agonistic features of this system only magnified as the country matured and expanded. Constitutional doctrine concerning individual rights, too, was not infrequently bent to accommodate radical exceptions, such as slavery, Native American genocide, and Jim Crow–era discrimination. American law still wavers on bedrock issues of equal protection. At the same time, Canada's judicial system has changed greatly, muddying the historical waters, so to speak. Canadian pundits frequently decry the "judicialization" of Canadian politics, and indeed, the courts have become more active in this respect. The passage of the 1982 Charter of Rights and Freedoms created for Canada an American-style list of federally guaranteed rights. This might thus be one area where Canadian politics are likely to converge with American, though the exact ramifications of this are hard to predict. In general, legal protections surrounding personal freedom and group rights seem more secure in Canada than in the United States. The federal courts in the United States are simply too powerful and unpredictable to know how issues such as abortion, same-sex marriage, immigration law, citizenship and voter rights, and the rights of "enemy combatants" will fare.

Identity politics. The comparative demographics of the United States and Canada have always been different—America's large African-American and Mexican-American populations and Canada's current influx of immigrants from South Asia and the Far East, for example. For both geographic and political reasons, Canada also does not currently have an illegal immigration "problem" like that festering in the United States. In fact, Canada is currently one of the world's most welcoming, fastest-growing immigration-intensive societies. Though some vestiges of nativism remain, native-born Canadians have had a relatively peaceable time accepting newcomers regardless of their race, religion, and cultural background. Canada has also made notable advances in addressing the political and social grievances of its aboriginal peoples. One might attribute all this to the peaceful good nature of Canadians, but it is more likely the result of legal precedents protecting minority group rights, coupled with current public policy designed to help new immigrants get established and comfortable in Canadian society.

Ironically, in the United States, where "rights talk" is paramount, decisions about the competing rights and externalities of personal freedom are extremely unpredictable. With so many points of entry into the policy-making arena, fringe interest groups can and do have disproportionate sway on such issues. A vibrant American tradition of outspokenness and paternalism with regard to morality also shapes American policy with respect to issues such as sexuality, substance use, and education. Americans seem unusually willing to legislate morality.

Nations, Nation Building, and Nationalism

Nation building is a tricky business. The modern concept of the nation-state is itself rather unusual. Rather than ruling through brute force, cultural hegemony, or economic coercion, modern nation-states exist largely as legal fictions, exerting power while attempting to use it as little as possible. They seek to command deference by fiat, not force. In most cases, modern nation-states handle the various functions of public administration by creating and regulating subordinate legal fictions—states, provinces, territories, counties, and municipalities, as well as private and public corporations, trusts, partnerships, and even marital unions.

This is a legal house of cards, so to speak, something much greater (and far more unstable) than the sum of its parts—which may help explain why dissolving nation-states are so hard to put back together again. Without the trappings of legal legitimacy, social order falls apart. Property rights fade, civil mandates melt away, and the state's monopoly on violence shatters. This is happening now, in the early twenty-first century world, with astonishing frequency.

One of the biggest internal threats a modern nation-state can ever face is domestic rejection of the legal order that holds it together. Violation of specific laws, particularly criminal laws, is a major problem, but rejection of the very jurisdictional infrastructure that holds together such systems of law is even more threatening. Rejection of jurisdictional claims constitutes a rejection of the state project itself, as occurred in the eighteenth-century American colonies, the nineteenth-century American South, and which threatens to occur on a regular basis in Quebec today. At the same time, the foregoing narrative supports the observation that jurisdictional tension—friction rather than outright rejection—can be beneficial, as it has been in contemporary Canada.

So too does Canadian history show that executive power, concerted and accountable at *both* the national and regional levels, is crucial to the fate of nations. Canada has only haltingly followed America's lead in opening politics to the people, yet it has a long and admirable history of ably serving its constituents. "Executive federalism," rather than popular democracy may thus be a workable model for nations that are struggling with the competing demands of modernization and multiculturalism.

A related set of observations has similar implications for global affairs. One of the primary concerns of this volume has been the role of state jurisdiction over the creation and regulation of intermediary associations—such as private groups of individuals legally enfranchised as corporations, congregations, charities, and clubs. Though one of the defining characteristics of modernity has been the rising power and prominence of such groups in civil society, they are actually creatures with a long lineage in the Western world. Having long ago seen the purpose of using state power to "incorporate" churches and colleges, states have been doing so since at least the Roman Empire. An important historical feature of this legal avatar is the expectation that corporations remain firmly under the control of the states. Revolutionary-era New Englanders thus opened a Pandora's box when they initiated a transformation in the relationship of Americans to the means of incorporation. In the early American colonies, the jurisdictional makeup of the corporation was hotly contested. "Freedom of incorporation" was not the dream of the Puritan founders—in fact, they viewed the corporation as a means of tying civil enterprise more closely to the state. But because their own struggles for state sovereignty were wrapped up in legal battles over the autonomy of corporations, the relationship between corporations and the state was unintentionally transformed in its wake. American law subsequently gave birth to the idea that the state should have only limited jurisdiction over so-called private actors—particularly corporations, but also individuals and groups. Today, many features of the American political landscape are products of the overweening influence of private business corporations, nonprofit organizations, and political action committees. Incorporation grants capital a source of state-divined power that was never imagined by its Roman inventors.

For a variety of reasons—not just the ones established here—the corporation has become the pinnacle of modern social enterprise worldwide. American commercial law is increasingly the standard in much of the rest of the world. Nonetheless, American civil society still seems to remain more open to corporate influence than its counterparts, the result of its long and liberal history with regard to corporate activity of all types.

Today, an analogous process appears to be occurring in the wider international domain. Multinational corporations and extranational militias appear to be rapidly chipping away at the power of the modern nation-state in the early twenty-first century. Both militias and multinationals operate under the radar of national jurisdiction, thus undermining the regulatory and tax powers of nation-states, as well as their claim to a monopoly over the legitimate means of violence. Both rely on the most advanced legal and financial techniques to harbor and deploy resources. They are powerful private interests that defy both the rule of law and its underpinning national jurisdictional regimes.

Like Canada and the United States, every nation contains within it many nations—subnational polities, as well as intermediary associations, and private citizens. Without the "iron cage" of nation-states, however, self-interest, entropy, and the battle of each against all spread and flow. Regrettably, contemporary efforts to reexert the powers of the nation-state—efforts such as those waged by the United States in Iraq and by the North Atlantic Treaty Organization (NATO) in Afghanistan—only appear to put those ailing states in further jeopardy. This is, at least in part, the result of systematic failure to comprehend the jurisdictional bases of social order and political development, the tricky mélange of relationships that is modern statecraft. On the ground, at the local level, residents need to feel a combined sense of autonomy, recognition, and protection from untoward threats and aggression. The American system of governance—the proposed model for American nation building abroad—seems perfectly suited to neglect at least two of these three "needs."

Canada and the United States have always had a unique relationship. This is the result of more than just proximity, anglophilia, or goodwill. Tocqueville, Franklin, and Adams may have been wrong in predicting unification, but they were warranted in seeing the potential for neighboring nations to build lasting ties by building conduits through which people, commerce, and ideas might readily flow. Unfortunately, this too is now under threat. American attempts to maintain "homeland security" have dramatically slowed the flow of traffic across the US/Canadian border. Regardless of whatever trade agreements are or are not sustained, the relationship between the United States and Canada lives and dies on the two-way intercourse of its people, organizations, and governments. Slower borders threaten not only the economic but also the diplomatic and cultural ties that bind. For two nations that share the closest economic, diplomatic, demographic, and cultural relationship in the world—and perhaps in world history—this is a perilous prospect, indeed.

Notes

Introduction

1. Alexis de Tocqueville, *Democracy in America,* trans. George Lawrence (New York [1966] 1988), 660.
2. Ibid., 661n2. Kant refers to this outcome as "perpetual peace."
3. Floyd W. Rudmin, *Bordering on Aggression: Evidence of US Military Preparations against Canada* (Hull, Canada, 1993).
4. Karen Orren and Stephen Skowronek, *The Search for American Political Development* (New York, 2004), esp. 126–127; Charles Tilly, *Identities, Boundaries, and Social Ties* (Boulder, CO, 2005); Mustafa Emirbayer and Jeff Goodwin, "Network Analysis, Culture, and the Problem of Agency," *American Journal of Sociology* 99 (1994): 1411–1454.
5. Ronald L. Watts, "The American Constitution in Comparative Perspective: A Comparison of Federalism in the United States and Canada," *Journal of American History* 74 (1987): 769–792; Kenneth Grant Crawford, *Canadian Municipal Government* (Toronto, 1954); Leonard P. Curry, *The Corporate City: The American City as a Political Entity, 1800–1850* (Westport, CT, 1997); Gerald Frug, "The City as a Legal Concept," *Harvard Law Review,* 93, no. 6 (1980): 1057–1154; Hendrik Hartog, *Public Property and Private Power: The Corporation in the City of New York in American Law, 1730–1870* (Chapel Hill, NC, 1983).
6. J. P. Nettl, "The State as a Conceptual Variable," *World Politics* 20 (1968): 559–592; Margaret R. Somers, "Citizenship and the Place of the Public Sphere: Law, Community, and Political Culture in the Transition to Democracy," *American Sociological Review* 58 (1993): 587–620; George M. Thomas, John W. Meyer, Francisco O. Ramirez, and John Boli, *Institutional Structure: Constituting State, Society, and the Individual* (Newbury Park, CA,

1987). The progenitor of this approach to the state is, of course, Max Weber.

7. Jason Kaufman, "Corporate Law and the Sovereignty of States," *American Sociological Review* 73 (2008): 402–425.

8. Elizabeth Mancke, *The Fault Lines of Empire: Political Differentiation in Massachusetts and Nova Scotia, ca. 1760–1830* (New York, 2005), 1.

9. Ibid., 161.

10. Robert Frost, "Mending Wall," in *North of Boston* (London, 1914).

11. Michael Adams, *Fire and Ice: The United States, Canada and the Myth of Converging Values* (Toronto, 2003); Edward Grabb and James Curtis, *Regions Apart: The Four Societies of Canada and the United States* (Toronto, 2004); Jeffrey Simpson, *Star-Spangled Canadians: Canadians Living the American Dream* (Toronto, 2000); Seymour Martin Lipset, *Continental Divide: The Values and Institutions of the United States and Canada* (New York, 1990); Neil Nevitte, *The Decline of Deference: Canadian Value Change in Cross-National Perspective* (Peterborough, Canada, 1996).

12. Daniel T. Rodgers, "Exceptionalism," in *Imagined Histories: American Historians and the Past,* ed. Anthony Mohlo and Gordon S. Wood (Princeton, NJ, 1998); Michael Kammen, "The Problem of American Exceptionalism: A Reconsideration," *American Quarterly* 45 (1993): 1–43; Mary Nolan, "Against Exceptionalism," *American Historical Review* 102 (1997): 769–774; Ian Tyrrell, "American Exceptionalism in an Age of International History," *American Historical Review* 96 (1991): 1031–1055; Sean Wilentz, "Against Exceptionalism: Class Consciousness and the American Labor Movement," *International Labor and Working Class History* 26 (1984): 1–24; Aristide R. Zolberg, "How Many Exceptionalisms?" in *Working Class Formation: Nineteenth Century Patterns in Western Europe and the United States,* ed. Ira Katznelson and Aristide R. Zolberg (Princeton, NJ, 1986); Bryon E. Shafer, ed., *Is America Different? A New Look at American Exceptionalism* (New York, 1991); Jack P. Greene, *The Intellectual Construction of America: Exceptionalism and Identity from 1492 to 1800* (Chapel Hill, NC, 1993); Rick Halpern and Jonathan Morris, eds., *American Exceptionalism? U.S. Working-Class Formation in an International Context* (New York, 1997); Seymour Martin Lipset and Gary Marks, *It Didn't Happen Here: Why Socialism Failed in the United States* (New York, 2000); Seymour Martin Lipset, *American Exceptionalism: A Double-Edged Sword* (New York, 1996).

13. Daniel Elazar, *The American Mosaic: The Impact of Space, Time and Culture on American Politics* (Boulder, CO, 1994); David Hackett Fischer, *Albion's Seed: Four British Folkways in America* (New York, 1989); Joel Garreau, *The Nine Nations of North America* (Boston, 1981); Grabb and Curtis, *Regions Apart.*

14. Halpern and Morris, *American Exceptionalism;* Lipset and Marks, *It Didn't Happen Here;* Michael Porter and Jeffrey Sachs, eds., *Global Competitiveness Report, 2001* (New York, 2001); Dan Zuberi, *Differences That Matter: Social Policy and the Working Poor in the United States and Canada* (Ithaca, NY, 2006).

15. "Human Development Report 2003," hdr.undp.org (accessed September 30, 2004); "Public Social Expenditure in 1998 as a Percentage of GDP," www.oecd.org (accessed March 16, 2004); Roger Gibbins and Neil Nevitte, "Canadian Political Ideology: A Comparative Perspective," *Canadian Journal of Political Science* 18 (1985): 577–598; Seymour Martin Lipset, *Agrarian Socialism: The Cooperative Commonwealth Federation in Saskatchewan—A Study in Political Sociology* (Berkeley, CA, 1950); Lipset, *Continental Divide.*

16. David E. Smith, *The Invisible Crown: The First Principle of Canadian Government* (Toronto, 1995), 11–13; Watts, "American Constitution in Comparative Perspective"; Robert C. Vipond, *Liberty and Community: Canadian Federalism and the Failure of the Constitution* (Albany, NY, 1991); Chester B. Martin, *Foundations of Canadian Nationhood* (Toronto, 1955); Bruce A. Ackerman, *The Failure of the Founding Fathers: Jefferson, Marshall, and the Rise of Presidential Democracy* (Cambridge, MA, 2005).

17. Mary Ann Glendon, *Rights Talk: The Impoverishment of Political Discourse* (New York, 1991); Richard A. Posner, *The Problems of Jurisprudence* (Cambridge, MA, 1990). Though perfectly comparable figures are hard to come by, the United States had about 3.2 lawyers per 1,000 inhabitants in 2004, while Canada had only about 1.95.

18. Mark Noll, *A History of Christianity in the United States and Canada* (Grand Rapids, MI, 1992); Irene Bloemraad, *Becoming a Citizen: Incorporating Immigrants and Refugees in the United States and Canada* (Berkeley, CA, 2006); S. D. Clark, *Church and Sect in Canada* (Toronto, 1948); Jill Vickers, *The Politics of Race: Canada, Australia, and the United States* (Ottawa, 2002).

19. Gosta Esping-Anderson, *The Three Worlds of Welfare Capitalism* (Princeton, NJ, 1990).

20. William Julius Wilson, *The Declining Significance of Race: Blacks and Changing American Institutions* (Chicago, 1978); Thomas B. Edsall, *Chain Reaction: The Impact of Race, Rights, and Taxes on American Politics* (New York, 1991); Paul Frymer, *Black and Blue: African Americans, The Labor Movement, and the Decline of the Democratic Party* (Princeton, NJ, 2008); C. Vann Woodward, *The Strange Career of Jim Crow* (New York, 1955). The literature on this topic is simply too immense to summarize in a citation or two.

21. James H. Webb, *Born Fighting: How the Scots-Irish Shaped America* (New York, 2004); Grabb and Curtis, *Regions Apart*. See also James Hunter, *A Dance Called America: The Scottish Highlands, the United States, and Canada* (Edinburgh, 1994).

22. Ira Katznelson, *City Trenches: Urban Politics and the Patterning of Class in the United States* (New York, 1981); Theodore Lowi, *At the Pleasure of the Mayor: Patronage and Power in New York City, 1898–1958* (New York, 1964); Paul M. Sniderman, Louk Hagendoorn, and Markus Prior, "Predisposing Factors and Situational Triggers: Exclusionary Reactions to Immigrant Minorities," *American Political Science Review* 98 (2004): 35–49; David Ward, *Cities and Immigrants: A Geography of Change in Nineteenth Century America* (New York, 1971).

23. Donald L. Horowitz and Gérard Noiriel, *Immigrants in Two Democracies: French and American Experience* (New York, 1992); Jason Kaufman, *For The Common Good? American Civic Life and the Golden Age of Fraternity* (New York, 2002); Jeffrey Reitz and Raymond Breton, *The Illusion of Difference: Realities of Ethnicity in Canada and the United States* (Toronto, 1994). Some examples of "ethnicist" thinking about the United States and Canada are: Daniel Elazar, *American Federalism: A View from the States* (New York, 1966); Marc Egnal, *Divergent Paths: How Culture and Institutions Have Shaped North American Growth* (New York, 1996); David Hackett Fischer, *Albion's Seed: Four British Folkways in America* (New York, 1989); Garreau, *Nine Nations of North America*.

24. Christopher Adamson, "God's Continent Divided: Politics and Religion in Upper Canada and the Northern and Western United States, 1775 to 1841," *Comparative Studies in Society and History* 36 (1994): 417–446; Clark, *Church and Sect*; Gerald M. Craig, *Upper Canada: The Formative Years, 1784–1841* (Toronto, 1963), 55; Grabb and Curtis, *Regions Apart,* 111–116.

25. Edwin Amenta, *Bold Relief: Institutional Politics and the Origins of Modern American Social Policy* (Princeton, NJ, 1998); Paul Burstein and April Linton, "The Impact of Political Parties, Interest Groups, and Social Movement Organizations on Public Policy," *Social Forces* 81 (2002): 380–408; Jacob S. Hacker, *The Divided Welfare State: The Battle over Public and Private Benefits in the United States* (New York, 2002); Paul Pierson, *Dismantling the Welfare State? Reagan, Thatcher and the Politics of Retrenchment* (New York, 1994); Theda Skocpol, *Protecting Soldiers and Mothers: The Political Origins of Social Policy in the United States* (Cambridge, MA, 1992); Sven Steinmo, Kathleen Thelen, and Frank Longstreth, eds. *Structuring Politics: Historical Institutionalism in Comparative Analysis* (New York, 1992).

26. Watts, "American Constitution in Comparative Perspective"; Peter Karsten, *Between Law and Custom: "High" and "Low" Legal Cultures in the Lands of the*

British Diaspora—The United States, Canada, Australia, and New Zealand, 1600–1900 (New York, 2002); Bora Laskin, *The British Tradition in Canadian Law* (London, 1969).

27. Seymour Martin Lipset, "Radicalism or Reformism: The Sources of Working-Class Politics," *American Political Science Review* 77 (1983): 1–19; Adam Przeworski, *Capitalism and Social Democracy* (New York, 1985).

28. Elisabeth Clemens and James Cook, "Politics and Institutionalism: Durability and Change," *Annual Review of Sociology* 25 (1999): 441–466; Frank Dobbin, "Cultural Models of Organization: The Social Construction of Rational Organizing Principles," in *The Sociology of Culture,* ed. Diana Crane (Cambridge, MA, 1994); Paul Pierson, *Politics in Time: History, Institutions, and Social Analysis* (Princeton, NJ, 2004); Steinmo, Thelen, and Longstreth, eds., *Structuring Politics;* Kathleen Thelen, "Historical Institutionalism in Comparative Politics," *Annual Review of Political Science* 2 (1999): 369–404; Thomas, Meyer, Ramirez, and Boli, *Institutional Structure;* Walter Powell and Paul DiMaggio, *The New Institutionalism in Organizational Analysis* (Chicago, 1991).

29. Louis Hartz, *The Liberal Tradition in America: An Interpretation of American Political Thought since the Revolution* (San Diego, CA [1955] 1991), 3; Kenneth McRae, "The Structure of Canadian History," in *The Founding of New Societies,* ed. Louis Hartz (New York, 1964); Gad Horowitz, "Conservatism, Liberalism, and Socialism in Canada: An Interpretation," *The Canadian Journal of Economics and Political Science* 32 (1966): 143–171.

30. Seymour Martin Lipset: "The Value Patterns of Democracy: A Case Study in Comparative Analysis," *American Sociological Review* 28 (1963): 515–31; *The First New Nation: The United States in Historical and Comparative Perspective* (New York, 1963); *Revolution and Counterrevolution* (New York, 1968); *Continental Divide;* Seymour Martin Lipset and Noah M. Meltz, *The Paradox of American Unionism: Why Americans Like Unions More than Canadians Do but Join Much Less* (Ithaca, NY, 2004).

31. Doug Baer, Edward Grabb, and William A. Johnston, "The Values of Canadians and Americans: A Critical Analysis and Reassessment," *Social Forces* 68 (1990): 693–713. See also Craig Crawford and James Curtis, "English Canadian-American Differences in Value Orientations," *Studies in Comparative International Development* 14 (1979): 23–44; Edward Grabb and James Curtis, "English Canadian-American Differences in Orientation toward Social Control and Individual Rights," *Sociological Focus* 21 (1988): 127–141; Tom Truman, "A Critique of Seymour M. Lipset's Article, Value Differences, Absolute or Relative: The English-Speaking Democracies," *Canadian Journal of Political Science* 4 (1971): 497–525.

32. Jason Kaufman, "Endogenous Explanation in the Sociology of Culture," *Annual Review of Sociology* 30 (2004): 335–357.
33. Lipset, *American Exceptionalism,* 91.
34. See n. 27, as well as Julia Adams, Elisabeth Clemens, and Ann Orloff, eds., *Remaking Modernity: Politics, History, and Sociology* (Durham, NC, 2005); Michèle Lamont and Laurent Thévenot, *Rethinking Comparative Cultural Sociology: Repertoires of Evaluation in France and the United States* (New York, 2000); James Mahoney and Dietrich Rueschemeyer, eds., *Comparative Historical Analysis in the Social Sciences* (New York, 2003); Orren and Skowronek, *Search for American Political Development;* Dietrich Rueschemeyer and Theda Skocpol, eds., *States, Social Knowledge, and the Origins of Modern Social Policies* (New York, 1996); George Steinmetz, ed., *State/Culture: State-Formation after the Cultural Turn* (Ithaca, NY, 1999); Tilly, *Identities, Boundaries, and Social Ties;* Margaret Weir, Ann Orloff, and Theda Skocpol, eds., *The Politics of Social Policy in the United States* (Princeton, NJ, 1988).
35. Lawrence M. Friedman, "Legal Culture and Social Development," *Law and Society Review* 4, no. 1 (1969): 34, 40; see also Konrad Zweigert and Hein Kötz, *Introduction to Comparative Law,* trans. Tony Weir (Oxford, [1977] 1998).
36. See, for example, Richard J. Ross, "The Legal Past of Early New England: Notes for the Study of Law, Legal Culture, and Intellectual History," *William and Mary Quarterly,* 3rd ser., 50, no. 1 (1993): 23–41; Patricia Ewick and Susan Silbey, *The Common Place of Law: Stories from Everyday Life* (Chicago, 1998); John David Skrentny, *The Minority Rights Revolution* (Cambridge, MA, 2002); Miriam Smith, "The Politics of Same-Sex Marriage in Canada and the United States," *PS: Political Science & Politics* (April 2005): 225–228.

1. Origins of the Colonial System

1. Karen Cerulo, *Identity Designs: The Sights and Sounds of a Nation* (New Brunswick, NJ, 1995); Jeffrey K. Olick and Joyce Robbins, "Social Memory Studies: From 'Collective Memory' to the Historical Sociology of Mnemonic Practices," *Annual Review of Sociology* 24 (1998): 105–140; Lyn Spillman, *Nation and Commemoration: Creating National Identities in the United States and Australia* (New York, 1997).
2. Ruth A. McIntyre, *Debts Hopeful and Desperate: Financing the Plymouth Colony* (Plymouth, MA, 1963); Charles M. Andrews, *The Colonial Period of American History* (New Haven, CT, 1934), I: 254, 266.
3. McIntyre, *Debts;* Andrews, *Colonial Period,* I: 272–283; see also Herbert L. Osgood, *The American Colonies in the Seventeenth Century* (New York, 1904), I.

4. William DeLoss Love Jr., *The Fast and Thanksgiving Days of New England* (Boston, 1895), 70–71; see also H. S. J. Sickel, *Thanksgiving: Its Source, Philosophy, and History with All National Proclamations and Analytical Study Thereof* (Philadelphia, PA, 1940).

5. One of the marked differences between the religious spirit of the Pilgrims of Plymouth Plantation and their subsequent Puritan neighbors to the north, at the Massachusetts Bay Colony, was that the latter held several important fasting days on Friday, "the day of the week popular among [Anglican] churchmen for fasting." Love, *Fast and Thanksgiving Days,* 93.

6. Love, *Fast and Thanksgiving Days,* 85, 90, 93, 99, 249.

7. Osgood, *American Colonies,* I: 109; see also Andrews, *Colonial Period,* I: 280–284; T. H. Breen, *Puritans and Adventurers: Change and Persistence in Early America* (New York, 1980); David Grayson Allen, *In English Ways: The Movement of Societies and the Transferal of English Local Law and Custom to Massachusetts Bay in the Seventeenth Century* (Chapel Hill, NC, 1981).

8. Andrews, *Colonial Period,* I: 291–292; William Bradford, George Morton, and Edward Winslow, *A Relation or Iournall of the Beginning and Proceedings of the English Plantation Setled at Plimoth in New England* [*Mourt's Relation*] (London, 1622 [1848]); McIntyre, *Debts.*

9. McIntyre, *Debts.*

10. Andrews, *Colonial Period,* I: 294, 297; Bradford, Morton, and Winslow, *Mourt's Relation.*

11. George Best, *A True Discourse of the Late Voyages of Discouerie: For the Finding of a Passage to Cathaya, by the Northvveast, Vnder the Conduct of Martin Frobisher Generall: Deuided into Three Bookes* (London, 1578), quoted in Robert McGhee, *The Arctic Voyages of Martin Frobisher: An Elizabethan Adventure* (Montreal, 2001), 112. It seems equally probable that earlier explorers, such Giovanni Caboto (John Cabot) or Jacques Cartier, would have held such services, but Frobisher is generally credited as the first, perhaps because a firsthand account exists of the actual service, led by minister Thomas Wolfall.

12. McGhee, *Arctic Voyages of Martin Frobisher;* James McDermott, *Martin Frobisher: Elizabethan Privateer* (New Haven, CT, 2001).

13. Harold A. Innis, *The Fur Trade in Canada: An Introduction to Canadian History* (Toronto, 1956); J. M. S. Careless, *Canada: A Story of Challenge,* 3rd ed. (Toronto, 1970); W. J. Eccles, *The Canadian Frontier, 1534–1760* (Albuquerque, NM, 1983).

14. Andrews, *Colonial Period,* I: 77.

15. In general, the sugar colonies of the British Atlantic were more carefully supervised than the remainder of British North America. I am grateful to

historian Ian Steele for this insight. See also Robert M. Bliss, *Revolution and Empire: English Politics and the American Colonies in the Seventeenth Century* (New York, 1990); Stephen Saunders Webb, *1676: The End of American Independence* (New York, 1984).

16. Andrew McFarland Davis, *Corporations in the Days of the Colony* (Cambridge, MA, 1894); Joseph Stancliffe Davis, *Essays in the Earlier History of American Corporations* (Cambridge, MA, 1917); Herbert L. Osgood, "The Corporation as a Form of Colonial Government," *Political Science Quarterly* 11 (1896): 259–277, 502–533, 694–715.

17. Andrews, *Colonial Period*, I: 91–94; Wesley Frank Craven, *Dissolution of the Virginia Company: The Failure of a Colonial Experiment* (New York, 1932); April Lee Hatfield, *Atlantic Virginia: Intercolonial Relations in the Seventeenth Century* (Philadelphia, PA, 2004).

18. Andrews, *Colonial Period*, I: 103, 112, 116–117, 119; Warren M. Billings, John E. Selby, and Thad W. Tate, *Colonial Virginia: A History* (White Plains, NY, 1986); Osgood, *American Colonies*, III: 28–36, 85–86; James R. Perry, *The Formation of a Society on Virginia's Eastern Shore, 1615–1655* (Chapel Hill, NC, 1990).

19. Andrews, *Colonial Period*, I: 178, 194, 200, 202, 204–205; Billings, Selby, and Tate, *Colonial Virginia*; John C. Rainbolt, *From Prescription to Persuasion: Manipulation of Eighteenth Century Virginia Economy* (Port Washington, NY, 1974).

20. Francis J. Bremer, *John Winthrop: America's Forgotten Founding Father* (New York, 2003).

21. Bremer, *Winthrop*, 152–153, 160–161; see also Andrews, *Colonial Period*, I: 344–374. Andrews discusses the probable fate of the missing transfer documents on p. 358, where he adds (n. 3), "The destruction of inconvenient documents was not unknown to the nonconformists of the seventeenth century."

22. Bremer, *Winthrop*, 235–236; John G. Reid, *Maine, Charles II, and Massachusetts: Governmental Relationships in Early Northern New England* (Portland, OR, 1977).

23. Bremer, *Winthrop*, 236, 239; Osgood, "Corporation as a Form of Colonial Government," 505; Jason Kaufman, "Corporate Law and the Sovereignty of States," *American Sociological Review* (2008).

24. Osgood, *American Colonies*, III: 4; see also Samuel Lucas, *Charters of the Old English Colonies in America* (London, 1850), 31; Andrews, *Colonial Period*, I: 371; Cradock quoted in Andrews, *Colonial Period*, I: 367.

25. Allen, *In English Ways*; see also Kenneth A. Lockridge, *A New England Town, the First Hundred Years: Dedham, Massachusetts, 1636–1736* (New York, 1970); Michael Zuckerman, *Peaceable Kingdoms: New England Towns in the*

Eighteenth Century (New York, 1970); T. H. Breen, "Who Governs: The Town Franchise in Seventeenth Century Massachusetts," *William and Mary Quarterly,* 3rd ser., 27 (1970): 460–474.

26. A copy of the charter is reprinted in Samuel Eliot Morison, *Harvard College in the Seventeenth Century* (Cambridge, MA, 1936), 5–8, 24–25.

27. Morison, *Harvard College,* 9–10.

28. Andrews, *Colonial Period,* I: 42n2; Simeon E. Baldwin, "History of the Law of Private Corporations in the Colonies and States," in *Select Essays in Anglo-American Legal History* (Boston, 1909), III: 241–242.

29. Increase Mather, "A Brief Account concerning Several of the Agents of New England, Their Negotiation at the Court of England, with Some Remarks on the New Charter Granted to the Colony of Massachusets [*sic*], etc." (London, November 16, 1691), 21.

30. Both passages are quoted in Davis (*Earlier History of American Corporations,* I: 18), though Davis's citation method is somewhat vague regarding their original provenance.

31. Patrick T. Conley, *Democracy in Decline: Rhode Island's Constitutional Development, 1776–1841* (Providence, RI, 1977); Irving Berdine Richman, *Rhode Island: A Study in Separatism* (Boston, 1905).

32. Bremer, *John Winthrop;* Bruce H. Mann, *Neighbors and Strangers: Law and Community in Early Connecticut* (Chapel Hill, NC, 1987); John Frederick Martin, *Profits in the Wilderness: Entrepreneurship and the Founding of New England Towns in the Seventeenth Century* (Chapel Hill, NC, 1991).

33. Martin, *Profits in the Wilderness,* 174, 185, 302.

34. Ibid., 258–259, 262–263; see also Shaw Livermore, *Early American Land Companies: Their Influence on Corporate Development* (New York, 1939).

35. Martin, *Profits in the Wilderness,* 55.

36. John Winthrop, "Speech to the General Court," in *The American Puritans: Their Prose and Poetry,* ed. Perry Miller (Garden City, NY, 1956), 91–92; Andrews, *Colonial Period,* I: 442, 445–447, 472; Bremer, *John Winthrop;* George Less Haskins, *Law and Authority in Early Massachusetts* (New York, 1960); Osgood, "Corporation as a Form of Colonial Government," III: 696.

37. Andrews, *Colonial Period,* I: 439–440, 460, 485, 519; Winthrop quoted in Osgood, *American Colonies,* I: 262, see also 225–255.

38. Osgood, *American Colonies,* I: 258–263, 266, 278–279, 285; Haskins, *Law and Authority.*

39. Osgood, *American Colonies,* I: 249, 265, 302–303, 306–308. New France practiced similar exclusion against Huguenots, but dissenters in this case were not allowed to wander off and form their own provinces, a key difference in the jurisdictional structure of the two emerging polities.

40. Innis, *Fur Trade.*

41. Careless, *Canada*, 23–28; Innis, *Fur Trade*.
42. Cartier was actually referring only to a short stretch of the St. Lawrence River in using the term, "River of Hochelaga, or the great river of Canada." See Francis Parkman, *The Struggle for a Continent*, ed. Pelham Edgar (Boston, 1903), 71; also Careless, *Canada*, 33.
43. Kenneth J. Banks, *Chasing Empire across the Sea: Communications and the State in the French Atlantic, 1713–1763* (Montreal, 2002), 15–16; Careless, *Canada*, 34–40; Eccles, *Canadian Frontier*, 6.
44. Innis, *Fur Trade*.
45. Banks, *Chasing Empire*, 19; Careless, *Canada*, 40–46; Innis, *Fur Trade*, 19, 31.

2. Expansion and Contraction

1. W.J. Eccles, *The Canadian Frontier, 1534–1760*, rev. ed. (Albuquerque, NM, 1983), esp. 53–54; Allan Greer, *The People of New France* (Toronto, 1997).
2. Richard White, *The Middle Ground: Indians, Empires, and Republics in the Great Lakes Region, 1650–1815* (New York, 1991).
3. From *Peter Kalm's Travels in North America*, trans. Adolph Benson (New York: Dover, 1937), quoted in Greer, *People of New France*, 84; Eccles, *Canadian Frontier*, xiii.
4. Eccles, *Canadian Frontier*, 80; Colbert à Talon quoted in Eccles, ibid., 104; see also Greer, *People of New France*; Richard Colebrook Harris, *The Seigneurial System in Early Canada: A Geographical Study* (Madison, WI, 1966).
5. Kenneth J. Banks, *Chasing Empire across the Sea: Communications and the State in the French Atlantic, 1713–1763* (Montreal, 2002), 140–141; Greer, *People of New France*, 37, 86–89.
6. Greer, *People of New France*, 37–40; Francis Parkman, *The Struggle for a Continent* (Boston, 1903), 121. One reason New France had such a limited population was that French Huguenots had been expelled from the colony by order of Cardinal Richelieu. More speculative is Parkman's assertion, "If, instead of excluding Huguenots, France had given them an asylum in the west [of Canada], and left them there to work out their own destinies, Canada would never have been a British province, and the United States would have shared their vast domain with a vigorous population of self-governing Frenchmen."
7. Greer, *People of New France*, 39; Harris, *Seigneurial System*, 192; Dale Miquelon, ed., *Society and Conquest: The Debate on the Bourgeoisie and Social Change in French Canada, 1700–1850* (Vancouver, BC, 1977).

8. Jean Claude Marsan, *Montreal in Evolution: Historical Analysis of the Development of Montreal's Architecture and Urban Environment* (Montreal, 1981), 21–24; 66–68; Allan Greer, *Peasant, Lord, and Merchant: Rural Society in Three Quebec Parishes, 1740–1840* (Toronto, 1985).

9. E. N. Hartley, *Ironworks on the Saugus: The Lynn and Braintree Ventures of the Company of Undertakers of the Ironworks in New England* (Norman, OK, 1957); Stephen Innes, *Creating the Commonwealth: The Economic Culture of Puritan New England* (New York, 1995), 61–62, 237–271; Bernard Bailyn, *The New England Merchants in the Seventeenth Century* (Cambridge, MA, 1979), 61–62, 74, 83.

10. Bailyn, *New England Merchants,* 110, 138–142; William B. Weeden, *Economic and Social History of New England, 1620–1789* (New York, 1963).

11. Innes, *Creating the Commonwealth,* 215–216; David Grayson Allen, *In English Ways: The Movement of Societies and the Transferal of English Local Law and Custom to Massachusetts Bay in the Seventeenth Century* (Chapel Hill, NC, 1981); George Lee Haskins, *Law and Authority in Early Massachusetts: A Study in Tradition and Design* (New York, 1960), 170–174; David Thomas Konig, *Law and Society in Puritan Massachusetts: Essex County, 1629–1692* (Chapel Hill, NC, 1979); Shaw Livermore, *Early American Land Companies: Their Influence on Corporate Development* (New York, 1939); John Frederick Martin, *Profits in the Wilderness: Entrepreneurship and the Founding of New England Towns in the Seventeenth Century* (Chapel Hill, NC, 1991).

12. Bailyn, *New England Merchants,* 103; Andro Linklater, *Measuring America* (New York, 2002), 35; Allen, *In English Ways,* 214; Irving H. Bartlett, *Daniel Webster* (New York, 1978); Oscar Handlin and Mary F. Handlin, *Commonwealth: A Study of the Role of Government in the American Economy, 1774–1861* (Cambridge, MA, 1969); Pauline Maier, "The Revolutionary Origins of the American Corporation," *William and Mary Quarterly,* 3rd ser., 50 (1993): 51–84; William E. Nelson, *Americanization of the Common Law: The Impact of Legal Change on Massachusetts Society, 1760–1830* (Cambridge, MA, 1975).

13. Charles M. Andrews, *The Colonial Period of American History* (New Haven, CT, 1934), I: 323.

14. Herbert L. Osgood, *The American Colonies in the Seventeenth Century* (New York, 1904), I: 398; Sung Bok Kim, *Landlord and Tenant in Colonial New York: Manorial Society, 1664–1775* (Chapel Hill, NC, 1978), 13; Robert C. Black III, *The Younger John Winthrop* (New York, 1966), 290; Martin, *Profits in the Wilderness.*

15. William G. McLoughlin, *Rhode Island: A Bicentennial History* (New York, 1978); Black, *Younger John Winthrop;* Livermore, *Early American Land Companies;* Martin, *Profits in the Wilderness.*

16. According to Osgood (*American Colonies*, 513), parliamentary activity with respect to the colonies was limited to "a half dozen acts which related to the subject of trade." See also Leonard Labaree, *Royal Government in America: A Study of the British Colonial System before 1783* (New York, 1958 [1930]).

17. Andrews, *Colonial Period of American History*, II: 156, 194, and III: 138–140, 157–158, 162; Livermore, *Early American Land Companies*; Mary Lou Lustig, *The Imperial Executive in America: Sir Edmund Andros, 1637–1714* (Madison, NJ, 2002), 110–113.

18. Black, *Younger John Winthrop*; Andrews, *Colonial Period*, II: 191.

19. Osgood, *American Colonies*, III: 309–335; Martin, *Profits in the Wilderness*, 262–266.

20. Lustig, *Imperial Executive*, 70, 82, 108; Jack M. Sosin, *English America and the Revolution of 1688: Royal Administration and the Structure of Provincial Government* (Lincoln, NE, 1982), 15–16, 25–27; Labaree, *Royal Government in America*, 173.

21. Osgood, *American Colonies*, III: 330–334; Sosin, *English America*; Lustig, *Imperial Executive*.

22. Lustig, *Imperial Executive*, 134–135.

23. Sosin, *English America*, 93–94; Lustig, *Imperial Executive*, 190–198.

24. Sosin, *English America*, 114; Andrews, *Colonial Period*, II: 109–110, 124–137.

25. Increase Mather, *A Brief Account concerning Several of the Agents of New England, Their Negotiation at the Court of England, with Some Remarks on the New Charter Granted to the Colony of Massachusets [sic]* (London, November 16, 1691), 16.

26. Samuel Eliot Morison, *Harvard College in the Seventeenth Century* (Cambridge, MA, 1936), II: 512, 516–517. There is good reason to believe that Mather himself doomed the 1697 charter to failure. After pining for years for an excuse to return to England, Mather wrote a letter to William Blathwayt, a member of the Board of Trade and Plantations, advising him to delay consideration of the college charter "until such Time, as I can be with you, which I hope may be in July or August next." Only a few days before Blathwayt received this note, the solicitor general of the Crown issued a positive report on the charter request, presumably because he had failed to note the colonists' refusal to admit the king's oversight of college affairs. Mather's self-serving request for delay had the unintended effect of subjecting the 1697 charter "to a new and more careful scrutiny. . . . Mather's craze for a trip to England simply called attention to a feature of the Charter which would otherwise have passed unnoticed among the mass of documents coming in from all parts of the Empire."

27. Morison, *Harvard College,* II: 518, 526–530; Richard Hofstadter, *Academic Freedom in the Age of the College* (New York, 1955), 106; Maier, "Revolutionary Origins of the American Corporation," 56n14.

28. Joseph Stancliffe Davis, *Essays in the Earlier History of American Corporations* (Cambridge, MA, 1917), I: 17; Harry A. Cushing, *History of the Transition from Provincial to Commonwealth Government in Massachusetts* (New York, 1896), 49–50; Herbert L. Osgood, "The Corporation as a Form of Colonial Government," *Political Science Quarterly* 11 (1896): 259–277, 502–533, 694–715. Virginia also was originally founded on these grounds, though it did not remain for very long. In 1624, with still scarcely more than a few hundred settlers, its charter was nullified and the territory was reinstated as a royal colony.

29. Hofstadter, *Academic Freedom,* 136; Samuel Sewall, *Letter Book of Samuel Sewall* (Boston, 1886–1888), I: 263–264, quoted in Davis, *Earlier History of American Corporations,* 21–22. Judge Sewall's advice is also discussed in Simeon E. Baldwin, *Modern Political Institutions* (Boston, 1898), 184.

30. Eleazar Wheelock to William Smith, quoted in John M. Shirley, *The Dartmouth College Causes and the Supreme Court of the United States* (New York, 1971 [1895]), 22, 25.

31. Simeon E. Baldwin, "History of the Law of Private Corporations in the Colonies and States," in *Select Essays in Anglo-American Legal History* (Boston, 1909), III: 242; Baldwin, *Modern Political Institutions,* 184–185; Frederic W. Maitland, *State, Trust, and Corporation,* ed. David Runciman and Magnus Ryan (New York, 2003), 42.

32. Shirley, *Dartmouth College Causes,* 24.

33. Simeon E. Baldwin, "Private Corporations, 1701–1901," in *Two Centuries Growth of American Law, 1701–1901* (New York, 1901), 312; Maier, "Revolutionary Origins of the American Corporation," 53; Cushing, *Transition from Provincial to Commonwealth Government,* 262; Andrew L. Creighton, *The Emergence of Incorporation as a Legal Form for Organizations* (PhD dissertation, Stanford University, Dept. of Sociology, 1990); Charles Perrow, *Organizing America: Wealth, Power, and the Origins of Corporate Capitalism* (Princeton, NJ, 2002); William G. Roy, *Socializing Capital: The Rise of the Large Industrial Corporation in America* (Princeton, NJ, 1997).

34. Simeon E. Baldwin, "Private Corporations," 247–249; Andrew McFarland Davis, *Corporations in the Days of the Colony* (Cambridge, MA, 1894); Oscar Handlin and Mary F. Handlin, "Origins of the American Business Corporation," *Journal of Economic History* 5 (1945): 4; Handlin and Handlin, *Commonwealth,* 96; Maier, "Revolutionary Origins of the American Corporation," 53, 56.

35. Andrews, *Colonial Period,* III: 183.
36. Osgood, *American Colonies,* III: 193–239.
37. Leonard Labaree, ed., *Royal Instructions to British Colonial Governors, 1670–1776* (New York, 1935).
38. Andrews, *Colonial Period,* III: 224–225.
39. Andrews, *Colonial Period,* II: 282; Osgood, "Corporation as a Form of Colonial Government."
40. Bernard Bailyn, *The Origins of American Politics* (New York, 1970).
41. Andrews, *Colonial Period,* II: 282, 348–349, 356, 375–376.
42. Mary Geiter, *William Penn* (Harlow, England, 2000). Geiter makes the strong but controversial argument that Penn should be viewed less as a religious missionary than as a practical, commercially minded speculator and politician. Compare Edwin B. Bronner, *William Penn's "Holy Experiment": The Founding of Pennsylvania, 1681–1701* (Westport, CT, 1978 [1962]; Hans Fantel, *William Penn: Apostle of Dissent* (New York, 1974); Harry Emerson Wildes, *William Penn* (New York, 1974).
43. Geiter, *William Penn.*
44. Andrews, *Colonial Period,* III: 268–328.
45. Ibid., 324, 326–327.
46. Ibid., 212–213, 220–222, 250–251; Peter Laslett, "John Locke, the Great Recoinage, and the Origins of the Board of Trade: 1697–1698," *William and Mary Quarterly,* 3rd ser., 14 (1957): 370–402; Labaree, *Royal Government in America.*
47. Thomas Perkins Abernethy, *From Frontier to Plantation in Tennessee: A Study in Frontier Democracy* (Chapel Hill, NC, 1932); Thomas D. Clark, *Three American Frontiers: Writings of Thomas D. Clark,* ed. Holman Hamilton (Lexington, KY, 1968); C. Vann Woodward, *The Burden of Southern History* (Baton Rouge, LA, 1993).
48. Isaac Rhys, *The Transformation of Virginia, 1740–1790* (Chapel Hill, NC, 1982).
49. Virginia banned men in the colony from giving legal counsel for profit in 1658. In the Carolinas, men were banned from asking courts for any kind of reward, monetary or otherwise. Michael Stephen Hindus, *Prison and Plantation: Crime, Justice, and Authority in Massachusetts and South Carolina, 1767–1878* (Chapel Hill, NC, 1980), xxvi; Andrews, *Colonial Period,* III: 216.
50. Osgood, *American Colonies,* III: 248–252.
51. Ibid., 251–252.
52. Nathaniel Bacon (June 18, 1676) quoted in Osgood, *American Colonies,* III: 264–265.
53. Lustig, *Imperial Executive,* 85–98.

54. Cf. Frederick Jackson Turner, *The Frontier in American History* (New York, 1996 [1920]).

3. Two Turning Points

1. Timothy J. Shannon, *Indians and Colonists at the Crossroads of Empire: The Albany Congress of 1754* (Ithaca, NY, 2000).
2. Ibid., 46–47, 109; see also Dorothy V. Jones, *License for Empire: Colonialism by Treaty in Early America* (Chicago, 1982).
3. Sung Bok Kim, *Landlord and Tenant in Colonial New York: Manorial Society, 1664–1775* (Chapel Hill, NC, 1978), 295–315.
4. Ibid., 346, 350, 350n14.
5. Ibid., 365; Shannon, *Indians and Colonists,* 162–171.
6. Julius Goebel Jr., "Introduction," in Shaw Livermore, *Early American Land Companies: Their Influence on Corporate Development* (New York, 1939), xxiii.
7. *Pennsylvania Gazette* (May 9, 1754) quoted in Shannon, *Indians and Colonists,* 83; Bruce E. Johansen, *Forgotten Founders: Benjamin Franklin, the Iroquois and the Rationale for the American Revolution* (Ipswich, MA, 1982).
8. Shannon, *Indians and Colonists,* 99, 179.
9. Ibid., 182.
10. Ibid., 61, 186; Leonard Woods Labaree, *Royal Government in America: A Study of the British Colonial System before 1783* (New York, 1958 [1930]); Philip Lawson, *The Imperial Challenge: Quebec and Britain in the Age of the American Revolution* (Montreal, 1989), 82, 87–88; Simeon Eben Baldwin, "History of the Law of Private Corporations in the Colonies and States," in *Select Essays in Anglo-American Legal History* (Boston, 1909), 236–240.
11. Shannon, *Indians and Colonists,* 208–212.
12. Guy Frégault, *Canada: The War of the Conquest,* trans. Margaret M. Cameron (Toronto, 1969), 18; Thomas Perkins Abernethy, *Western Lands and the American Revolution* (New York, 1959), 8–10.
13. Frégault, *Canada: The War of The Conquest,* 17–18; Fred Anderson, *Crucible of War: The Seven Years' War and the Fear of Empire in British North America, 1754–1766* (New York, 2000), 615.
14. Frégault, *Canada: The War of the Conquest,* 29–33, 38–39; Matthew C. Ward, *Breaking the Backcountry: The Seven Years' War in Virginia and Pennsylvania, 1754–1765* (Pittsburgh, PA, 2003).
15. Both letters quoted in Frégault, *Canada: The War of the Conquest,* 244–245. See also David R. Starbuck, *Massacre at Fort William Henry* (Hanover, NH, 2002); Ian K. Steele, *Betrayals: Fort William Henry and the Massacre* (New York, 1990). The latter two books seek to correct James Fenimore Cooper's depiction of the battle in *The Last of the Mohicans.*

16. J. Hector St. John de Crévecoeur, *Letters from an American Farmer,* ed. Albert E. Stone (New York, 1981 [1782]), 69.

17. Frégault, *Canada: The War of the Conquest,* 35, 239.

18. Anderson, *Crucible of War.*

19. Lawson, *Imperial Challenge,* 3–24; Frégault, *Canada: The War of the Conquest,* 231, 235, 266, 291, 305.

20. Kenneth J. Banks, *Chasing Empire across the Sea: Communications and the State in the French Atlantic, 1713–1763* (Montreal, 2002); A. L. Burt, *The Old Province of Quebec, Vol. 1* (Toronto, 1968); Lawson, *Imperial Challenge.*

21. Lawrence Henry Gipson, *The British Empire before the American Revolution, Vol. 9—The Triumphant Empire: New Responsibilities within the Enlarged Empire, 1763–1766* (New York, 1956), 197.

22. Jean-Claude Marsan, *Montreal in Evolution* (Montreal, 1981), 128–129.

23. Anderson, *Crucible of War,* 611; John Phillip Reed, *Constitutional History of the American Revolution: The Authority to Tax* (Madison, WI, 1987); Pauline Maier, *From Resistance to Revolution: Colonial Radicals and the Development of American Opposition to Britain, 1765–1776* (New York, 1972), 100–106; John W. Tyler, *Smugglers and Patriots: Boston Merchants and the Advent of the American Revolution* (Boston, 1986), 88.

24. Reid, *Constitutional History,* 51, 98–99, 177, 282; Anderson, *Crucible of War,* 608; Labaree, *Royal Government in America.*

25. Anderson, *Crucible of War,* 612; Robert L. Brunhouse, *The Counter-Revolution in Pennsylvania, 1776–1790* (Philadelphia, PA, 1942).

26. Louise Burnham Dunbar, *A Study of "Monarchical" Tendencies in the United States from 1776 to 1801* (Urbana, IL, 1923), 10–11, 13.

27. Kim, *Landlord and Tenant;* Michael A. Bellesiles, *Revolutionary Outlaws: Ethan Allen and the Struggle for Independence on the Early American Frontier* (Charlottesville, VA, 1993); Matt Bushnell Jones, *Vermont in the Making, 1750–1777* (Cambridge, MA, 1939).

28. Alan Taylor, *Liberty Men and Great Proprietors: The Revolutionary Settlement on the Maine Frontier, 1760–1820* (Chapel Hill, NC, 1990), 4, 11–14, 181.

29. Richard Maxwell Brown, *The South Carolina Regulators* (Cambridge, MA, 1963), 39.

30. Taylor, *Liberty Men and Great Proprietors,* 4, 181; Leonard L. Richards, *Shay's Rebellion: The American Revolution's Final Battle* (Philadelphia, PA, 2002), 63–67; George Rude, *The Crowd in History: A Study of Popular Disturbances in France and England, 1730–1848* (New York, 1964), 42; Brown, *South Carolina Regulators,* 42, 51, 137; Richard Lyman Bushman, "Farmers in Court: Orange County, North Carolina, 1750–1776," in *The Many Legalities of Early America,* ed. Christopher L. Tomlins and Bruce H. Mann (Chapel Hill, NC, 2001).

31. D. G. Creighton, *The Commercial Empire of the St. Lawrence, 1760–1850* (Toronto, 1937); Robert McConnell Hatch, *Thrust for Canada: The American Attempt on Quebec in 1775–1776* (Boston, 1979); Lawson, *Imperial Challenge;* William Renwick Riddell, *The Bar and the Courts of the Province of Upper Canada or Ontario* (Toronto, 1928), 5–6. The admission of Catholics into the Canadian legal system was not a product of the Quebec Act of 1774, but came from a 1764 decision by the Lords of Trade in response to an explicit ban on Catholic service.

32. Harold Innis, *The Fur Trade in Canada: An Introduction to Canadian Economic History* (Toronto, 1956); Peter C. Newman, *Empire of the Bay* (Toronto, 1998); Richard Colebrook Harris, *The Seigneurial System in Early Canada: A Geographical Study* (Madison, WI, 1966); Peter N. Moogk, *La Nouvelle France: The Making of French Canada—A Cultural History* (East Lansing, MI, 2000); Fernand Ouellet, *Histoire Economique et Sociale du Quebec, 1760–1850: Structures et Conjonctures* (Ottawa, 1980 [1966]); Dale Miquelon, ed., *Society and Conquest: The Debate on the Bourgeoisie and Social Change in French Canada, 1700–1850* (Vancouver, BC, 1977); Gipson, *British Empire;* R. Cole Harris and John Warkentin, *Canada before Confederation: A Study in Historical Geography* (New York, 1974); Chester Martin, *Foundations of Canadian Nationhood* (Toronto, 1955).

33. J. M. S. Careless, *Canada: A Story of Challenge* (Toronto, 1970), 100–104; Gipson, *British Empire,* 45–46; Innis, *Fur Trade,* 175–180.

4. The Birth Pangs of Nationalism

1. William Pitt quoted in Philip Lawson, *The Imperial Challenge: Quebec and Britain in the Age of the American Revolution* (Montreal, 1989), 144; Robert McConnell Hatch, *Thrust for Canada: The American Attempt on Quebec in 1775–1776* (Boston, 1979), 11; Samuel Adams (April 11, 1768) quoted in Charles H. Metzger, *The Quebec Act: A Primary Cause of the American Revolution* (New York, 1936), 24, 61, 77, 109; *Georgia Gazette* (December 14, 1774) quoted in Reba Carolyn Strickland, *Religion and the State in Georgia in the Eighteenth Century* (New York, 1939), 140; James Lowell Underwood, "The Dawn of Religious Freedom in South Carolina: The Journey from Limited Tolerance to Constitutional Right," in *The Dawn of Religious Freedom in South Carolina,* ed. James Lowell Underwood and W. Lewis Burke (Columbia, SC, 2006), 26–27.

2. Alfred Leroy Burt, *The Old Province of Quebec* (Toronto, 1968), I: 182–224; Hatch, *Thrust for Canada,* 13; see also F. Murray Greenwood, *Legacies of Fear: Law and Politics in Quebec in the Era of the French Revolution* (Toronto, 1993).

3. Gorman Condon, *The Envy of the American States: The Loyalist Dream for New Brunswick* (Fredericton, NB, 1984), 79; J. M. S. Careless, *Canada: A Story of Challenge* (Toronto, 1970), 111; Arthur Granville Bradley, *Colonial Americans in Exile: Founders of British Canada* (New York, 1932); John Barlet Brebner, *The Neutral Yankees of Nova Scotia: A Marginal Colony during the Revolutionary Years* (New York, 1937); Wilfred Brenton Kerr, *The Maritime Provinces of British North America and the American Revolution* (Sackville, New Brunswick, 1941); Elizabeth Mancke, *The Fault Lines of Empire: Political Differentiation in Massachusetts and Nova Scotia, 1760–1830* (New York, 2005).

4. Hatch, *Thrust for Canada,* 14–16.

5. Peter S. Onuf, *Jefferson's Empire: The Language of American Nationhood* (Charlottesville, 2000), 60–61.

6. Jack P. Greene, *The Intellectual Construction of America: Exceptionalism and Identity from 1492 to 1800* (Chapel Hill, NC, 1993); Pauline Maier, *From Resistance to Revolution: Colonial Radicals and the Development of American Opposition to Britain, 1765–1776* (New York, 1972), 16–18. Dalrymple and Alden quoted in John Philip Reid, *In Defiance of the Law: The Standing-Army Controversy, the Two Constitutions, and the Coming of the American Revolution* (Chapel Hill, NC, 1981), 79–80, 206–207, 214–215.

7. William H. Nelson, *The American Tory* (Oxford, 1961), 87, 92; Wallace Brown, *The Good Americans: The Loyalists in the American Revolution* (New York, 1969); Esther Clark Wright, *The Loyalists of New Brunswick* (Fredericton, New Brunswick, 1955); Claude Halstead Van Tyne, *The Loyalists in the American Revolution* (Gloucester, MA, 1959); Thomas Perkins Abernethy, *Western Lands and the American Revolution* (New York, 1959), 277–278.

8. Van Tyne, *Loyalists in the American Revolution,* 209–210, 215–216, 280.

9. Gordon Wood, *The Creation of the American Republic, 1776–1787* (Chapel Hill, NC, 1998 [1969]), 75–76; Bernard Bailyn, *The Origins of American Politics* (New York, 1967); Leonard Woods Labaree, *Royal Government in America: A Study of the British Colonial System before 1783* (New York, 1958 [1930]).

10. Wood, *Creation of the American Republic,* 162–187, 208, 218, 513; Jack N. Rakove, *Original Meanings: Politics and Ideas in the Making of the Constitution* (New York, 1996).

11. Jefferson quoted in Wood, *Creation of the American Republic,* 213; James Albert Woodburn, "Western Radicalism in American Politics," *Mississippi Valley Historical Review* 13 (1926): 143–168.

12. Wood, *Creation of the American Republic,* 205; Rakove, *Original Meanings,* 250–252; Alexander Keyssar, *The Right to Vote: The Contested History of Suffrage in the United States* (New York, 2000).

13. Adams (May 12, 1776) quoted in Wood, *Creation of the American Republic,* 225.

14. Wood, *Creation of the American Republic,* 270; Simeon Eben Baldwin, "History of the Law of Private Corporations in the Colonies and States," in *Select Essays in Anglo-American Legal History* (Boston, 1909 [1901]), 240; Maier, *From Resistance to Revolution,* 238–239. On the violation of native treaties, see Onuf, *Jefferson's Empire,* 37–41; Dorothy V. Jones, *License for Empire: Colonialism by Treaty in Early America* (Chicago, 1982); Francis Paul Prucha, *American Indian Treaties: The History of a Political Anomaly* (Berkeley, CA, 1994).

15. Wood, *Creation of the American Republic,* 283; Michael G. Kammen, *A Machine That Would Go of Itself: The Constitution in American Culture* (New York, 1986).

16. Michael A. Bellesiles, *Revolutionary Outlaws: Ethan Allen and the Struggle for Independence on the Early American Frontier* (Charlottesville, VA, 1993), 108–109; John Jay (October 7, 1779) quoted in Peter S. Onuf, "State-Making in Revolutionary America: Independent Vermont as a Case Study," *Journal of American History* 67 (1981): 801.

17. Washington quoted in Leonard L. Richards, *Shays's Rebellion: The American Revolution's Final Battle* (Philadelphia, PA, 2002), 131–132.

18. Wood, *Creation of the American Republic,* 410, 412, 432.

19. Ibid., 403–413, 475.

20. Ibid., 356–357, 359; Jackson Turner Main, *The Sovereign States, 1775–1783* (New York, 1973).

21. Clinton Rossiter, ed., *The Federalist Papers* (New York, 1999), esp. *Federalist* no. 10, 27, 46, 58–60; James A. Morone, *The Democratic Wish: Popular Participation and the Limits of American Government* (New Haven, CT, 1998), 62–73.

22. Wood, *Creation of the American Republic,* 485; Ralph Ketcham, ed., *The Anti-Federalist Papers and the Constitutional Convention Debates* (New York: Penguin, 1986).

23. Wood, *Creation of the American Republic,* 531, 533, 599, 601–602; Kammen, *A Machine That Would Go of Itself.*

24. Rakove, *Original Meanings,* 330–331.

25. "A Freeman of Virginia," in *The Freeman's Remonstrance against an Ecclesiastical Establishment* (Williamsburg, VA, 1777), quoted in Thomas E. Buckley, *Church and State in Revolutionary Virginia, 1776–1787* (Charlottesville, VA, 1977), 40, 27; Anson Phelps Stokes, *Church and State in the United States* (New York, 1950).

26. Jacob C. Meyer, *Church and State in Massachusetts from 1740 to 1833: A Chapter in the History of the Development of Individual Freedom* (Cleveland,

OH, 1930); William G. McLoughlin, *New England Dissent, 1630–1833: The Baptists and the Separation of Church and State* (Cambridge, MA, 1971); Strickland, *Religion and the State in Georgia*; James Lowell Underwood, "The Dawn of Religious Freedom in South Carolina." State incorporation rates and regulations come from the published session laws of each state legislature. It is difficult to know exactly how many groups were chartered specifically under general incorporation laws, since such charters did not require special acts of the legislature and no other records of their passage are generally available.

27. Buckley, *Church and State in Revolutionary Virginia.*
28. Ibid., 180–181.
29. John S. Moir, *The Church in the British Era: From the British Conquest to Confederation* (Toronto, 1972), 77–78, 107. In this respect, one might consider the parallel case of New Orleans, another primarily Catholic polity in which "immoral" behavior was, and is, unusually widespread and largely tolerated by civil authorities.
30. George Rawlyk and Mark Noll, eds., *Amazing Grace: Evangelicalism in Australia, Britain, Canada and the United States* (Grand Rapids, MI 1994); George Rawlyk, *Is Jesus Your Personal Saviour? In Search of Canadian Evangelicalism in the 1990s* (Montreal and Kingston, 1996); Mark Regnerus, David Sikkink, and Christian Smith, "Voting with the Christian Right: Contextual and Individual Patterns of Electoral Influence" *Social Forces* 77 (1999): 445–457; Sam Reimer, *Evangelicals and the Continental Divide: The Conservative Protestant Subculture in Canada and the United States* (Montreal and Kingston, 2003); Sam Reimer, "A Look at Cultural Effects on Religiosity: A Comparison between the United States and Canada," *Journal for the Scientific Study of Religion* 34 (1995): 445–457.
31. Seymour Martin Lipset, *The First New Nation: The United States in Historical and Comparative Perspective* (New York, 1979 [1963]; Lipset, *Continental Divide: The Values and Institutions of the United States and Canada* (New York, 1990); Samuel P. Huntington, *Who Are We? The Challenges to America's National Identity* (New York, 2004); Northrop Frye, *The Bush Garden: Essays on the Canadian Imagination* (Toronto, 1971).
32. Wallace Brown, *The Good Americans: The Loyalists in the American Revolution* (New York, 1969), 192; Robert McCluer Calhoon, *The Loyalists in Revolutionary America, 1760–1781* (New York, 1973), 501; Ann Gorman Condon, *The Envy of the American States: The Loyalist Dream for New Brunswick* (Fredericton, New Brunswick, 1984); Paul H. Smith, "The American Loyalists: Notes on Their Organizational and Numerical Strength," *William and Mary Quarterly* 25 (1968): 259–277; A. G. Bradley, *Colonial Americans in Exile: Founders of British Canada* (New York, 1932), 108.

33. Brebner, *North Atlantic Triangle*, 69; Condon, *Envy of the American States;* Bradley, *Colonial Americans in Exile;* D. W. Meinig, *The Shaping of America: Vol. 1, Atlantic America, 1492–1800* (New Haven, CT, 1986), 323–332; *St. John's* [sic] *Gazette and Nova Scotia Intelligencer* (February 26, 1784).

34. Condon, *Envy of the American States*, 137.

35. Carleton to Sydney (June 25, 1785) quoted in Condon, *Envy of the American States*, 137–138, emphasis added; Wright, *Loyalists of New Brunswick*, 148–150.

36. Condon, *Envy of the American States*, 140, 142; Wright, *The Loyalists of New Brunswick;* James W. St. Gême Walker, *The Black Loyalists: The Search for a Promised Land in Nova Scotia and Sierra Leone, 1783–1870* (London, 1976).

37. Brebner, *North Atlantic Triangle*, 79–80; Chester Martin, *Dominion Lands Policy* (Toronto, 1973), 132–133; Donald G. Creighton, *The Commercial Empire of the St. Lawrence, 1760–1850* (Toronto, 1937), 28.

38. Fred Landon, *Western Ontario and the American Frontier* (Toronto, 1941), 2, 15–16; Albert B. Corey, *Canadian-American Relations along the Detroit River* (Detroit, MI, 1957); Gerald M. Craig, *Upper Canada: The Formative Years, 1784–1841* (Toronto, 1963); G. P. deT. Glazebrook, *Life in Ontario: A Social History* (Toronto, 1968); Marcus Lee Hansen, *The Mingling of the Canadian and American Peoples* (New Haven, CT, 1940).

39. Meinig, *The Shaping of America* (New Haven, CT, 1986), I: 284–288; Robert Livingston Schuyler, *The Fall of the Old Colonial System: A Study in British Free Trade, 1770–1870* (London, 1945).

40. Abernethy, *Western Lands and the American Revolution*, 369.

41. "Washington once admitted that he was willing to break 'the letter of the law' when it came to land speculation"—Thomas Slaughter, *The Whiskey Rebellion: Frontier Epilogue to the American Revolution* (New York, 1986), 284n16, also 79–89. Slaughter attributes Washington's admission to *The Writings of George Washington*, ed. John C. Fitzpatrick (Washington, DC, 1931–1944), III: 498–499.

42. Abernethy, *Western Lands and the American Revolution*, 239.

43. Ibid., 242–257; Robert Levere Brunhouse, *The Counter-Revolution in Pennsylvania, 1776–1790* (Philadelphia, PA, 1942).

44. Peter S. Onuf, *Statehood and Union: A History of the Northwest Ordinance* (Bloomington, IN, 1987).

45. Thomas Perkins Abernethy, *Three Virginia Frontiers* (Gloucester, MA, 1962), 67–68, 80–81; Lowell H. Harrison and James C. Klotter, *A New History of Kentucky* (Lexington, KY, 1997).

46. Abernethy, *Three Virginia Frontiers*, 76–77.

47. Harrison and Klotter, *New History of Kentucky*, 55; Wallace (July 12, 1785) quoted in Abernethy, *Western Lands and the American Revolution*, 297.
48. Onuf, *Origins of the Federal Republic*, 11.
49. Kenneth R. Bowling, *The Creation of Washington, D.C.: The Idea and Location of the American Capital* (Fairfax, VA, 1991).
50. Ibid.; Slaughter, *The Whiskey Rebellion*, 89; James Thomas Flexner, *George Washington* (Boston, 1965–1972), IV: 46, 157, 163.
51. Brunhouse, *Counter-Revolution in Pennsylvania*, 135–140.
52. Alpheus H. Snow, *The Administration of Dependencies: A Study of the Evolution of the Federal Empire, with Special Reference to American Colonial Problems* (New York, 1902), 472; Bowling, *Creation of Washington, D.C.*, 30–42.
53. Peter S. Onuf, *The Origins of the Federal Republic: Jurisdictional Controversies in the United States, 1775–1787* (Philadelphia, PA, 1983), 23.
54. Thomas Jefferson, *Notes on the State of Virginia* (New York, 1999 [1975]), 98; see also Jack Ericson Eblen, *The First and Second United States Empires: Governors and Territorial Government, 1784–1912* (Pittsburgh, PA, 1968); Drew R. McCoy, *The Elusive Republic: Political Economy in Jeffersonian America* (Chapel Hill, NC, 1980); Onuf, *Jefferson's Empire*, 18–52.
55. Eblen, *First and Second United States Empires*; Onuf, *Origins of the Federal Republic*.
56. Beverley W. Bond Jr., *Civilization of the Old Northwest: A Study of Political, Social, and Economic Development, 1788–1812* (New York, 1934), 144–147.

5. Nationhood Begins, and Almost Ends

1. Whether or not either country had a right to annex these territories is not directly at issue here, though the manner in which they did so is examined in detail. Frazer Ells Wilson, *Arthur St. Clair: Rugged Ruler of the Old Northwest, An Epic of the American Frontier* (Richmond, VA, 1944), 46; Alpheus H. Snow, *The Administration of Dependencies: A Study of the Evolution of the Federal Empire, with Special Reference to American Colonial Problems* (New York, 1902), 360–362; Paul W. Gates, *History of Public Land Law Development* (Washington, DC, 1968), 72.
2. Beverly W. Bond Jr., *The Civilization of the Old Northwest: A Study of Political, Social, and Economic Development, 1788–1812* (New York, 1934); Jack Ericson Eblen, *The First and Second United States Empires: Governors and Territorial Government, 1784–1912* (Pittsburgh, PA, 1968).
3. Wilson, *Arthur St. Clair.*
4. Ibid.
5. Ibid., 47; Bond, *Civilization of the Old Northwest*, 55–59; Eblen, *First and Second United States Empires*, 72–86.

6. D. W. Meinig, *The Shaping America, Vol. 1: Atlantic America, 1492–1800* (New Haven, CT, 1986), 390–393, 409–412; Eblen, *First and Second United States Empires*, 86, 90; Peter S. Onuf, *The Origins of the Federal Republic: Jurisdictional Controversies in the United States, 1775–1787* (Philadelphia, PA, 1983).

7. Shaw Livermore, *Early American Land Companies: Their Influence on Corporate Development* (New York, 1939), ix–xxvi, 134–146; Rudolf Freund, "Military Bounty Lands and the Origins of the Public Domain," *Agricultural History* 20 (1946): 8–18; James W. Oberly, *Sixty Million Acres: American Veterans and the Public Lands before the Civil War* (Kent, OH, 1990); Bond, *Civilization of the Old Northwest*, 55–56, 141–147.

8. Simcoe quoted in Fred Landon, *Western Ontario and the American Frontier* (Toronto, 1941), 1.

9. Mary Beacock Fryer and Christopher Cracott, *John Graves Simcoe, 1752–1806: A Biography* (Toronto, 1998).

10. Sir Andrew Agnew, *From Lochnaw to Manitoulin: A Highland Soldier's Tour through Upper Canada* (Toronto, 1999); Cunningham Geike, *Life in the Woods: A Boy's Narrative of the Adventures of a Settler's Family in Canada* (Boston, 1865); Edwin Clarence Guillet, *Pioneer Days in Upper Canada* (Toronto, 1968); Susanna Moodie, *Roughing It in the Bush* (Toronto, 2006); M. R. Redclift, *The Frontier Environment and Social Order: The Letters of Francis Codd from Upper Canada* (Northampton, MA, 2000); Gary Thomson, *Village Life in Upper Canada* (Belleville, ON, 1988); Louis Tivy, *Your Loving Anna: Letters from the Ontario Frontier* (Toronto, 1972); Catherine Parr Traill, *The Backwoods of Canada* (Toronto, 2006).

11. Jane Errington, *The Lion, the Eagle, and Upper Canada: A Developing Colonial Ideology* (Kingston, ON, 1987), 15; Fryer and Cracott, *John Graves Simcoe*.

12. Gerald M. Craig, *Upper Canada: The Formative Years, 1784–1841* (Toronto, 1963), 55; W. Stewart Wallace, *The Family Compact: A Chronicle of the Rebellion in Upper Canada* (Toronto, 1915), 61–62; Marcus Lee Hansen, *The Mingling of the Canadian and American Peoples, Vol. 1* (New Haven, CT, 1940); Douglas McCalla, *Planting the Province: The Economic History of Upper Canada, 1784–1870* (Toronto, 1993); Alan Taylor, *William Cooper's Town: Power and Persuasion on the Frontier of the Early American Republic* (New York, 1995).

13. Fryer and Cracott, *John Graves Simcoe*, 157; Craig, *Upper Canada*; Landon, *Western Ontario and the American Frontier*.

14. Michel Brunet, "La Conquête anglaise et la déchéance de la bourgeoisie canadienne (1760–1793)," in *Society and Conquest: The Debate on the Bourgeoisie and Social Change in French Canada, 1700–1850*, ed. Dale Miquelon

(Vancouver, BC, 1977), 153; F. Murray Greenwood, *Legacies of Fear: Law and Politics in Quebec in the Era of the French Revolution* (Toronto, 1993).

15. Allan Greer, *Peasant, Lord, Merchant: Rural Society in Three Quebec Parishes 1740–1840* (Toronto, 1985); Fernand Ouellet, *Economic and Social History of Quebec, 1760–1850* (Ottawa, 1980 [1966]).

16. Greenwood, *Legacies of Fear*; William M. Weekes, "The War of 1812: Civil Authority and Martial Law in Upper Canada," in *The Defended Border: Upper Canada and the War of 1812*, ed. Morris Zaslow (Toronto, 1964); Ernest A. Cruikshank, "A Study of Disaffection in Upper Canada in 1812–15," in Zaslow, *Defended Border.*

17. Brian Young, *The Politics of Codification: The Lower Canadian Civil Code of 1866* (Montreal, 1994), 46.

18. Young, *Politics of Codification*; Donald W. Fyson, ed., *The Court Structure of Quebec and Lower Canada, 1764 to 1860* (Montreal, 1994); Donald Fyson, Colin M. Coates, and Kathryn Harvey, eds., *Class, Gender, and the Law in Eighteenth- and Nineteenth-Century Quebec: Sources and Perspectives* (Montreal, 1993).

19. Mark F. Fernandez, *From Chaos to Continuity: The Evolution of Louisiana's Judicial System, 1712–1862* (Baton Rouge, LA, 2001), 57; Samuel C. Hyde Jr., *Pistols and Politics: The Dilemma of Democracy in Louisiana's Florida Parishes, 1810–1899* (Baton Rouge, LA, 1996), 18–22.

20. Fernandez, *From Chaos to Continuity*, 57, 88; Ouellet, *Economic and Social History of Quebec,* 364.

21. Though the Ordinance of 1787 banned slavery from the Northwest Territory, St. Clair ruled that it was not retroactive, thus appeasing existing French slaveholders who threatened to flee across the Mississippi to Spanish Territory, where slavery faced no similar restriction. This provided the leading edge for proslavery advocates in the territories in later years. Bond, *Civilization of the Old Northwest*, 62–63.

22. Landon, *Western Ontario and the American Frontier,* 8.

23. Bond, *Civilization of the Old West*, 64–71, 77–79, 86; Eblen, *First and Second United States Empires*, 87–113.

24. Robert E. May, *Manifest Destiny's Underworld: Filibustering in Antebellum America* (Chapel Hill, NC, 2002); Donald W. Meinig, *The Shaping of America, Vol. 2: Continental America, 1800–1867* (New Haven, CT, 1993); John Anthony Caruso, *The Appalachian Frontier: America's First Surge Westward* (Knoxville, TN, 2003 [1959]).

25. Lillian F. Gates, *Land Policies of Upper Canada* (Toronto, 1968).

26. Gates, *Land Policies of Upper Canada*; J. E. Hodgetts, *Pioneer Public Service: An Administrative History of the United Canadas, 1841–1867* (Toronto, 1955), 128–137.

27. Gates, *Land Policies of Upper Canada,* 100.

28. Wallace, *Family Compact,* 30–41.

29. William Renwick Riddell, *The Bar and the Courts of the Province of Upper Canada, or Ontario* (Toronto, 1928); Patrick Brode, *Sir John Beverley Robinson: Bone and Sinew of the Compact* (Toronto, 1984).

30. Gates, *Land Policies of Upper Canada,* 112; Wallace, *Family Compact,* 34–41.

31. Wallace, *Family Compact,* 44, 50, 51, 53; John Sewell, *Mackenzie: A Political Biography of William Lyon Mackenzie* (Toronto, 2002).

32. Frances Wright D'Arusmont, *Views of Society and Manners in America in a Series of Letters, during the Years 1818, 1819, and 1820* (London, 1821) quoted in Wallace, *Family Compact,* 63.

33. Errington, *The Lion, the Eagle, and Upper Canada,* 195n4; George Parkin de Twenebroker Glazebrook, *Life in Ontario: A Social History* (Toronto, 1968), 88; S. D. Clark, *Church and Sect in Canada* (Toronto, 1948).

34. Reginald C. Stuart, *United States Expansionism and British North America, 1775–1871* (Chapel Hill, NC, 1988), 51.

35. Stuart, *United States Expansionism,* xi, 34, 50; Marcus Lee Hansen and John Bartlett Brebner, *The Mingling of the Canadian and American Peoples,* vol. 1 (New Haven, CT, 1940).

36. John Quincy Adams (August 31, 1811) quoted in Worthington Chauncey Ford, ed., *Writings of John Quincy Adams* (New York, 1914), IV: 209.

37. Errington, *The Lion, the Eagle, and Upper Canada.*

38. McCalla, *Planting the Province,* 162–178.

39. Brode, *Sir John Beverly Robinson,* 21–25.

40. Walter R. Borneman, *1812: The War That Forged a Nation* (New York, 2004); Stuart, *United States Expansionism,* 39, 201, 258.

41. Clay quoted in Borneman, *1812,* 57; Gallatin quoted ibid., 304.

42. Phillip A. Buckner, *The Transition to Responsible Government: British Policy in British North America, 1815–1850* (Westport, CT, 1985); Brebner, *North American Triangle.*

43. Borneman, *1812;* Gates, *History of Public Land Law Development.*

6. Federalism Suborned

1. Malcolm Rohrbough, *The Land Office Business: The Settlement and Administration of American Public Lands, 1789–1837* (New York, 1968), 4; Everett Dick, *The Lure of the Land: A Social History of the Public Lands from the Articles of Confederation to the New Deal* (Lincoln, NE, 1970), 50; Benjamin Horace Hibbard, *A History of the Public Land Policies* (Madison, WI, 1965); Peter S. Onuf, *The Origins of the Federal Republic: Jurisdictional Controversies in the United States, 1775–1787* (Philadelphia, PA, 1983); Richard

White, *The Middle Ground: Indians, Empires, and Republics in the Great Lakes Region, 1650–1815* (New York, 1991).

2. Dick, *Lure of the Land,* 50.

3. Paul W. Gates, *Landlord and Tenants on the Prairie Frontier: Studies in American Land Policy* (Ithaca, NY, 1973), 30–43; Lowell H. Harrison and James C. Klotter, *A New History of Kentucky* (Lexington, KY, 1997).

4. Benjamin Rush (October 26, 1786) quoted in Robert F. Berkhofer Jr., "The Northwest Ordinance and the Principle of Territorial Evolution," in *The American Territorial System,* ed. John Porter Bloom (Athens, GA, 1973), 50.

5. Jefferson quoted in Berkhofer, "Northwest Ordinance," 50; Lee quoted in Paul W. Gates, *History of Public Land Law Development* (Washington, DC, 1968), 72.

6. Richard White, *"It's Your Misfortune and None of My Own": A New History of the American West* (Norman, OK, 1991), 58.

7. Jack Ericson Eblen, *The First and Second United States Empires: Governors and Territorial Government, 1784–1912* (Pittsburgh, PA, 1968), 42; Peter S. Onuf, *Statehood and Union: A History of the Northwest Ordinance* (Bloomington, IN, 1987).

8. Eblen, *First and Second United States Empires,* 49.

9. Theda Skocpol, *Protecting Soldiers and Mothers: The Political Origins of Social Policy in the United States* (Cambridge, MA, 1992); Stephen Skowronek, *Building a New American State: The Expansion of National Administrative Capacities, 1877–1920* (New York, 1982).

10. James W. Oberly, *Sixty Million Acres: American Veterans and the Public Lands before the Civil War* (Kent, OH, 1990); Dick, *Lure of the Land;* White, *Your Misfortune.*

11. Rohrbough, *Land Office Business,* 13, 19.

12. Dick, *Lure of the Land,* 35; Frederick S. Calhoun, *The Lawmen: United States Marshals and Their Deputies, 1789–1989* (Washington, DC, 1989), 16; Rohrbough, *Land Office Business,* 126.

13. Rohrbough, *Land Office Business,* 36, 38, 161; Andro Linklater, *Measuring America: How an Untamed Wilderness Shaped the United States and Fulfilled the Promise of Democracy* (New York, 2002); Hildegard Binder Johnson, *Order upon the Land: The U.S. Rectangular Land Survey and the Upper Mississippi Country* (New York, 1876).

14. Rohrbough, *Land Office Business,* 89, 131–132; Richard Slotkin, *Regeneration through Violence: The Mythology of the American Frontier, 1600–1860* (Norman, OK, 1973); White, *Your Misfortune;* White, *Middle Ground.*

15. Roger L. Nichols, *Indians in the United States and Canada: A Comparative History* (Lincoln, NE, 1998), 141–147; Olive Patricia Dickason, *Canada's*

First Nations: A History of Founding Peoples from Earliest Times (Don Mills, ON, 2002).

16. Terry G. Jordan and Matti Kaups, *The American Backwoods Frontier: An Ethnic and Ecological Interpretation* (Baltimore, MD, 1989), 69; Dick, *Lure of the Land,* 53–54; Gates, *History of Public Land Law;* Slotkin, *Regeneration through Violence.*

17. Rohrbough, *Land Office Business,* 110; Dick, *Lure of the Land,* 74–76; David J. Langum, *Law and Community on the Mexican California Frontier: Anglo-American Expatriates and the Clash of Legal Traditions, 1821–1846* (Norman, OK, 1987).

18. Dick, *Lure of the Land,* 55; McLean (January 19, 1816) quoted in Rohrbough, *Land Office Business,* 95.

19. Rohrbough, *Land Office Business,* 21; Allan G. Bogue and Margaret Beattie Bogue, "'Profits' and the Frontier Land Speculator," *Journal of Economic History* 17 (1957): 1–24; Robert P. Swierenga, "Land Speculation and Its Impact on American Economic Growth and Welfare: A Historiographical Review," *Western Historical Quarterly* 8 (1977): 283–302; John Denis Haeger, *The Investment Frontier: New York Businessmen and the Economic Development of the Old Northwest* (Albany, NY, 1981); Beverly Bond, *The Civilization of the Old Northwest: A Study of Political, Social, and Economic Development, 1788–1812* (New York, 1934), 226–228.

20. Dick, *Lure of the Land,* 42, Eau Claire on 44; see also Gates, "Landlords and Tenants"; Gates, *History of Public Land Law,* 123, on rules barring land officers from personally profiting from land sales.

21. Dick, *Lure of the Land,* 46, 48.

22. Rohrbough, *Land Office Business,* 136.

23. Caruso, *Appalachian Frontier.*

24. *Charles City Intelligencer* (September 1, 1859) quoted in Donald W. Meinig, *The Shaping of America: Continental America, 1800–1867* (New Haven, CT, 1993), 245.

25. Gates, *History of Public Land Law,* 30–32, 66; White, *Your Misfortune,* 57–59.

26. James McPherson, *Battle Cry of Freedom: The Civil War Era* (New York, 1988), 42, 126; Boyd, *Civilization of the Old Northwest,* 225–226; Gates, *History of Public Land Law,* 18; Eric Foner, *Politics and Ideology in the Age of the Civil War* (Oxford, 1980).

27. Lillian F. Gates, *Land Policies of Upper Canada* (Toronto, 1968), 303–304; *The British American Guide-Book for 1859, First Edition* (Montreal, 1859), esp. 39–40.

28. Ann M. Carlos and Stephen Nicholas, "Agency Problems in Early Chartered Companies: The Case of the Hudson's Bay Company," *Journal of Economic History* 50 (1990): 853–875; Elizabeth Mancke, *A Company of Businessmen:*

The Hudson's Bay Company and Long Distance Trade, 1670–1730 (Winnepeg, 1988).

29. Peter C. Newman, *Empire of the Bay: The Company of Adventures that Seized a Continent* (New York, 1998), 263; Jean Murray Cole, *Exile in the Wilderness: The Life of Chief Factor Archibald McDonald, 1790–1853* (Seattle, WA, 1979); John S. Galbraith, *The Little Emperor: Governor Simpson of the Hudson's Bay Company* (Toronto, 1976).

30. Marcel Giraud, *The Métis in the Canadian West*, 2 vols., trans. George Woodcock (Edmonton, AB, 1986 [1945]).

31. Newman, *Empire of the Bay*, 115.

32. Giraud, *Métis in the Canadian West*, I: 363–364.

33. Cole, *Exile in the Wilderness*, 35, 37.

34. Ibid., 51.

35. Newman, *Empire of the Bay*, 410, 420–421; J. M. S. Careless, *Canada: A Story of Challenge* (Toronto, 1970), 143. The Red River settlement was actually returned to the jurisdiction of Hudson's Bay Company in 1836. Lewis Herbert Thomas, *The Struggle for Responsible Government in the North-West Territories, 1870–97*, 2nd ed. (Toronto, 1978 [1956]), 21.

36. Charles Adams, *When in the Course of Human Events: Arguing the Case for Southern Secession* (Lanham, MD, 2000), 15.

37. Adams, *When in the Course of Human Events*, 13, 44; Albert Taylor Bledsoe, *Is Davis a Traitor; or Was Secession a Constitutional Right Previous to the War of 1861?* (Richmond, VA, 1907).

38. Lincoln quoted in McPherson, *Battle Cry of Freedom*, 247.

39. Philip S. Foner, *Business and Slavery: The New York Merchants and the Irrepressible Conflict* (Chapel Hill, NC, 1941); Robert V. Remini, *The Revolutionary Age of Andrew Jackson* (New York, 1976); George Rogers Taylor, *The Transportation Revolution, 1815–1860* (New York, 1951); Jason Kaufman, *Sometimes Civil Society: Urban Development, Municipal Politics, and the Impact of the Communications Revolution on 19th Century American Cities* (Princeton, NJ, 1999).

40. Emory M. Thomas, *The Confederate Nation: 1861–1865* (New York, 1979), 6; see also David Brion Davis, *The Problem of Slavery in Western Culture* (Ithaca, NY, 1966); McPherson, *Battle Cry of Freedom*, 99; Orlando Patterson, *Slavery and Social Death: A Comparative Study* (Cambridge, MA, 1982).

41. Jeffrey Rogers Hummel, *Emancipating Slaves, Enslaving Free Men: A History of the American Civil War* (Chicago, 1996), 9, 44, 57; Eugene D. Genovese, *Roll, Jordan, Roll: The World the Slaves Made* (New York, 1974).

42. Hummel, *Emancipating Slaves, Enslaving Free Men*, 52; Davis, *Problem of Slavery;* Claudia Goldin, "The Economics of Emancipation," *Journal of Economic History* 33 (1973): 66–85; Roger L. Ransom and Richard Sutch, "Capitalists without Capital: The Burden of Slavery and the Impact of Emancipation," *Agricultural History* 62 (1988): 133–160.

43. *Prigg v. Pennsylvania,* 16 Peters 539 (1842); Frederick S. Calhoun, *The Lawmen: United States Marshals and Their Deputies, 1789–1989* (Washington, DC, 1990); Stanley W. Campbell, *The Slave Catchers: Enforcement of the Fugitive Slave Law, 1850–1860* (Chapel Hill, NC, 1970); Don E. Fehrenbacher, *The Dred Scott Case: Its Significance in American Law and Politics* (New York, 1978).

44. Robin W. Winks, *Canada and the United States: The Civil War Years* (Baltimore, MD, 1960), 10; Fred Landon, "The Negro Migration to Canada after the Passing of the Fugitive Slave Act," *Journal of Negro History* 5 (1920): 22; Benjamin Drew, *The Refugee: or the Narratives of Fugitive Slaves in Canada. Related by Themselves, with an Account of the History and Condition of the Colored Population of Upper Canada* (Toronto, 2000 [1856]).

45. Thomas, *Confederate Nation,* 19; Charles S. Sydnor, "The Southerner and the Laws," *Journal of Southern History* 6 (1940): 3–23.

46. Thomas, *Confederate Nation,* 4.

47. Lincoln quoted in McPherson, *Battle Cry of Freedom,* 90.

48. Adams, *When in the Course of Human Events.*

49. McPherson, *Battle Cry of Freedom,* 147–148, 214, 223; Dick, *Lure of the Land,* 136.

50. Robert E. May, *Manifest Destiny's Underworld: Filibustering in Antebellum America* (Chapel Hill, NC, 2002), 3, 78, 153.

51. Adams, *When in the Course of Human Events,* 36–45; McPherson, *Battle Cry of Freedom,* 250, 276–338; May Spencer Ringold, *The Role of the State Legislatures in the Confederacy* (Athens, GA, 1966).

52. John Bartlet Brebner, *North Atlantic Triangle: The Interplay of Canada, the United States, and Great Britain* (Toronto, 1966 [1945]), 163; Eric Foner, *Nothing but Freedom: Emancipation and Its Legacy* (Baton Rouge, LA, 1983), 10; Hummel, *Emancipating Slaves, Enslaving Free Men,* 20, 27, 353; Orlando Patterson, *The Ordeal of Integration: Progress and Resentment in America's "Racial" Crisis* (Washington, DC, 1997).

53. See, for example, Stephen Cresswell, *Rednecks, Redeemers, and Race: Mississippi after Reconstruction, 1877–1917* (Jackson, MS, 2006); C. Vann Woodward, *Origins of the New South, 1877–1913* (Baton Rouge, LA, 1951); C. Vann Woodward, *Strange Career of Jim Crow* (New York, 1955); John B. Boles and Bethany L. Johnson, eds., *Origins of the New South Fifty Years Later: The Continuing Influence of a Historical Classic* (Baton Rouge, LA,

2003); Thomas D. Clark and Albert D. Kirwan, *The South Since Appomattox: A Century of Regional Change* (New York, 1967).

54. Jason Kaufman, "Americans and Their Guns: Civilian Military Organizations and the Destabilization of American National Security," *Studies in American Political Development* 15 (2001): 88–102; W. Craig Riddell, "Unionization in Canada and the United States: A Tale of Two Countries," in *Queen's Papers in Industrial Relations* (Kingston, ON, 1993).

55. Kaufman, "Americans and Their Guns"; Josh Sugarman, *National Rifle Association: Money, Firepower, and Fear* (Washington, DC, 1992).

56. Winks, *Canada and the United States: The Civil War Years.*

57. Ibid., 86–87, 94–95, 98.

58. Donald F. Warner, *The Idea of Continental Union: Agitation for the Annexation of Canada to the United States, 1849–1893* (Lexington, KT, 1960), 33, 35; see also Brebner, *North Atlantic Triangle,* 150–168; Robert Livingston Schuyler, *The Fall of the Old Colonial System: A Study in British Free Trade, 1770–1870* (London, 1945); Reginald C. Stuart, *United States Expansionism and British North America, 1775–1871* (Chapel Hill, NC, 1988).

59. Stuart, *United States Expansionism*; Brebner, *North Atlantic Triangle.*

60. Jane Errington, *The Lion, the Eagle, and Upper Canada: A Developing Colonial Ideology* (Kingston, ON, 1987); David Mills, *The Idea of Loyalty in Upper Canada, 1784–1850* (Kingston, ON, 1988).

61. Winks, *Canada and the United States: The Civil War Years,* 112–114; Stuart, *United States Expansionism*; Warner, *Idea of Continental Union.*

62. Winks, *Canada and the United States: The Civil War Years,* 155–158, 167–168; S. F. Wise and Robert Craig Brown, *Canada Views the United States: Nineteenth-Century Political Attitudes* (Toronto, 1967); Stuart, *United States Expansionism*; Warner, *Idea of Continental Union.*

63. Jean Barman, *The West beyond the West: A History of British Columbia,* rev. ed. (Toronto, 1991).

64. Brebner, *North Atlantic Triangle,* 165–166; Winks, *Canada and the United States: The Civil War Years,* 178–205.

65. Winks, *Canada and the United States: The Civil War Years,* 132, 136.

66. Ibid., 220.

67. Ibid., 303, 307.

68. Ibid., 326–331.

7. Completing the Journey West

1. S. F. Wise, "The Annexation Movement and Its Effect on Canadian Opinion, 1837–67," in *Canada Views the United States: Nineteenth-Century*

Political Attitudes, ed. S. F. Wise and Robert Craig Brown (Toronto, 1967), 97.

2. Wise, "Annexation Movement," 94, emphasis added.

3. R. Cole Harris and John Warkentin, *Canada before Confederation: A Study in Historical Geography* (New York, 1974), chap. 4; David Mills, *The Idea of Loyalty in Upper Canada, 1784–1850* (Kingston, ON, 1988); Jane Errington, *The Lion, the Eagle, and Upper Canada: A Developing Colonial Ideology* (Kingston, ON, 1987); William Westfall, *Two Worlds: The Protestant Culture of Nineteenth-Century Ontario* (Kingston, ON, 1989).

4. Gerald M. Craig, *Upper Canada: The Formative Years, 1784–1841* (Toronto, 1963); S. D. Clark, *The Social Development of Canada* (Toronto, 1942); George Emery and J. C. Herbert Emery, *A Young Man's Benefit: The Independent Order of Odd Fellows and Sickness Insurance in the United States and Canada, 1860–1929* (Montreal, 1999).

5. Harris and Warkentin, *Canada before Confederation*; Charles E. Rosenberg, *The Cholera Years: The United States in 1832, 1849, and 1866* (Chicago, 1962).

6. S. D. Clark, *Movements of Social Protest in Canada* (Toronto, 1959); David Flint, *William Lyon Mackenzie: Rebel against Authority* (Toronto, 1971); Sir Francis B. Head, *The Emigrant* (London, 1852), 130.

7. Jacques Monet, *The Last Cannon Shot: A Study of French-Canadian Nationalism, 1837–1850* (Toronto, 1969); Fernand Ouellet, *Lower Canada, 1791–1840: Social Change and Nationalism,* trans. Patricia Claxton (Toronto, 1980).

8. Allan Greer, *The Patriots and the People: The Rebellion of 1837 in Rural Lower Canada* (Toronto, 1993), esp. 120–188; Fernand Ouellet, *Economic and Social History of Quebec, 1760–1850*; Ouellet, *Structures and Conjunctures* (Ottawa, 1980 [1966]).

9. Ian Radforth, "Sydenham and Utilitarian Reform," in *Colonial Leviathan: State Formation in Mid-Nineteenth-Century Canada,* ed. Ian Radforth and Allan Greer (Toronto, 1992), 65.

10. J. M. S. Careless, *The Union of the Canadas: The Growth of Canadian Institutions, 1841–1857* (Toronto, 1967).

11. J. E. Hodgetts, *Pioneer Public Service: An Administrative History of the United Canadas, 1841–1867* (Toronto, 1955), 88.

12. Phillip A. Buckner, *The Transition to Responsible Government: British Policy in British North America, 1815–1850* (Westport, CT, 1985); Hodgetts, *Pioneer Public Service,* 34; Allan Greer, "The Birth of the Police in Canada," in *Colonial Leviathan: State Formation in Mid-Nineteenth Century,* ed. Allan Greer and Ian Radforth (Toronto, 1992), 40.

13. J. L. Morison, *British Supremacy and Canadian Self-Government, 1839–1854* (Glasgow, 1919); David E. Smith, *The Invisible Crown: The First Principle of Canadian Government* (Toronto, 1995), 23; J. M. S. Careless, *Canada: A Story of Challenge* (Toronto, 1970), 230–276; Robert C. Vipond, *Liberty and Community: Canadian Federalism and the Failure of the Constitution* (Albany, NY, 1991).

14. Ronald L. Watts, "The American Constitution in Comparative Perspective: A Comparison of Federalism in the United States and Canada," *Journal of American History* 74 (1987): 769–792; Kenneth Grant Crawford, *Canadian Municipal Government* (Toronto, 1954); Leonard P. Curry, *The Corporate City: The American City as a Political Entity, 1800–1850* (Westport, CT, 1997); Gerald Frug, "The City as a Legal Concept," *Harvard Law Review* 93, no. 6 (1979): 1057–1154; Hendrik Hartog, *Public Property and Private Power: The Corporation in the City of New York in American Law, 1730–1870* (Chapel Hill, NC, 1983).

15. Smith, *Invisible Crown*, 23; Careless, *Canada*, 230–276; Vipond, *Liberty and Community*.

16. William L. Morton, *The Critical Years: The Union of British North America, 1857–1873* (New York, 1964); Emily Barman, *The West beyond the West: A History of British Columbia*, rev. ed. (Toronto, 1996), 105.

17. Careless, *Canada*, 268, 364.

18. Doug Owram, *Promise of Eden: The Canadian Expansionist Movement and the Idea of the West, 1856–1900* (Toronto, 1992); Richard Simeon and Ian Robinson, *State, Society, and the Development of Canadian Federalism* (Toronto, 1990).

19. Careless, *Canada*, 294–295.

20. Careless, *Canada*, 370–372; Simeon and Robinson, *State, Society, and the Development of Canadian Federalism*, 52–53; Alan Cairns, "The Judicial Committee and Its Critics," *Canadian Journal of Political Science* 4 (1971): 301–345; Peter Hogg, *Constitutional Law in Canada*, 2nd ed. (Toronto, 1985); Vipond, *Liberty and Community*. Today, Quebec is guaranteed three of the nine seats on the Supreme Court; Ontario normally receives three, the western provinces two, and the Atlantic provinces one, thus perpetuating remnants of decentralized federalism on the nation's highest federal court.

21. Alvin C. Gluek Jr., *Minnesota and the Manifest Destiny of the Canadian Northwest: A Study in Canadian-American Relations* (Toronto, 1965).

22. Gluek, *Minnesota*, 86, emphasis added.

23. Ibid., 78.

24. Harold R. Lamar, *Dakota Territory, 1861–1889: A Study of Frontier Politics* (New Haven, CT, 1956), 28, 36–40; Harold Edward Briggs, *Frontiers of the Northwest: A History of the Upper Missouri Valley* (New York, 1940).

25. Lamar, *Dakota Territory,* 40, 68, 71, 73.

26. Ibid., 41–50, 52–53; Everett N. Dick, *The Sod-House Frontier, 1854–1890: A Social History of the Northern Plains from the Creation of Nebraska to the Admission of the Dakotas* (Lincoln, NE, 1979 [1954]).

27. Andrew P. Morriss, "'Miners' Law': Informal Law in Western Mining Camps," in *Law in the Western United States,* ed. Gordon Morris Bakken (Norman, OK, 2000), 209; John R. Umbeck, *A Theory of Property Rights* (Ames, IA, 1981), 132.

28. Charles Howard Shinn, *Mining Camps: A Study in American Frontier Government* (New York, 1885).

29. Raymond S. August, *Law in the American West: A History of Its Origins and Its Dissemination* (Ann Arbor, MI, 1987), 179, 197–201; David J. Langum, *Law and Community on the Mexican California Frontier: Anglo-American Expatriates and the Clash of Legal Traditions, 1821–1846* (Norman, OK, 1987); Carolyn Strange and Tina Loo, *Making Good: Law and Moral Regulation in Canada, 1867–1939* (Toronto, 1997), 34.

30. David Alan Johnson, *Founding the Far West: California, Oregon, and Nevada, 1840–1890* (Berkeley, CA, 1992); August, *Law in the American West;* Lawrence M. Friedman, *A History of American Law,* 2nd ed. (New York, 1985), 365–366.

31. August, *Law in the American West,* 205–212.

32. Ibid., 205, 208.

33. Andrew P. Morriss, "The Reception of Mexican Land Law in the United States: *Hornsby v. United States,*" in *Law in the Western United States,* ed. Gordon Morris Bakken (Norman, OK, 2000), 313–315; Donald J. Pisani, "Squatter Law in California, 1850–1858," *Western Historical Quarterly* 25 (1994): 277–310; Malcolm Ebright, ed., *Spanish and Mexican Land Grants and the Law* (Manhattan, KS, 1989); Alan Watson, "Aspects of Reception of Law," *American Journal of Comparative Law* 44 (1996): 335–351.

34. Donald W. Meinig, *The Shaping of America: A Geographical Perspective on 500 Years of History, Volume 3: Transcontinental America, 1850–1915* (New Haven, CT, 1998), 50–51.

35. Mark Twain, *Roughing It* (New York, 1962 [1872]), 230–231.

36. Richard White, *"It's Your Misfortune and None of My Own": A History of the American West* (Norman, OK, 1991), 135, 147; Thomas G. Alexander, *A Clash of Interests: Interior Department and Mountain West, 1863–96* (Provo, UT, 1977), 33.

37. Richard Erdoes, *Saloons of the Old West* (New York, 1979); Johnson, *Founding the Far West,* 72–89; Christian G. Fritz, "Constitution Making in the Nineteenth-Century American West," in *Law for the Elephant, Law for the Beaver: Essays in the Legal History of the North American West,* ed. John

McLaren, Hamar Foster, and Chet Orloff (Pasadena, CA, 1992); Twain, *Roughing It*, 150–151.

38. Gordon Morris Bakken, *The Development of Law on the Rocky Mountain Frontier: Civil Law and Society, 1850–1912* (Westport, CT, 1983), 13–15.

39. August, *Law in the American West*; Bakken, *Development of Law on the Rocky Mountain Frontier.*

40. Gilman M. Ostrander, *Nevada: The Great Rotten Borough, 1859–1964* (New York, 1966), 28–29.

41. Ibid., 27–28.

42. Meinig, *Transcontinental America*, III: 37–39, 68–69, 70–71; Johnson, *Founding the Far West*; Charlene Porsild, *Gamblers and Dreamers: Women, Men, and Community in the Klondike* (Vancouver, BC, 1998); Barman, *West beyond the West*; William R. Morrison, *Showing the Flag: The Mounted Police and Canadian Sovereignty in the North, 1894–1925* (Vancouver, BC, 1985); Jim Wallace, *Forty Miles to Bonanza: The North-West Mounted Police in the Klondike Gold Rush* (Calgary, 2000).

43. Martha Sonntag Bradley, *ZCMI: America's First Department Store*, (Salt Lake City, UT, 1991); Meinig, *Transcontinental America*, III: 103–104, 108; Bakken, *Development of Law on the Rocky Mountain Frontier*, 116.

44. Johnson, *Founding the Far West*; White, *Your Misfortune*, 164–168.

45. White, *Your Misfortune*, 168–169.

46. Ibid.

47. Edward Leo Lyman, *Political Deliverance: The Mormon Quest for Utah Statehood* (Urbana, IL, 1986); Alexander, *A Clash of Interests*, 133, 175, 184; Fernand Ouellet, *Economic and Social History of Quebec, 1760–1850* (Toronto, 1980 [1966]).

48. August, *Law in the Western United States*, 10, 312.

49. John G. Wells, ed., *Wells' Every Man His Own Lawyer, and United States Form Book: Being a Complete Guide in All Matters of Law and Business Negotiations, For Every State in the Union* (New York, 1860).

50. A Retired Officer [Richard E. Goodridge], *A Year in Manitoba: Being the Experience of a Retired Officer in Settling His Sons*, 2nd ed. (London, 1882), 27, 78–80, 84; Mrs. Edward Copleston, *Canada: Why We Live in It, and Why We Like It* (London, 1861), 27; Rudyard Kipling, *Letters to the Family: Notes on a Recent Trip to Canada* (Toronto, 1908), 33–34.

51. Henry N. Copp, ed. *The American Settler's Guide: A Brief Exposition of the Public Land System of the United States of America* (Washington, DC, 1880).

52. Ibid.

53. Ibid., 82.

54. William B. Matthews, *Matthews's Guide: for Settlers upon the Public Lands, Land Attorneys, Land Agents, Clerks of Courts, Notaries, Bankers, Brokers and*

All Persons Interested in the Public Lands of the United State[s], and Having Business before the District Land Offices, the General Land Office and the Department of the Interior (Washington, DC, 1889), xi–xiv.

55. Lamar, *Dakota Territory,* 80, 103.

56. Ibid., 105.

57. Ibid.

58. Ibid., 102.

59. Moses Armstrong, *The Early Empire Builders of the American West* (St. Paul, MN, 1901 [1866]), quoted in Lamar, *Dakota Territory,* 101; Stutsman quoted in Lamar, *Dakota Territory,* 100, see also 109; cf. Theda Skocpol, *Protecting Soldiers and Mothers: The Political Origins of Social Policy in the United States* (Cambridge, MA, 1992).

60. Lamar, *Dakota Territory,* 74–75.

61. Ibid., 79–80.

62. Ibid.

63. Erdoes, *Saloons of the Old West,* 205–206, 223; Richard Maxwell Brown, *No Duty to Retreat: Violence and Values in American History and Society* (New York, 1991).

64. John Phillip Reid, *Law for the Elephant: Property and Social Behavior on the Overland Frontier* (San Marino, CA, 1980), 352, 354–355, emphasis added.

65. John Phillip Reid, "The Layers of Western Legal History," in *Law for the Elephant, Law for the Beaver: Essays in the Legal History of the North American West,* ed. John McLaren, Hamar Foster, and Chet Orloff (Pasadena, CA, 1992), 43.

66. British Columbia Provincial Archives, Series GR-0328, Great Britain, Colonial Office, Transcript, 1847–1851, emphasis added. No date or names are given in this document, though details appear to date it on or about 1848, deriving from the British Colonial Office to its representatives in British Columbia.

67. Earl S. Pomeroy, *The Territories and the United States, 1861–1890: Studies in Colonial Administration* (Philadelphia, PA, 1947), 97, 106; Lewis Herbert Thomas, *The Struggle for Responsible Government in the North-West Territories, 1870–97,* 2nd ed. (Toronto, 1978 [1956]), 262; Morton, *Critical Years.*

68. S. W. Horrall, "Sir John A. Macdonald and the Mounted Police Force for the Northwest Territories," *Canadian Historical Review* 53 (1972): 180.

69. Horrall, "Macdonald and the Mounted Police Force," 190; Jim Wallace, *A Double Duty: The Decisive First Decade of the North West Mounted Police* (Winnipeg, 1997), 235, 246.

70. Wallace, *Double Duty,* 30–32; R. C. MacLeod, *The NWMP and Law Enforcement, 1873–1905* (Toronto, 1976).

71. Louis A. Knafla, "Violence on the Western Canadian Frontier: A Historical Perspective," in *Violence in Canada: Sociopolitical Perspectives,* ed. Jeffrey Ian Ross, 2nd ed. (New Brunswick, NJ, 2004), 29–30; R. C. Macleod, "Law and Order on the Western-Canadian Frontier," in *Law for the Elephant, Law for the Beaver: Essays in the Legal History of the North American West,* ed. John McLaren, Hamar Foster, and Chet Orloff (Pasadena, CA, 1992), 95; Hamar Foster, "Long-Distance Justice: The Criminal Jurisdiction of Canadian Courts West of the Canadas, 1763–1859," *American Journal of Legal History* 34 (1990): 1–48; Desmond H. Brown, "Unpredictable and Uncertain: Criminal Law in the Canadian North West Before 1886," *Alberta Law Review* 17 (1979): 497–512; Reid, "Layers of Western Legal History," 46–55. Royal Canadian Mounted Police report quoted in Strange and Loo, *Making Good,* 22–23.
72. Retired Officer [Goodridge], *Year in Manitoba,* 24.
73. Ibid., 28; Wallace, *Double Duty,* 208, 160; MacLeod, *NWMP and Law Enforcement.*
74. John Phillip Reid, *Patterns of Vengeance: Crosscultural Homicide in the North American Fur Trade* (Pasadena, CA, 1999); Wallace, *Double Duty,* 160, 216; Reid, "Layers of Western Legal History," 46–55; R. C. Macleod, "Law and Order on the Western-Canadian Frontier," 102.
75. Wallace, *Double Duty,* 122.
76. Louis A. Knafla, "From Oral to Written Memory: The Common Law Tradition in Western Canada," in *Law and Justice in a New Land: Essays in Western Canadian Legal History,* ed. Louis A. Knafla (Toronto, 1986), 60, 73.
77. Ibid., 65, 70.
78. Thomas, *Struggle for Responsible Government,* 35–37.
79. Ibid., 18–44; Gerald Friesen, *The Canadian Prairies: A History* (Lincoln, NE, 1984), 120–126; Bob Beal and Rod Maclead, *Prairie Fire: The 1885 North West Rebellion* (Edmonton, Canada, 1984); Marcel Giraud, *The Métis in the Canadian West,* II, trans. George Woodcock (Edmonton, Canada, 1986).
80. Thomas, *Struggle for Responsible Government,* 60–61, 145; see also Morton, *Critical Years;* Smith, *Invisible Crown;* Vipond, *Liberty and Community.*
81. Bakken, *Development of Law on the Rocky Mountain Frontier,* 114, 127.
82. Retired Officer [Goodridge], *Year in Manitoba,* 74; Thomas, *Struggle for Responsible Government,* 63, 66–67.
83. Friesen, *Canadian Prairies,* 239.
84. Bill McKee and Georgeen Klassen, *Trail of Iron: The CPR and the Birth of the West, 1880–1930* (Vancouver, BC, 1983); cf. Frank Dobbin, *Forging Industrial Policy: The United States, Britain, and France in the Railway Age* (New York, 1994).
85. Wallace, *Double Duty.*

86. Roger L. Nichols, *Indians in the United States and Canada: A Comparative History* (Lincoln, NE, 1998); Olive Patricia Dickason, *Canada's First Nations: A History of Founding Peoples from Earliest Times*, 3rd ed. (Don Mills, ON, 2002); Alexander, *Clash of Interests*.

87. Meinig, *Transcontinental America*, III: 218; White, *Your Misfortune*, 159.

88. White, *Your Misfortune*, 246–247; Bakken, *Development of Law on the Rocky Mountain Frontier*.

89. For example, William Shaw, ed., *Sioux City Directory, 1871–72* (Sioux City, IA, 1871).

90. Henry N. Copp, *The American Settler's Guide: A Brief Exposition of the Public Land System of the United States of America* (Washington, DC, 1880), back pages (unnumbered).

91. Robert R. Dykstra, *The Cattle Towns* (New York, 1968); Howard R. Lamar, *The Far Southwest, 1846–1912: A Territorial History* (New Haven, CT, 1966), 135, 146; Bakken, *Development of Law on the Rocky Mountain Frontier*, 23–24.

92. Lamar, *Far Southwest*, 135.

93. Ostrander, *Nevada*; cf. William E. Nelson, *Americanization of the Common Law: The Impact of Legal Change on Massachusetts Society, 1760–1830* (Athens, GA, 1994).

94. Alexander, *Clash of Interests*, 76–78.

95. Ibid., 111, 173, emphasis added.

96. Ibid., 182; White, *Your Misfortune*, 174–175.

97. White, *Your Misfortune*, 354.

98. Alexander, *Clash of Interests*, 176; White, *Your Misfortune*, 176.

99. White, *Your Misfortune*, 333; Johnson, *Founding the Far West*; Lamar, *Far Southwest*.

100. White, *Your Misfortune*, 177.

101. Ibid.

8. Nations Reborn

1. Frederic L. Paxson, *American Democracy and the World War: Pre-War Years, 1913–1917* (Boston, 1936).

2. Jason Kaufman, "Americans and Their Guns: Civilian Military Organizations and the Destabilization of American National Security," *Studies in American Political Development* 15 (2001): 88–102.

3. Paxson, *American Democracy and the World War*, esp. 289–307; Thomas Fleming, *The Illusion of Victory: America in World War I* (New York, 2003).

4. Elizabeth H. Armstrong, *The Crisis of Quebec, 1914–1918* (Toronto, 1974), 79.

5. David W. Love, *"A Call to Arms": The Organization and Administration of Canada's Military in World War One* (Winnepeg, 1999), 52–53; Desmond Morton and J. L. Granatstein, *Marching to Armageddon: Canadians and the Great War, 1914–1919* (Toronto, 1989); David J. Carter, *Behind Canadian Barbed Wire: Alien, Refugee and Prisoner of War Camps in Canada, 1914–1946* (Calgary, 1980).

6. Armstrong, *Crisis of Quebec*, 198, 227, 230.

7. Floyd W. Rudmin, *Bordering on Aggression: Evidence of US Military Preparations against Canada* (Hull, Quebec, 1993), 95–99.

8. Paxson, *American Democracy and the World War.*

9. Fleming, *Illusion of Victory,* 107–110.

10. Pierre Berton, *The Great Depression, 1929–1939* (Toronto, 1990), 95; Don H. Tolzman, ed., *German-Americans in the World Wars,* vol. 1 (München, Germany, 1995).

11. Fleming, *Illusion of Victory,* 107–110.

12. Charles Perrow, *Organizing America: Wealth, Power, and the Origins of Corporate Capitalism* (Princeton, NJ, 2002); William Roy, *Socializing Capital: The Rise of the Large Industrial Corporation in America* (Princeton, NJ, 1997); Kenneth Norrie, Douglas Owram, and J. C. Herbert Emery, *A History of the Canadian Economy,* 3rd ed. (Scarborough, ON, 2002).

13. Robert Muccigrosso, "The City Reform Club: A Study in Late Nineteenth-Century Reform," *New York Historical Quarterly* 52 (1968): 240; Michael E. McGerr, *The Decline of Popular Politics: The American North, 1865–1928* (New York, 1986), 61; Martin J. Schiesl, *The Politics of Efficiency: Municipal Administration and Reform in America, 1800–1929* (Berkeley, CA, 1977), 13–14; William Howe Tolman, *Municipal Reform Movements in the United States* (New York, 1895), 75.

14. Richard L. McCormick, *From Realignment to Reform: Political Change in New York State, 1893–1910* (Ithaca, NY, 1981), 185–186.

15. William G. Domhoff, *Who Really Rules? New Haven and Community Power Reexamined* (Santa Monica, CA, 1978), 161; Kenneth Finegold, *Experts and Politicians: Reform Challenges to Machine Politics in New York, Cleveland, and Chicago* (Princeton, NJ, 1995); Kenneth Fox, *Better City Government: Innovation in American Urban Politics, 1850–1937* (Philadelphia, PA, 1977); Norman N. Gill, *Municipal Research Bureaus: A Study of the Nation's Leading Citizen-Supported Agencies* (Washington, DC, 1944); Roy Lubove, *The Professional Altruist: The Emergence of Social Work as a Career, 1880–1930* (New York, 1983 [1965]), 137–156; William Bennett Munro, *The Government of American Cities* (New York, 1916); Daniel T. Rodgers, *Atlantic Crossings: Social Politics in a Progressive Age* (Cambridge, MA, 1998); Schiesl, *The Politics*

of Efficiency, 111–132; Theda Skocpol, *Protecting Soldiers and Mothers: The Political Origins of Social Policy in the United States* (Cambridge, MA, 1992), 340–354.

16. Edwin Lawrence Godkin, "The Duty of Educated Men in a Democracy," *Forum* (March 1894), reprinted in Godkin, *Problems of Modern Democracy: Political and Economic Essays* (New York, 1897), 208. See also James Bryce, *The American Commonwealth* (New York, 1920), II: 406–425; Lincoln Steffens, "Philadelphia: Corrupt and Contented," *McClure's Magazine* (July 1903), reprinted in Steffens, *The Shame of the Cities* (New York, 1948), 193–229, esp. 195–197.

17. Charles H. Parkhurst, *Our Fight with Tammany* (New York, 1895), 10, 126, 161; William T. Stead, *If Christ Came to Chicago* (New York, 1964 [1894]), 182, 342, 357; Paul S. Boyer, *Urban Masses and Moral Order in America, 1820–1920* (Cambridge, MA, 1978), 164–165, 184–187; Joel A. Tarr and Gabriel Dupuy, eds., *Technology and the Rise of the Networked City in Europe and America* (Philadelphia, PA, 1988).

18. Edward W. Bemis, "Regulation or Ownership?" in *Municipal Monopolies: A Collection of Papers by American Economists and Specialists,* ed. Edward W. Bemis, rev. ed. (New York, 1899), 656–660.

19. Gustavus Myers, *History of Public Franchises in New York City* (New York, 1974 [1900]), 206.

20. Samuel Whinery, *Municipal Public Works: Their Inception, Construction and Management* (New York, 1903), 189; Robert P. Porter, *The Dangers of Municipal Ownership* (New York, 1907); Carl D. Thompson, *Municipal Ownership: A Brief Survey of the Extent, Rapid Growth, and the Success of Municipal Ownership throughout the World, Presenting the Arguments against Private Ownership, the Failure of Regulation and the Advantages of Municipal Ownership* (New York, 1917).

21. David Hammack, *Power and Society: Greater New York at the Turn of the Century* (New York: Russell Sage, 1982), 56; Melvin G. Holli, *Reform in Detroit: Hazen S. Pingree and Urban Politics* (Westport, CT, 1981), esp. 74–124; Frederic C. Howe, *The Confessions of a Reformer* (Kent, OH, 1988 [1925]), esp. 113–126; Morton Keller, *Regulating a New Economy: Public Policy and Economic Change in America* (Cambridge, MA, 1990); McCormick, *From Realignment to Reform;* David E. Nye, *Electrifying America: Social Meanings of a New Technology, 1880–1940* (Cambridge, MA, 1990), esp. 178–181; Rodgers, *Atlantic Crossings,* 144–159; David P. Thelen, *The New Citizenship: Origins of Progressivism in Wisconsin, 1885–1900* (Columbia, 1972), esp. 223–289; Carl D. Thompson, *Public Ownership: A Survey of Public Enterprises, Municipal, State, and Federal in the United States and Elsewhere* (New York, 1925).

22. William D. Harpine, *From the Front Porch to the Front Page: McKinley and Bryan in the 1896 Presidential Campaign* (College Station, TX, 2005); Clarence Ames Stern, *Resurgent Republicanism: The Handiwork of Hanna* (Ann Arbor, MI, 1963); Herbert Croly, *Marcus Alonzo Hanna: His Life and Work* (New York, 1912); Michael McGerr, *The Decline of Popular Politics: The American North, 1865–1928* (New York, 1986); K. D. Ewing, *Money, Politics, and Law: A Study of Electoral Campaign Finance Reform in Canada* (Oxford, 1992); Arthur B. Gunlicks, ed., *Campaign and Party Finance in North America and Western Europe* (Boulder, CO, 1993).

23. Steffens, "Philadelphia: Contented," *McClure's Magazine* (July 1903), reprinted in Steffens, *Shame of the Cities,* 196.

24. Seymour Martin Lipset and Noah M. Meltz, *The Paradox of American Unionism: Why Americans Like Unions More than Canadians Do, but Join Much Less* (Ithaca, NY, 2004).

25. H. A. Logan, *Trade Unions in Canada: Their Development and Functioning* (Toronto, 1948), 38, author's emphasis; James Weinstein, *The Decline of Socialism in America, 1912–1925* (New York, 1967); Seymour Martin Lipset, *Agrarian Socialism: The Cooperative Commonwealth Federation in Saskatchewan: A Study in Political Sociology* (Berkeley, CA, 1950); Paul F. Sharp, *The Agrarian Revolt in Western Canada: A Survey Showing American Parallels* (Regina: Canadian Plains Research Center, 1997 [1948]); Martin Robin, *Radical Politics and Canadian Labour, 1880–1930* (Kingston, ON, 1968); Jason Kaufman, "Rise and Fall of a Nation of Joiners: The Knights of Labor Revisited," *Journal of Interdisciplinary History* 31 (2001): 553–579; Kim Voss, *The Making of American Exceptionalism: The Knights of Labor and Class Formation in the Nineteenth Century* (Ithaca, NY, 1993).

26. Kenneth D. Tunnell, "Worker Insurgency and Social Control: Violence by and against Labour in Canada," in *Violence in Canada,* ed. Jeffrey Ian Ross (New Brunswick, NJ, 2004), 79; Carolyn Strange and Tina Loo, *Making Good: Law and Moral Regulation in Canada, 1867–1939* (Toronto, 1997), 19–20; Irving Abella and David Millar, *The Canadian Worker in the Twentieth Century* (Toronto, 1978); Stuart M. Jamieson, *Times of Trouble: Labour Unrest and Industrial Conflict in Canada, 1900–1966* (Ottawa, 1968).

27. Robert H. Jackson, *The Struggle for Judicial Supremacy: A Study of a Crisis in American Power Politics* (New York, 1941), 40, 59–60; Clarence E. Bonnett, *Employers' Associations in the United States: A Study of Typical Associations* (New York, 1922); Philip S. Foner, *History of the Labor Movement in the United States: Volume II* (New York, 1975 [1955]); Selig Perlman, "Upheaval and Reorganisation," in John R. Commons, *History of Labour in the United States,* vol. 2 (New York, 1926); Voss, *Making of American Exceptionalism.*

28. Foner, *History of the Labor Movement,* II: 247–249.

29. Ibid., 257–259.

30. Clarence E. Bonnett, *Employers' Associations in the United States: A Study of Typical Associations* (New York, 1922), 21–22; see also Clarence E. Bonnett, *History of Employers' Associations in the United States* (New York, 1956), 241. It was estimated that some 50 percent of the nation's railroad workers were employed by roads affiliated with the General Managers' Association (Foner, *History of the Labor Movement,* II: 260).

31. Foner, *History of the Labor Movement,* II: 261–263.

32. Ibid., 264–265.

33. Ibid., 266–268; Gabriel Kolko, *The Triumph of Conservatism: A Re-Interpretation of American History 1900–1916* (New York, 1963), 62.

34. Samuel Gompers, *Seventy Years of Life and Labor: An Autobiography* (New York, 1925), 403–416, esp. 412; Foner, *History of the Labor Movement,* II: 272–275; Kaufman, "Rise and Fall of a Nation of Joiners."

35. *U.S. v. Debs,* 64 Fed. 724 (1894) and *In re Debs,* 158 U.S. 564 (1895). Lawrence M. Friedman, *A History of American Law* (New York: Simon and Schuster, 1985 [1973]), 557–563; see also Perlman, "Upheaval and Reorganisation," 500–503, 508–509.

36. European Trade Union Institute, *Trade Unions and Industrial Relations in the USA and Canada: A Comparative Study of the Current Situation* (Brussels, 1992); Lipset and Marks, *It Didn't Happen Here;* Pradeep Kumar, *From Uniformity to Divergence: Industrial Relations in Canada and the United States* (Kingston, ON, 1993).

37. Lipset, *Agrarian Socialism;* Lipset and Meltz, *Paradox of American Unionism;* Logan, *Trade Unions in Canada;* Abella and Millar, *Canadian Worker.*

38. Albert Finkel, *The Social Credit Phenomenon in Alberta* (Toronto, 1989); Sharp, *Agrarian Revolt in Western Canada* (Regina, 1997 [1948]); Jason Kaufman, Lydia Bean, and Marco Gonzalez, "Are American Evangelicals More Politically Conservative than Canadian Evangelicals? An Empirical Investigation Using Multiple Data Sources" (working paper, Harvard University, Cambridge, MA, 2006).

39. Finkel, *Social Credit Phenomenon in Alberta,* 106, 155.

40. Strange and Loo, *Making Good,* 20–22; Leslie A. Pal, "Gun Control," in *The Government Taketh Away: The Politics of Pain in the United States and Canada,* ed. Leslie A. Pal and R. Kent Weaver (Washington, DC, 2003), 236, 245.

41. Strange and Loo, *Making Good,* 23, 27–28; Kenneth Grant Crawford, *Canadian Municipal Government* (Toronto, 1954).

42. Robert A. Campbell, "'Profit Was Just a Circumstance': The Evolution of Government Liquor Control in British Columbia, 1920–1988," in Warsh, *Drink in Canada,* 172–173.

43. Gord Steinke, *Mobsters and Rumrunners of Canada: Crossing the Line* (Alberta, 2003).
44. Ernest R. Forbes, "The East-Coast Rum-Running Economy," in Warsh, *Drink in Canada*, 166–167.
45. Steinke, *Mobsters and Rumrunners of Canada*.
46. Malcolm Rorabaugh, *Alcoholic Republic: An American Tradition* (New York, 1979), 84–91; Warsh, *Drink in Canada*, 12; James M. Clemens, "Taste Not, Touch Not, Handle Not: A Study of the Social Assumptions of the Temperance Literature and Temperance Supporters in Canada West between 1839 and 1859," *Ontario History* 64 (1972): 142–143; Forbes, "East-Coast Rum-Running Economy," 168–169; Campbell, "'Profit Was Just a Circumstance,'" 172–173.
47. Gerald L. Hallowell, *Prohibition in Ontario, 1919–1923* (Ottawa, 1972), 5.
48. Jacques Paul Couturier, "Prohibition or Regulation? The Enforcement of the Canada Temperance Act in Moncton, 1881–1896," in Cheryl Krasnick Warsh, ed. *Drink in Canada: Historial Essays* (Montreal, 1993), 148.
49. Ibid., 151.
50. Ibid., 156.
51. Ibid., 160.
52. Ibid., 160–161.
53. Ibid., 162–164.
54. Strange and Loo, *Making Good*, 150–151.
55. James R. Mallory, *Social Credit and the Federal Power in Canada*, 2nd ed. (Toronto, 1976), 56.
56. Keith G. Banting, *The Welfare State and Canadian Federalism*, 2nd ed. (Kingston, ON, 1987), 172; Richard Simeon and Ian Robinson, *State, Society, and the Development of Canadian Federalism* (Toronto, 1990).
57. James T. Patterson, *The New Deal and the States: Federalism in Transition* (Princeton, NJ, 1969), 3–4.
58. Patterson, *The New Deal and the States*, 4, 25.
59. Simeon and Robinson, *State, Society, and the Development of Canadian Federalism*; Blair Neatby, *The Politics of Chaos: Canada in the Thirties* (Toronto, 1972); Herbert F. Quinn, *The Union Nationale: Québec Nationalism from Duplessis to Levesque*, 2nd ed. (Toronto, 1979).
60. Patterson, *The New Deal and the States*, 26, 30; Jason Scott Smith, *Building New Deal Liberalism: The Political Economy of Public Works, 1933–1956* (New York, 2006), 26–28; Arthur D. Gayer, *Public Works in Prosperity and Depression* (New York, 1935); Udo Sautter, *Three Cheers for the Unemployed: Government and Unemployment before the New Deal* (New York, 1991).
61. Gerald William Boychuk, *Patchworks of Purpose: The Development of Provincial Social Assistance Regimes in Canada* (Montreal, 1998).

62. Berton, *The Great Depression;* Michael Horn, ed. *The Dirty Thirties: Canadians in the Great Depression* (Toronto, 1972); James Struthers, *No Fault of Their Own: Unemployment and the Canadian Welfare State, 1914–1941* (Toronto, 1983).

63. Berton, *The Great Depression,* esp. 325, 362, 426, 445.

64. Edwin Amenta, *Bold Relief: Institutional Politics and the Origins of Modern American Social Policy* (Princeton, NJ, 1998); Kenneth Finegold and Theda Skocpol, *State and Party in America's New Deal* (Madison, WI, 1995); Smith, *Building New Deal Liberalism;* Patterson, *The New Deal and the States,* 37–38, 102–105.

65. Robert H. Jackson, *The Struggle for Judicial Supremacy: A Study of a Crisis in American Power Politics* (New York: Knopf, 1941), 197–235.

66. Jackson, *The Struggle for Judicial Supremacy,* 41–43, 165–168, 183, 185.

67. Amenta, *Bold Relief;* Finegold and Skocpol, *State and Party in America's New Deal;* William E. Leuchtenburg, *Franklin D. Roosevelt and the New Deal* (New York: Harper and Row, 1963); Smith, *Building New Deal Liberalism;* Patterson, *The New Deal and the States,* 121, 128, 139.

68. Smith, *Building New Deal Liberalism,* 47–48.

69. Patterson, *The New Deal and the States,* 207; see also Alan Brinkley, *The End of Reform: New Deal Liberalism in Recession and War* (New York, 1995); Mark H. Leff, *The Limits of Symbolic Reform: The New Deal and Taxation, 1933–1939* (New York, 1984); Colin Gordon, *New Deals: Business, Labor, and Politics in America, 1920–1935* (New York, 1994); Christopher L. Tomlins, *The State and the Unions: Labor Relations, Law, and the Organized Labor Movement in America, 1880–1960* (New York, 1985).

9. The Vagaries of National Political Development

1. W. Craig Riddell, "Unionization in Canada and the United States: A Tale of Two Countries," in *Queen's Papers in Industrial Relations* (Kingston, ON, 1993), 33–34.

2. Riddell, "Unionization in Canada and the United States," 33–34.

3. Stephen Skowronek, *Building a New American State: The Expansion of National Administrative Capacities, 1877–1920* (New York, 1982). On comparative campaign finance law, see: K. D. Ewing, *Money, Politics, and Law: A Study of Electoral Campaign Finance Reform in Canada* (Oxford, 1992); Arthur B. Gunlicks, ed., *Campaign and Party Finance in North America and Western Europe* (Boulder, CO, 1993).

4. James Madison, *The Federalist Papers* (New York [1788] 1961); David R. Mayhew, *Congress: The Electoral Connection,* 2nd ed. (New Haven, CT, 2004).

5. Mildred A. Schwartz, *Party Movements in the United States and Canada: Strategies of Persistence* (Lanham, MD, 2006); Alan C. Cairns, "The Governments and Societies of Canadian Federalism," *Canadian Journal of Political Science* 10 (1977): 659–725; Gunlicks, *Campaign and Party Finance in North America and Western Europe.*

6. Jacob S. Hacker, "The Historical Logic of National Health Insurance: Structure and Sequence in the Development of British, Canadian, and U.S. Medical Policy," *Studies in American Political Development* 12 (1998): 57–130; Jill Quadagno, *One Nation Uninsured: Why The US Has No National Health Insurance* (Oxford, 2005); Theda Skocpol, *Protecting Soldiers and Mothers: The Political Origins of Social Policy in the United States* (Cambridge, MA, 1992); Paul Starr, *The Social Transformation of American Medicine* (New York, 1982).

7. A. W. Johnson, *Dream No Little Dreams: A Biography of the Douglas Government of Saskatchewan, 1944–1961* (Toronto, 2004); E. A. Tollefson, *Bitter Medicine: The Saskatchewan Medicare Feud* (Saskatoon, Canada, 1964).

8. David T. Beito, *From Mutual Aid to the Welfare State: Fraternal Societies and Social Services, 1890–1967* (Chapel Hill, NC, 2000); Terry Boychuk, *The Making and Meaning of Hospital Policy in the United States and Canada* (Ann Arbor, MI, 1999); Jacob Hacker, *The Divided Welfare State: The Battle over Public and Private Social Benefits in the United States* (New York, 2002).

9. Medicaid figure from "Annual Statistical Supplement, 1975," *Social Security Bulletin,* quoted in Allen J. Matusow, *The Unraveling of America: A History of Liberalism in the 1960s* (New York, 1984), 231; Hacker, "Historical Logic of National Health Insurance"; David Cutler, *Your Money or Your Life: Strong Medicine for America's Health Care System* (Oxford, 2004).

10. For example, Sven Steinmo, "Rethinking American Exceptionalism," in *The Dynamics of American Politics: Approaches and Interpretations,* ed. Lawrence C. Dodd and Calvin Jillson (Boulder, CO, 1994); Mayhew, *Congress.*

11. Keith G. Banting, *The Welfare State and Canadian Federalism,* 2nd ed. (Kingston, ON, 1987); Dennis Guest, *The Emergence of Social Security in Canada,* 3rd ed. (Vancouver, BC, 1997); Johnson, *Dream No Little Dreams.*

12. John David Skrentny, *The Ironies of Affirmative Action: Politics, Culture, and Justice in America* (Chicago, 1996); John David Skrentny, *The Minority Rights Revolution* (Cambridge, MA, 2002); Brian Steensland, *The Failed Welfare Revolution: America's Struggle over Guaranteed Income Policy* (Princeton, NJ, 2007).

13. "Civil Incorporation of Church Property," *Catholic Encyclopedia on CD-ROM,* www.newadvent.org (accessed August 26, 2006), emphasis added; North American Mission Board, "Basic Administration of a CCSB Church

Plant," *Church Planting Basic Training Manual,* www.ccsb.ca (accessed August 26, 2006); Internal Revenue Service, "Publication 557: Tax-Exempt Status for Your Organization," (2005). In its section on "Churches," IRS Publication 557 notes, "Although a church, its integrated auxiliaries, or a convention or association of churches is not required to file Form 1023 to be exempt from federal income tax or to receive tax deductible contributions, the organization may find it advantageous to obtain recognition of exemption. In this event, you should submit information showing that your organization is a church, synagogue, association or convention of churches, religious order, or religious organization that is an integral part of a church, and that it is engaged in carrying out the function of a church."

14. Roger Finke and Rodney Stark, *The Churching of America: Winners and Losers in our Religious Economy* (New Brunswick, NJ, 1992); Jason Kaufman, "The Political Economy of Inter-Denominational Competition in Late 19th century American Cities," *Journal of Urban History* 28 (2002): 445–465.

15. Samuel P. Huntington, *Political Order in Changing Societies* (New Haven, CT, 1968), 122; Donald V. Smiley, *Constitutional Adaptation and Canadian Federalism since 1945* (Ottawa, 1970); see also Peter H. Russell, *Constitutional Odyssey: Can Canadians Become a Sovereign People?* 2nd ed. (Toronto, 1993).

16. "Voting Rights," Committee on the Judiciary, Senate Hearings (1965), quoted in Matusow, *Unraveling of America,* 181; Alexander Keyssar, *The Right to Vote: The Contested History of Democracy in the United States* (New York, 2000).

17. Marshall quoted in Matusow, *Unraveling of America,* 78, emphasis added.

18. Matusow, *Unraveling of America,* 187, emphasis added.

19. See, for example, Thomas J. Sugrue, *The Origins of the Urban Crisis: Race and Inequality in Postwar Detroit* (Princeton, NJ, 1996); Douglas Massey and Nancy Denton, *American Apartheid: Segregation and the Making of the Underclass* (Cambridge, MA, 1993).

20. Matusow, *Unraveling of America,* 245–246, 265; Daniel P. Moynihan, *Maximum Feasible Misunderstanding: Community Action in the War on Poverty* (New York, 1969); John D. Skrentny, *Ironies of Affirmative Action.* For an entertaining but less objective account, see Tom Wolfe, *Radical Chic and Mau-Mauing the Flak Catchers* (New York, 1970).

21. Robert Putnam, "Bowling Alone: America's Declining Social Capital," *Journal of Democracy* 6 (1995): 65–78; Putnam, *Bowling Alone: The Collapse and Revival of American Community* (New York, 2000); Marvin Olasky, *The Tragedy of American Compassion* (Wheaton, IL, 1992); Peter Berger and Richard John Neuhaus, *To Empower People: From State to Civil Society,* 20th

anniversary ed. (Washington, DC, 1996); Benjamin R. Barber, *A Place for Us: How to Make Society Civil and Democracy Strong* (New York, 1998); David T. Beito, *From Mutual Aid to the Welfare State: Fraternal Societies and Social Services, 1890–1967* (Chapel Hill, NC, 2000). For critical perspectives, see Jason Kaufman, *For the Common Good? American Civic Life and the Golden Age of Fraternity* (New York, 2002); Alejandro Portes and Patricia Landholt, "The Downside of Social Capital," *American Prospect* 26 (May/June 1996): 18–21.

22. Richard Hofstadter, *The Paranoid Style in American Politics and Other Essays* (New York, 1965).

23. Jason Kaufman, "Americans and Their Guns: Civilian Military Organizations and the Destabilization of American National Security," *Studies in American Political Development* 15 (2001): 88–102; Leslie A. Pal, "Gun Control," in *The Government Taketh Away: The Politics of Pain in the United States and Canada,* ed. Leslie A. Pal and R. Kent Weaver (Washington, DC, 2003).

24. OECD Society at a Glance 2002, Annex CO: Social Cohesion Indicators (CO1 to C06): Data Chart CO3.1; Nationmaster 2004, "Map and Graph Crime, Murder Per Capita and Prisoners Per Capita"; Richard Block, "Firearms in Canada and Eight Other Western Countries: Selected Findings of the 1996 International Crime (Victim) Survey," Canada Firearms Centre, Department of Justice Canada, 1998.

25. Kaufman, "Americans and Their Guns"; Jeffrey Ian Ross, ed., *Violence in Canada: Sociopolitical Perspectives,* 2nd ed. (New Brunswick, NJ, 2004).

26. Robert H. Jackson, *The Struggle for Judicial Supremacy: A Study of a Crisis in American Power Politics* (New York, 1941), 10–11; Mark Tushnet, *A Court Divided: The Rehnquist Court and the Future of Constitutional Law* (New York, 2005).

27. Graham Parker, "Canadian Legal Culture," in *Law and Justice in a New Land: Essays in Western Canadian Legal History,* ed. Louis Knafla (Toronto, 1986), 4; William P. LaPiana, *Logic and Experience: The Origin of Modern American Legal Education* (New York, 1994); Samuel Herbert Fisher, *The Litchfield Law School, 1775–1833* (New Haven, CT, 1933). Lawyer per capita numbers come from International Labour Office Bureau of Statistics, *Laborsta database.* US data are for 1996; Canada data are for 2000.

28. Russell, *Constitutional Odyssey,* 42; see also Keith Banting and Richard Simeon, eds., *And No One Cheered: Federalism, Democracy, and the Constitution Act* (Toronto, 1983); Paul Howe and Peter Russell, eds., *Judicial Power and Canadian Democracy* (Montreal, 2001); Christopher P. Manfredi, *Judicial Power and the Charter: Canada and the Paradox of Liberal Constitutionalism* (Don Mills, ON, 2001); F. L. Morton, *Pro-Choice vs. Pro-Life: Abortion and the Courts in Canada* (Norman, OK, 1992).

29. F . L. Morton, *Pro-Choice v. Pro-Life: Abortion and the Courts in Canada* (Norman, OK, 1992), 274; Raymond Tatalovich, *The Politics of Abortion in the United States and Canada: A Comparative Study* (Armonk, NY, 1997); Drew Halfmann, "Institutional Democracy and Interest Construction: The Politics of Abortion Policy in the United States, Britain and Canada, 1960–2000" (Working paper, Dept. of Sociology, New York University, 2001).

30. Morton, *Pro-Choice v. Pro-Life,* 69.

31. Leon Dion, *Quebec: The Unfinished Revolution* (Montreal, 1976); Ramsay Cook, *Canada, Québec and the Uses of Nationalism,* 2nd ed. (Toronto, 1995 [1986]).

32. Russell, *Constitutional Odyssey;* Donald V. Smiley, *The Federal Condition in Canada* (Toronto, 1987).

33. Samuel V. LaSelva, *The Moral Foundations of Canadian Federalism: Paradoxes, Achievements, and Tragedies of Nationhood* (Montreal, 1996); Miriam Smith, "The Politics of Same-Sex Marriage in Canada and the United States," *PS: Political Science & Politics* (April 2005): 225–228.

34. Richard Simeon, "Debating Secession Peacefully and Democratically: The Case of Canada" (working paper, Third General Assembly, Club de Madrid, 2003).

Conclusion

1. Jason Kaufman and Matthew Kaliner, "History Repeats Itself, until It Doesn't: The 'Re-Accomplishment of Place' in 20th Century Vermont" (Working paper, Dept. of Sociology, Harvard University, 2007).

Index